D1498117

SWIFT'S LANDSCAPE

THE JOHNS HOPKINS UNIVERSITY PRESS
Baltimore and London

Swift's Landscape

Carole Fabricant

PR
3728
S46
F3
1982

The Johns Hopkins University Press, Baltimore, Maryland 21218
The Johns Hopkins Press Ltd., London

Library of Congress Cataloging in Publication Data

Fabricant, Carole.
Swift's landscape.

Includes bibliographical references and index.
1. Swift, Jonathan, 1667-1745—Settings.
2. Swift, Jonathan, 1667-1745—Criticism and
interpretation. I. Title
PR3728.S46F3   828'.509   82-165
ISBN 0-8018-2721-3   AACR2

Frontispiece: A section of a map of Dublin from John Rocque's *Exact Survey of the City and Suburbs of Dublin* (Dublin, 1756). Courtesy of the National Library of Ireland. For purposes of orientation, note that the right side of the map is north and, for example, the Castle is northeast of St. Patrick's.

For my mother, Shelley Dorenbaum Fabricant

Contents

Acknowledgments

My first and foremost debt is to Ronald Paulson, for his generosity, encouragement, and support over the past decade, and for first opening my mind to the crucial interconnections between verbal, visual, and topographical structures. His pioneering work in the areas of eighteenth-century satiric art, aesthetic theory and practice, and popular culture has, I daresay, been seminal for an entire generation of younger scholars.

I am also grateful to those friends and colleagues who, by reading portions of my manuscript and commenting, criticizing, praising, and challenging, helped me clarify my ideas, test the validity of my conclusions, and tighten my argument: Jim Dean, Lois Chaber, Richard Helgerson, David James, Steven Axelrod, and Sean Shesgreen. My research assistant, Jay Salter, reading an earlier (and longer) version of the book, not with but through the eye, saw the shape of things both immanent and to come, and helped me make it a perceptible reality. Claude Rawson was kind enough to read my manuscript in its entirety and send me comments. Bliss Carnochan's criticisms and suggestions proved helpful in the final stages of preparing my manuscript for publication.

An NEH Summer Fellowship in 1977 made it possible for me to spend several months in England and Ireland, doing research work relevant to my book; and an ACLS grant-in-aid in the same year enabled me to continue working full time on the book through the fall of 1977. I remember with fondness and gratitude those newly made friends in Ireland who not only helped make my visits pleasurable but also gave me insights into Swift's Dublin that are unobtainable from books and libraries.

I wish to thank the Committee on Research of the University of California, Riverside, for their consistent and generous financial support of this project. In addition, I am grateful to the Affirmative Action Committee of the University of California, Riverside Academic Senate for awarding me a special two-quarter leave of absence during the fall and winter of 1979–1980; without this extended period of released time, this book might now still be a work-in-progress. An earlier version of certain parts of my discussion in this book appeared in "The Garden as City: Swift's Landscape of Alienation," *ELH* 42 (1975): 531–55. I benefited from the expert typing skills of Clara Dean for all earlier drafts and versions of this book; in the later stages of manuscript preparation, I was fortunate to have the typing assistance of Helen Curtis.

I am very glad not to have to acknowledge a debt to any self-sacrificing, long-suffering soul who stayed at home and endured so that I could carry on my work.

My last but obviously not least debt is to Swift himself, for affording me many years of instruction and delight, for presenting me with a constant reminder of the vanity of words divorced from deeds, and for demonstrating the fullness of a life nourished by committed worldly involvements and enlightened social action. I am infinitely richer for the experience of having spent the past seven years in his continually disruptive presence.

List of Abbreviations

The following abbreviations appear in the text:

C: *The Correspondence of Jonathan Swift*, 5 vols., ed. Harold Williams (Oxford: Clarendon Press, 1963–1965).

JS: Swift, *Journal to Stella*, 2 vols., ed. Harold Williams (1948; Oxford: Basil Blackwell, 1974).

P: *The Poems of Jonathan Swift*, 3 vols., ed. Harold Williams, 2d ed. (Oxford: Clarendon Press, 1958).

PW: *The Prose Works of Jonathan Swift*, 14 vols., ed. Herbert Davis (Oxford: Basil Blackwell, 1939–1968).

TT: Swift, *A Tale of A Tub &c.,* ed. A. C. Guthkelch and D. Nichol Smith, 2d ed. (Oxford: Clarendon Press, 1958).

A Section of a Map of Dublin from John Rocque's *Exact Survey of the City and Suburbs of Dublin* (Dublin, 1756).

CHAPTER · I

Introduction: Landscape as Vision and Place

i

My aim in this book is to reconstruct and explore the significance of what I call Swift's landscape, by which I mean both the actual features of his physical surroundings and the idiosyncratic, highly distinctive way in which he perceived them, as evidenced by their recurring, often obsessive depiction throughout his writings. Transformed alternately (or simultaneously) into political, symbolic, and satiric statement, these features constitute an all-encompassing ideological landscape, a country of the mind as well as a concrete habitation for the body. Examining his works, we discover that for Swift, the geographic and architectural aspects of his environment were invariably linked to prevailing social and economic conditions, which is why in his case it would be pointless to talk about the aesthetics of landscape: It was an inescapably and pervasively *political* landscape that regularly caught Swift's eye and monopolized his attention. One could, of course, argue—as I myself would want to do, in agreement with insightful critics like John Barrell and James Turner[1]—that the perception or poetic re-creation of landscape is *always* inextricably bound up with broadly political considerations, whether or not they are openly acknowledged. I deliberately lay special stress upon them in Swift's case, however, since they are treated by him with an exceptional degree of clarity and explicitness. Swift once observed to his friend Charles Ford that ". . . as the World is now turned, no Cloyster is retired enough to keep Politicks out" (C, 2:330), and generally speaking, there was no part of his mind or psyche, just as there was no part of his geographic environs, that could remain entirely aloof from prevailing political conditions. Not even the pulpit was a refuge from them, as is evident from the urgently

1

topical nature of several of his extant sermons. His letters are a continuing
testimonial to the fact that for him, there was no escape from the urgencies and intrusions of public affairs.

Swift's physical surroundings played a central role in his life and his
literary work alike. In very concrete ways, they helped to shape his outlook on life, his class consciousness, and the literary styles he consistently
employed as his mode of expression. At the same time, they themselves
were reshaped and redefined as a result of the impact upon them of
Swift's vision: an eminently active mode of perception that, as we see
from the example of *Gulliver's Travels,* could profoundly affect the
shapes and sizes of viewed objects in the environment. The relationship,
in other words, was a reciprocal one—so much so, indeed, that the line
between inner and outer comes to seem at times a rather arbitrary demar-
cation. J. H. Van Den Berg, in commenting generally upon the link between environment and human perception, expresses the matter well:
"The relationship of man and world is so profound, that it is an error to
separate them. If we do, then man ceases to be man and the world to be
world. The world is our home, our habitat, the materialization of our subjectivity. Who wants to become acquainted with man, should listen to the
language spoken by the things in his existence. Who wants to describe man
should make an analysis of the 'landscape' within which he demonstrates,
explains and reveals himself."[2]

This book is not intended as a phenomenological study, and it often
in effect distinguishes between the internal and the external aspects of
Swift's landscape, focusing now on one, now on the other as the occasion
demands. Nevertheless, its goal is to explore, not so much a body of external objects or facts that happened to be observed and recorded by
Swift, but precisely "the materialization of [Swift's] subjectivity" insofar
as we can reconstruct it from "the 'landscape' within which he demonstrates, explains, and reveals himself." Although I devote a substantial portion of my study to discussions of a historical nature, intended to provide
pertinent background and contexts for Swift's own revelations of his landscape, my primary aim in doing so is not to present a particular interpretation of eighteenth-century Irish history, but rather to illuminate the
peculiar urgencies that moved Swift to act as he did and the abiding preoccupations that shaped the way in which he viewed—hence depicted—his
world. In a sense the book's historical commentary is intended to enable
the reader to hear more clearly the "language spoken by the things in
[Swift's] existence": a language at all times temporally bound and invariably possessing political overtones. The commentary is intended at the
same time to shed crucial light upon the abiding structures and characteristic workings of Swift's consciousness.

I might put the matter another way. In our act of recovering the peculiar contours of Swift's surroundings, we find that they become "literally and figuratively, a place to stand, an angle of vision."[3] This phrase is used by Maynard Mack to describe Pope's combined physical, artistic, and mythopoeic creation of his Twickenham estate. In applying the phrase to Swift, I mean to underscore two quite different points. The first is the existence of a similarity between the two writers, to the extent that each of them transformed the concrete features of his environment into a symbolic depiction of his society and his own position (or lack of position) within it. The second, finally more crucial point is the existence of a fundamental contrast between the two writers and their modes of perception. For to explore their respective landscapes is to journey through two separate countries marked by very different physical and ideological terrain. The contrast, by implication, points up the fallacy of attempting to define a single, monolithic "Augustan outlook" presumably shared by all the major writers of the period.[4] What we find instead are several coexisting but quite divergent outlooks (as well as "lookouts") held by writers who may have been friends, members of the same political party, and espousers of the same philosophic beliefs and moral norms, but who nevertheless occupied different positions in their landscape and who therefore saw things differently. In saying this, I do not mean to suggest that one cannot talk of a prevailing orthodoxy during this period—a body of assumptions, values, and myths embraced by a significant number of the age's leading thinkers and writers. (I elaborate upon this issue at the beginning of chapter 4, in my discussion of ruling-class ideology in relation to the country house ideal.) Indeed, it is precisely within the context of such an orthodoxy that I explore Swift's vision in this book. Nevertheless, my study demonstrates, both directly and indirectly, the fallacies that result from failing to make necessary distinctions—specifically, from according these dominant ideas a universality and a homogeneity they did not possess.

The distortion that inevitably follows from the indiscriminate grouping of "Augustans" under a single rubric, such as "the Christian humanist tradition," may be seen in Martin C. Battestin's reflections upon "the principle of Order, on which [the Augustans'] faith was founded."[5] In the space of little more than a page, Battestin brings together Palladio, Burlington, Pope, Shaftesbury, Newton, Swift, and Dennis as essentially interchangeable representatives of this principle. The idea of Order becomes a procrustean bed into which all the works of these diverse individuals are made to fit, at the price of disregarding specific contexts and the occasionally unorthodox ways in which conventional motifs were used. Battestin's revealing (and what I take to be characteristic) misrepresentation of a passage from Swift's *Journal to Stella* has already been remarked upon by C. J. Rawson,[6] so I will not belabor the point here. A similar distortion, although expressed in quite different terms, is produced by Isaac Kramnick's lumping together of Pope and Swift as fellow members of Bolingbroke's "Circle" and as exemplars of the same ideological stance.[7] The "common alienation from the age" and the "politics of nostalgia" that Kramnick indiscriminately ascribes to both take on a very different character in each case, as a consequence of their having been shaped by two distinct sensibilities and modes of perception.

Thus we have on the one hand the rather studied, literary, and "sociable" alienation reflected in Pope's Horation retirement to Twickenham, where he could remain apart from the world, yet be in the midst of a civilized Augustan community surrounded by "Chiefs, out of War, and Statesmen, out of Place" (*Imitations of Horace, Satire II, i,* 126)[8]—a posture reminiscent of Bolingbroke's self-indulgent dream of ". . . buying the Dominion of Bermuda, and spending the remainder of my days as far as possible from those people wth whom I have past the first & greater part of my Life," which prompted his asking Swift, "will you . . . transplant yr self wth me into the middle of the Atlantick ocean? we will form a society, more reasonable, & more useful than that of Dr Berkley's Colledge . . ." (C, 3:82). These expressions of disaffection, which might be said to signify the romantic longings of the affluent or would-be aristocrat for an elegant refuge from the messiness of contemporary urban, middle-class society, bear only a superficial resemblance to the embittered, self-mocking, deeply personal alienation Swift displayed in his periodic flights to Thomas Sheridan's "obscure Irish Cabbin" to "forget and to be forgotten" (C, 3:84, 76) (always with the gnawing realization that this was an unattainable goal), in his insistence that "there is not a Clergyman on the top of a mountain who so little converses with mankind" as himself (C, 4:4), and in his characterization of himself as "a poisoned rat in a hole" (C, 3:383). Swift's words combine a hostile rejection of contemporary society with a terrifying, even if at times comically depicted, sense of isolation that has little affinity with the spirit informing Pope's vision.

To be sure, this isolation did not constitute the last word for Swift, however much it continued with him throughout his life. (In chapter 6, for example, I suggest the ways in which it was tempered and at least partially transformed as a result of his political activism.) Nevertheless, very different structures of feeling characterize Pope's and Swift's respective withdrawals from society. Swift himself attested to his awareness of this difference when he wrote to Pope, "I have no very strong Faith in you pretenders to retirement; you are not of an age for it, nor have you gone through either good or bad Fortune enough to go into a Corner and form Conclusions de contemptu mundi et fuga Seculi, unless a Poet grows weary of too much applause as Ministers do with too much Weight of

Business" (C, 2:464-65). This statement, part of a letter (written in 1723) that contrasts Pope's fortunate situation and accompanying "Security of Mind" with Swift's more wretched and precarious plight, as a man "condemned to another Scene" and doomed to suffer for ". . . being so Strongly attached to Traytors (as they call them) and Exiles, and State Criminalls," reminds us that the "alienation from the age" experienced by the Augustan writers cannot be interpreted in the same way for Pope and for Swift.

The differences in outlook that I have been discussing can be understood only if we examine each writer's landscape, in the concrete, inclusive sense in which I am using the term here, rather than abstractly considering the concepts they officially espoused. To the extent that we limit our concerns to the latter, we can have no serious quarrel with Kramnick's conclusion that, for Swift, "degree and order ruled both God's universe and man's world,"[9] nor with Basil Hall's picture of Swift as a sober, pious churchman who consistently extols the idea of limitation and who "believes profoundly in the moral realism of the traditional Christian doctrine of Original Sin."[10] However much these descriptions may strike us as being somehow irrelevant to our *experience* in reading Swift's works, it is only after we have moved from the realm of doctrinal allegiances to the world of concrete shapes and images, from public maxims to personal perceptions, that we are in a position to argue the inadequacy (even if not necessarily the technical inaccuracy) of such formulations. John Traugott has remarked upon the fallacies of these overgeneralizing and abstracting tendencies in Swift criticism with incisiveness and an appropriate degree of caustic wit: "The sociology of this phenomenon of modern academia by which a demonic writer like Swift is 'elevated' by being reduced to a proper cleric is beyond the scope of this essay ["*A Tale of a Tub*"]. Suffice it to say that it is a form of the pseudo-scientific determinism in scholarship that explains (away) a refractory writer by a system of ideas which were, we are told, his heritage and environment. This Swift comes to seem much like a university lecturer."[11]

There is no danger that the reader of this book will encounter a Swift thus diminished. Not that my book questions Swift's scholarly learning, nor his role and the conscientious execution of his duties (interpreted in his own unique light) as clergyman. But placed within the larger context of an active public life and a body of writings that spanned over half a century, they assume a different significance and resist the anemic and misleading abstractions that are too often applied to Swift. Peter Steele has skillfully (if indirectly) called these abstractions into question by demonstrating how Swift's role as preacher is inextricably bound up with that of jester and buffoon—influenced by ". . . his own capacity for extravagance—his ability to combine a hectic fancy with a sober expression."[12] My own study shows how these two roles are further linked to other recurring Swiftian roles, including that of social commentator and political activist. The sum total of the diverse yet interrelated roles Swift played, both in his life and in his writings, help make up what I have termed his landscape.

An exploration of Swift's landscape, as recorded in his writings, reveals a world expressed through images of metamorphosis and confusion, of profound instability at times verging on chaos, far more frequently than through images of a divinely ordained chain of being: a world pervaded by forces inherently subversive of the traditional hierarchic order. It is only here that we can discover the author of *A Tale of a Tub*, the emphatically unPope-like versifier of pieces like *Helter Skelter* and *The Revolution at Market-Hill*, and the man who devised a project "To build a House for Fools and Mad" (*Verses on the Death of Dr. Swift*, 480). Moreover, it is this world alone that allows us to understand why Swift's political influence on future ages was felt most acutely by men like the revolutionary republican Henry Yorke and the egalitarian Thomas Spence, and that therefore helps explain the largely but not wholly ironic fact that, as Caroline Robbins notes, "Readers of [Swift's] works, listeners to his sermons, were likely to derive liberal rather than Tory politics from them."[13] To put it another way, the examination of Swift's concrete landscape provides indispensable access to those "anarchic" elements in Swift's writings which have been periodically acknowledged by critics in the past (though at times with considerable reluctance, dismay, or abhorrence) and which must necessarily be apparent to any sensitive reader with no stake in making Swift into a respectable, conservative Anglican dean.

We need not wander far afield, among Swift's obscurer works, in order to find these elements. His two best-known fictive identities, the Tale-teller and Gulliver, are marginal men who dramatize an anarchic dispersion of energies through their respective peregrinations and digressions, whether of a physical or a mental nature. The works in which they appear exploit formally loose, open-ended literary genres—that is, picaresque fiction and satiric anatomy—that accentuate the fragmentation of traditional hierarchic organization and institutionalized order: the collapse of tight, coherent systems and centers of unquestioned authority. There are, of course, significant differences between the works, reflecting in part the passage of three decades between the composition of each. In the earlier *Tale* there is still (technically) a center of sorts (in literary terms, the official text, the allegory of the three brothers; in ideological terms, the authority of the ancients and classical learning, which the author is ostensibly defending), although even here the center cannot hold. It exists, moreover, as little more than a hypothetical construct, an implied antithesis to what *is,* so that all of the most appealing, vital energies seem to be located on the fringes, manifested in the speaker's wild mental excursions and imaginative flights (in the "Digressions") rather than in the central, didactic text. By the time we get to *Gulliver's Travels,* we find a disjointed, fragmented world wholly lacking a single center of authority or legitimacy—a world whose hero moves and acts entirely on the periphery as he continually embarks on journeys characterized by shipwrecks and lost bearings, by endless digressions and detours. Like the whale mentioned in the *Tale,* Gulliver is led astray by an assortment of tubs, but there is no longer a ship either capable or worthy of being preserved. The "centers" of political power encountered by Gulliver in his travels belong to a world of relativity and flux; they appear and vanish suddenly, change size and shape at the drop of a hat (or the readjustment of Gulliver's spectacles), and function according to arbitrary laws that bespeak their insular nature. They are either too big or too small, too debased or too ideal, for human consumption. The political "center" of Gulliver's homeland "appears" only in absentia; it exists solely in storytelling and hearsay. From what we learn of it through Gulliver's sometimes deliberately, sometimes unwittingly incriminating narrative, it operates through deception, hypocrisy, and blatant exploitation—above all, through a fundamental inauthenticity that substitutes might for right, money for virtue, and the plunder and pillaging of a "Crew of Pyrates" for "a new Dominion acquired with a Title by *Divine Right*" (PW, 11:294).

The peculiarly anarchic tendencies so evident throughout Swift's writings, as exemplified in his two most famous works, written near the beginning and toward the end of his literary career, are placed in an interesting perspective by Edward W. Said, who argues that rather than viewing Swift "as an Anglican divine whose life can be described as a sequence of events over a period of time. . . . we do him a greater service if we accept the discontinuities he experienced in the way he experienced them: as either actual or imminent losses of tradition, heritage, position, history, losses located at the center of his disjointed verbal production."[14] Although I strongly take issue with certain important aspects of Said's position (as will become evident in chapter 6, where I examine these matters in a concretely political context and argue for Swift's "gains" as well as his "losses," for the "presences" as well as the "absences" marking his existence), Said's comments succeed in underscoring some of the reasons why Swift cannot be looked at in traditional terms. A similar function is served by the criticism of C. J. Rawson, the most insightful commentator on Swift's anarchic proclivities. His discussion of what he terms Swift's "unofficial energies," "active and radical ambiguity," and "self-implicating sense of our anarchic tortuosity" crystallizes the ways in which Swift defies common preconceptions about "the Augustan world view" and dif-

fers profoundly from Pope.[15] As my previous comments about the concretely geographic and profoundly political dimensions of Swift's outlook
would suggest, however, in trying to understand the precise textures and
nuances of Swift's thought we must finally go beyond considerations of
sensibility and of what Rawson refers to as "authorial temperaments and
styles." A single-minded focus upon the latter can, somewhat paradoxically, produce its own kind of abstractness. Therefore, although I do not
by any means question the aspects of temperament and psychological disposition stressed by Rawson, in the following chapters I place them
within the broader, more concrete context of what was for Swift perceived and felt reality: the immediate daily observations and experiences
of a life that for the most part functioned simultaneously on public and
private levels.

A few more words remain to be said about the nature of my study
and its mode of proceeding. Given my definition of Swift's landscape and
the comprehensive scope of my subject matter, it follows that this book is
(among other things) a canon study, which uses as many of Swift's writings
as possible to provide insights into his peculiar angle of vision. Too frequently, critical studies of Swift have isolated a single work or a carefully
selected group of works for discussion. (Interpretations of either *Gulliver's Travels* or *A Tale of a Tub,* along with generic examinations of his
satire, are the most obvious examples, with the recent spate of books
and articles on his suddenly rediscovered poetry basically perpetuating
this trend.) Although some of these studies are unquestionably instructive
and illuminating, the general approach they represent has tended to produce narrowly formalistic analyses that examine Swift's verbal structures
in a vacuum, divorced from the mind and personality that created them,
as well as from the soil that fertilized them. Any generalizations about
Swift himself derived from such studies must necessarily be suspect, given
their exclusive focus upon what tends to be only a minute proportion of
Swift's total output—chosen, moreover, on the basis of carefully defined
aesthetic or generic criteria that often have little relevance to Swift. My
own study, while it in no way questions the existence of formal differences among Swift's works, and while it on many occasions looks
closely at the structural, rhetorical, or imagistic aspects of specific works,
ranges freely over the entire spectrum of his writings without separating
them into neat generic cubbyholes or adhering to any rigid distinction between his "literary" and his "nonliterary" works, and without according
any particular works a privileged status within his canon. All are treated
as revelatory of Swift's mode of perception—as equal (though distinct)
expressions of his consciousness. My approach in this regard, I would
argue, is particularly appropriate to Swift, who in his writings consistently
transgressed the formal boundaries scrupulously drawn or invoked by

modern critics and who, as any reader of his poetry (of his entire poetic output rather than of the handful of "Augustan" verses regularly anthologized and discussed) realizes, would have had little patience with the combined isolation and elevation of "high" or "pure" art, or with the almost religious exaltation of "literary" over "nonliterary" works. He would have seen such an apotheosis as one more mystification of the sort he scornfully exposed throughout his life.

Finally, it follows from my understanding of Swift's landscape that this book has a significant biographical dimension, although it is not, I hasten to add, a biography in any strict or conventional sense of the term. It does not, for example, treat biographical details in and of themselves, for their own sake, nor does it examine Swift's writings in chronological sequence. Irvin Ehrenpreis's standard biography of Swift, an admirable piece of scholarship, more than adequately fills the need for such a study.[16] My own book addresses a very different set of needs and concerns. It is biographical in the special sense in which Georges Poulet uses the term when, observing that a book is "the means by which an author actually preserves his ideas, his feelings, his modes of dreaming and living" and that "every word of literature is impregnated with the mind of the one who wrote it," he explains: "It is not the biography which explicates the work, but rather the work which sometimes enables us to understand the biography."[17] By exploring Swift's canon, in other words, we can establish intimate contact with the mind that produced it and can come to "know" Swift in a way we could never do by simply learning the facts of his life.

Because my study deals simultaneously with a consciousness and a history, it functions at once synchronically and diachronically. It is concerned both with the fixed, simultaneously existing and interconnected structures of Swift's landscape and with its development over time. My discussion of Swift's antipastoral perspective and his subversion of the country house ideal, for example, reveals the unchanging aspect of his attitude toward these matters throughout his lifetime—no doubt the result of a skeptical and demystifying bent that was temperamental in origin—even as it traces the shifts in emphasis and direction that these attitudes underwent as a result of Swift's deepening involvement in Irish affairs and his growing insistence upon dealing with empirical realities, which produced an increasingly cynical stance toward all forms of literary and political romanticization. In this connection, a central and striking paradox is evident in Swift's writings: a coexistence of antithetical forces exerting a strong pull both outward, into the world of time and history, and inward, into the world of Swift's stubbornly persistent mental fixations. Few if any writers have produced a body of work so pervasively and consistently occasional, so inextricably linked to historical events or situations that are by their very nature evanescent,

doomed to temporal dispersion. Yet at the same time few writers have so
thoroughly and distinctively impressed their own style and peculiar mode
of obsessiveness upon their works, making them unique and unmistakable
signatures that pugnaciously call attention to their own eccentric character and, to that extent, defy the world of flux. As the organization of
my book suggests, the exploration of Swift's landscape entails both a
linear journey that parallels the course of eighteenth-century history and
a continuous circling around the fixed patterns of Swift's mind.

ii

The exploration of Swift's landscape is a major undertaking, for his
landscape (unlike Pope's, which has been written about exhaustively[18])
remains to this day largely virgin territory for eighteenth-century scholarship. A part of the explanation for this may be inferred from Pat Rogers's
remark: "All his days, Pope was a poet of daylight and champaign; with
Swift we think of the windy downs about Letcombe or the desolate
landing-stage at Holyhead."[19] The terms with which Rogers describes
the Swiftian milieu are ones that by their very nature defy the carefully
formulated, officially recognized categories that both eighteenth-century
theorists and twentieth-century critics have regularly applied to their
perception of landscape—even more, have used as criteria for defining
what is a landscape and thus, by implication, what is *not*. Holyhead's
"desolate" expanses and Letcombe's "windy downs" are irreconcilable
with our expectations, as contemplators of landscape, of picturesque
scenes, prospects, chiaroscuro effects, and the like. Our inclination,
especially if we are students of eighteenth-century topography, is to regard Swift's environs not as a *different type* of landscape from Pope's, but
rather, as a *non*landscape—as "mere" terrain not worthy of special attention either for itself or for its connection with Swift.

The problem I raise here centers upon the word "landscape," which,
although innocent and neutral-looking enough, is in fact a rather loaded
term and was especially so throughout the eighteenth century. Barrell
suggests the reasons for this when he observes: "There is no word in
English which denotes a tract of land, of whatever extent, which is apprehended *visually* but not, necessarily, *pictorially*. . . . The word we do use,
of course, is 'landscape': we can speak of the 'landscape' of a country,
but in doing so we introduce, whether we want to or not, notions of value
and form which relate, not just to seeing the land, but to seeing it in a
certain way—pictorially."[20] Now Swift's landscapes, as recorded in his
various writings, can on occasion be quite visually precise and detailed,
but they *never* lend themselves to being apprehended pictorially. Indeed,

a crucial aspect of Swift's vision—perhaps its most characteristic feature—
is its fundamental antagonism to the artistic framing and other forms of
aesthetic organization so integral to the vision of contemporaries like
Pope and Thomson. Swift's landscapes lack visual resolution just as his
poetry lacks the aesthetic resolution derived from elegant heroic couplets,
and just as his satires lack the clear moral resolution provided by neatly
defined ethical norms and an absolute distinction between good and evil.
Swift continually presents us with images that refuse to be contained
within the frames, and frameworks, customarily set up by other writers
of the period.

In the single instance where the word "landscape" appears in Swift's
poetry, it is associated with transient shapes as well as visual distortion:
When Cartesian artists " . . . catch the living landscape thro' a scanty
light,/ The figures all inverted shew,/ And colours of a faded hue. . ."
(*Ode to Dr. William Sancroft*, 30-32). This landscape is characterized
by disproportioned and chaotic forms.

> Here a pale shape with upward footstep treads,
> And men seem walking on their heads;
> There whole herds suspended lie
> Ready to tumble down into the sky;
> . . . .
> Disjointing shapes as in the fairy-land of dreams,
> Or images that sink in streams. . . .
>
> (33-36, 39-40)

Although the ode is technically part of a particular literary and philosophic tradition (its description of the earth as " . . . this inferior world
[which] is but Heaven's dusky shade" [21] points to Platonic influences,
for example), it bears only a superficial resemblance to the grotesquely
disproportioned pastoral scene and upside-down world described by
Marvell in *Upon Appleton House* (stanzas 58-60), or to Pope's depiction
of an inverted world in *Windsor-Forest:*

> In her chast Current oft the Goddess [Diana] laves,
> And with Celestial Tears augments the Waves.
> Oft in her Glass the musing Shepherd spies
> The headlong Mountains and the downward Skies,
> The watry Landskip of the pendant Woods,
> And absent Trees that tremble in the Floods;
> In the clear azure Gleam the Flocks are seen,
> And floating Forests paint the Waves with Green.
> Thro' the fair Scene rowl slow the lingring Streams,
> Then foaming pour along, and rush into the *Thames.*
>
> (209-18)

What we see here is not Swift's misshapen and frighteningly unpredictable world, but rather a serene, harmonious, and aesthetically pleasing
picture of a topsy-turvy world—a world that, for all its apparent confusion,
never threatens to burst out of its frame (or to escape the "Glass" upon
which the "musing Shepherd" gazes), resolving itself instead into a "fair
Scene" painted with the help of nature's artistry and controlled by the
poet's visual imagination. Neatly balanced couplets, the continuity embodied by literary tradition (Pope is here imitating Ausonius), and explicit
pictorial techniques work together in this instance to reaffirm the principle of order on all levels. Although Swift's lines in the *Ode to Dr. William
Sancroft* are also technically related to the familiar commonplace of the
world upside down, the poet's emphasis is upon a scene that seems to
elude the grasp of both literary tradition and pictorial re-creation. Swift's
landscape is not simply inverted but is in a disconcerting state of uncertainty and flux; it is a landscape on the brink of upheaval, threatening
imminent collapse or dissolution, composed of things about to "tumble
down" or melt into "fairy-land" or "sink" into watery depths.

    Similarly, Swift's Latin verses *Carberiae Rupes,* which record his per-
ceptions of the terrain he encountered during his travels through the south
of Ireland in 1723, describe the Carbery Rocks in a state of violent upheaval, at once the agents and the victims of a storm that threatens the
very existence of the craggy shore. The opening lines convey the radical
instability and the sense of uncontrollable forces that characterize both
the external setting and the poem itself: "Ecce ingens fragmen scopuli
quod vertice summo/Desuper impendet, nullo fundamine nixum/Decidit
in fluctus. . ." (1-3). Or, as it is expressed in William Dunkin's translation,
which Swift allowed to be published alongside his own poem in Faulkner's
1735 edition:

> Lo! from the Top of yonder Cliff, that shrouds
> Its airy Head amidst the azure Clouds,
> Hangs a huge Fragment; destitute of props
> Prone on the Waves the rocky Ruin drops.
>
>   (P, 1:318)

Typically, Swift's poem eschews a resolution that depicts the calm following the storm or that hints at a subsequent rebirth; instead it portrays
"Piscator terrâ" (31)—in Dunkin's words, "The frighted Fisher with
desponding Eyes"—who "[lies] trembling in the Harbour" ("in portu
tremebundus"), doubtful whether he will ever again "behold the Skies
serene" ("aera sudum/Haud sperans. . ."). The scene depicted in *Carberiae
Rupes* conveys its own kind of vividness and power, but it is hardly what
one would call beautiful.

    In Swift's actual and epistemological as well as his verbally reconstructed landscapes, there was little place for pretty scenes, for visually satisfying spectacle. When, for example, he enumerated the advantages of living at the deanery in a letter to Pope, who was at the time contemplating a visit to Ireland, he recommended its large garden and its general spaciousness but went on to assert that it is "without any beauty" (C, 4:170). Although eager to improve his grounds at Laracor, he took exception to Reverend Thomas Wallis's landscaping plan, protesting that " . . . it is very pretty, too pretty for the use I intend to make of Laracor" (C, 2:409). His terse, offhand reference to Laracor's attractions for the benefit of Esther Vanhomrigh (C, 1:373) contrasts strikingly with, say, Thomson's luxuriant and expansive description of Hagley Park in letters to Elizabeth Young.[21] Similarly, after viewing the spectacular salmon leap at Leixlip, a noted scenic attraction of the day, Swift laconically reported to a friend that he "got to Leixlip between three and four, saw the curiosities there, and the next morning came to Dublin. . ." (C, 2:408). This reaction is a far cry from that of another, much more typical eighteenth-century visitor, John Bush, who devoted several pages to an enthusiastic description of Leixlip's visual marvels, including "the most diverting kind of entertainment" provided by the salmon's ascent of the waterfall.[22] In viewing his landscape in general, Swift either failed to see any beauty or else willfully banished it from his realm, judging it to be incompatible with practical use, with his financial capabilities, or with existing conditions. Swift's mode of describing landscape suggests that he was either hostile to or incapable of detached aesthetic contemplation of natural beauty. It suggests, moreover, that he might well have considered such contemplation little more than pretense—an act of romantic indulgence or self-delusion, or perhaps a deliberate striving to ignore harsh realities. Swift's demythologizing outlook resulted in a cynical view of arcadian scenes set in contemporary topography. Hence he scornfully abandoned his plan to build a noble "Mansion" on "Drapier's Hill" (near Market-Hill), chiding himself for his momentary folly: "How could I form so wild a vision,/To seek, in deserts, Fields Elysian?" (*The Dean's Reasons For not Building at Drapier's Hill,* 15-16).

We can see from the preceding why Swift is rarely discussed in terms of eighteenth-century landscape, traditional conceptions of which involve the idealization of actual physical terrain through its association with art in a general sense (that is, with ideas of perfection and transcendence) and with specific works of art, such as the paintings of Claude Lorrain, Nicholas Poussin, and Salvator Rosa.[23] The creation of landscape during this period, at least in its most widely recognized and generally accepted signification, was a means of translating the mutable shapes of an aging world into the permanent forms of paradise—a means of converting the disproportions of everyday mortal existence into emblems of divinelike harmony. Swift, although he had little to do with these tendencies himself, perceived very clearly their relevance for the Popeian landscape. He noted in a letter to Pope: "I have been long told by Mr Ford of your great Atchivements in building and planting and especially of your Subterranean Passage to your Garden whereby you turned a blunder into a beauty which is a Piece of Ars Poetica" (C, 3:103).

The process of "turn[ing] a blunder into a beauty" and of containing wild nature in "a Piece of Ars Poetica" (or within a picture frame) is at the heart of what we have come to associate with "the" eighteenth-century landscape. Unquestionably it was a central aspect of one major conception of landscape during this period, the one characterized by Horace Walpole in his statement that "Poetry, Painting & Gardening, or the science of Landscape will forever by men of Taste be deemed Three Sisters, or the *Three New Graces* who dress and adorn Nature."[24] Continually we find variations on the theme of ugliness turned into beauty. Joseph Addison, for example, in celebrating the attractions of Kensington, praised " . . . the fine Genius for Gardening, that could have thought of forming such an unsightly hollow into so beautiful an Area."[25] Making nature more perfect through human artistry became the great endeavor, so that, according to Sir Thomas Whately, the gardener's aim "is to . . . discover and to show all the advantages of the place upon which he is employed; to supply its defects, to correct its faults, and to improve its Beauties."[26] A similar aim was shared by contemporary poets. As John Dixon Hunt observes, "The dominant idea of [Pope's] *Pastorals*—celebration of a golden age and its corollary, the golden kingdom of art—is expressed in landscapes of pastoral perfection and artistry that recall the ideal paintings of Claude and Poussin."[27]

With such "landscapes" and "artistry" Swift had nothing in common. The one elaboration upon the concept of *ut pictura poesis* that appears in his verse makes reference not to Claude or Poussin but to Hogarth, and functions within a poem (*A Character, Panegyric, and Description of the Legion Club*) that describes the very antithesis of an ideal world—describes, indeed, a world of rampant madness where the Irish Parliament House assumes the identity of an insane asylum: "How I want thee, humorous *Hogart*?/Thou I hear, a pleasant Rogue art;/Were but you and I acquainted,/Every Monster should be painted. . ." (219–22). When Swift shifted his gaze from human to topographical shapes, his observations were often similarly Hogarthian, producing images of comic disproportion, grotesqueness, or chaos. Disorder, indeed, is a conspicuous and recurring feature of Swift's landscapes, viewed alternately from a somber and a comic perspective. We might note, in this connection, a comment Swift made in a letter to Bolingbroke:

Pray my Lord how are the gardens? have you taken down the mount, and removed the yew hedges? . . . I built a wall five years ago, and when the masons played the knaves, nothing delighted me so much as to stand by while my servants threw down what was amiss: I have likewise seen a Monkey overthrow all the dishes and plates in a kitchen, merely for the pleasure of seeing them tumble and hearing the clatter they made in their fall. I wish you would invite me to such another entertainment. . . . (C, 3:383)

It is difficult to imagine a stance vis-à-vis landscape development that could be more antithetical to Pope's than this. We might well be tempted to conjecture that Swift was perhaps more interested in "turning a beauty into a blunder" than vice versa, more committed to making self-destructing earth works than to creating "a Piece of Ars Poetica." He seems in a sense desirous of turning the tables on a major aspect of contemporary land-scaping theory by insisting upon the transient shapes of a fallen world rather than the permanent forms of an artfully restored paradise. We perceive here Swift's highly idiosyncratic, predictably parodic, and almost literally subversive version of the detached aesthetic contemplation of nature. It can be argued, indeed, that the passage just quoted presents the closest Swift ever comes to such disinterested aesthetic enjoyment. There was a part of Swift (an important, even central part) that automatically gravitated toward, and delighted in, scenes of chaos and disintegration, much as a pig, eschewing greener—and cleaner—pastures, delightedly wallows in mud. An examination of Swift's landscape might well lead us to conclude that order was in some fundamental way alien to his mode of perceiving and locating himself in the world.

His writings tend to resemble his physical environs in their similar emphasis upon the forces of confusion and their similar reliance on col-lapsing structures—the spire of Castleknock Church, which tumbled to the ground "with a prodigious Fall," is a typical example (*On the Little House by the Church Yard of Castleknock,* 8). Like the masons' flawed constructions, doomed to be raised one day and thrown down the next, the narrative edifices set up in works like *A Tale of a Tub* and *Gulliver's Travels* are designed to self-destruct, whether as a result of the self-incriminating ramblings of an ex-Bedlamite or the appearance of Sinon to remind us that all is a lie. And, just as Swift raises up a wall one moment only to destroy it the next, so too he " . . . write[s] Pamphlets and follys meerly for amusement, and when they are finished, as I grow weary in the middle, I cast them into the fire, partly out of dislike, and chiefly because I know they will signify nothing" (C, 3:434). The tone is a more somber one in this instance, but it does not negate the aspect of sheer "amusement"; we are struck here by the extent to which, in Swift's case, it is often impossible to distinguish clearly between delight and despondency, between mischievous glee and despair. Swift, a man obsessed with transience throughout his lifetime, in many ways chose to become its co-conspirator and acting agent rather than, like Pope, waging all-out war on it with the weapons of his art. (This was, perhaps, his ultimate, his most brilliant stroke of self-irony.) As the author primarily of occasional writings, he was only too well aware of the obsolescence of words. It is *his* voice, along with the Tale-teller's, that we hear in the "Epistle Dedicatory to Prince Posterity," uttering a kind of primal outcry against the prospect of literary extinction and noting that "Books, like Men their Authors, have no more than one Way of coming into the World, but there are ten Thousand to go out of it, and return no more" (TT, 36). When Swift directed his attention and energies to his external environment, it is therefore not surprising that he became a combined overseer-creator (as well as, at times, a destroyer) of what might be termed "occasional" landscapes: ones whose architectural structures, like his linguistic constructions, were radically implicated in the world of mutability.

For Swift, painting, as well as landscape gardening, was inextricably bound to the world of temporal flux, and thus was capable of conferring neither perfection nor permanence upon living reality. Conceived as a tactile medium divorced from all notions of high art, paint is subject to the same ills as mortal man: It can crack, smear, and fade, or even decay altogether. As part of the cosmetic arsenal of Celia, who "By help of Pencil, Paint and Brush" strives to perfect her image, it fully reveals its inadequacy: "The Paint by Perspiration cracks,/And falls in Rivulets of Sweat. . ." (*The Progress of Beauty*, 46, 37-38). Even when applied to a far more worthy and enduring subject—Stella—paint cannot transcend life's vicissitudes or the ravages of time. In *Stella's Birth-day. 1720-21,* Swift's companion is represented as an inn that cheerily beckons all travelers: "And though the Painting grows decayd/The House will never loose it's Trade" (7-8). However "angelic" her mind, however immortal her spirit, Stella—along with the art that aspires to capture her in one everlasting moment beyond time's reach—must remain vulnerable to the inexorable march of years: "Now, this is Stella's Case in Fact;/An Angel's Face, a little crack't;/(Could Poets or could Painters fix/How Angels look at thirty six)" (15-18).

When he confronts the problem of how to depict the "Thought of Fame" accurately, Swift concludes:

Less should I dawb it o're with transitory Praise,
And *water-colours* of these Days,
These Days! where ev'n th' Extravagance of Poetry
Is at a loss for Figures to express

Men's Folly, Whimsyes, and Inconstancy,
And by a faint Description make them less.

(Ode to the Athenian Society, 169-74)

Paint and language alike, in other words, prove to be inadequate media
for portraying what actually exists. Contemporary art forms can only
imperfectly convey or distort outright what they are designed to give
permanent definition to, whether because the subject matter is too
exalted (as in the case of fame) or because it is too debased (as in the
case of prevailing human follies). Art is, in effect, placed in a no-win
situation, fated to come in second best no matter what the precise nature
of its endeavor. Contrary to a dominant strain of eighteenth-century
aesthetic theory, art forms as treated by Swift can neither idealize nor
magically transmute the intractable realities of life.

Later, as his attention became increasingly riveted on the harsh
realities of the Irish landscape and as he turned more and more frequently
to the printed (or at least the written) word in his desire to expose these
realities, Swift centered his thoughts on the medium of language rather
than painting. Here again a form designed to contain and crystallize aspects of human existence was apt to prove inadequate for the task.
Despite his life-long insistence upon the importance of a plain and simple
prose style whereby words never lose their basic connection to things,
Swift's numerous experimentations with "little languages" (*Journal to
Stella*), invented languages (*Gulliver's Travels*), word games (letters to
Sheridan, verse riddles), and dialects and "street" language (both verse and
prose pieces incorporating Dublin street cries), however comic their effects, indicate a profounder awareness: an awareness of the inability of
established, officially sanctioned modes of expression to deal with certain
kinds of reality, certain kinds of experience.

Swift's realization that "official" contemporary art forms, such as
neoclassical landscape painting and pastoral poetry, were inadequate
for conveying (for example) the facts of Irish life as he knew and observed them on a daily basis reinforced his preference for literary forms
such as burlesque and travesty, his reliance upon a popular satiric tradition
represented in broadsides and ballads, and his consistent use of *mock*-
pastoral throughout his verse. In virtually all of his works, we may discern
themes, energies, or (anti-) structures that are fundamentally inimical to
the ordering, idealizing Augustan mind as we have come to understand it
in terms of someone like Pope. They remain unalterably resistant to all
those forces particularly evident in Augustan poetry that transform local
ugliness into cosmic beauty—those forces lending support to Pope's assertion that "All Nature is but Art, unknown to thee;/All Chance, Direction,
which thou canst not see;/All Discord, Harmony, not understood;/All

partial Evil, universal Good. . ." (*Essay on Man,* Epistle I, 289-92). As a consequence, Swift's landscape stands as a concrete as well as a theoretic denial of Pope's "one [clear] truth": Whatever IS, is RIGHT" (294). We can see here the specifically ideological dimensions of the concept of landscape. For the pictorializing and idealizing techniques we have noted, although generally interpreted in terms of aesthetics, were closely allied in the eighteenth century to a stance of cosmic Toryism. Visually and structurally, they tend to support a conservative world view that justifies the status quo even as it *seems* to reject the latter for a vision of heavenly perfection.

Pope was, of course, quite capable of conveying a darker or more negative vision of things. In poems like the *Epistle II, i* ("To Augustus") from his *Imitations of Horace* and the *Epilogue to the Satires,* where he satirically exposed what he saw as the corruptions of the Hanoverian reign and the Walpole ministry, we are hardly moved to celebrate the status quo. Like most human beings, Pope revealed a complexity of moods and outlooks throughout his lifetime. Nevertheless, his temperamental propensity toward accommodation and reconciliation made his most characteristic mode of perception, as well as the ideological stance growing out of it, very different from Swift's. Writing to his friend in Ireland, Pope in various ways reiterated his optimistic belief in the fundamental rightness of things. Luxuriantly picturing the moment when the two men would stroll into the grave together, "contentedly and chearfully," much as they had previously sauntered through the gardens at Twickenham, he asserted, " . . . it suffices me to know [the country beyond the grave] will be exactly what region or state our Maker appoints, and that whatever *Is,* is *Right*" (C, 4:147). Industriously constructing an image of himself that he wished to leave to posterity, Pope elsewhere averred, "I will not quarrel with the present Age" and advised his friend, "Do not you be too angry at it . . . it has done and can do neither of you [Swift or Bolingbroke] any manner of harm, as long as it has not, nor cannot burn your works. . ." (527).

By contrast, Swift, in his epistolary replies, rejected assurances of ultimate resolution or vindication. (Tellingly, Swift foresaw the time when "His famous LETTERS [would be] made waste Paper" [*Drapier's Hill,* 17].) He consistently resisted the tendency (and strong temptation) to turn away from the assorted ills visible all around him and to escape instead into a world of ideal forms and pictorial representations. His continued observations of everyday reality convinced him that "whatever is" was most definitely *not* "right," as his repeated, almost obsessive recountings of Ireland's miseries indicate. What *he* saw was a world where numerous evils ". . . operate more every day, [so that] the kingdom is absolutely undone" (C, 3:341). The word "undone" echoes like a refrain throughout Swift's writings and reminds us that, for Pope's anticipations of spiritual or artistic consummation and his images of comic apocalypse, Swift substituted his own vision of nihilistic dissolution. His manner of perceiving the world made him incapable of accepting the aesthetic and ideological "solutions" offered him by Pope. "You advise me right, not trouble my self about the World: But oppressions torture me . . . ," he explained to Pope in a letter that insists upon conveying the desperate reality of a country " . . . now absolutely starving; by the means of every Oppression that can possibly be inflicted on mankind" (C, 4:385). When it was *his* turn to give advice, Swift told his correspondent, "I heartily wish you were what they call disaffected, as I, who detest abominate & abhor every Creature who hath a dram of Power in either Kingdom. . ." (383).

Implicit throughout the preceding discussion is the fact that we cannot speak intelligently about Swift's landscape—whether physical, aesthetic, mental, or ideological—without speaking of a specifically *Irish* landscape. Born in Dublin in 1667, Swift spent eighteen of his first twenty-one years in Ireland and, except for several lengthy periods spent in England during the next twenty years, followed by four years in London (1710–1714) working for the Tory ministry and two brief (half-year) visits to England in 1726 and 1727, Swift lived out his long life in his native country. By the time of his death in 1745, he had been a resident of Ireland for well over half a century and a politically involved actor in its internal affairs for almost as long. Although a handful of scholars have dealt with Swift's crucial and abiding ties to Ireland (apart from Ehrenpreis, the names of Louis A. Landa and Oliver W. Ferguson immediately come to mind[28]), Swift criticism in the main has had either the consciously desired or the indirect effect of making Swift into an eighteenth-century *Englishman:* a companion of Pope and Gay, a member of Bolingbroke's Circle—even, if we are to believe Edward Malins and the Knight of Glin, a typical Augustan landscape designer who managed to carry on his existence as though he were residing in the midst of an English garden (albeit one that happened to be located in Ireland). Reading the descriptions by Malins and the Knight of Glin of Swift and his friend Patrick Delany being "swept into the full tide of landscaping by Pope and his friends when they stayed at Twickenham in 1726 and 1727," and of their becoming "the chief precursors of the romantic-poetic garden in Ireland,"[29] one might be led to think that Swift presided over Paradise Hall rather than his small urban orchard, Naboth's Vineyard; that he lived on the banks of a re-created Lake Nemi rather than beside the polluted, frequently overflowing Poddle; and that his imagination was captured by the elegant artistries of Twickenham rather than the barren wilds of Cavan.

There were, to be sure, a number of people residing in Ireland during

this period whose energies were devoted largely to remaking portions of
the Irish landscape into little replicas of England—to surrounding themselves with artificial environments capable of sustaining the illusion that
they were in the midst of Somerset or Richmond. Several of these individuals, indeed, were included among Swift's friends—for example, Patrick
Delany, Lord Orrery, and Charles Ford. Orrery spent so much money on
building and landscaping projects designed to beautify his Irish estate at
Caledon (including the construction of a bone house modeled upon Lady
Curzon's at Kedleston, Derbyshire) that he eventually went bankrupt and
had to be bailed out by his daughter-in-law's father, Henry Hoare, the
prominent banker (as well as creator of Stourhead).[30]

Astute observer of human nature that he was, Swift understood very
well those impulses in the Anglo-Irish gentry which prompted them to
strive to become more English than the English themselves. His response
to these impulses alternated between indulgent amusement at his friends'
foibles and scathing denunciation of those aspects of the Anglicized outlook which he felt lent support to England's oppressions. The former attitude is exemplified in his verse *To Charles Ford Esqr. on his Birth-day,
1722-3*. Ford, increasingly disenchanted with life in Ireland, began residing in London for extended periods, and Swift's poem is in part a
response to his friend's expressed preference for England and his gradual
abandonment of Ireland. "In London! what would You do there?" the
poet asks incredulously (35), reminding Ford of the political repression
under "bloody Townshend" (Viscount Charles Townshend, Secretary of
State under George I and brother-in-law of Walpole) as well as of the
"swarms of Bugs and Hanoverians" he will be forced to contend with in
that city (43-46, 50). He then proceeds to assure Ford that, if he still
pines away for the supposedly superior attributes of England, they can
if necessary be reproduced in the midst of Ireland itself:

> If you have London still at heart
> We'll make a small one here by Art:
> The Diff'rence is not much between
> St James's Park and Stephen's Green;
> And, Dawson street will serve as well
> To lead you thither, as Pell-mell,
> (Without your passing thro the Palace
> To choque your Sight, and raise your Malice). . . .
>
> (57-64)

As we can see from this verse, Swift was quite willing to humor
his friends' cultivated, urbane tastes in landscape and their longing for
a specifically English environment. For his own part, however, Swift
showed little inclination to transform his Irish surroundings into a carbon

copy of the English landscape. Despite the profound ambivalence he felt toward his native country, and despite his frequent insistence upon emphasizing its most negative and unpleasing aspects, Swift demonstrated a willingness to accept the Irish landscape on its own terms. There was something about the country's sprawling disorder, about the angularities and eccentricities of her topography, that in the final analysis proved oddly congenial to Swift's own temperament and predilections: "I live in a cabin and in a very wild country [Cavan]; yet there are some agreeablenesses in it, or at least I fancy so..." (C, 3:60). At a time when gardening enthusiasts in Ireland were in a virtual frenzy to obtain exotic plants and trees from abroad, Swift took pride in his unexotic Dublin elms (C, 2:436), tended the trees in Naboth's Vineyard, and otherwise confined his attention to his cherished willows, a tree indigenous to Ireland and peculiarly adapted to its soil.

Repeatedly, Swift made it clear that his overriding concern was with practical considerations related to the native topography. When he was not commenting somberly on the land's impoverishment and desolation (usually for a specific political purpose), he was suggesting improvements designed to bring out the inherent capabilities of the Irish landscape rather than to cover them over with a veneer of English (or Continental) elegance. For example, after carefully observing the peculiar characteristics of the Irish climate, especially the direction of its winds, he asserted, "I do not believe that a greater and quicker profit could be made, than by planting large groves of ash, a few feet asunder, which in seven years would make the best kind of hop-poles," and he assured his readers that it would be "...of great use and beauty in our desert scenes, to oblige all tenants and cottagers to plant ash or elm before their cabbins, and round their potatoe-gardens" (PW, 12:88). Swift's advice for improving the management of the bogs likewise demonstrated his familiarity with the native Irish terrain and his desire to effect necessary changes without doing violence to its basic character: "For the main bog, although perhaps not reducible to natural soil, yet, by continuing large, deep, straight canals through the middle, cleaned at proper times, as low as the channel or gravel, would become a secure summer-pasture; the margins might, with great profit and ornament, be filled with quickins, birch, and other trees proper for such a soil, and the canals be convenient for water-carriage of the turf..." (87). "Profit and ornament," "use and beauty": this is the language of contemporary landscaping manuals, the kind of words we are likely to find in a work like *The Nobleman's, Gentleman's and Gardener's Recreation* by Stephen Switzer (1715). But how differently they are used by Swift, who is concerned here, as well as elsewhere, not with the combined aesthetic and economic enhancement of private property, but with the improvement of public welfare; not with the sophisticated, rich appetites of noblemen and gentlemen gardeners, but with the basic (and hitherto sadly neglected) needs of average country dwellers and travelers. Above all, it is not an affluent but an impoverished landscape that Swift observes around him, precisely because he chooses to see an *Irish* landscape instead of restricting his vision to those carefully circumscribed pockets of "little England" scattered throughout the island.

Given Swift's ties to his native terrain, attempts to assimilate him into the environs of Twickenham or Cirencester or Marble-Hill are sadly misguided. Even those who do not try to make Swift into an English country gentleman generally fail to locate him in his proper landscape. We may recall Pat Rogers's comment, cited earlier, that in contradistinction to Pope's "daylight and champaign," "with Swift we think of the windy downs about Letcombe or the desolate landing-stage at Holyhead." Now this remark certainly comes closer to conveying the basic spirit behind Swift's outlook than those made by Malins and the Knight of Glin, but, once we give a little further thought to this statement, the rather astonishing realization hits us that of the two places identified most intimately with Swift, neither happens to be in Ireland. Why, at the mention of Swift, should we think of Letcombe, the small Berkshire village near Wantage where he spent less than three months in the summer of 1714 before returning to Ireland, or why, even, should we immediately think of Holyhead, an area admittedly occupying an important place in his thought as well as in his writings but where he spent a matter of mere days in a lifetime that spanned seventy-eight years? Why, instead, do we not automatically associate Swift with the places he observed, traveled through, resided in, and wrote about most frequently: Cavan, Glasnevin, Belcamp, Market-Hill, Laracor, Trim, and—most obvious of all—Dublin?

I suspect that the explanation for this is similar to the reasons why, when we discuss Swift as satirist, we tend immediately to think of the Moderns, the Royal Society, Grub Street hacks, Robert Walpole, and King George—those butts, in other words, whom Swift shares in common with his fellow satirists in England. Often it is only as an afterthought that we call to mind (if we bother to do so at all) such names as Sir Thomas Prendergast, Lord Chief Justice Whitshed, "Booby" Bettesworth, and Lord Allen: men who played a far more immediate and direct role in Swift's life and who occupied a good deal of both his political and his literary attentions. There is a particular irony here when we recall Swift's letter to Pope after reading *The Dunciad,* in which he expressed concern that " . . . it will be a great disadvantage to the poem, that the persons and facts will not be understood, till an explanation comes out, and a very full one" (C, 3:293). Swift's insistence upon preserving the historical particularities and local details informing a literary work should serve as a model for our treatment of Swift's own writings. That this model has not been followed nearly as much or as closely as it ought to be may well reflect certain shortcomings in our established critical framework, which are not unrelated to the problems surrounding the term "landscape." In our attempts, whether conscious or otherwise, to confer sanction upon given writers by subsuming them into what we loosely—but then again, not so loosely—understand to be the English literary tradition, we have too often accorded Swift a small corner of Pope's landscape rather than allowing him to inhabit his own. The following chapters are intended to correct this fundamental misperception by restoring Swift to his proper environs.

CHAPTER • 2

Central Features of Swift's Landscape

Excremental Vision vs. Excremental Reality

i

That the imaginative and satiric world of Swift's writings derives a good part of its meaning from the geographic and political world of eighteenth-century Ireland becomes evident in the course of a reappraisal of those images and preoccupations which have given rise to the term "excremental vision." Critics have interpreted them as expressions of the psyche or the subconscious, as the subject for psychobiography or psychoanalysis.[1] It is true that the peculiarly obsessive quality of Swift's excremental references makes explanations based only on (say) satiric strategy seem woefully inadequate, and we might well conjecture that the frequency of these references points to an important aspect of Swift's mode of apprehending his world. But what has generally been ignored is the fact that Swift actually lived in a landscape in which excrement was a prominent—not to mention highly visible and necessarily obtrusive—feature. He had only to leave the immediate confines of the deanery and walk down any neighboring street, or through most other parts of Dublin for that matter, in order to see omnipresent signs of human ordure amidst other assorted offal. Such sights were of course not unique to Dublin, being in some measure endemic to all urban areas during this period: a period that had neither plumbing nor centralized, technologically efficient methods of sanitation. We know from Hogarth's prints, from Gay's city perambulations, and from Pope's depiction of the place " . . . where Fleet-ditch with disemboguing streams / Rolls the large tribute of dead dogs to Thames" (*The Dunciad*, Book II, 271–72), not to mention from Swift's

24

own account of the "Filth of all Hues and Odours" flowing to Holborn Bridge (*A Description of a City Shower*, 55–60), that these were aspects of the London scene as well. The approaches to the city were especially stench-ridden, and the Ditch extending from Fleet Bridge to Holborn Bridge was nothing more than an open sewer.[2]

But to an even greater extent than London, and for a longer span of time, Dublin in the eighteenth century was a place of conspicuous and widespread uncleanness. When Arthur Young visited Dublin at the start of his Irish tour thirty years after Swift's death, he complained of dirty accommodations and remarked that walking in the streets of the city was "a most uneasy and disgusting exercise," due to a combination of narrow thoroughfares, overcrowding, and filth.[3] Writing in 1847, John Edward Walsh observed: "For want of sewers, the filth and water [in the streets] were received in pits, called cesspools, dug before the doors [of houses], and covered in; and those continued in Sackville Street, and other places, long after the year 1810; and many now remember the horrid sight and smell which periodically offended the inhabitants in even the most fashionable streets, when those stygian pools were opened and emptied."[4] The lateness of the date cited here suggests that this problem was more serious and tenacious in Dublin than in London, where major improvements in sanitary conditions began taking place by the middle of the eighteenth century.[5]

The situation was particularly bad in the Liberties, the southwest area of Dublin where St. Patrick's Cathedral stood (and still stands), which was at once the oldest and poorest part of the city. (In addition to the Liberty of St. Patrick's, this area included the Liberties of Christchurch and St. Sepulchre's, as well as the Liberties of Thomas Court and Donore, which lay mostly within the boundaries of the Earl of Meath's estate. All were exempt from the city jurisdiction.) Constantia Maxwell notes that "in the filthy and squalid quarters [of Dublin], especially around St. Patrick's Cathedral, housing conditions were very bad, and sanitary arrangements almost nonexistent."[6] When the Reverend James Whitelaw took his census of Dublin at the end of the century, it was the Liberties he singled out as the most grimly vivid embodiment of the city's miserable conditions. This dubious distinction was based to a large extent on the Liberties' pervasively excremental character:

The streets [in the Liberties] are generally narrow; the houses crowded together; the rears or back-yards of very small extent, and some without any accommodation of any kind. . . . I have frequently surprised from ten to sixteen persons, of all ages and sexes, in a room not 15 feet square, stretched on a wad of filthy straw, swarming with vermin and without any covering, save the wretched rags that constituted their wearing apparel. . . . This crowded population

A SECTION OF A MAP OF DUBLIN FROM JOHN BUSH'S *HIBERNIA CURIOSA*
(LONDON, 1768).

wherever it obtains is almost universally accompanied by a very
serious evil—a degree of filth and stench inconceivable except by
such as have visited these scenes of wretchedness. Into the backyard
of each house, frequently not 10 feet deep, is flung from the windows of each apartment, the ordure and other filth of its numerous

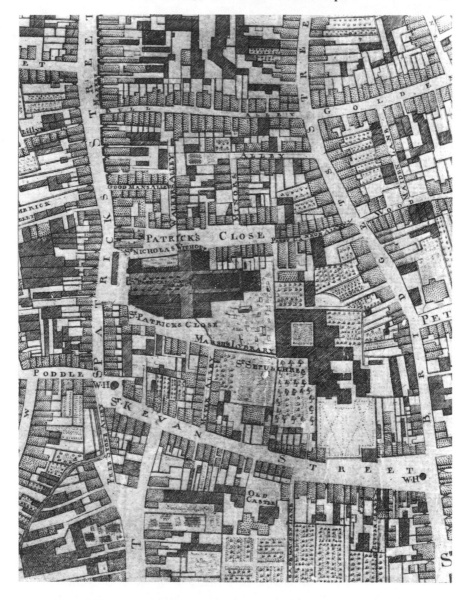

A SECTION OF A MAP OF DUBLIN FROM JOHN ROCQUE'S *AN EXACT SUR-
VEY OF THE CITY AND SUBURBS OF DUBLIN* (DUBLIN, 1756).
Courtesy of the National Library of Ireland

inhabitants; from which it is so seldom removed, that I have seen it nearly on a level with the windows of the first floor; and the moisture that, after heavy rains, oozes from this heap, having frequently no sewer to carry it off, runs into the street, by the entry leading to the staircase.[7]

Had the Huguenot weavers who settled the area of the nearby Coombes in such large numbers been permitted to carry on their trade without outside interference, that area might well have developed into a thriving middle-class neighborhood, exuding that robust glow likely to accompany successful applications of the Protestant Ethic. But England's harsh economic sanctions, designed to protect her own clothing industry and to convert Ireland into a dumping ground for English manufactured goods, replaced potential prosperity with immediate hardship and had the effect of turning the Liberties into an increasingly poorer working-class area plagued by widespread unemployment. It became a natural haven for abandoned refuse and for the human "refuse" of a highly stratified class society—in Swift's own words, "that great Number of Poor, who under the Name of common Beggars, infest our Streets, and fill our Ears with their continual Cries" (PW, 9:205).

The first half of the eighteenth century was already witnessing what Maurice Craig terms "the unique eastward tendency in Dublin" whereby "the fashionable-residential could only spread east"[8]—a tendency soon to result in the division of the city into the "two Dublins" noted by a visitor in the following century: the east, comprising the "handsomest parts of the city," being "airy [and] elegant" with "spacious squares and streets"; and "the western end of this city, denominated by the citizens the *Liberty*," which presented "a complete contrast" to the former, filled with "mostly narrow" streets and dilapidated houses "excessively crowded together," along with "the accumulation of filth, stench, and every variety of wretchedness resulting from this union of obnoxious circumstances. . . ." A footnote adds that "the rears, or back-yards, of these houses are in general the *only* receptacles for the ordure and filth of their numerous occupants."[9] Thus whereas Pope, from his distant, richly landscaped suburban villa, satirically reproduced the *westward* progress of the Dunces through London, Swift bemusedly watched the exodus of the Anglo-Irish gentry *eastward*, to the spacious, elegant environs of Dawson Street, Merrion Square, and St. Stephen's Green, abandoning Swift himself to the "filth, stench, and . . . wretchedness" that permeated the environs of the deanery. (See map of Dublin on p. xii.)

Exacerbating these unsanitary conditions was the fact that St.

WEST FRONT OF ST. PATRICK'S CATHEDRAL, DUBLIN. ILLUSTRATION BY
J. MALTON (LONDON, 1793).
Courtesy of the National Library of Ireland

Patrick's stood on very low ground. John Loveday of Caversham, during
his visit to the cathedral in 1732, admired its elevated tower but noted
that "St Werburgh's new and new-fashioned Tower seems to overtop It,
That Church standg upon high Ground, whereas This is seated just by ye
Butchery, in a low part of Dublin."[10] Thomas Cromwell, visiting the
cathedral some years later, went further, proclaiming the site of St.
Patrick's "the lowest ground in Dublin."[11] Its situation meant that St.
Patrick's—along with the Liberties in general—was particularly vulnerable to the frequent flooding caused by the Liffey and the underground
Poddle near the cathedral, which inevitably increased the filth and stench.
William Monck Mason describes one such disaster that occurred in early
December 1687, after two months of incessant rain: ". . . the houses, in
the lower parts of the city, were filled with water above the first floor;
the flood continued to rise during the two following days, and during that
period boats plied in Patrick-street and the Coombe. . . . The cathedral
and its chapels suffered much, as the water rose above the desks, and the
books were almost all destroyed."[12] A century later, James Malton noted,

in the description appended to his view of St. Patrick's: "The Cathedral
Church of St. Patrick, has not the advantage of contributing to the splen-
dour of Dublin, owing as much to the meanness of the surrounding dwellings, as to its situation, which is as uneligible as possible; being built quite
in a hollow, which occasions the whole Church, with the surrounding
Close and contiguous Streets, at the time of heavy rains, to be under water
even to the depth of seven or more feet; this keeps it very damp and dirty,
and is bringing it quickly to ruin."[13] Swift attested to the immediate
effects these heavy rains and consequent flooding had upon him. In a
letter to Sheridan he mentions one particular inundation from the Poddle
that caused "Havock in *Naboth*'s Vineyard"—that is, in Swift's orchard
just beyond the deanery (C, 3:298). (The Poddle eventually became an
open sewer and had to be filled in.) That the Liberties were situated on
such low ground adds a special literalness to Swift's preoccupation with
murky depths and nether regions. Whereas his contemporaries deliberately
sought out *elevated* sites that could offer them a vantage point from
which to *oversee* their world, Swift remained in an area *depressed* in every
way, topographically as well as economically, which is one reason, perhaps, why he so consistently kept his nose to the ground and his eyes
fixed on the objects in his immediate purview.

Excrement, then, was very much a fact of life for Swift; his landscape was literally as well as linguistically full of it. His satiric piece, *An
Examination of Certain Abuses, Corruptions, and Enormities, in the City
of Dublin,* suggests just how literal a fact it was. Pointing out that "Every
Person who walks the Streets, must needs observe the immense Number
of human Excrements at the Doors and Steps of waste Houses, and at the
Sides of every dead Wall," Swift proceeds with a graphic comparison between the *"British Anus"* and the *"Hibernian"* one in order to discredit
the malicious rumor "that these Heaps were laid there privately by *British
Fundaments,* to make the World believe, that our *Irish* Vulgar do daily eat
and drink" (PW, 12:220). Despite the grotesquely exaggerated and comically absurd world set into motion by the satire, the descriptions abound
in empirical detail ("coming up *Fishamble-street,*" listening to the varied
Dublin street cries) and convince us of the excremental *reality,* not simply
the "excremental vision," of this world. With the statement that the street
cry, *"Dirt to carry out,"* has been "so effectually observed, that the true
political Dirt is wholly removed, and thrown on its proper Dunghills, there
to corrupt and be no more heard of," we find ourselves in a realm between literal fact and figure of speech. The "Dunghills" here point both
outward, to the external environment, and inward, to Swift's own be-
fouled and stench-ridden world of satiric fictions. It takes only one more

small step in the direction of metaphor to produce the passage in *A Pane-gyric on the Reverend D——n S——t, In answer to the Libel on Dr. D——y, and a Certain Great L——d,* which describes

> . . . how *Statesmen* oft are stung
> By Gnats, and draw the Nation's *Dung,*
> The *stinking* Load of all the Crimes,
> And *Nastiness* of modern Times,
> Not only what themselves have ——
> For that were not unjust a Bit,
> But all the *Filth* both *Spiss,* and *Sparse*
> Of e'ery Rogue that wears an ——

(114-21)*

The sticky, besmeared world of the Liberties is not left behind here but is simply spread around over a wider area, with its putrefaction shown to extend to the highest levels of government.

Similarly, in *A Character, Panegyric, and Description of the Legion Club* we see the Irish politicians "dabbl[ing] in their Dung" (52) and "Toast[ing] *old Glorious* in [their] Piss" (152). Their entire world is defined by "Ordure" (19), "Dirt" (74), and "stink" (154). Swift's mock-epic descent into the hellish interior of the Parliament House is on one level a satiric fantasy expressed through excremental imagery, but when we realize the conditions in which Swift actually lived, we are less likely to attribute this passage to satiric convention or psychological fixation only and more inclined to consider its relationship to external realities:

> *Clio* stifled with the Smell,
> Into Spleen and Vapours fell;
> By the *Stygian* Steams that flew,
> From the dire infectious Crew.
> Not the Stench of Lake *Avernus,*
> Could have more offended her Nose;

*There have been some questions raised about the attribution of this poem. James Woolley, for example, presents a credible but by no means definitive case for its having been written by James Arbuckle rather than Swift (see "Arbuckle's 'Pane-gyric' and Swift's Scrub Libel: The Documentary Evidence," in *Contemporary Studies of Swift's Poetry,* ed. John Irwin Fischer and Donald C. Mell, Jr. [Newark: University of Delaware Press, 1981], pp. 191-209). Although doubts about the poem's author-ship remain (and, indeed, date back to Swift's printer, George Faulkner, who also attributed it to Arbuckle), I find the *Panegyric* not at all uncharacteristic of Swift in its vituperative and self-defamatory tone and have followed the two modern editors of Swift's poetry, Ball and Williams, in accepting it as part of Swift's canon.

Had she flown but o'er the Top,
She would feel her Pinions drop,
And by Exhalations dire,
Though a Goddess must expire.
In a Fright she crept away,
Bravely I resolved to stay.

                                                                (121-32)

An inspection of many Irish buildings at the time (even if not the
Parliament House per se) could undoubtedly have provided a factual basis
for the kind of hellish tour just depicted and, at least by the end of the
century, particularly in districts like the Liberties, could easily have
matched one's wildest stygian fantasies. Reverend Whitelaw tells us that
when he and his assistants explored some of these "wretched habitations"
in the summer of 1798, they encountered "degrees of filth, stench, and
darkness inconceivable by those who have not experienced them," and he
recounts one incident when his entry into a house was impeded "by an
inundation of putrid blood, alive with maggots, which had from an adjacent slaughter yard burst the back door, and filled the hall to the depth
of several inches."[14] St. Patrick's Cathedral was itself located right near a
butchery,[15] and we are reminded of the "Sweepings from Butchers Stalls,
Dung, Guts, and Blood" revealed in *A Description of a City Shower* (61)
as well as of Swift's general preoccupation with parasitic creatures. In
Part II of *Gulliver's Travels,* for example, he depicts Gulliver encountering
crowds of beggars while riding through downtown Brobdingnag: "But, the
most hateful Sight of all was the Lice crawling on their Cloaths: I could
see distinctly the Limbs of these Vermin with my naked Eye, much better
than those of an *European* Louse through a Microscope; and their Snouts
with which they rooted like Swine" (PW, 11:113). Maggots, lice, fleas,
stripped carcasses, heaps of dung, cellars, and garrets—these, the recurring
features of Swift's satiric world, were at the same time features of his
geographic and sociological landscape.

The daily aspects of Swift's life in the Liberties profoundly affected
his way of seeing the world; that is, his specific, immediate perceptions of
basic power relationships and class interactions within society, as well as
of the dramatically differing physical landscapes that the latter inevitably
produce. To maintain that Swift kept his gaze unwaveringly fixed upon
the Great Chain of Being or upon the symmetrical beauties of Divine
Providence as he daily plowed through the muck and ruins of his Dublin
neighborhood, past the now-empty weavers' shops, the filthy, over-
crowded tenements, and the teeming mass of lice-infested beggars who
came pouring into the Liberties from all regions of Ireland, is in effect to

argue that Swift was a far less observant and sensitive human being than his writings continually reveal him to be. Swift's physical surroundings were far more likely to inspire visions of a cosmic dung heap than visions of " . . . blushing Flora paint[ing] th' enamel'd Ground" (*Windsor-Forest,* 38) or even of a " . . . Garden, tempting with forbidden fruit" (*Essay on Man,* Epistle I, 8). These surroundings stood as a visible reminder that the "fruit" had already been eaten, and that the "Garden" had long since gone to seed and become a receptacle for waste matter rather than a producer of divine nutriments.

ii

Swift's excremental environment was not limited to urban poverty and congestion; it extended to the land outside Dublin as well. Swift's comment to Sheridan, "*You live among ill Folks in a Dunghill*" (C, 4:502), though appearing in an exchange of playful verses, has literal application to an existing landscape: Cavan, where Sheridan lived "among a Million of wants" in "a little obscure Irish Cabbin about fourty miles from Dublin" in "a very wild country" (C, 3:89, 84, 60). In his verse *To Quilca, a Country House in no very good Repair,* Swift describes Sheridan's habitation as "A rotten Cabbin, dropping Rain," where "The Goddess *Want* in Triumph reigns" together with "*Dirt*" as one of her "chief Officers of State" (2, 10-12). He stresses the cabin's generally filthy condition in *The Blunders, Deficiencies, Distresses, and Misfortunes of Quilca* also, offering, among other things, "A Proverb on the Laziness and Lodgings of the Servants: *The worse their Stye, the longer they lie*" (PW, 5:221). In his lampoon against Sir Thomas Prendergast, Swift underscores his victim's rural origins and then exclaims, "Just Heaven! to see the Dunghill dastard Brood/Survive in thee. . ." (*On Noisy Tom,* 17-18). Reflecting upon Ireland's "Nurseries" for young criminals, Swift points to "the barbarous and desert Part of the Country, from whence such Lads come up hither to seek their Fortunes, who are bred up from the Dunghill in Idleness, Ignorance, Lying, and Thieving" (PW, 9:203).

Here again, what we might be tempted to explain simply in terms of either satiric technique or mental fixation turns out to have a concrete historical as well as geographical dimension. Contemporary travelers through the Irish countryside frequently remarked upon the enormous dunghills surrounding the Irish cabins that at times appeared to be inseparable from both the houses and the inhabitants. John Dunton, arriving in 1699 in Rathcoole, a village six miles from Dublin, made note of "several little children as naked as ever they were born easing themselves on the dunghills before the doors of the cabins," and a half-century later Edmund Burke asserted that "it is no uncommon Sight to see half a dozen Children run quite naked out of a Cabin, scarcely distinguishable from the Dunghill. . . ."[16] Arthur Young's comment that the poorly repaired roofs of many cabins conveyed "the appearance of a weedy dunghill"[17] functions somewhere between empirical observation and metaphoric description—so omnipresent was the excrement that it permeated language as well as landscapes, shaping one's frame of reference as well as one's field of vision. Another contemporary traveler, viewing these generally chimneyless and windowless cabins from a distance after fires had been lit from within, compared them to "heaps of dung reeking with the steam of their own fermentation."[18] Accounts like these give added immediacy and relevance to Swift's terminology in his sermon, *Doing Good*. Speaking of those who would introduce infected goods (here referring to Wood's halfpence) into a country for personal gain, he declares: "Let those among us consider this and tremble, whose houses are privately stored with those materials of beggary and desolation, lately brought over to be scattered like a pestilence among their countrymen, which may probably first seize upon themselves and their families, until their houses shall be made a dunghill" (PW, 9:237).

Swift explores the excremental realities of rural life in two distinct, indeed antithetical, ways. On the one hand, he stresses their negative association with nastiness, gross physicality, and barbarism; on the other, he suggests their connection with an appealing form of naturalness and spontaneity. The former view is expressed in his depiction of the Yahoos in Part IV of *Gulliver's Travels*. The Houyhnhnm master refers disdainfully to their "strange Disposition to Nastiness and Dirt," one that makes them susceptible to various diseases, which they cure with "a Mixture of *their own Dung* and *Urine,* forcibly put down [their] Throat" (PW, 11: 262-63). In Gulliver's first encounter with them, they "discharge[d] their Excrements on [his] Head," causing him to become "almost stifled with the Filth, which fell about [him] on every Side" (224). Later, "a young Male of three Years old" rebuffed his overtures of tenderness and "voided its filthy Excrements of a yellow liquid Substance, all over [his] Cloaths" (265-66). Despite the fact that he claims to have discovered a kind of Edenic realm presided over by perfect beings, Gulliver in Houyhnhnmland, like his creator in the Liberties, finds himself in the midst of a dung-filled, stench-ridden environment, forced repeatedly to negotiate his way through the muck and to confront physically repugnant aspects of his surroundings in very immediate ways. He, like Swift, displays a rather unseemly preoccupation with his messy fate and disgustedly lashes out against it—although he, of course, lacks Swift's capacity for dealing both

humorously and realistically with similarly unpleasant features of his landscape.

In many ways, the depiction of the Yahoos, as Sir Charles Firth
noted, "recalls the description given by Swift, in prose pamphlets written about the same time, of the people whom he terms 'the savage old
Irish.'"[19] More broadly, the Yahoos embody characteristics that Swift
periodically observed in the Irish people as a whole: slovenliness, squalor,
and a certain kind of barbarity, paradoxically coexisting with an excessive
submissiveness to authority (the Yahoo leader's favorite would *"lick his
Master's Feet and Posteriors"* [262])—not to mention their basic position
as a servant class to a ruling elite, who seem to have established a kind of
Equestrian Ascendancy. On one level the Yahoos are the Irish as perceived with lofty disdain by a highly cultivated elite who have fully sub-
limated all biological and emotional urges to higher forms of rational
thought and civilized behavior. They are the Irish adjudged by English
(hence also Gulliverian) standards as subhuman (or rather, subequestrian)
creatures whose excremental activities bespeak an atavistic force that must
be kept under tight control—creatures who must be "inclosed" (271),
tamed as draught or carriage animals (271), and consigned to "Huts"
(266) perhaps not very different from the notorious Irish "cabbins,"
finally to be deemed unfit for anything but extermination.[20]

The satire of Part IV cuts both ways, casting a critical light on
both the brutish, slavish Yahoos and (though less obviously) on their
icily detached, colonial masters. Swift was himself at various periods in
his life a Yahoo bent on denying his true origins in order to be accepted as
a Houyhnhnm before he, like Gulliver, was "exiled" and forced to return
to "Yahooland." In this sense, Gulliver in Part IV is the Swift who on
occasion repudiated his links to his fellow countrymen, choosing to see
the Irish as little better than dabblers in, and devourers of, their own
excrement—as wallowers in filthy conditions that were self-generated
rather than created by external circumstances.

The point to be stressed in all of this is that the complex, shifting
perspectives explored in Gulliver's fourth voyage are inextricably linked to
an existing landscape and to its actual inhabitants. Thomas M. Curley
maintains that the Yahoos "have much in common with the benighted
Australian aborigines of Dampier's New Holland,"[21] but I am arguing they
have even more in common with the "aborigines" of eighteenth-century
Ireland, whom Swift, indeed, on several occasions likened to Laplanders,
Hottentots, and other exotic creatures living wild, primitive existences in
remote parts of the world. In one instance he avers that "whatever Stranger took such a Journey [through Ireland], would be apt to think himself
travelling in *Lapland,* or *Ysland*. . ." (PW, 12:10). Swift's personal travels

through the more isolated regions of Ireland gave him firsthand knowledge
of the omnipresent squalor, visibly dramatized by the excremental realities, that characterized the Irish countryside. In Part IV of *Gulliver's
Travels,* the brutish, dung-filled world of the Irish is treated largely with
revulsion and contempt; elsewhere in Swift's writings, this world is treated
with alternating pity, anguish, and outrage against the external forces
responsible for these conditions.

If Gulliver in Houyhnhnmland champions the biological repressions
required for the advancement of civilization (and for the maintenance of
a ruling class), the persona of *A Panegyrick on the D——n, in the Person of
a Lady in the North* takes the opposite position. In this verse, the Golden
Age is portrayed in terms of an excremental plenitude. Addressing the
"bounteous Goddess *Cloacine,*" whom now, unjustly, "To Temples . . .
we confine" and "Forbid in open Air to breath" (229-31), the speaker
recalls a more natural and innocent time when

> Ten Thousand Altars *smoaking* round
> Were built to thee, with Off'rings crown'd:
> And here thy daily Vot'ries plac't
> Their Sacrifice with Zeal and Haste:
> The Margin of a purling Stream,
> Sent up to thee a grateful Steam.

> (237-42)

Swift's reference elsewhere to the "gaudy Tulips rais'd from Dung" (*The
Lady's Dressing Room,* 142) gains added emphasis from his description
here of the prolific offerings made "in some flow'ry Vale" (247), as a
result of which "many a Flow'r abstersive grew" (249). The basic distinction between the Golden Age and "our degen'rate Days" (287) is
conveyed through contrasting images of unnatural confinement on the
one hand, and of freedom and unconstraint on the other: "None seek
thee now in open Air;/To thee no verdant Altars rear;/But, in their Cells
and Vaults obscene/Present a Sacrifice unclean" (281-84).

All the devaluative terms in the poem ("Stealth," "Confin'd," "Cell,"
"Forbid") have to do with forms of repression. The *Panegyrick* is part of
Swift's idiosyncratic and extremely complicated version of "Civilization
and Its Discontents"; his allegiances remain, here as elsewhere, equivocal.
The sheer exuberance communicated by those passages dealing with spontaneous self-expression betrays whatever "official" position Swift might
have in the matter. Yet Swift cunningly protects himself by ascribing the
sentiments in these passages to his poetic persona, the "Lady in the North"
(Lady Acheson), while he himself is portrayed as one whose actions are
designed to *promote* the forces of repression: as a builder of "Palladian"
outhouses where "In sep'rate Cells the He's and She's/Here pay their

Vows with *bended Knees...*" (207–8). Viewed in ideological terms, the
verse dramatizes the ironic tensions between the "Tory" and the "anarchist" elements that are ever present in Swift; that is, between his theoretic belief in the societal need for sublimation and his temperamental
antipathy to all forms of restraint. The entire series of *Market-Hill* poems,
indeed, may be considered in this light, with the figures of Lady Acheson
and "the Dean" taking turns playing the roles of the Urizenic naysayer
and the Orc-like figure of rebelliousness or misrule.

There is a further ideological dimension to the poem that is relevant
to the issue of Swift's "excremental vision." The contrast between the
"degen'rate" present and the "golden" age comes to be seen in terms of
an opposition between "Ye Great ones" (291) and "our harmless Northern Swains" (300)—between, in other words, two very different classes in
society, whose respective styles of excreting in a sense represent their antithetical styles of living. The "Great ones" are rebuked for "disdain[ing] /
To pay [their] Tribute on the Plain," and the speaker demands to know
of them

> Why will you place in lazy Pride
> Your Altars near your Couches Side?
> When from the homeliest Earthen Ware
> Are sent up Off'rings more sincere
> Than where the haughty Dutchess Locks,
> Her Silver Vase in Cedar-Box.
>
> (293–98)

The repression of natural instincts in the cause of civilized society here
results merely in pride, haughtiness, and ostentation. The "Northern
Swains," on the contrary, happily retain "some Devotion" to Golden
Age practices, for their "Off'rings plac't in golden Ranks,/Adorn our
chrystal River's Banks:/Nor seldom grace the flow'ry downs,/With spiral
Tops, and Copple-Crowns..." (301–4). It is the second of these alternative excremental styles (so to speak) that strikes us as the more appealing,
although it need hardly be pointed out that the latter description in no
way constitutes an unironic tribute to living "according to nature."

The *Panegyrick* indirectly attests not only to Swift's "obsession
with" excrement but also to the omnipresent *fact* of excrement in Swift's
life: the "loads of sh—— almost choking the way" that daily assaulted his
eyes and nose and that threatened at any moment to impede his passage
through streets or countryside. However much involved it is in a world of
fantasy, the *Panegyrick* underscores this reality, its insistence and ines-
capability, when the (mock) idealized setting of an excrementally adorned
Eden abruptly turns into a world of immediate (all-too-immediate) experience. Just as the description of the swains' "Off'rings plac't in golden

Ranks" *seems* on the verge of becoming an artifact, an autonomous scene carefully framed as though on canvas, it suddenly repudiates its idealized status and asserts its eminently palpable presence in the world of everyday existence. Hence, following a literary allusion that momentarily encourages our expectations of an aesthetic transformation ("[So Poets sing, with golden Bough/The *Trojan* Heroe paid his Vow]"), we are unceremoniously catapulted from the realm of high art right smack into the midst of an effluvial heap, accompanied by the now-soiled poetic speaker:

> Hither by luckless Error led,
> The crude Consistence oft I tread.
> Here, when my Shoes are out of case,
> Unweeting gild the tarnish'd Lace:
> Here, by the sacred Bramble ting'd,
> My Petticoat is doubly fring'd.

(309–14)

Lest the references to "gilding" and "fringing" tempt the reader to speculate that perhaps another form of aesthetic transformation is in the offing, the speaker hurriedly assures us that "the zealous *Hannah*" will be directed "To wash [Cloacine's] injur'd Off'rings out" (317–18)—a discreet reminder that these "Off'rings," no matter how "arcadian" or ritualistically significant, are in the last analysis simply dirty.

Although "fresh vomit" and ordure's "magic juices" are very much part of the world portrayed in *The Dunciad,* there the nastiness *is* aesthetically contained and transformed: Smedley, for example, rises from Fleet Ditch's foul waters "bear[ing] no token of the sabler streams" and, in an artistic apotheosis not wholly unlike that of Belinda's lock, " . . . mounts far off among the Swans of Thames" (Book II, 297–98). Even more to the point, the nastiness is an aspect of the *Dunces'* milieu, *not* Pope's: It reflects the world inhabited by Grub Street hacks and other promoters of popular culture, *not* by the cultural elite who have effected a would-be Horatian retreat into the country (or, in many cases, the suburbs) to escape the "contamination" of unruly urban mobs and their messy cityscapes.

In Swift's *Panegyrick,* on the contrary, no distance is established between the depicted setting and the poet himself; indeed, the latter is not only presented in the very midst of this setting, he is also shown to be an eager participant in its mode of existence. The "Lady in the *North*" calls him "Our Thatcher, Ditcher, Gard'ner, [and] Baily" (156) and commends him for his willingness "To sweep the Mansion-house they [the Poultry] dwell in;/And cure the Rank unsav'ry Smelling" (165–66). It is the "Lady" who finally steps in the mess, but it could just as well have been Swift himself, who is at the moment sharing his hostess's landscape and who, as other verses in the *Market-Hill* series indicate, is even more prone than she to wander through its grounds. The landscape described here is not some satirically grotesque projection of the world of (say) the Dunces, but rather the actual surroundings (comically heightened, to be sure) that Swift saw and smelled, labored in and walked through, during his extended stays at Market-Hill.

The references to "North" and "Northern," in connection with both the "Lady" and the "Swains," underscore the verse's relevance to Market-Hill, since the Achesons' residence was situated in county Armagh, in what is today part of Northern Ireland. The "Swains" may function as imaginary figures in a mock-pastoral verse, but at the same time they take their place among the rural laborers actually living in the neighborhood of Market-Hill. Although the nearby town of Armagh would later in the century become noted for its distinguished architecture and prosperous appearance, thanks to the costly improvements made by Archbishop Robinson, in Swift's time it must have been almost as primitive (as "arcadian" or mock-arcadian) as other provincial areas of Ireland, even though it was better off economically on the strength of its linen trade.[22] Indeed, almost a half-century later, Arthur Young, approaching Market-Hill from Newry, observed that "this road is abominably bad, continually over hills, rough, stony, and cut up" (we may recall Swift's emphasis upon sharp stones and potentially bruised "bums" in his mock-pastoral poems), and, although admiring how Armagh was in the process of becoming "a well-built city of stone and slate," he noted that Archbishop Robinson had initially "found it in a nest of mud cabbins."[23] The "Swains" and "Cowboys" (80) who appear in the *Panegyrick* are, then, denizens of the same historical world ironically portrayed in Swift's *Answer to the Craftsman*: a world in which "the industrious Shepherd and Cow-herd may sit, every Man under his own Blackberry Bush, and on his own Potatoe-Bed, whereby this happy Island will become a new *Arcadia*" (PW, 12:176).

In short, the landscape presented in the *Panegyrick* is firmly rooted in historical and topographical reality as well as in specific autobiographical detail. What Swift saw in front of him, what he smelled in the air, what his hostess stepped in—all are details belonging to a particular place at a particular point in time. This is one more reason, we might note in passing, why Swift's topographical verse is not usually thought of in connection with eighteenth-century landscape poetry, since the latter, for all its often abundant pictorial detail, necessarily sacrifices genuine individuation and true specificity for the creation of a rural scene general (or emblematic) enough to evoke immediate associations with an *ideal* landscape.

iii

Swift's insistence upon describing landscapes where excrement is a matter to be dealt with both literally and figuratively, both in empirical and in verbal terms, dramatizes the profound differences between Swift's perception of his world and the perceptions of writers like Pope and Thomson. One need hardly point out that no similar insistence characterizes their landscape depictions, which, indeed, have been antiseptically purged of all such features. It would be virtually impossible to conceive of (let us say) Lord Lyttelton and his "loved Lucinda" coming upon a heap of dung on their leisurely strolls through Hagley Park, either in real life or in a Thomsonian re-creation. If we consider for a moment why this should be so (manure is, after all, a common fact of rural existence) we come to realize that the style of life aristocrats like Lyttelton led, as well as the style of life commemorated by aristocratically supported poets like Thomson, was not a genuine rural existence, but rather an existence artificially produced, carefully protected from the outside world, and aesthetically elevated to a "finer"—which is to say, among other things, a less smelly and messy—tone. It was a style of life growing out of what Raymond Williams in a different context calls "a rentier's vision: the cool country that is . . . not that of the working farmer but of the fortunate resident," representing "not a rural but a suburban or dormitory dream."[24] The absence of excrement from the landscapes of Lyttelton and his poetic commemorator points to their freedom from all sorts of human odors, embarrassments, and physical discomforts. Reflecting further upon this issue, we realize that Lord Lyttelton must have arranged his entire life, just as Thomson arranged his art, so as to avoid having to deal with excremental matters, along with all they imply. Both men, in their own respective ways, succeeded in creating landscapes filled with a variety sufficiently wide to produce the illusion of comprehensiveness, but also sufficiently controlled to keep out all hints of ugliness and squalor, as well as to prevent disagreeable "accidents" like stepping into dunghills or being confronted face to face with the human "offspring" of these dunghills.

We can think of this matter in slightly different terms. In the society in which Swift lived, one's relationship to excremental realities was necessarily determined by social and economic class. Not everyone (indeed, very few) could afford to keep these realities at a safe and comfortable remove. There were, in fact, a vast number of people whose entire existence was literally engulfed in excrement on a daily basis, both because they lived in an impoverished, dilapidated area and because they obtained their livelihood by maintaining the cleanliness of the environs inhabited by the more prosperous and fortunate few—by ensuring that all offensive

matter was disposed of before it could infect the latter's immediate surroundings or spoil their view. In a world without plumbing and modern
sanitation, whole groups in society were employed for the sole purpose of
tending to another, more privileged group's waste matter. James L.
Clifford, in his fascinating exploration of "The Other Side of the Enlight-
enment," mentions several of these groups: for example, the "Night
Men," who regularly emptied London's privies, drains, and cesspools by
carrying away the contents in wagons, and who were exposed to occupa-
tional hazards such as befell several of their number when, in the process
of emptying a public house vault in Southwark, they were overcome by
the stench and died.[25] The Night Men's (and other workers') daily, intimate contact with an excremental world allowed other segments of English
society to minimize their own contact with it, even to ignore its existence
entirely, and to occupy instead a world of idealized, as well as sanitized,
neoclassical environs and forms. Clifford points to the example of Joshua
Reynolds, who had a privy in his garden at a comfortable remove from his
house in Leicester Fields—a private staircase led to it from his studio so
that he could hurriedly pay his calls to nature and then return without
delay to his purer, more exalted pursuits.[26]

In eighteenth-century England and Ireland, then, the relationship
between the upper and lower classes, between master and servant, was defined, at least in part, excrementally. We have already noted the contrast
Swift draws between the Yahoos and the Houyhnhnms, and between the
"Northern Swains" and the "Great ones" in the *Panegyrick on the D——n.*
We may recall another example from *Gulliver's Travels*, where Gulliver
describes how his bodily needs were taken care of in Lilliput: "From this
Time my constant Practice was, as soon as I rose, to perform that Business
in open Air, at the full Extent of my Chain; and due Care was taken every
Morning before Company came, that the offensive Matter should be carried off in Wheel-barrows, by two Servants appointed for that Purpose"
(PW, 11:29). Here again we are presented with a menial class whose status
in society is inseparable from its immediate and constant involvement
with offal. Lilliput's servants, like London's "Night Men," have been relegated to a world defined both by man's nether regions and by the lower
parts of human society.

Similarly, Swift's *Directions to Servants* presupposes a stratified
social order in which one class is responsible for cleaning up the mess
made by another. The household duties of specific servants, as characterized by Swift's ironic admonitions, are shown to consist largely of dis-
posing of their master's or mistress's bodily wastes. In his "Directions to
the Chamber-Maid," for example, Swift declares: "Do not carry down the
necessary Vessels for the Fellows to see, but empty them out of the Win-

dow, for your Lady's Credit. It is highly improper for Men Servants to know that fine Ladies have Occasion for such Utensils; and do not scour the Chamber pot, because the Smell is wholesome" (PW, 13:53). If these words function as a satiric comment upon the ignorant and slovenly behavior of chambermaids, they function no less satirically as an exposure of the absurd priggishness and anality of the "fine Ladies," who, like the "Great ones" depicted in the *Panegyrick on the D——n,* are incapable of dealing honestly and openly with the physical facts of life, but must rely instead both upon elaborate modes of concealment and upon the existence of others hired specifically to mediate between themselves and reality. Another version of this excremental concealment and mediation appears in the "Directions to the House-Maid," where Swift's ironic net captures at once the indolent, unthinking servants, who shamelessly expose what should be dealt with in a quietly efficient and discreet fashion, and their "proud," "lazy" mistresses, who do their business in "a dark Closet" and then leave it for others to take care of while they themselves can pretend to the world that they are fragile creatures "above" such gross physicality (60-61).

The *Directions* presents a vivid picture of a class society as it translates into a clear-cut division of excremental labor and responsibility. Swift, to be sure, does not consciously argue for a more equitable distribution of these labors. (He was, after all, a master of servants himself, and an especially demanding one at that.) Nevertheless, Swift's repeated linguistic participation in the world of maids and footmen (see also his pamphlet, *The Humble Petition of the Footmen in and about the City of Dublin* [PW, 12:235], as well as his poem, *The Humble Petition of Frances Harris*)—more specifically, his own mental and verbal "dabbling in other Folks Urine" (*Directions to Servants* [PW, 13:61])—creates a bond of imaginative identification between himself and the servant class and makes him a figure who seems far more at home in the cramped, stench-filled alleys of the Liberties than in the fashionable, expansive landscapes of a typical Augustan estate.

In sum, Swift's excremental universe is at once vision and reality, something that can be explained adequately in terms of neither satiric theme nor mental fixation. For Swift, this universe was an outgrowth both of seeing what actually existed around him and of according these realities a special prominence and significance in his larger scheme of things. To understand fully the role "excremental vision" plays in Swift's writings is to understand also the yawning epistemological, ideological, and literary gap separating Swift from the idealized, manureless environs of the affluent Augustans' sumptuously re-created and elegantly versified Edens.

Stone Walls vs. Prisons of the Mind

i

The concreteness as well as the historicity of Swift's writings, resulting from their inextricable ties to the shapes and the conditions of his landscape, is further evidenced by the theme of imprisonment pervading his work. Hopewell R. Selby, defining it in mental and epistemological terms, talks of Swift's "fictive prisons" as a "metaphor of the mind."[27] In a related vein, C. J. Rawson explores the theme via a combination of psychological, existentialist, and rhetorical considerations. Using ideas given currency by "modern psychiatric or metapsychiatric literature" in order to explain such aspects of Swift's writing as the interplay between openness and enclosure, he argues that "closest to Swift . . . and directly imbued with his spirit, are those Beckettian heroes, whose minds and lives are trapped in those very prisons of the self which Swift mocked, and suffered, as symptoms of the radical madness of the race."[28] Both views have validity, and Rawson's in particular is provocative as well as illuminating; yet neither comes to terms with the historical and the environmental immediacy communicated by Swift in his treatment of confinement.

Confinement for Swift was an external act as well as a state of mind; it was a physical condition defined by architectural structures or geographical spaces, and a political condition produced by specific forms of oppression. There is a frightening literalness and concreteness to Swift's growing persuasion, expressed in a letter to Pope, that "a Dagger is at my Throat, a halter about my Neck, or Chains at my Feet, all prepared by those in Power" (C, 2:465). Whatever role paranoia or existential angst may have played in these fears, it is clear that the contemporary situation in Ireland justified them to a considerable extent by providing objective correlatives for his images of imprisonment. (The experience of his printer Waters, who not only landed in jail but died there, attests to the reality of Swift's perceptions.) Swift understood very well the way in which geography and politics could combine to produce a state of enslavement: "Were not the People of *Ireland* born as *free* as those of *England*? . . . Am I a *Free-man* in *England,* and do I become a *Slave* in six Hours, by crossing the Channel?" (PW, 10:31).

The *Holyhead Journal*—at once a kind of "prison diary" and a cry for freedom[29]—dramatizes the terrifying immediacy associated with Swift's sense of confinement, which goes much beyond his simple assertion that he "shall always fret at the remembrance of this imprisonment" in a Welsh inn while awaiting passage to Ireland (PW, 5:205). The entire

Journal is suffused with a feeling of physical oppressiveness, with an almost unbearably claustrophobic quality. Swift laments that while the rain continues relentlessly, he must "confine my self to my narrow chambr in all unwalkable hours" (205). His accommodations at the inn seem virtually interchangeable with a prison cell, for he is "cooped up in a room not half so large as one of the Deanry Closets" (207). The room "smoaks into the bargain," which adds to its stifling aspect. When he does venture forth from the inn, he winds up having to take shelter from "a furious shower" in yet another prisonlike structure—"a welch cabin, almost as bad as an Irish one" (206). (Irish cabins, noted for their diminutive proportions and their state of congestion, were no less an emblem of hellish confinement than Defoe's Newgate.[30])

Swift on occasion experienced his life in Ireland in similar terms of spatial enclosure. He observes to Sheridan that the Irish "all live in a wretched, dirty Doghole and Prison" (C, 3:140), likens himself to "a poisoned rat in a hole" who is "pin[ing] away in this kingdom" (383), and complains that because of his deafness he is "not in a Condition to go beyond the Deanry Garden, to which I have been confined four Months" (46). He tends to conceive of the habitations of his Irish friends as diminutive, cramped structures: Sheridan's "little obscure Irish Cabbin"; Archdeacon Walls's "Little House by the Church Yard of Castleknock," into which he ". . . once a Week creeps in,/ [and] Sits with his Knees up to his Chin" (19–20); Henry Leslie's residence at Market-Hill, ". . . a [repaired] cabin gone to ruin,/Just big enough to shelter two in" (*Robin and Harry,* 21–22); and the Pilkingtons' "Lilliputian Palace."[31] Similar images of architectural enclosure are often used to describe his own residence at the deanery. This is explicable in light of the actual physical environs of the deanery, which even more than other congested urban areas tended to be cramped and constrictive. An early nineteenth-century visitor observed: "Both [St. Patrick's Cathedral and Christ Church] are placed in such narrow, dirty, and obscure parts of the town that their founders may be supposed to have been influenced in their choice of such inconvenient situations from a pious regard to what was said by the great Founder of our religion of the road to Heaven, that 'strait is the gate, and narrow is the way.'"[32] Even in those instances where he acknowledges the largeness of the house, Swift portrays himself confined within one small area of it. He declares to Pope, "I live in the corner of a vast unfurnished house" (C, 2:177), and describes himself to another correspondent as "the Dean of St. Patrick's sitting like a toad in a corner of his great house" (C, 3:114).

Swift's view of confinement acquired an increasingly greater degree of concreteness, as well as a heightened sense of urgency, from the cumulative effect of his many long years of experience with oppression in Ire-

land. In an early work like *A Tale of a Tub,* we find an emphasis upon the
exploration of inner space—on the delusive expansiveness combined with
the claustrophobic constraints of the Tale-teller's wandering, circling,
fabricating mind. As W. B. Carnochan suggests, the work on at least
one level is a "chronicle of a brooding, solitary, shut in subjectivity"—one
that "shows the world turned inward against itself as a metaphorical
prison. . . ."[33] Yet even the *Tale* depicts an imprisonment that extends
beyond the concentric circles of the Hack's consciousness into the external shapes and structures of his environment. The inextricable, at once
comic and terrifying links between body and soul that characterize the
activities of the Aeolists are also aspects of Swift's own world: a world in
which the realms of mind and spirit never wholly (and only on rare
occasions even partially) escape their ties to physical reality. The Tale-
teller, having formerly been incarcerated in Bedlam, is now confined to his
Grub Street garret and is spatially as well as perceptually restricted to a
world epitomized by the "Poet's Chamber (who works for [his] Shop) in
an Alley" and by the dank habitations of his fellow "wits," accessible
only via "a prodigious Number of dark, winding Stairs" (TT, 24). Imprisoned within such external enclosures, he reinforces his own condition
of entrapment by projecting the erection of an academy to contain the
wits in the country (41), by converting mental systems into *"Edifices in
the Air"* (56), and by imposing geographical limits upon his mobility:
"Thus, *Wit* has its Walks and Purlieus, out of which it may not stray the
breadth of a Hair, upon peril of being lost. The *Moderns* have artfully
fixed this *Mercury,* and reduced it to the Circumstances of Time, Place,
and Person. Such a Jest there is, that will not pass out of *Covent-Garden;*
and such a one, that is no where intelligible but at *Hide-Park* Corner"
(43). In an early variation on a theme that Swift would later in his career
treat in a specifically political context—the tendency of oppressed beings
not to seek their own liberation but to pass their oppression on to others—
the Tale-teller proposes an experiment whereby "every Prince in *Christen-
dom* will take seven of the *deepest Scholars* in his Dominions, and shut
them up close for *seven* Years, in *seven* Chambers, with a Command to
write *seven* ample Commentaries on this comprehensive Discourse" (185).
In this way the text itself will be imprisoned within multiple layers of
commentary, just as the Tale-teller's life is confined within a seemingly
endless series of enclosing structures and takes place in a landscape whose
"Frontiers of Height and Depth, [very nearly] border upon each other,"
so that a soarer into the heights inevitably "falls down plum into the
lowest Bottom of Things; like one who travels the *East* into the *West;* or
like a strait Line drawn by its own Length into a Circle" (158).

The satiric butts of Swift's later works find themselves less enclosed
within "prisons of the self" and more explicitly confined within exter-

nally defined spaces and stone walls. The members of the Irish House of
Commons carry on their activities within an edifice that assumes the
dimensions of a combined jail and madhouse. When viewed from the
outside, the building appears "large and lofty," but the interior is quite
another matter, providing only enough space for the "Club" members
" . . . to dwell/Each within his proper Cell;/With a Passage left to creep
in,/And a Hole above for peeping" (*The Legion Club,* 43–46). The edifice
housing the "Legion Club" is not merely a mental construct but an eminently concrete and visible reality in the world Swift inhabited. Indeed,
Swift makes a point of situating it as a recognizable feature of the landscape—more specifically, as the new Irish Parliament House (designed by
Sir Edward Lovet Pearce and begun in 1729, seven years before the
composition of Swift's verse), which stood opposite Trinity College and
next to St. Andrew's Church:

> As I strole the City, oft I
> Spy a Building large and lofty,
> Not a Bow-shot from the College,
> Half the Globe from Sense and Knowledge.
> By the prudent Architect
> Plac'd against the Church direct. . . .
>
> (1–6)

It is interesting, and finally very revealing, that the object of Swift's
virulently satiric deflation (we have already noted the pervasively excremental character he ascribes to it) was "the earliest important public
building in these islands to embody the full Burlingtonian ideals of correctness," designed by "the foremost exponent of Palladianism in Ireland."[34] We have here one more indication of Swift's general indifference
to "ideals of correctness" considered in purely aesthetic terms, of his
inability or unwillingness to contemplate the principles of Augustan high
art (as well as their architectural embodiments) in the abstract, divorced
from the social or political purposes to which they have been put.

Gulliver's Travels, a work explicitly and pervasively concerned with
the theme of confinement, reveals most clearly the objective correlatives
of mental entrapment—that is, the assorted ways in which the external
world alternately creates, mirrors, and reinforces the state of human captivity. The imagistic suggestions of enclosure with which the work opens
("a small Estate," "a narrow Fortune") soon become translated into
actual confinement in Lilliput. Gulliver's progress through his four voyages
is marked by a continual falling into captivity and a simultaneous endeavor to obtain his "liberty," the latter word echoing like a refrain
throughout Part I in particular. This captivity is concretely embodied in
the various architectural structures Gulliver inhabits during his journeys:

the house in Lilliput that he got into "with some Difficulty" (not unlike the Irish cabins that required creeping into) and where he "lay on the Ground" for "about a Fortnight" (PW, 11:31); the box in Brobdingnag "close on every Side, with a little Door for me to go in and out, and a few Gimlet-holes to let in Air" (97); the "wooden Chamber of sixteen Foot square" built by the Brobdingnag Queen's personal cabinetmaker, for whose door Gulliver, in an ironically self-imprisoning gesture, demands a lock (105); and the "travelling Closet" he occupies when accompanying Glumdalclitch, each of whose three windows "was latticed with Iron Wire on the outside" (113). Gulliver's final confinement takes place within the boundaries of his stable, into which he retreats in order to escape the society of his family and to converse with his horses.

Now there is, I think, a good deal of validity in Ronald Paulson's emphasis upon the self-imprisoning tendencies in Gulliver's character. (Paulson sees Gulliver as "a foolish, subservient man, easily enchained by plausible knaves and apparent authority" who invariably "allowed himself to be convinced that he was a servant or captive."[35]) Swift's understanding of this basic human issue was at all times complex and often revealed his awareness of the subtle, ironic interdependencies existing between master and slave—more specifically, of the latter's at-times overwhelming complicity in his own state of servitude. Nevertheless, I wish to shift the focus here (as I believe Swift finally shifted it) from self-enslavement to external oppression, from the gull's tragicomic subservience to the master's far more culpable despotic impositions. If many of Swift's accounts suggest that he viewed his countrymen in much the same light that Hogarth conceived Gulliver in "The Punishment of Lemuel Gulliver" (bending over with bared behinds, ready to receive whatever their "masters" chose to shove up them), it is nonetheless true that Swift increasingly directed his gaze, as well as his wrath, not upon the willingly proffered asses, but upon those doing the shoving. Frequently there is an emphasis in his writings upon a sheer, brute force that in effect renders the whole question of choice between resistance and acquiescence rather academic: "For in *Reason,* all *Government* without the Consent of the Governed,* is the *very Definition of Slavery:* But in *Fact, Eleven Men well armed, will certainly subdue one single Man in his Shirt*" (PW, 10:63).

For Swift, confinement and servitude were above all the result of public policy and concrete exertions of power, not of psychological self-entrapment or a Dostoevskian urge to flee the terrible burden of freedom. Always an astute observer of the way in which power works in society, Swift was very well aware of the cunning strategies used by those in power both to perpetuate and to rationalize their rule—if need be, to place the blame for its excessive rigors on the subjects themselves. When England passed an act in 1720 decreeing the subordinate status of the Parliament of Ireland and negating the powers of the Irish House of Lords, Swift succinctly explained the basic issue involved: "The Question is whether People ought to be Slaves or no. It is like the Quarrell against Convocations; they meet but seldom, have no Power, and for want of those Advantages, cannot make any Figure when they are suffered to assemble. You fetter a Man seven years, then let him loose to shew his Skill in dancing, and because he does it awkwardly, you say he ought to be fetterd for Life" (C, 2:342).

Along with this insight into the subtler arts of political repression, Swift possessed a keen awareness of the latter's harsher, more brutal aspects, which can be seen in the instance where Gulliver is used as a mouthpiece for exposing the nature of colonialist rule. His descriptions do not allow us the comfort of pretending that the enslaved actively promote, or willingly consent to, the conditions of their servitude:

> A Crew of Pyrates are driven by a Storm they know not whither; at length a Boy discovers Land from the Top-mast; they go on Shore to rob and plunder; they see an harmless People, are entertained with Kindness, they give the Country a new Name, they take formal Possession of it for the King, they set up a rotten Plank or a Stone for a Memorial, they murder two or three Dozen of the Natives, bring away a Couple more by Force for a Sample, return home, and get their Pardon. Here commences a new Dominion acquired with a Title by *Divine Right*. Ships are sent with the first Opportunity; the Natives driven out or destroyed, their Princes tortured to discover their Gold; a free Licence given to all Acts of Inhumanity and Lust; the Earth reeking with the Blood of its Inhabitants: And this execrable Crew of Butchers employed in so pious an Expedition, is a *modern Colony* sent to convert and civilize an idolatrous and barbarous People. (PW, 11:294)

Lest we still miss the point, Gulliver reiterates his determination not to inform England about the lands he visited, since "those Countries which I have described do not appear to have a Desire of being conquered, and enslaved, murdered or driven out by Colonies. . ." (295).

A similar point is made in Swift's allegorical tract, *The Story of the Injured Lady*, which shows that not even a "fallen" woman, such as the "Injured Lady" (who represents Ireland), harbors the slightest wish to be dominated by her lover (in this case, the "Gentleman in the Neighbourhood" who represents England), although she may eventually be forced into a degrading accommodation with her new circumstances in order to ensure her own survival. The lady is condemned to an imprisonment, in very literal as well as figurative terms: one acted out within the specific confines of her house and within the geographical bounds of her now-decaying estate (" . . . I was born to a good Estate, although it now turn-

eth to little Account under the Oppressions I endure. . ." [PW, 9:4]).
No part of her life remains free of her lover's constant scrutiny and often
outright intrusions, as one by one his retainers infiltrate her household
and assume control over all her actions (5-8). The initial act of seduction
("half by Force, and half by Consent, after solemn Vows and Protestations of Marriage" [5]), manifested by the lover's physical invasion of the
lady's body, is in effect continued and extended through his repeated
invasions of both her privacy and her property. The protective boundaries
of her home turn into the constraining environs of a jail.

References to a "prison of the mind" seem very much beside the
point when we are confronted with this overwhelming, almost unbearably
physical weight of oppression being exerted on the "Injured Lady," imposed from without by a nameable and recognizable embodiment of
external reality. What this story portrays, above all, is the plight of a
victim, and the fact that she is shown to be in certain ways a victim of her
own ignorance as well as overcomplaisance pales into relative insignificance beside the obvious fact that she is a victim of sexual violation, political despotism, and economic exploitation. Swift, I believe, realized very
well that the crucial insight regarding the complex interdependencies between tyrant and slave (note the phrase, "half by Force, and half by Consent") can be turned all too easily into the facile and finally meaningless
assertion that slaves are themselves the producers of tyranny, the builders
of their own prisons—an assertion that, in effect, absolves tyrants of responsibility for their acts and denies the reality of stone walls. However
frequently he acknowledged the validity of the insight throughout his
writings, Swift emphatically repudiated the fallacious conclusions drawn
from it with all the rhetorical and satiric weapons at his disposal.

ii

Swift at all times displayed a healthy appreciation for the reality of
stone walls. As we have already seen, he, no less than the "Injured Lady,"
experienced a sense of stifling oppressiveness, and he too succumbed to a
pervasive dread of external intrusions on his privacy. His *Letter from Dr
Swift to Mr Pope* (1721), which critics generally cite (if at all) as a calm,
straightforward exposition of Swift's conservative political principles,
ranks in many ways with the *Holyhead Journal* as a "prisoner's" combined testimony to, and outcry against, the circumstances of his confinement. In this case, the "jail" is not a Welsh inn but the nation of Ireland
itself. Swift presents himself at the outset as an innocent man having to
defend himself in a court of "law" so thoroughly corrupt that it has lost
all vestiges of moral authority even though it continues to exercise judicial (now interchangeable with political) power: "I rather chuse to appeal

to you [Pope] than to my Lord Chief Justice Whitshed. . . . You are a
much fitter Judge. . . . I doubt, whether the Arguments I could suggest
to prove my own innocence would be of much weight from the gentlemen of the Long-robe to those in Furs. . ." (PW, 9:25). Like the "Injured Lady," Swift emerges as the quintessential victim ("a person so
ill treated as I have been. . ." [31])—a powerless creature, also depicted as
a naïf, who is subjected to continual persecutions ("it is with great injustice I have these many years been pelted by your [England's] Pam-
phleteers" [30]). He must do his best to survive in an atmosphere of
widespread political paranoia and repression reminiscent of the Popish
Plot hysteria in England forty-three years earlier.[36] We glimpse Swift
anxiously hunched over his writings in what ought to be, but no longer is,
the privacy of his own home: "These papers, at my few hours of health
and leisure, I have been digesting into order by one sheet at a time, for I
dare not venture any further, lest the humour of searching and seizing
papers should revive. . ." (26). Both his person and his property seem in
imminent danger from what he terms "the whole Tribe of Informers, the
most accursed, and prostitute, and abandoned race, that God ever permitted to plague mankind" (32-33). He is trapped in a part Orwellian,
part Kafkaesque world in which he "dare not venture to publish" his
work, since "however orthodox they may be while I am now writing, they
may become criminal enough to bring me into trouble before midsum-
mer"; it is a world where the powers that be "will just give themselves
time to libel and accuse me, but cannot spare a minute to hear my defence" (33). All notions of individual liberty and private conscience, not
to mention basic human justice, necessarily disappear within an established
order that sustains its rule through "diligent enquiries into remote and
problematical guilt, with a new power of enforcing them by chains and
dungeons to every person whose face a Minister thinks fit to dislike. . ."
(32).

    This totalitarian nightmare, complete with hints of a medieval tor-
ture chamber, comes perilously close to sounding like some wild fantasy
projected by the Tale-teller's imagination; but Swift makes certain to
anchor it in empirical reality by relating it to specific contemporary
events. Recounting Lord Chief Justice Whitshed's prosecution (or, to be
more precise, *per*secution) of the printer of *A Proposal for the Universal
Use of Irish Manufacture*, Swift reminds the reader that he himself is living
in the midst of the society portrayed in the *Letter* and can therefore attest
to its atrocities from personal experience: "The Printer was seized, and
forced to give great bail: After his trial the Jury brought him in Not
Guilty, although they had been culled with the utmost industry; the Chief
Justice sent them back nine times, and kept them eleven hours. . ." (27).
The "chains and dungeons" thus belong to the physical world of eigh-

teenth-century Ireland as much as to the mental world of a deranged Modern. In their final appearance toward the end of the *Letter,* we must accept them not only as literal fact but also as an immediate threat to Swift's own existence: "So in a plot-discovering age, I have often known an innocent man seized and imprisoned, and forced to lie several months in chains, while the Ministers were not at leisure to hear his petition, until they had prosecuted and hanged the number they proposed" (33). The danger posed to all men, no matter how guiltless, by the arbitrary workings of power is a theme in Swift's verses as well. He ends his lampoon of Sir Thomas Prendergast with a similar vision of corrupted justice allied with false imprisonment: "Then vote a worthy Citizen to Jail,/In Spight to Justice, and refuse his Bail" (*On Noisy Tom,* 19–20). That these lines are a specific topical reference to one such living "worthy Citizen" ("Mr. G— F— [George Faulkner], a very honest and eminent Printer in Dublin, who was voted to Newgate upon a ridiculous Complaint of one Serjeant Bettesworth") underscores the reality, even as it in certain ways magnifies the nightmarish quality, of the world Swift depicts.

Prisons, then, are recurring features of Swift's landscape—as important to the way in which he experienced space and viewed his surroundings as Palladian or Claudian structures were to the way in which Pope perceived his world. Even in those instances where the prisons are invoked either hypothetically or metaphorically, they convey a sense of immediacy and never stray very far from the conditions of existing society. Speaking as the Drapier, for example, Swift offers a hypothetical projection that is at the same time a logical extension of prevailing circumstances: "And as it often happens at Play, that Men begin with *Farthings,* and go on to *Gold,* till some of them lose their Estates and die in Jayl: So it may possibly fall out in my Case, that by *playing* too long with Mr. *Wood*'s Half-pence, I may be drawn in to pay a *Fine,* double to the Reward for *Betraying* me; be sent to Prison, and *not be delivered thence until I shall have payed the uttermost Farthing*" (PW, 10:83–84). Extending the implications of this repressive society even further, Swift elsewhere justifies his allegedly trivial complaints about one small aspect of Ireland's ills by observing: "And yet a poor Fellow going to the *Gallows,* may be allowed to feel the Smart of *Wasps* while he is upon *Tyburn-Road*" (PW, 12:55). Imprisonment is shown to be the result not of retributive justice but of power relationships that are inherently predatory; thus the lower clergymen promoted to a bishopric have escaped "Labour, Confinement, and Subjection . . . *like a Bird out of the Snare of the Fowler*" (192).

Making the terrors of confinement even more vivid are the suggestions of accompanying physical torture. Although invoked primarily as figures of speech, they too retain a close connection with existing reality. The Drapier emphasizes the extremity of the current state of affairs by pointing out that "those who have used *Power* to cramp *Liberty,* have gone so far as to resent even the *Liberty* of *Complaining; although* a Man upon the Rack, was never known to be refused the Liberty of *roaring* as loud as he thought fit" (PW, 10:63). Swift here uses metaphor, not simile—that is, he chooses to establish identity rather than mere resemblance—in juxtaposing the political prisoner with the "Man upon the Rack." Prevailing economic practices are similarly conceived of as a form of torture; hence landlords are censured for the "unmeasurable *screwing* and *racking* [of] their Tenants all over the Kingdom. . ." (PW, 9:21). These examples might suggest that when Swift told Pope that "oppressions torture me" (C, 4:385), he was speaking far more literally than we would ever suspect at first glance.

Swift's view of confinement necessarily implies a particular attitude toward its opposite, freedom. The latter is likewise defined in combined spatial and political terms. We may note, for example, a passage from Letter V of *The Drapier's Letters,* where Swift is addressing Viscount Molesworth: "Since your last Residence in *Ireland,* I frequently have taken my Nag to ride about your Grounds; where I fancied my self to feel an Air of *Freedom* breathing round me. . . . But I have lately sold my Nag, and honestly told his greatest Fault, which was that of snuffing up the Air about *Brackdenstown;* whereby he became such a Lover of *Liberty,* that I could scarce hold him in" (PW, 10:93). We know from numerous passages in his letters that Swift was an enthusiastic, even at times fanatic, horseman. His equestrian travels apparently included occasional trips to the estate of Lord Molesworth, located approximately seven miles north of Dublin (see, e.g., C, 2:285).

In various places in his writings we find an implied connection between horseback riding and freedom—a typically Swiftian kind of freedom that, like his conception of imprisonment, cannot be understood apart from the concrete shapes and physical spaces of his landscape. The association is made explicit in a letter to Pope where he boasts of the ease with which he can move about through Dublin, in contrast with London where there are numerous lords "to turn me out of the road, or run over me with their Coaches & six." In light of this difference he chooses to remain in Ireland, "to be a freeman among slaves, rather than a slave among freemen" (C, 4:171). This is one of the rare instances in which Swift characterizes himself as a "freeman" rather than as a man who must share the enslavement of his countrymen. He does so not by citing theoretical rights he possesses, but by stressing physical mobility and the absence of territorial barriers—by substituting images of spatial expanse for his more usual images of claustrophobic enclosure. Swift's freedom, in other words, is above all the freedom of a prisoner—or rather, the type of freedom a prisoner would most readily relate to. It is a freedom best appreciated by one habitually cooped up in narrow places, who is permitted moments of reprieve when he can breathe in open air again and move through unrestricted space.

The image of the liberty-loving nag he uses in Letter V of *The Drapier's Letters* is peculiarly apt under the circumstances. For Swift, on those occasions when he was not a toad confined to a corner or a rat trapped in a hole, was very much like a horse chomping at the bit or a rebellious colt ready to spring over the fence. Indeed, in the previously cited letter to Pope, Swift notes "the indifference, the love of quiet, the care of health, &c. that grow upon men in years" but goes on to declare: " . . . yet at your or his [Bolingbroke's] time of life, I could have leapt over the moon" (C, 4:171). (It could be argued that his moon-leaping days were not yet at an end.) What is here only an implied analogy becomes explicit, if also somewhat more prosaic, elsewhere: " . . . so I am like a horse which though off his mettle, can trot on tolerably" (C, 3:341). The metaphoric truth of this statement blends easily into the literal reality of Swift's life: " . . . and this comparison puts me in mind to add that I am returned to be a rider. . . ." Whether as horse or as rider, Swift continually rejected the stifling immobility of the dungeon dweller and endeavored to extend the physical boundaries of his being.

The passage from Letter V of *The Drapier's Letters* (PW, 10:93) thus functions on several levels simultaneously; it is at once an autobiographical, a political, and a topographical statement indicating Swift's stance in and toward the world. The nag who, after "snuffing up the Air about *Brackdenstown,*" can scarcely be controlled is a descendant of the Pegasus we encounter in the *Ode to Sir William Temple,* who " . . . like an unruly Horse/Tho' ne'er so gently led/To the lov'd Pasture where he us'd to feed,/Runs violently o'er his usual Course" (146–49). The nag also displays certain affinities with the Tale-teller's "Imaginations" in that the latter are "hard-mouth'd, and exceedingly disposed to run away with his *Reason,* which [he has] observed from long Experience, to be a very light Rider, and easily shook off. . ." (TT, 180). To that extent the nag embodies something both beyond and anterior to explicitly political attitudes—an unruly, anarchic force central to Swift's nature (even when transferred to a satiric butt), which he alternately urged on and guiltily reined in throughout his life. At the same time, the nag has specifically imbibed the spirit of *"Liberty"* from the air surrounding Molesworth's country house near Swords—inevitably a rather heady element, considering what Herbert Davis terms its inhabitant's "dangerously liberal" views (PW, 10:xxiv) on issues ranging from Irish independence to widespread religious toleration.[37] Indeed, we can see why Swift himself might not have dared to venture on these grounds in print without assuming the disguise of an anonymous tradesman and performing a symbolic act of expiation by selling the nag for being too unmanageable. As in traditional country house literature, Molesworth's estate is the concrete embodiment of the values of its owner. In this case, however, they are hardly the orthodox ruling-class values typical of the conservative aristocrat. In short, on the grounds of Brackdenstown as presented by Swift, temperament and politics, ideology and landscape come together. In doing so, they serve as a reminder that for Swift, confinement—along with its opposite, liberty—was neither a "fiction" nor a "metaphor of the mind," but rather an empirical reality, however rich in symbolic implications, that could be breathed and felt, and that at all times retained firm links (or should we say "fetters"?) to an external world that was only too much with him at every moment of his life.

CHAPTER • 3

Swift's Antipastoral Vision and Ireland's Antipastoral Reality

i

It is no accident that Swift's verse on "The Plagues of a Country Life" is three times longer than his verse enumerating "The Blessings of a Country Life." Throughout his writings we find a denigration of the supposedly innocent, simple joys of rural existence that are extolled in eighteenth-century pastoral poetry. Many of Swift's verses explicitly mock the genre in both their language and their angle of vision, in effect subverting Pope's conception of a pastoral poem, which assumes the necessity of "some illusion to render [it] delightful" and which "consists in exposing the best side only of a shepherd's life, and in concealing its miseries."[1] Countering what he construed to be the coarseness and the indecorous absurdities of Ambrose Philips's pastorals, Pope affirmed that "pastoral is an image of what they call the Golden age," so that poets "are not to describe our shepherds as shepherds at this day really are, but as they may be conceiv'd then to have been; when the best of men follow'd the employment." Fontenelle's essay, "Of Pastoral," embodies a similar perspective: "Pastoral Poetry cannot be very charming if it is as low and clownish as Shepherds naturally are; or if it precisely runs upon nothing but rural Matters. For, to hear one speak of Sheep and Goats, and of the care that ought to be taken of these Animals, has nothing which in it self can please us; what is pleasing is the Idea of quietness, which is inseparable from a Pastoral Life."[2] Pope's and Fontenelle's outlook indirectly points up the paradox that is at the heart of the eighteenth-century attitude toward nature: the simultaneous embrace of the pastoral mode and the rejection of rural realities.

55

The views expressed by Pope and Fontenelle reinforce Renato Poggioli's observation that "the pastoral ideal shifts on the quicksands of
wishful thought" and that "the bucolic dream has no other reality than
that of imagination and art."[3] Given Swift's radical skepticism toward
the realms of both imagination and art and his insistence upon acknowledging existing realities in all situations, it is not surprising that when he
turned his attention to country life, he showed little inclination to embrace Pope's "illusion" or his contemporaries' "bucolic dream." His
farewell to "High Raptures, and romantick Flights;/To Goddesses so
heav'nly sweet,/[and] Expiring Shepherds at their Feet," occasioned
by Chloe's "unthinkable act" (*Strephon and Chloe*, 198-200), ultimately
justifies the need to deal with *all* forms of reality, historical and geographical as well as biological.

Swift's scornful stance vis-à-vis the realm of illusion was consistent
throughout his life. In *On Dreams; An Imitation of Petronius*, he dismisses
dreams that " . . . with false flitting Shades our Minds delude"; denying
supernatural explanations, he insists that " . . . all are meer Productions of
the Brain,/And Fools consult Interpreters in vain" (2, 5-6). What Pope
saw as necessary and delightful "illusion" was, from Swift's perspective,
absurd and pernicious *de*lusion. In the *Ode to the Athenian Society*,
Swift portrays the "transported Muse" (48), seduced by her vision of an
imaginary paradise (58-59), ". . . grop[ing] her uncouth way/After a
mighty Light that leads her wandring Eye" (66-67); he concludes that
"No wonder then she quits the *narrow Path of Sense*/For a dear Ramble
thro' Impertinence" (68-69). Swift's own answer was to cling, at times
almost fanatically, to "the narrow Path of Sense," personally eschewing
any similar "rambles" along the illusory paths of a re-created Eden. The
unbridgeable gap Swift perceived between the fictions of the pastoral ideal
and the intractable realities of life is implicitly acknowledged in the *Ode
to Sir William Temple*, where the same muse, presumably still young
though now perforce somewhat less virginal, "soars clear out of sight"
into "Paradises of her own" (144-45). The concrete surroundings of Moor
Park are thus shown to be clearly distinct from the Edenic realm inhabited
by the poetic muse, which exists in a world of mental fantasy and illusion
only.

For Swift, the pastoral ideal could never be embodied in an existing
landscape such as Temple's garden, since realities could only mock or challenge visionary ideals, not concretely express them. Swift's comic reduction of "Paradise," Sir John Stanley's villa near Fulham, to a watering
hole for horses, merely one of "ten thousand such paradises in this kingdom" familiar to his own bay mare (C, 4:455), is despite its flippancy part
of an extended poetic and epistolary statement that Eden no longer exists

in contemporary topography; it can be characterized only by images of an emphatically postlapsarian garden:

> Our British soil is over-rank, and breeds
> Among the noblest flow'rs a thousand pois'nous weeds,
>   And ev'ry stinking weed so lofty grows,
>   As if 'twould overshade the Royal Rose. . . .
>   (*Ode to Dr. William Sancroft*, 101-4)

The poem *To Mr. Congreve* contains a passage that highlights the drama of the death of pastoral existence. The muse, this time conceived as a shepherdess "who on shady banks has joy'd to sleep/Near . . . her father's sheep" (221-22), witnesses the invasion of her landscape by a throng of odious creatures and is forced to withdraw, into regions yet more distant from and unconnected with the existing world: "'Tis time to bid my friend a long farewell,/The muse retreats far in yon chrystal cell;/Faint inspiration sickens as she flies,/Like distant echo spent, the spirit dies" (227-30). We see here the death of an entire way of life, a way of both seeing and singing in the world.

Another version of this fateful—not to mention fatal—change occurs in Swift's later poem, *On Cutting Down the Old Thorn at Market-Hill*, which conveys its own unique interpretation of Man's Fall and the latter's impact upon the landscape. Time's "Iron Teeth" have cankered a "spacious Thorn" (17, 4), the venerable relic of a former Golden Age represented by "Sir *Archibald* [Acheson] that val'rous Knight,/The Lord of all the fruitful Plain" (9-10). In a symbolically revealing act, Swift cuts down the now "aged, sickly, sapless Thorn" with his "sacrilegious Hand" (21, 24). In other words, he responds in a pragmatic way to the reality of its present condition and thereby rejects its (necessarily sentimental) claims to a mythic status. His action is greeted by the burlesque equivalent of nature's response to Adam and Eve's eating the apple in *Paradise Lost*:

> Dame Nature, when she saw the Blow,
> Astonish'd gave a dreadful Shriek;
> And Mother *Tellus* trembled so
> She scarce recover'd in a Week.
>
>   (25-28)

The event, although primarily treated in a tone that combines travesty and mock-heroic, on a more serious level tolls the end of an era, the destruction of an untainted and well-protected pastoral existence: "The Owl foresaw in pensive Mood/The Ruin of her antient Seat;/And fled in Haste with all her Brood/To seek a more secure Retreat" (37-40). This symbolic act of withdrawal may well remind us of the one previously described in *To Mr. Congreve*.

Although Swift hardly sympathizes with the forces of contemporary reality, he shows even less sympathy in his writings for any kind of wishful embrace of, or sentimental allegiance to, an unreal (or perhaps only once real) way of life. His poem *Occasioned by Sir William Temple's Late Illness and Recovery* is a scathing denunciation of the visionary muse, now conceived as a "Malignant goddess" (81), and affirms a resolve to turn away completely from the realm of murky imaginings, of chimeras rather than actualities. The poem is also an exorcism of those tendencies in Swift himself toward a variety of mental peregrinations and errancies:

> Ah, should I tell a secret yet unknown,
> That thou ne'er hadst a being of thy own,
> But a wild form dependent on the brain,
> Scatt'ring loose features o'er the optic vein;
> Troubling the chrystal fountain of the sight,
> Which darts on poets eyes a trembling light;
> Kindled while reason sleeps, but quickly flies,
> Like antic shapes in dreams, from waking eyes. . . .
>
> (93–100)

The verse ends with a renunciation having profound implications for both the form and the content of Swift's subsequent poetry, which becomes increasingly more topical and more dependent upon empirically observed detail, as well as increasingly less indulgent of the vagaries of the imagination:

> There thy enchantment broke, and from this hour
> I here renounce thy visionary pow'r;
> And since thy essence on my breath depends,
> Thus with a puff the whole delusion ends.
>
> (151–54)

The dismissal of "the whole delusion" includes the banishment of those private paradises and imaginary groves which are given an almost palpable but finally illusory existence by the trickster muse.

With the muse's "enchantment" thus dispelled, it is not surprising that Swift's subsequent "pastoral" verses are completely devoid of Popeian shepherds—that they insist upon treating, at times in graphic detail, the tangible, empirically observable aspects of the landscape and its inhabitants. In Swift's hands, the charming innocence and simplicity of Pope's rustic scenes become translated into coarseness and often gross physicality. Swift continually reminds us that things like buttocks, sweat, and lust exist even in the most "pastoral" of surroundings, in somewhat the same way that the Earl of Rochester keeps reminding us (in verses like *A Dialogue between Strephon and Chloe* and "As Chloris in a pigsty lay") that erect penises, wet dreams, and masturbation are integral parts of "pastoral" life:

> Sheelah
> Thy Breeches torn behind, stand gaping wide;
> This Petticoat shall save thy dear Back-side;
> Nor need I blush, although you feel it wet;
> *Dermot,* I vow, 'tis nothing else but Sweat.
>   . . .
> When you with *Oonah* stood behind a Ditch,
> I peept, and saw you kiss the dirty Bitch.
> *Dermot,* how could you touch those nasty Sluts!
> I almost wisht this Spud were in your Guts.
>   (*A Pastoral Dialogue,* 21-24; 37-40)

Dermot's and Sheelah's language is rooted in the empirical realities of their surroundings; it assumes its peculiar character as well as its color from the weeds and thorns growing around them in an actual landscape: "My Love to *Sheelah* is more firmly fixt/Than strongest Weeds that grow these Stones betwixt:/My Spud these Nettles from the Stones can part,/No Knife so keen to weed thee from my Heart" (9-12). The language of Swift's rustics is "natural" and "organic" with a vengeance. Stubbornly refusing to transmute environmental realities, Swift resists the temptation to make luscious peaches and unblemished apples (let alone thornless roses) out of "strongest Weeds," just as he elsewhere rejects his own fantasy to create "Fields Elysian" out of "deserts" (*The Dean's Reasons For not Building at Drapier's Hill,* 16). By contrast, the language used by Pope's shepherds is consistent with his recommendations in "A Discourse on Pastoral Poetry": "As there is a difference between simplicity and rusticity, so the expression of simple thoughts should be plain, but not clownish. . . . The expression [should be] humble, yet as pure as the language will afford; neat, but not florid; easy, and yet lively."[4] Pope's carefully balanced, euphuistic prose demonstrates, among other things, that he wants to have his cake and eat it too, so to speak—that he wants to have his shepherd and his cultivated, genteel courtier at the same time.

We can better understand Swift's version of pastoral language in light of the closing lines to the *Ode to Sir William Temple:*

> In vain all wholsome Herbs I sow,
>   Where nought but Weeds will grow.
> Whate'er I plant (like Corn on barren Earth)
>   By an equivocal Birth
> Seeds and runs up to Poetry.
>   (208-12)

The metaphorical link established here between Swift's literary and gardening endeavors helps to explain why the structure and the language of his verse so closely resemble the shapes and textures of his landscape. It is a reciprocity at once analogous in principle but antithetical in substance to the bonds uniting Pope's landscape and art, as defined by the equation Swift himself indicated between Twickenham's grotto and "a Piece of Ars Poetica" (C, 3:103).

Swift's *Pastoral Dialogue* does more than satirically undermine poetic conventions. It also makes a serious statement about the nature of the land and its relationship to those who depend upon it for their survival. Traditionally, pastoral literature bases its vision on a garden world filled with all the goods of the earth: a world characterized by plenitude and fecundity—or, at the very least, in certain types of hard primitivism, total sufficiency. Want or unfulfilled need is unknown here. Edenic life, as described by Milton in *Paradise Lost,* epitomizes one important strain of English pastoral:

> . . . .Thus was this place,
> A happy rural seat of various view:
> Groves whose rich Trees wept odorous Gums and Balm,
> Others whose fruit burnisht with Golden Rind
> Hung amiable, *Hesperian* Fables true,
> If true, here only, and of delicious taste:
> Betwixt them Lawns, or level Downs, and Flocks
> Grazing the tender herb, were interpos'd,
> Or palmy hillock, or the flow'ry lap
> Of some irriguous Valley spread her store,
> Flow'rs of all hue, and without Thorn the Rose. . . .
>
> (Book IV, 246-56)[5]

The earth's treasures yield themselves up willingly, even eagerly, to man's touch and taste, thereby making strenuous toil unnecessary. Adam and Eve, for example, feast upon "Nectarine Fruits which the compliant boughs/Yielded them. . ." (Book IV, 332-33). Man's labors are portrayed not as a source of pain and travail in fulfillment of God's curse after the Fall, but rather as an expression of love and gratitude. Work becomes literally a labor of love symbolizing the reciprocal bonds between man and nature—the as yet unruptured links between man and God. Thus Adam and Eve partake of their supper ". . . after no more toil/Of thir sweet Gard'ning labor than suffic'd/To recommend cool *Zephyr,* and made ease/More easy. . ." (Book IV, 327-30).

Robert Herrick, depicting scenes from rural life in the postlapsarian world of seventeenth-century England, indirectly acknowledges the often arduous exertions involved in farm labor, but at the same time he glosses

over them, assimilating them into a mythic vision of renewal and festivity
symbolized by the harvest:

> Come Sons of Summer, by whose toile,
> We are the Lords of Wine and Oile:
> By whose tough labours, and rough hands,
> We rip up first, then reap our lands.
> Crown'd with the eares of corne, now come,
> And, to the Pipe, sing Harvest home.
>
>   . . .
>
> Drink frollick boyes, till all be blythe.
> Feed, and grow fat; and as ye eat,
> Be mindfull, that the lab'ring Neat
> (As you) may have their fill of meat.
>   (*The Hock-cart; or, Harvest home,* 1-6, 43-46)[6]

The pastoral genre, then, is capable of raising serious issues concerning
mortal existence and does not necessarily exclude all reference to back-
breaking toil, here vividly suggested by Herrick's analogy between the
farm workers and the beasts of burden ("the lab'ring Neat"). Nevertheless,
it functions through ideological and rhetorical strategies designed to
ignore the consequences and implications of these issues. In the final
analysis it dissolves all hardships into a combined social and cosmic ritual
marked by singing, dancing, and feasting. The abundant culinary delights
enumerated by Herrick (28-34) remind us that in the pastoral world there
can be no hunger, since it provides an endless supply of food for stomach
and soul alike. Boethius's rather more austere vision of mankind's "first
white age" would tend to reject such gustatory delights along with all
forms of "soft luxurious Diet" that have since "Effeminated men."[7]
Nevertheless, its exaltation of a time "when wee/Lived by the Earths
meere Charitie," supping upon "coarse Mast, or simple honey," suggests
a world likewise devoid of hunger and basically compatible with Raphael's
picture of a world whose members feed and are in turn fed by one another
as part of a cosmic banquet (*Paradise Lost,* Book V, 414-33).

Swift's version of pastoral existence contrasts in every way with
these traditional conceptions. References to briars that tear the flesh and
sharp stones that "bruise bums" attest to the fact that the harmonious relationship between man and nature associated with the Golden Age no
longer exists. Nature does not fulfill the role of fertile and nurturing
mother, but instead is a source of deprivation, a creator of snares and
obstacles. The "old stubborn Root" that Dermot grapples with in *A Pastoral Dialogue* (25) suggests the earth's general attitude of defiance toward
man. Lacking all traces of that profusion of succulent and nourishing victuals conventionally ascribed to pastoral realms, Swift's world conveys

instead a general sense of insufficiency with regard to food, as well as to other of man's needs. It is a world resembling a wasteland, epitomized by Holyhead's desolate terrain: " . . . this bleaky shore/Where loudest winds incessant roar/Where neither herb nor tree will thrive,/Where nature hardly seems alive" (Holyhead. Sept. 25. 1727, 29-32). The landscape surrounding Quilca, Thomas Sheridan's house in Cavan, is depicted similarly. Nature, once (perhaps) gloriously fruitful and generous to man, now displays only a grotesque sterility, a recalcitrance to all human desire and effort:

> Here Elements have lost their Uses,
> Air ripens not, nor Earth produces:
> In vain we make poor *Sheelah* toil,
> Fire will not roast, nor Water boil.
>
> *(To Quilca, A Country House
> in no very good Repair, 5-8)*

On the whole, Swift's delineations of the country constitute a negation of all those features and characteristics which Ernst Curtius associates with the *locus amoenus.*[8] Journeying through Swift's landscape, we find few traces indeed of any "pleasant place," let alone a resurrected Eden. It is thus not surprising to read of Swift's complaint to one correspondent that "I never yet saw in Ireland a spot of earth two feet wide, that had not in it something to displease" (C, 4:33-34). He goes on in the same letter to observe: "I think I was once in your county, Tipperary, which is like the rest of the whole kingdom, a bare face of nature, without houses or plantations. . ." (34). Variations on this "bare face of nature" also appear in fictionalized form in Swift's writings. When Gulliver first set foot on Brobdingnag, for example, he "walked alone about a Mile" and "observed the Country all barren and rocky" (PW, 11:85). Later, during his visit to Balnibarbi, he recounts his journey with Lord Munodi to the latter's country house:

> We passed through one of the Town Gates, and went about three Miles into the Country, where I saw many Labourers working with several Sorts of Tools in the Ground, but was not able to conjecture what they were about; neither did I observe any Expectation either of Corn or Grass, although the Soil appeared to be excellent. . . . I made bold to desire my Conductor, that he would be pleased to explain to me what could be meant by so many busy Heads, Hands and Faces, both in the Streets and the Fields, because I did not discover any good Effects they produced; but on the contrary, I never knew a Soil so unhappily cultivated, Houses so ill contrived and so ruinous, or a People whose Countenances and Habit expressed so much Misery and Want. . . . During our Journey, he [Lord Munodi] made me observe the several Methods used by Farmers in managing their

Lands; which to me were wholly unaccountable: For except in some few Places, I could not discover one Ear of Corn, or Blade of Grass. (PW, 11:174-75)

As we shall see later in this chapter, the preceding account is a thinly disguised description of the actual conditions prevailing in the Irish countryside, as Swift observed them on a regular basis. In both cases, we encounter a dramatic reversal of the situation defining traditional pastoral life, in which, despite the lack of arduous labors, production is always more than adequate to meet the consumers' needs. In Balnibarbi as in eighteenth-century Ireland, however, constant toil is demanded but very little (if anything) is produced.

ii

Swift's antipastoralism was an important expression of his psyche and his temperament. In proposing that the Golden Age "is a dream, based perhaps on childhood," Laurence Lerner points to the links between an idealized vision of mankind's first age on earth and the nostalgic recollection of one's own first age, the desire to go back to one's beginnings.[9] Certainly on a psychological level, pastoral creation and childhood revery are closely related. So it is significant, and hardly surprising under the circumstances, that Swift was rarely moved to record his memories of his own early years, and that the few that do exist in print possess a cold metallic quality and are devoid of all lyricism or nostalgia.

In his autobiographical fragment, *The Family of Swift,* he adopts a tone of icy detachment. He refers to himself throughout in the third person. His terse reflections center upon loss and deprivation and stress the misfortunes he encountered as a result of his parents' "indiscreet" marriage: "And his son [Swift himself] (not then born) hath often been heard to say that he felt the consequences of that marriage not onely through the whole course of his education, but during the greatest part of his life" (PW, 5:192). A posthumous child, he lacked the strong, loving guidance of a father. And at the age of one year, he was kidnapped by his nurse and carried aboard ship with her to Whitehaven, "where he continued for almost three years," thus being early deprived of a maternal presence as well. Although he was subsequently reunited with his mother, his stay with her seems to have been short-lived, for "after his return to Ireld, he was sent at six years old to the School of Kilkenny," where he remained until the age of fourteen. Swift relates this in an utterly matter-of-fact fashion, without further comment or elaboration, but we have to believe that a second prolonged separation from his mother while he was still so young, coming so soon on the heels of the first, must have made a deep and lasting impression on him. His pained awareness of separation was undoubtedly intensified, moreover, by his mother's departure from Ireland for Leicester shortly thereafter. Swift's statement that he began his schooling at the age of six is especially significant in light of the fact that the age of boys entering Kilkenny College (at least in 1684–1686) ranged from nine to fifteen.[10] If Swift's account is accurate here, it would seem to indicate a rather unseemly haste on the part of Abigail Swift to rid herself of her young son's charge. If incorrect, the statement would tend to indicate Swift's subjective feelings of having been unwanted, hence shipped off to school by his mother at an unnaturally early age. In either case, the coldly detached recollection cloaks a deep-seated sense of rejection and abandonment.

The autobiographical fragment contains no recollection of his eight boyhood years in Kilkenny but instead hurries on to record that "at fourteen [Swift] was admitted into the University at Dublin, where by the ill Treatment of his nearest Relations, he was so discouraged and sunk in his Spirits, that he too much neglected his Academical Studyes. . ." (192). The remainder of the fragment can be said to constitute additional testimony to his "ill Treatment" and sunk spirit. Nowhere in the piece do we find any happy remembrance of childhood, any memory capable of evoking associations with a time of innocence or joy. On the contrary, feelings of alienation and estrangement appear to have suffused his earliest years. Leave-taking, and everything attendant upon it, was a central and recurring experience of this period in his life. Swift was an exile from the garden, separated from the love and tranquillity it symbolizes, even before he took his first steps, and his subsequent life is conceived of as a series of reenactments of this initial banishment. When we read that Swift "happened before twenty years old, by a Surfeit of fruit to contract a giddyness and coldness of Stomach, that almost brought him to his Grave, and this disorder pursued him with Intermissions of two or thre years to the end of his Life" (193), we cannot help thinking of another fruit whose consumption had catastrophic consequences and marked the beginning of man's sufferings in a fallen world. The one difference is that, whereas Adam and Eve enjoyed their brief moment in paradise, Swift seems to have been born outside its gates, hence deprived of even that fleeting taste of idyllic existence.

It is revealing, in this connection, to compare Swift with his fellow countryman, Oliver Goldsmith, who likewise felt deep ambivalence toward his homeland and who clung to never-forgotten humiliations he suffered as a youth growing up in Ireland: "Unaccountable, that he should still have an affec[tion for] a place, who never received when in it above civil [contem]pt, [and] who never brought out of it [anything], except his brogue [an]d his blunders. . . ." Yet Goldsmith was also capable of evoking blissful memories of his early years and of expressing nostalgic feelings for his boyhood surroundings, describing to one friend his "desire of seeing Ireland" and insisting that "I am frequently tempted ... to return home. . . ." His remembrance of old friends who had remained behind in Lissoy, in the Midlands, produced "the pangs I feel in seperation."[11] Helping to shape Goldsmith's consciousness were not only the cherished memories of loved ones but also the recollections of a landscape radiant with innocent pleasures, suffused with the colors of childhood: "If I climb Flamstead hill where nature never exhibited a more magnificent prospect; I confess it fine but then I had rather be placed on the little mount before Lishoy gate, and take in, to me, the most pleasing horizon in nature."[12]

These illuminations from a distant but mentally restorable past were later transformed into aspects of Goldsmith's literary world. Childhood memories of Lissoy underlie his poetic apostrophe to "Sweet AUBURN! lovliest village of the plain" and his re-creation of those "Dear lovely bowers of innocence and ease,/Seats of my youth, when every sport could please" (*The Deserted Village,* 5-6).[13] The "neighbouring hill" in this once paradisal village (12) might well have been modeled upon the "little mount before Lishoy gate," which in times past had provided the youthful Goldsmith with access to "the most pleasing horizon in nature." Similarly, the yearning "Around my fire an evening groupe to draw,/And tell of all I felt, and all I saw" (91-92) seems a likely outgrowth of the memory, recorded in his letters, of happy family gatherings around the Lissoy fireside.[14] Various passages in *The Deserted Village* tend to confirm the notion that the pastoral dream is a form of homesickness—an expression of the desire to return to one's beginnings in childhood: "In all my wanderings round this world of care,/In all my griefs—and GOD has given my share—/I still had hopes my latest hours to crown,/Amidst these humble bowers to lay me down. . ." (83-86). We might thus conclude that Goldsmith's blissful memories of childhood actively influenced his adult conception of an idyllic pastoral world.

For Swift, on the contrary, austere memories of a bleak, joyless childhood contributed to an emphatically antipastoral perspective—to the adult denial of an idyllic age located in the past and at least potentially restorable in the present. Thus the few early memories that he records in places other than *The Family of Swift* also prove inimical to an Edenic vision and serve to contradict the idea, put forth by Gaston Bachelard, that childhood is "the archetype of simple happiness" and that it is "an image within us, a center for images which attract happy images and repulse the experiences of unhappiness."[15] Typical of Swift is the recollection appearing in a letter addressed jointly to Bolingbroke and Pope:

> I never wake without finding life a more insignificant thing than it was the day before ... but my greatest misery is recollecting the scene of twenty years past, and then all on a sudden dropping into the present. I remember when I was a little boy, I felt a great fish at

the end of my line which I drew up almost on the ground, but it dropt in, and the disappointment vexeth me to this very day, and I believe it was the type of all my future disappointments. (C, 3:329)

The wording here is curious and revealing, for the observation about life's daily loss of significance, coupled with the "misery" Swift confesses to feeling in juxtaposing the past with the present, prepares us for a reference to some idyllic "scene" from an earlier time that would serve to highlight, through contrast, the debased state of present affairs. Yet when Swift does produce the expected image from the past, it proves to be not so much a contrast as an analogy to the present. Fishing through his memories of childhood, Swift can come up with only the origins of his adult pain and the "type" of his present unhappiness, not with the tranquillity and innocence that anteceded it. In place of Goldsmith's remembered springtime of youthful pleasures and happiness, or Bachelard's "summers of our childhood [that] bear witness to 'the eternal summer,'"[16] Swift conveys an initial and thereafter continually recurring winter of discontent.

The cited recollection is especially significant since fishing, as both fact and metaphor, has regularly been used by writers to represent a condition of spiritual tranquillity and contentment. Izaak Walton, in *The Compleat Angler,* specifically differentiates fishermen from "men that spend all their time first in getting, and next in anxious care to keep it" and confidently affirms that "we [anglers] enjoy a contentedness above the reach of such dispositions." Here the sea, like the earthly garden, is a symbol of divine and natural plenitude; indeed, Walton's "Piscator" argues that "The *Water* is more productive than the *Earth.*"[17] We are reminded of Pope's "patient Fisher," who is likewise confronted with the water's blessed abundance: "Our plenteous Streams a various Race supply..." (*Windsor-Forest,* 137–38, 141). John Gay also presents us with the figure of an expectant angler whose endeavors are assured of success because he lives in a world where nature generously rewards his labors. As he ties "the treach'rous hook" while eagerly anticipating the sport, "His bosom glows with treasures yet uncaught,/Before his eyes a banquet seems to stand,/Where ev'ry guest applauds his skilful hand" (*Rural Sports,* Book I, 144–48).[18]

Swift's version of the fisherman of both Pope and Gay is the "frighted Fisher with desponding Eyes" in *Carbery Rocks,* for whom nature is a fierce adversary, not an affectionate and generous ally. We find throughout Swift's poetry images, not of "plenteous Streams" abounding in fish, but of empty waters pillaged and drained of them. The ballad *The* [National] *Bank thrown down* declares, "The DAMS and the WEIRS must all be your own,/You get all the FISH, while others get none,/We look for a SALMON, you leave us a *Stone*" (6–8), and the verse *To Mr. Gay* conjures up the image of "some *imperious Neighbour* sink[ing] the Boats,/And drain[ing] the *Fish-ponds...*" (89–90). In yet another poem, we meet "Th' amphibious Tyrant, with his rav'nous Band" who "Drains all [Ireland's] Lakes of Fish, of Fruits [her] Land" (*Verses occasioned by the sudden drying up of St. Patrick's Well,* 63–64). Given this abiding perception of nature's depleted state and the consequent impoverishment of those dependent on nature for sustenance, it is little wonder that Swift's writings are devoid of the kind of triumphant apostrophe we find, for example, in Gay's verse: "Now, happy fisherman, now twitch the line!/ How thy rod bends! behold, the prize is thine!" (*Rural Sports,* Book I, 155–56). For Swift, in his own life as well as in his poetic depictions, the piscatory "prize" was never there to "behold" (much less to possess), having either escaped or been snatched away before his hungry eyes. Viewed in its widest context, Swift's choice of a boyhood fishing episode as "the type of all [his] future disappointments" can be interpreted as one more expression of his antipastoral vision.

By temperament stubbornly resistant to the common tendencies in man to idealize the past, Swift once remarked to Charles Ford that "men are never more mistaken, than when they reflect upon passt things" because "our Memoryes lead us onely to the pleasant side. . . . So I formerly used to envy my own Happiness when I was a Schoolboy, the delicious Holidays, the Saterday afternoon, and the charming Custards in a blind Alley; I never considered the Confinement ten hours a day, to nouns and Verbs, the Terror of the Rod, the bloddy [*sic*] Noses, and broken Shins" (C, 1:109). Having dismissed his few fleeting memories of boyhood pleasures as distorted perception and mere wishful thinking, Swift in subsequent recollections stuck to variations on the confinement, terror, and "broken Shins." Reflecting back on his youthful years spent at Moor Park, Swift turned a potential source of Edenic reminiscence into memories of pain and alienation as he called to mind Sir William Temple's chilling remoteness and his penchant for treating Swift "like a schoolboy" (JS, 1:230). Over a decade after his final departure from Moor Park, he would demand of Stella, "Don't you remember how I used to be in pain when Sir William Temple would look cold and out of humour for three or four days, and I used to suspect a hundred reasons?" (231).

Dreams of both paradise and childhood tend to reflect strains of self-indulgence. They are marked by fantasies of self-gratification, of being the center of one's universe and having one's every desire and need instantly and miraculously fulfilled. Swift's memories have nothing in common with such dreams. His mind, rummaging through the past as through a decaying and deserted attic, seized instead upon remembrances of cruel neglect, cold indifference, or condescension directed toward him. Such remembrances convey his acute sense of residing at the periphery rather than at the center of his world, of being treated as an outsider or an insignificant figure in the landscape and of having to endure the pangs of unfulfilled longing from a remote corner of the universe—hence his description of himself as "the Dean of St. Patrick's sitting like a toad in a corner of his great house" (C, 3:114) and his feeling of having been relegated to "a dirty obscure nook of the world" (C, 2:417).

Thus an exploration of Swift's landscape does not lend itself to the type of investigation that Bachelard calls "topophilia," which consists in studying "simple images of *felicitous space*," or "the sorts of space that may be grasped, that may be defended against adverse forces, the space we love."[19] (If anything, the Swiftian landscape would require an investigation centered upon images reflecting "topo*phobia*.") Swift, looking out over his environs both past and present, saw primarily hostile and alien space: space that was associated with anxiety and frustration, not love, and that had already been contaminated by "adverse forces." We find nothing in Swift's writings that would substantiate Bachelard's contention that "before he is 'cast into the world,' as claimed by certain hasty metaphysics, man is laid in the cradle of the house. . . . Life begins well, it begins enclosed, protected, all warm in the bosom of the house."[20] What many of his writings dramatize is precisely the experience of having been "cast into the world," and what his writings conspicuously fail to convey is any sense of having once been at home, embosomed in a warm, protective place. Instead we find passages like the one from the *Ode to Sir William Temple* where Swift, as aspiring poet, characterizes himself through imagery suggesting a state of perennial wandering: "In vain I strive to cross this spacious Main,/In vain I tug and pull the Oar,/And when I almost reach the Shore/Strait the Muse turns the Helm, and I launch out again" (192-95). Interestingly, in his poem *Horace, Book I, Ode XIV, Paraphrased and inscribed to Ir——d*, Swift uses identical imagery to characterize Ireland, that *"Poor floating Isle, tost on ill Fortune's Waves"* ("The Inscription," 1). He opens the poem with the lament: "Unhappy Ship, thou art return'd in Vain:/New Waves shall drive thee to the Deep again" (9-10). As both poet and Irishman, Swift was doubly doomed to a life "at sea": a life defined by its insurmountable distance from the safe, protective bosom of the shore.

iii

Swift's temperamental disposition toward the antipastoral was reinforced as well as concretely shaped by his personal experiences while living and working in Ireland. For his first clerical appointment in Ireland, Swift took up residence in Kilroot, located in the bleak northern region near Carrickfergus Bay, in Belfast Lough. As Louis A. Landa notes, "Swift did not enter a healthy and flourishing diocese"; instead, "the decayed temporalities were before his eyes in the form of ruined churches and alienated glebe lands." The poor state of both the land itself and its architectural structures provides an additional insight into the generally desolate and often dilapidated features of Swift's landscape:

> In County Antrim, where Swift's parishes lay, the dire condition of the Church in the middle of the seventeenth century is indicated by an Inquisition of 1657, which revealed that in the 65 parishes 30 churches were in ruins, 27 had no incumbents, 51 had no glebes, and the tithes of 32 were impropriate to laymen. And in 1693, a bare two years before Swift's incumbency, another report on Down and Connor emphasized its lamentable condition. . . . Kilroot was a small parish, extending 'about a mile over every way' and containing only four townlands with an unimpressive number of profitable acres. . . . There is no evidence that [Swift] had a glebe to cultivate or a manse house to live in, and there is definite evidence that he had no church to preach in. The extant visitations for Kilroot in the seventeenth century record the church as ruinous, and omit any mention of glebe or manse.[21]

Undoubtedly the bitter memory of his brief stay in Kilroot lay behind many of his subsequent references to the miserable lot of the lower-ranked clergy. In a pamphlet written more than three decades after his Kilroot experience, Swift protests that "the Maintenance of the *Clergy*, throughout the Kingdom, is precarious and uncertain" and argues that "an *English Vicar* of 40*l*. a Year, lives much more comfortably than one of double the Value in *Ireland*" (PW, 12:191, 197). He continues by stressing "how difficult it is upon any reasonable Terms, [for the inferior clergy] to find a Place of Habitation" (200). Comments such as these add a further dimension to Swift's cynical view of pastoral existence, in every sense of the term. The pastor's calling, as well as the shepherd's occupation, was doomed to be acted out amidst a bleak and dilapidated landscape incapable of fulfilling human needs.

Swift's second church appointment sent him to the vicarage of Laracor, in the diocese of Meath, which initially presented little improvement over the conditions he encountered in Kilroot. As Landa notes, "The temporalities of the Church in Meath matched those of Down and Connor in decay and neglect. A few years before Swift appeared at Laracor, Anthony Dopping, then Bishop of Meath, reported that the diocese contained 197 parish churches, of which only 43 were in repair."[22] Writing to Jane Waring in the spring of 1700, several months after being appointed to Laracor, Swift declared, "The dismal account you say I have given you of my livings I can assure you to be a true one; and, since it is a dismal one even in your own opinion, you can best draw consequences from it" (C,

1:34). In the absence of a manse on the glebe, Swift had literally to build
a roof to cover his head and four walls to shelter his body from the elements. He slept on "a field-bed and an Earthen floor" (373) in what was
described by a visitation report of 1723 as "a neat cabin."[23] This term
does not adequately convey to us the extent of the structure's primitive
nature, for the word "cabin" (which Swift himself applied to his habitation) designated a very specific type of abode native to the Irish countryside in the eighteenth century. Contemporary accounts by Bush, Young,
and others attest to the appalling condition of these mud, straw-thatched,
windowless abodes.[24] After explaining in detail the way in which Irish
cabins were constructed, John Dunton concluded: "Their [sic] buildings
of Versailles are so very magnificent as not capable of such a description
that may give a just idea of them; so these in the other extreme are so
very wretched things that perhaps the pen of the noblest architect would
be very defective in describing them."[25] Swift's Laracor habitation may
not have been in this poor a state, but his "neat cabin" had more than a
nominal kinship with these others, as we can infer from Swift's remarks
to Bolingbroke upon returning to Ireland from England in 1714: "I would
retire too, if I could; but my country-seat [Laracor], where I have an acre
of ground, is gone to ruin. The wall of my own apartment is fallen down,
and I want mud to rebuild it, and straw to thatch it. Besides, a spiteful
neighbour has seized on six feet of ground, carried off my trees, and spoiled
my grove. All this is literally true, and I have not fortitude enough to go
and see those devastations" (C, 2:130). When he finally did acquire "fortitude enough" to inspect his grounds, what confronted him was in fact
the feared "devastation": "I saw the Gardens at Laracor, and the Grove
too . . . and they all look sadly desolate" (193).

To be sure, Swift improved his Laracor environs considerably over
the years, planting trees and tending to grounds that included a canal and
river walk. As he observed in a letter to Esther Vanhomrigh, " . . . I am
now fitter to look after Willows, and to cutt Hedges than meddle with Affairs of State. I must order one of the Workmen to drive those Cows out
of my Island, and make up the Ditch again; a Work much more proper for
a Country Vicar than driving out Factions and fencing against them"
(C, 1:373). Nevertheless, Landa's view that Swift's attitude toward "his
little acre of ground" at Laracor was largely "that of the gentleman bent
on improving his estate"[26] misses the basic tone and spirit of Swift's endeavors in this respect, which are best characterized in light of his comment, written while at Sheridan's Quilca, that he was "levelling mountains
and raising stones, and fencing against inconveniencies of a scanty lodging" (C, 3:60). Just as he had earlier devoted his energies to "fencing
against" factions, so now he was busy "fencing against" the hostile ele-

ments of his environment. These endeavors were performed not in the spirit of a gentleman's leisure pursuit but rather as an act of urgency and necessity. Swift's attempts to improve the land, like his political and religious activities, revealed a profound and continuing struggle against antagonistic forces.

Although his interest in enhancing the condition of the land persisted, as he grew older he increasingly transformed aspects of his immediate environs into symbolic statements about the irrevocable loss of Eden and the consequent obsolescence of the pastoral mode. His version of "Henry Hoare's Paradise" (Hoare's gardens at Stourhead) or Lord Cobham's Elysian Fields at Stowe was a two-acre plot of ground near the deanery (unfortunately, also near the frequently flooding Poddle), which he pointedly called Naboth's Vineyard, after an orchard cursed by God, and which seemed singularly determined to live up (or rather, down) to its name, judging from Swift's recurring references to the exhausting, often fruitless toil and the exorbitant expenses required for its upkeep. Described to Mrs. Pilkington as "a garden that I [Swift] cheated one of my neighbours out of,"[27] Naboth's Vineyard comes to represent a postlapsarian garden in every sense—an arena for the flawed actions of fallen men. Within its boundaries, Swift is at once sinner and sinned against, at once exploiter and exploited. Thus the masons hired to build a wall around the vineyard "as often as they could . . . put in a rotten stone"; only after Swift asserts himself as "absolute monarch in the *Liberties*" are the laborers persuaded to remain honest.[28] In place of the "Paradise Well" and "Paradise Temple" which Hoare lovingly built and presided over, Swift presents us with "a cursed wall" that he predicts "will ruin both my Health and Fortune, as well as humor" and whose construction he later bitterly repents, since it entailed "squandering all I had saved" (C, 3:14–15, 60). His fruit is continually being blasted and his hay ruined by the onslaughts of "Northeast winds" and by periodic flooding (458–74). If it is true, as Sir William Temple affirmed, that "God Almighty esteemed the life of man in a Garden the happiest he could give him, or else he would not have placed Adam in that of Eden,"[29] one would never know it from the disasters and the general sense of sometimes tragic, sometimes comic futility that characterize Swift's "garden" existence. In the rare instance where Swift evokes his orchard's Edenic associations, his words are fraught with irony. We see him as a ludicrous, distracted, slightly senile Adam, "keep[ing] a clatter about my little garden, where I pretend to have the finest paradise stocks of their age in Ireland," but growing so old and despondent that his "Eden" faces the threat of withering away from lack of care (199).

iv

Swift's anti- and mock-pastoral depictions also constitute an important aspect of his continuing, as well as developing, political and social commentary on contemporary society. His mock-pastoral verses are offered as one of the very few types of expression appropriate for an age witnessing the systematic debasement of the land. On the broadest level, the one especially evident in his writings before 1715, they form part of Swift's devastating critique of capitalism as the latter was beginning to develop and expand throughout the first half of the eighteenth century.[30] A number of his *Examiner* essays were written to expose both the corruptions and the disruptions produced by the new economic order—more specifically, to decry the consequences of the fact that "*Power,* which, according to the old Maxim, was used to follow *Land,* is now gone over to *Money*" (PW, 3:5). The formerly exalted status and importance of the land is progressively being destroyed by a society that now computes all value according to "the Rise and Fall of Stocks" (6): a society that is being ruled to an ever greater extent by a nouveau riche class composed of city bankers, stock jobbers, and the like, who are referred to variously as "assuming Upstarts" (151), "*Retailers of Fraud*" (137), and "Engrossers of Money" (169).

Several of the *Examiner* essays exploit the contrast between the stable, firmly fixed Tories ("in or out of Favour, you see no Alteration [in them]" [PW, 3:126]), and the "*high-flying Whigs*" (109), men "under the Dominion of the *Moon,* [who] are for perpetual *Changes,* and perpetual *Revolutions*" (147)—between a landed aristocracy rooted in the *terra firma* and a class of assorted "retailers," unpropertied beings associated with "transient or imaginary" things (119). In both prose and poetry, Swift demonstrates that the disappearance of paradise is the result, not only of Man's Fall, but also of the present age's economic folly, which is systematically converting the British soil into a wasteland: "The bold Encroachers on the Deep,/Gain by Degrees huge Tracts of Land,/'Till Neptune with a Gen'ral Sweep/Turns all again to barren Strand" (*The Run upon the Bankers,* 1-4). A new breed of financial speculators—"new dextrous Men [introduced] into Business and Credit" (PW, 3:6)—has either directly appropriated or indirectly contaminated the physical terrain, with the result that the eminently solid and firmly rooted features of Eden become transformed into ambiguous shapes of watery illusion:

> Thus the deluded Bankrupt raves,
> Puts all upon a desp'rate Bett,
> Then plunges in the *Southern* Waves,
> Dipt over head and Ears—in Debt.

So, by a Calenture misled,
The Mariner with Rapture sees
On the smooth Ocean's azure Bed
Enamell'd Fields, and verdant Trees;

With eager Hast he longs to rove
In that fantastick Scene, and thinks
It must be some enchanted Grove,
And in he leaps, and down he sinks.

(The Bubble, 21–32)

When the land is not dissolving into water, it is threatening to vanish in thin air. Swift in this regard exploits the symbolic and imagistic as well as the literal significance of the South Sea Bubble, the eighteenth century's first stock market crash.[31] He uses the myth of Icarus to emblematize the destructiveness of the new capitalist society and the folly of those who are seduced by it: "On *Paper* Wings he takes his Flight,/With *Wax* the *Father* bound them fast,/The *Wax* is melted by the Height,/And down the towring Boy is cast" (*The Bubble,* 37–40).

But the contrast Swift drew here between a landed gentry and a class of urban capitalists, between a stability associated with the soil and a mutability evidenced by fluctuating stocks, gradually gave way to his far more significant and original insight that, in the final analysis, the traditional distinction between country and city no longer applied. This is particularly relevant to our concerns here since, as Frank Kermode observes, "The first condition of pastoral poetry is that there should be a sharp difference between two ways of life, the rustic and the urban."[32] It may well be that originally (as Cowper put it) "God made the country and man made the town," but Swift's writings continually underscore the fact that in eighteenth-century England and Ireland, the country along with the town was being created (or, to be more precise, uncreated and then re-created) by man: with man's money, in man's own image, for man's self-interest. Swift's recurring historical perceptions serve to confirm Raymond Williams's analysis of the perversely reciprocal relationship between country and city in eighteenth-century England: "The exploitation of man and of nature, which takes place in the country, is realized and concentrated in the city. But also, the profits of other kinds of exploitation—the accumulating wealth of the merchant, the lawyer, the court favorite—come to penetrate the country...."[33] Swift repeatedly points to the way in which capitalist values have infiltrated country and town alike, destroying all alternative modes of existence. In his *Pastoral Dialogue between Richmond-Lodge and Marble-Hill,* he has the latter house foresee its own doom as a result of capitalism's encroachments:

> Some *South Sea* Broker from the City,
> Will purchase me, the more's the Pity,
> Lay all my fine Plantations waste,
> To fit them to his Vulgar Taste. . . .

(67-70)

The mansion's reminder that "My Groves, my Ecchoes, and my Birds,/ Have taught [Pope] his poetick Words" (91-92) suggests that its own destruction will mean the demise of poetry (more specifically, pastoral poetry) as well. In light of the changes being perpetrated on the land by the inexorable movement from town to country, pastoral existence—and the literary genre associated with it—can be no more than an anachronistic fiction. It must necessarily give way to the contemporary reality of a land ravaged by the acquisitive and avaricious spirit characteristic of the new economy, typified by "The neighbouring Country Squires always watching like Crows for a Carcase over every Estate that was likely to be sold" (C, 4:319).

In *Part of the Seventh Epistle of the First Book of Horace, Imitated,* Swift portrays himself attempting to establish a country seat in Ireland but becoming mired in degrading financial transactions that create an inevitable alienation from the soil and its former values:

> Now all the Doctor's Money's spent,
> His Tenants wrong him in his Rent;
> The Farmers, spightfully combin'd,
> Force him to take his Tythes in kind;
> And *Parvisol* discounts Arrears,
> By Bills for Taxes and Repairs.

(107-12)

We see here the very antithesis of the traditional, idyllic (and, on another level, falsely romanticized) pastoral realm, marked by harmonious and joyful coexistence and functioning through a primitive but equitable economy—what Poggioli calls "home economics in the literal sense of the term." As he explains it, "Pastoral economy seems to realize the contained self-sufficiency that is the ideal of the tribe, of the clan, of the family. . . . Money, credit, and debt have no place in an economy of this kind."[34] The economic relationships described by Swift therefore presuppose, by their very nature, an antipastoral mode of existence. Swift's rural world grotesquely mirrors the city's depersonalization of human relationships—its conversion of human values into monetary ones. Hence the conventional contrast between town and country (or garden and city) loses its meaning, for literary myth and political ideology alike. The Dean's "Seat" is a place of turmoil and class warfare, not cosmic harmony, and therefore fails to reflect even the faintest traces of Eden.

If Swift's country world reflects the influence of the city, his depictions of the city often mirror or parody aspects of country life. It is not coincidental that Swift sets his mock-eclogue, *A Description of the Morning*, and his mock-georgic, *A Description of a City Shower*, in decidedly urban environs, heralding in the former "Ruddy Morns Approach" (2) in the midst of London's squalor and substituting the turnkey's "Flock" (15) for the shepherd's. Moreover, in *A Beautiful Young Nymph Going to Bed*, Swift creates what is on at least one level a mock-pastoral set in the midst of eighteenth-century London's "inner city," describing the life of a most cosmopolitan "Nymph" who plies her trade in Drury Lane and then returns to her shabby fourth-story "Bow'r" (8).

Swift's later writings, growing directly out of his daily experiences while living in Ireland, remind us in other ways too of the perverse bonds existing between country and city. In his tract *Maxims Controlled in Ireland*, for example, Swift notes the "concourse to this beggarly city [Dublin]" of "miserable farmers and cottagers," who in their desperate attempt to escape the poverty of the countryside only wind up bringing it with them into their new urban surroundings (PW, 12:135). Likewise, in one of his sermons he decries the great masses of "Strolers [and Vagabonds] from the Country" who daily swarm into Dublin, intensifying its level of poverty (PW, 9:207). Finally one cannot distinguish between city and country, because they have become basically interchangeable embodiments of Ireland's wretchedness and general deterioration. The very terms "country" and "town" are often deliberately coupled, as in the allusion to "the vast Number of ragged and naked Children in Town and Country" (201). In the world described by Swift, it makes little difference whether one walks through the streets of Dublin or along isolated provincial roads; the sights one sees are fated to prove equally pitiable and repellent in either case.

As the preceding examples hint at, Swift's general critique of capitalism and its adverse effects upon the British landscape increasingly gave way to a more specific (as well as more impassioned) exposure of the ills inflicted on the Irish soil by England's colonialist policies. In his Irish tracts of the 1720s and 1730s, Swift dramatizes the consequences arising from England's treatment of Ireland precisely by showing how this treatment has changed a potential green world—"a Country so favoured by Nature as ours, both in Fruitfulness of Soil, and Temperature of Climate" (PW, 12:10)—into a devastated garden where, as he sarcastically described it in one tract, "the People live with Comfort on Potatoes and Bonnyclabber" (178). Swift's ironical description of Ireland in 1731 as a would-be arcadia boasting of blackberry bushes and potato beds (176) reminds us that the debased landscape inhabited by Sheelah and Dermot is not a satiric fiction so much as a comically heightened historical fact.

A similarly debased landscape reflecting historical fact appears in
Swift's cynical exposures of the paradisal myths about the New World.
Decrying "the strong delusion in [the Irish] by false allurement from
America," he invokes the authority of Sir William Penn, who "did assure
me that his Country wanted the shelter of mountains, which left it open
to the Northern winds from Hudson's bay and the frozen sea, which
destroyed all Plantations of Trees, and was even pernicious to all common vegetables" (PW, 12:78, 76). Pennsylvania, as described here, invites
comparison with Holyhead's "bleaky shore," where "nature hardly seems
alive" (*Holyhead. Sept. 25. 1727,* 29, 32) and with the wilds of Cavan,
where "Air ripens not, nor Earth produces" (*To Quilca,* 6). Swift goes on
to emphasize the connections between England's colonialist policies and
the creation of an antipastoral landscape, between Edenic myths and
political propaganda. If the Irish who remain in their homeland "live
worse than *English* Beggars," without even "a House so convenient as an
English Hog-sty, to receive them" (PW, 12:11, 10), then their fellow countrymen who leave for America in order to escape "their present insupportable Condition at home" find themselves in even more pitiable straits,
compelled to perform the role of those "barbarous People, whom the
Romans placed in their Armies, for no other Service than to blunt their
Enemies Swords, and afterwards to fill up Trenches with their dead
Bodies" (60). Within the context of eighteenth-century English colonialism, paradisal vision can at any moment turn into genocidal nightmare.

The niggardly and unproductive soil depicted throughout Swift's
mock-pastoral verses, symbolic of postlapsarian starvation rather than
Edenic feasting, was likewise a historical and topographical reality, however much this reality may have taken on certain heightened dimensions
through the workings of Swift's consciousness. Again and again, Swift
directed his reader's or correspondent's attention to the terrible famine
engulfing the land, insisting upon the urgency of the situation. In a letter
to Pope he notes that in Ireland "there have been three terrible years
dearth of corn, and every place strowed with beggars," and concludes
that "the kingdom is absolutely undone" (C, 3:341). Responding to the
writer of a paper recommending as a solution to Ireland's food problem
the importation of corn from plantations abroad, Swift counters with
his own combined proposal and warning:

> If you will propose a general Contribution, in supporting the Poor
> in *Potatoes* and *Butter-milk,* till the new Corn comes in, perhaps you
> may succeed better; because the Thing, at least, is possible: And, I
> think, if our Brethren in *England* would contribute, upon this Emer-
> gency, out of the Million they gain from us every Year, they would
> do a Piece of *Justice* as well as *Charity.* In the mean Time, go and
> preach to your own Tenants, to fall to the Plough as fast as they can;

and prevail with your neighbouring 'Squires to do the same with theirs; or else die with the Guilt of having driven away half the Inhabitants, and starving the rest. (PW, 12:22)

In a similar vein, the sermon *Causes of the Wretched Condition of Ireland* calls attention to the tragic fact that "our Tradesmen and Shopkeepers, who deal in Home-Goods, are left in a starving Condition" (PW, 9:201). The scarcity of food is attributable not to any inherent limitations of Ireland's terrain—which, as Swift stresses, "is capable of producing all Things necessary, and most Things convenient for Life, sufficient for the Support of four Times the Number of its Inhabitants" (199)—but rather, to man-made policies, particularly as they emanate directly from England's colonialist rule. The "Injured Lady," a personification of Ireland, laments that "we must send all our Goods to his [England's] Market just in their Naturals; the Milk immediately from the Cow without making it into Cheese or Butter; the Corn in the Ear; the Grass as it is mowed; the Wool as it cometh from the Sheeps Back; and bring the Fruit upon the Branch, that he might not be obliged to eat it after our filthy Hands" (6). Whereas in Marvell's garden world, "Luscious Clusters of the Vine" along with "The Nectaren, and curious Peach" eagerly submit themselves to man's mouth and reach (*The Garden,* 35–38),[35] in Swift's mock-arcadia, Ireland's milk, corn, and "Fruit upon the Branch" are in effect snatched away by England's grasping fingers, to vanish into England's ravenous maw. It is hardly surprising, therefore, that Swift's portrait of an English statesman is of

A bloated M[iniste]r in all his Geer,
With shameless Visage, and perfidious Leer,
Two Rows of Teeth arm each devouring Jaw;
And, *Ostrich*-like, his all-digesting Maw.

(*To Mr. Gay,* 33–36)

This imagistic depiction occurs elsewhere. In *A Panegyric on the Reverend D——n S——t,* Swift notes that men like Swift and Delany "So long *unbishoprick'd* lie by" (147) while others (those sent or supported by England) "Devour the *Church's tiddest Bits*" (150), and in a contemporary tract he declares that "at this day there is hardly any remainder left of Dean and chapter lands in Ireland; that delicious morsel swallowed so greedily in England under the fanatick Usurpations" (PW, 12:185–86).

This latter reference to the "long wars between the Invaders and the Natives," during which "the Conquerors always seized what lands they could with little ceremony" (183), reminds us that underlying Swift's characterization of Ireland's plight was a long history of violence and oppression: a history rooted in the extremes of famine and devouring. Testimony to this fact appears in Spenser's *A View of the Present State of*

Ireland, where Irenius's prediction of the outcome of the wars against the Desmonds (at which time the English would finally wipe out the "stout and obstinate rebels") paints a grisly picture of widespread starvation and the bestiality resulting from it:

> The end I assure me will be very short and much sooner than can be in so great a trouble (as it seemeth) hoped for. Although there should none of them fall by the sword, nor be slain by the soldier, yet thus being kept from manurance, and their cattle from running abroad by this hard restraint, they would quickly consume themselves and devour one another. The proof whereof I saw sufficiently ensampled in those late wars in Munster, for notwithstanding that the same was a most rich and plentiful country, full of corn and cattle, that you would have thought they would have been able to stand long, yet ere one year and a half they were brought to such wretchedness, as that any stony heart would have rued the same. Out of every corner of the woods and glens they came creeping forth upon their hands, for their legs could not bear them. They looked anatomies of death, they spake like ghosts crying out of their graves, they did eat of the dead carrions, happy were they could find them, yea and one another soon after in so much as the very carcasses they spared not to scrape out of their graves, and if they found a plot of water cress or shamrocks, there they flocked as to a feast for the time, yet not able long to continue therewithal, that in short space there were none almost left and a most populous and plentiful country suddenly left void of man or beast.[36]

On whatever level and to whatever extent this aspect of Irish history affected Swift's consciousness, the fact is that he repeatedly described the inherently exploitative relationship between England and Ireland, not only through references to starvation, but also through images suggesting perverted acts of eating, including cannibalism. In a poem attacking Lord Allen, for example, he asserts: "Hence he draws his daily Food,/From his Tenants vital Blood" (*Traulus, The Second Part,* 41–42). This image is reinforced elsewhere by the poetic persona representing St. Patrick, who grimly foresees in Ireland's future a time "When Shells and Leather shall for Money pass,/Nor thy oppressing Lords afford thee Brass./But all turn Leasers to that Mongril Breed,/Who from thee sprung, yet on thy Vitals feed" (*Verses occasioned by the sudden drying up of St. Patrick's Well,* 93–96). (The "Mongril Breed" in this passage refers, as a contemporary footnote to the poem indicates, to "The Absentees, who spend the Income of their *Irish* Estates, Places and Pensions in *England*" [P, 3: 794]).

The hellish situation in which children feed themselves by devouring their mother's substance leads, with its own kind of satanic logic, to the

situation described in *A Modest Proposal*, where parents must have recourse to eating their offspring: "A Child will make two Dishes at an
Entertainment for Friends; and when the Family dines alone, the fore
or hind Quarter will make a reasonable Dish; and seasoned with a little
Pepper or Salt, will be very good Boiled on the fourth Day, especially in
Winter" (PW, 12:112). We can, if we wish, discuss the preceding as a
satiric fiction, but only if we simultaneously acknowledge its inextricable
links to what was, for Swift, economic and political reality. Despite its
gruesomely bizarre and surreal character, the image of a child served up
as a family's evening repast is, viewed in the broadest perspective, only a
slightly fictionalized extension of "those *voluntary Abortions,* and that
horrid Practice of *Women murdering their Bastard Children* . . . sacrificing
the *poor innocent Babes,* I doubt, more to avoid the Expence than the
Shame" (110); it is no more monstrous or incredible than "that vast
Number of poor People, who are Aged, Diseased, or Maimed" and who
are "every Day *dying,* and *rotting,* by *Cold* and *Famine,* and *Filth,* and
Vermin, as fast as can be reasonably expected" (114). Contrary to Oliver
W. Ferguson's contention that Swift's wrath in this work was directed
"not against England, or callous economists, or visionary projectors, but
against Ireland herself,"[37] *A Modest Proposal* is governed by a central
metaphor that for Swift automatically conveyed a definite political and
economic—specifically anticolonialist—statement: one that assumed the
existence of close ties between Ireland's self-destructive tendencies and
England's brutal oppressions. As Swift saw it, England's lawless seizure of
Ireland's earthly produce, like Eve's willful plunder of the forbidden fruit,
generated a fundamentally anarchic and predatory world founded upon a
grotesque Chain of Devouring. It is a world in which parents consume
children while themselves becoming the repast of others: "I grant this
Food will be somewhat dear, and therefore very *proper for Landlords;*
who, as they have already devoured most of the Parents, seem to have the
best Title to the Children" (112). Ultimately even the Irish landlords,
along with their less fortunate countrymen, become potential food for
another: ". . . this Kind of Commodity will not bear Exportation; the
Flesh being of too tender a Consistence, to admit a long Continuance in
Salt; *although, perhaps, I could name a Country, which would be glad to
eat up our whole Nation without it*" (117).

Swift incorporated into his writings numerous variations on this
basic vision of a cannibalistic world. His versified parable *Desire and Possession* concludes with a portrayal of Possession expiring beneath the
heavy weight of his load: "The Raven, Vulture, Owl, and Kite,/At once
upon his Carcase light;/And strip his Hyde, and pick his Bones,/Regard-
less of his dying Groans" (55-58). *On Poetry: A Rapsody* presents a similar vision of bestiality:

Hobbes clearly proves that ev'ry Creature
Lives in a State of War by Nature.
The Greater for the Smallest watch,
But meddle seldom with their Match.
A Whale of moderate Size will draw
A Shole of Herrings down his Maw.
A Fox with Geese his Belly crams;
A Wolf destroys a thousand Lambs.

(319-26)

The sea, like the land, functions on this principle of mutual devouring.
Hence we have " . . . Anarchy at Sea,/Where Fishes on each other prey;/
Where ev'ry Trout can make as high Rants/O'er his Inferiors as our Tyrants. . ." (*On a Printer's being sent to Newgate, by* ———, 3-6). The
explicitly topical subject matter of this verse (the imprisonment of Swift's
printer, George Faulkner, for a piece he had published) underscores the
links between Swift's images of a predatory world and his perception
of the contemporary political situation. As the counterpart to the piscatory world where the trout tyrannizes over his inferiors, though he
"hide[s] his coward Snout in Mud" at the appearance of "a lordly Pike"
(10, 8), we are elsewhere shown a human world rooted in *"universal Oppression,"* where *"Slaves* have a natural Disposition to be *Tyrants;* [so]
that when my *Betters* give me a Kick, I am apt to revenge it with six
upon my *Footman"*—even though, it is strongly implied, the real cul-
prits are his superiors, in the figure of such as *"their Worships* the Landlords" (PW, 9:21). However much Swift's recurring images of a fiercely,
often grotesquely predatory world may have grown out of satiric convention, and however much they may express a deep-seated Christian pessimism concerning man's fallen nature, on some (I would argue, profound)
level they were shaped, imbued with a special cogency and force, by
Swift's perception of the historical plight of Ireland, as a country being
systematically devoured by her "superiors."

The *Verses occasioned by the sudden drying up of St. Patrick's
Well* provides particularly powerful testimony to the historical basis of
Swift's imagery. The curse incurred by man as a consequence of his sin
finds its Swiftian counterpart in this poem, where the wrathful God-like
speaker (St. Patrick) describes the sufferings he has imposed on the
"spurious and degenerate Line" (101) now inhabiting Ireland—fallen
creatures who "in Vice and Slavery are drown'd" (38). This piece vividly
underscores Swift's simultaneous rage against the English for their oppressions and his disgust with the Irish for their cowardly acquiescence in their
own enslavement. The poem presents Swift's version of the destruction of
paradise—of the " . . . happy Island, *Pallas* call'd her own,/When haughty
Britain was a Land Unknown" (9-10)—through a kind of serpentine infil-
tration by "base Invaders" (22) who gradually conquered the land:

Britain, by thee we fell, ungrateful Isle!
Not by thy Valour, but superior Guile:
Britain, with Shame confess, this Land of mine
First taught thee human Knowledge and divine;
My Prelates and my Students, sent from hence,
Made your Sons Converts both to God and Sense:
Not like the Pastors of thy rav'nous Breed,
Who come to fleece the Flocks, and not to feed.

(25-32)

Swift metaphorically exploits here the historical fact that the well located near Trinity College suddenly dried up in 1729: "Where is the sacred Well, that bore my Name?/Fled to the Fountain back, from whence it came!/ Fair Freedom's Emblem once, which smoothly flows,/And Blessings equally on all bestows" (65-68). It is characteristic of Swift that he should have chosen to poetically commemorate the demise of the well rather than celebrate the renewal of its waters several years later, as did other contemporary versifiers. By placing the disappearance of St. Patrick's Well in a specifically political context, Swift emphasizes the fact that, for him, contemporary reenactments of Man's Fall were directly linked to England's colonialist policies and Ireland's colonized mentality.

Confronted with the spread of "Vice" and "Slavery" in his adopted isle (38), St. Patrick heralds forth a postlapsarian world where predatory creatures devour one another while the threat of barrenness and starvation looms ever larger:

I sent the Magpye from the *British* Soil,
With restless Beak thy blooming Fruit to spoil,
. . . .
See, where the new-devouring Vermin runs,
Sent in my Anger from the Land of *Huns;*
With harpy Claws it undermines the Ground,
And sudden spreads a numerous Offspring round;
Th' amphibious Tyrant, with his rav'nous Band,
Drains all thy Lakes of Fish, of Fruits thy Land.

(45-46, 59-64)

As the verse makes clear, Ireland does not lack harvests, but these are "waste[d] in Luxury" by those who systematically transport the country's "Treasures" to England, "yon rav'nous Isle" (97-98). This blatantly inequitable system has given rise to the spectre of famine amidst plenty, so that St. Patrick foresees the rapidly approaching time "When, for the Use of no *Hibernian* born,/Shall rise one Blade of Grass, one Ear of Corn" (91-92). The last line cited echoes almost verbatim part of Gulliver's description of Balnibarbi's countryside, where, "except in some very few Places," he "could not discover one Ear of Corn, or Blade of Grass"

(PW, 11:175), once again directing our attention to the fact that even Swift's fictionalized depictions of landscape never stray very far afield from the actual landscape amidst which he spent his life.

v

That Swift's metaphoric and symbolic re-creations of topography grew out of the physical terrain he knew so well becomes even clearer when we read his continuing commentary on the state of the Irish country-side, which appeared throughout the tracts he wrote in the 1720s and early 1730s. These tracts protest against what amounted to an official and systematic discouragement of agriculture, which Swift invariably linked to his bête noire, "that abominable Race of Graziers, who, upon Expiration of the Farmers Leases, are ready to engross great Quantities of Land" (PW, 12:17–18). He repeatedly condemned "the Desolation made in the Country by engrossing Graziers" (PW, 9:47). Swift's choice of words is significant, for it suggests that he viewed the graziers in a light similar to the one in which he perceived the city bankers and stock jobbers, those "Engrossers of Money" whom he attacks in his *Examiner* essays. For Swift, both groups were detestable outgrowths of an economic system based on seemingly endless expansion and uncontrollable greed. Constantia Maxwell describes the graziers as "lazy and extravagant" beings who "formed a class apart" in eighteenth-century Ireland and who habitually "neglected their duty as farmers."[38] This neglect, manifested by abundant, potentially fecund lands that were allowed to fall into disuse and by the striking juxtaposition of affluence and seeming penury, was attested to in the accounts written by eighteenth-century travelers to Ireland. John Loveday, for example, traveling through the countryside surrounding Kilkenny in 1732, noted: "The S[outh] runs all upon Sheep-walks; sometimes You see a patch of excellent Corn, but ride many miles on farther, & You may meet-with no more."[39] Some three decades later, John Bush observed that "though by nature, a very considerable part of [Irish lands are] rich and fertile, yet they almost universally wear the face of poverty, for want of good cultivation. . . ." These unfortunate circumstances were, according to him, directly traceable to the graziers and their effect upon the soil: "With respect to grazing, which is, at present [ca. 1768], the most profitable kind of agriculture, and which annually extends in this kingdom[,] . . . that insatiable avarice of most of the stock farmers, as they are called here, after black cattle (bullocks,) will, in time, spoil much of the best pasturage in Ireland."[40] Swift was also struck by the "insatiable avarice" of the graziers. In emphasizing the adverse consequences of their activities for the Irish countryside, Swift repeatedly pointed to two interrelated manifestations: the depopulation of the land and its almost criminal neglect as a result of lack of cultivation. Explaining how a farmer was "too easily tempted" by the monetary offers of a rich grazier, he concluded: "Thus, a vast Tract of Land, where Twenty or Thirty Farmers lived together, with their Cottagers, and Labourers in their several Cabins, became all desolate, and easily managed by one or two Herdsmen, and their Boys; whereby the Master-Grazier, with little Trouble, seized to himself the Livelyhood of a Hundred People" (PW, 12:18). And, in *A Short View of the State of Ireland,* he castigated those who, "by running into the Fancy of Grazing, after the Manner of the *Scythians,* are every Day depopulating the Country" (8).

Testimony to this depopulation, which occurred for the most part in Ulster and which generally took the form of emigrations to various parts of America,[41] appears in a number of contemporary accounts, including Bishop Boulter's in the late 1720s, which reports that "above 4200 men, women, and children have been shipped off . . . within three years, and of these above 3100 this last summer. . . . The whole north is in a ferment at present, and people every day engaging one another to go next year to the *West Indies.* The humour has spread like a contagious distemper. . . ."[42] This situation was particularly tragic since, as Swift keeps reminding us in these tracts, people are—or at any rate would be under all normal circumstances—the riches of a nation (see, e.g., PW, 12:89, 135). Indeed, as Landa points out, "In eighteenth-century mercantilist theory it was agreed 'that the natural Strength of a Nation consists in the Number' and increase of its inhabitants. . . . People were thought to be, as one writer stated, 'the chiefest, most fundamental, and precious commodity.'"[43] Instead of providing work and sustenance for her "most precious commodity," however, Ireland's economic system had placed the native inhabitants in a position where they "must either beg, steal, or starve, or be forced to quit [their] country" (PW, 12:136).

This situation was likewise protested against by another socially conscious Anglican churchman, Bishop Berkeley, who in his *Querist* posed the questions "Whether it be not a sure Sign of or Effect of a Countries thriving, to see it well cultivated, and full of Inhabitants? And, if so, whether a great Quantity of Sheep-Walk be not ruinous to a Country, rendering it Waste and thinly Inhabited?"[44] It was left to Swift, however, to turn rhetorical questions into powerful polemic and to fully exploit the bitter irony of a situation in which animals thrived and multiplied while humans disappeared:

> The *Grazier's* Employment is to feed great Flocks of *Sheep,* or *Black Cattle,* or both. . . . And, the Good of it is, that the more *Sheep* we have, the fewer human Creatures are left to wear the *Wool,* or eat the *Flesh. Ajax* was mad when he mistook a Flock of *Sheep* for his Enemies: But we shall never be sober, until we have the same Way of Thinking.
>
> The other Part of the *Grazier's* Business is, what we call *Black-*

Cattle; producing *Hides, Tallow,* and *Beef* for Exportation. . . . However, to bestow the whole Kingdom on *Beef* and *Mutton,* and thereby drive out half the People who should eat their Share, and force the rest to send sometimes as far as *Egypt,* for Bread to eat with it; is a most peculiar and distinguished Piece of publick Oeconomy; of which I have no Comprehension. (PW, 12:18-19)

That the average Irishman's sufferings were caused in part by sheep—animals so significant, both literally and symbolically, for the pastoral vision and the vision of a Christian community alike—gives us additional insight into the cynicism and the bitter irony underlying Swift's depictions of rural existence, as well as of that ravenous breed of high-ranking churchmen (especially bishops) sent by England to "fleece" the Irish in every way possible.

Viewed in the broadest perspective, the desolation of the land was a result of two opposite though interdependent extremes: the overuse of the land on the one hand, and its almost total disuse on the other. With regard to the former, Swift condemned "the shameful Practice of too many *Irish* Farmers, to wear out their Ground with Plowing; while, either through Poverty, Laziness, or Ignorance, they neither took Care to manure it as they ought; nor gave Time to any Part of the Land to recover itself." The situation was aggravated by the fact that "when their Leases were near expiring, being assured that their Landlords would not renew, they Ploughed even the Meadows," thereby wreaking untold "Havock" upon the soil (PW, 12:17). The agricultural abuses described by Swift suggest a kind of sexual exploitation and exhaustion: Excessive "plowing," without allowing sufficient time for "recovery," results in the soil's becoming both physically fatigued and "worn out of Heart" (18). Swift makes it clear that this state of affairs is part of a larger economic system founded upon the continuous abuse of the land and ultimately traceable to the wealthy absentee landlords and their supporters in England. This group's egregious mistreatment of Ireland is expressed through images of sexual exploitation followed by criminal neglect. As the "Injured Lady" mournfully explains, "I was reckoned to be as handsome as any in our Neighborhood, until I became pale and thin with Grief and ill Usage. . . . They that see me now will hardly allow me ever to have had any great Share of Beauty; for besides being so much altered, I go always mobbed and in an Undress, as well out of Neglect, as indeed for want of Cloaths to appear in" (PW, 9:4). Just as the farmers are "wear[ing] out their Ground with Plowing," the English colonializers are in the process of "drain[ing Ireland] and [her] Tenants so dry" (8). The result is the same in both cases: Through continued abuse, Ireland has become a haggard, scrawny woman, grown old before her time, having no more favors to give. We find a variation on this image in the Reverend Thomas Campbell's *Philo-*

sophical Survey of the South of Ireland, written later in the century: "My picture of Ireland should be *mulier formosa superne*—a woman exquisitely beautiful, with her head and neck richly attired, her bosom full, but meanly dressed, her lower parts lean and emaciated, half-covered with tattered weeds, her legs and feet bare, with burned shins, and all the squalor of indigent sloth."[45] The repeated assault on Ireland's body and her consequent exhaustion prompted Swift to deliver a warning to England, ostensibly for the latter's own good: " . . . *when the Hen is starved to Death, there will be no more Golden Eggs"* (PW, 12:12).

The sexual dimension of England's oppressive behavior is dramatized by Swift in more explicit and graphic terms elsewhere. In *An Excellent New Ballad: Or, The true English Dean to be hang'd for a Rape,* the true case of Dr. Sawbridge, Dean of Ferns, who was indicted for rape although he later succeeded in buying off the victim, is converted into a mordantly humorous parable of England's general treatment toward Ireland. "Our Brethren of *E——nd* who love us so dear" are blessed for having sent over "For the Good of our Church a true *En——sh* D——n" (1, 4), who proceeds to convert Dublin into his own private whorehouse (19–30) and then turns to rape in order to gratify his increasingly jaded appetites (55–60). An earlier verse, *The Description of a Salamander,* depicts Lord Cutts, appointed commander-in-chief in Ireland in 1705, as a repulsive lecher who has infected the country with venereal disease:

> And should some Nymph who ne'er was cruel,
> Like *Carleton* cheap, or fam'd *Duruel,*
> Receive the Filth which he ejects,
> She soon would find, the same Effects,
> Her tainted Carcase to pursue,
> As from the *Salamander's* Spue;
> A dismal shedding of her Locks
> And, if no Leprosy, a Pox.
>
> (61–68)

The physical manifestations of Ireland's ill usage can be represented with equal appropriateness by the ravages of syphilis on the female body and by the scarred, overplowed face of the Irish landscape.

If the overuse of Ireland's resources was a major cause of Ireland's distress, the other side of the coin, equally pernicious, was their systematic *non*use and neglect. Swift rebukes the "cruel Landlords" for "every Day unpeopling their Kingdom, by forbidding their miserable Tenants to till the Earth, against common Reason and Justice, and contrary to the Practice and Prudence of all other Nations" (PW, 9:201). L. M. Cullen claims that Swift exaggerated the situation due to his dislike of the Irish gentry,[46] but if Cullen is right, we would have to conclude that a large proportion of the period's leading political observers and public figures were equally guilty of such distortion, including Lord Carteret and the members of the Irish Privy Council, who in 1727 were moved to recommend passage of a tillage bill to require large landholders to cultivate at least a portion of their acreage. Their justification was that ". . . of late years many landlords have begun a practice to tye down their tenants by express covenants not to break up or plow their lands, by which covenants (highly prejudicial to the public good of the country) our desolation and want of tillage is increasing."[47]

The conditions recorded here constitute a negation of the traditional pastoral realm that, in its ability to reconcile all potential conflicts, comprehends pasture and tillage as two harmonious and mutually supportive aspects of the same flourishing landscape. In this landscape sheep can graze to their hearts' content without in any way interfering with the soil's well-being and the abundant growth, as we see from the following verse written by an otherwise unidentified "J. M." in 1600:

> Fields were over-spread with flowers,
> Fairest choise of *Floraes* treasure:
> Shepheards there had shadie Bowers,
> Where they oft repos'd with pleasure.
>   Meadowes flourish'd fresh and gay,
>   Where the wanton Heards did play.[48]

Pope's "Spring," the first of his *Pastorals,* likewise pictures thriving flora, beasts of labor, and grazing flocks that coexist within a landscape seemingly capable of sustaining all forms of life and livelihood at once. Such harmonious coexistence can prevail only in an imaginary world where the laws of the marketplace do not operate—a world where there are no conflicting claims for land usage, no competition for limited natural resources. Swift, realizing this, eschewed a literary escape into pastoral fantasy and instead chose to record the antipastoral reality of a world where the conflicting needs of farmer and shepherd, of grower and grazier, remained irreconcilable.

Swift was not, of course, the only writer in the eighteenth century to point out the links between the new economic order and the desolation of the land. Goldsmith, for another, described how the system of agricultural enclosure in mid-century England resulted in depopulation and barrenness even amidst seeming splendor. In his poem *The Traveller,* he asks rhetorically whether we have not "Seen opulence, her grandeur to maintain,/ Lead stern depopulation in her train" (401–2). And in *The Deserted Village* he devotes a lengthy passage to a consideration of the adverse consequences of the appropriation of extensive tracts of farmland by an affluent class:

. . . .The man of wealth and pride,
Takes up a space that many poor supplied;
Space for his lake, his park's extended bounds,
Space for his horses, equipage, and hounds;
The robe that wraps his limbs in silken sloth,
Has robbed the neighbouring fields of half their growth. . . .

(275-80)

There is an unmistakable note of anger and protest in both poems, but the cutting edge of their indictment is significantly blunted as the poet's dissatisfaction with the present becomes subsumed by his nostalgic re-creations of the past and his Christian-Stoic affirmation of the future. However memorable the passages describing " . . . trade's unfeeling train / Usurp[ing] the land and dispossess[ing] the swain" (63-64), *The Deserted Village* has its greatest emotional impact in those passages in which Goldsmith lovingly, lingeringly reflects upon the Edenic joys of a former time: "Sweet was the sound when oft at evening's close,/Up yonder hill the village murmur rose;/There as I past with careless steps and slow,/The mingling notes came softened from below" (113-16). Moreover, Goldsmith's denunciations of contemporary practices affecting the land are further blunted by his tendency to idealize, as well as sentimentalize, the lot of the poor. Although the necessity of labor is acknowledged, it quickly "len[ds] its turn to play" (16), and the sports engaged in "With sweet succession, taught even toil to please" (32). Goldsmith locates the Golden Age in an era, only recently departed, that could boast of "a bold peasantry, their country's pride" (55), whose "best companions" were "innocence and health" and whose "best riches" were "ignorance of wealth" (61-62). The impression conveyed is that the poor are (or at least would be, were it not for the tragic consequences of enclosure) essentially more fortunate than the wealthy, enjoying greater health, greater innocence, even finally greater happiness, than their more affluent countrymen.

    In Goldsmith's prose we can find a similar treatment of specifically Irish rural existence. The essay "A Description of the Manners and Customs of the Native Irish. In a Letter from an *English* Gentleman," written for the *Weekly Magazine* in 1759, after initially depicting certain aspects of the country in terms of a traditional pastoral realm, proceeds with a delineation of the wretched conditions in which the Irish peasants live, but it is a delineation that, characteristically, culminates in an affirmation of their joys. The speaker sets out on horseback for Ireland's western shore, "resolved to observe the manners of the inhabitants more minutely than they had been examined before":

    When I had got about forty miles from the capital, I found the country begin to wear a different appearance from what it before appeared to me in. The neat inclosures, the warm and well built houses, the fine cultivated grounds, were no more to be seen, the prospect now changed into, here and there a gentleman's seat, grounds ill cultivated, though seemingly capable of cultivation, little irregular fences made of turf, and topped with brush wood, cut from some neighbouring shrub, and the peasants houses wearing all the appearance of indigence and misery. You will not be surprized, sir, as you know me, that I had curiosity enough to enter one of those mansions, which seemed by its appearance to be the habitation of despair. . . .[49]

Thus far Goldsmith's description is consistent with Swift's accounts of his countrymen's wretched conditions. Once Goldsmith enters the hovel, however, his description turns into romance. Despite the meanness of the cabin and the absence of a chimney, which causes eyes to become "bleared with smoak," Goldsmith immediately finds comfort in the sight of a young girl of about fifteen, "beautiful as an angel." Having been invited to stay for dinner, the visitor delivers a glowing testimonial to the hospitality, good breeding, and social graces of the members of the peasant family, who, like England's "bold peasantry" in *The Deserted Village,* embody the superior virtues of the lower classes. Although we cannot help being somewhat dismayed by the meagerness of the dinner fare ("Supper was soon upon the table, which consisted of nothing more than potatoes and milk, for the rest of the family, but for the father and me, we were honoured each with a wooden knife, and a print of butter"), our attention is at once directed away from the starvation diet and toward the conviviality of the gathering. What we are left with, finally, is a sentimental, idealized picture that all but denies the terrible realities previously acknowledged: "We accordingly fell to, and as I had a good appetite, I assure you I never made a more comfortable meal. . . . The circulation of the beer soon threw us all into tip top spirits, I could not behold without the utmost satisfaction the faces of my fellow creatures which were but a little before wrinkled with fatigue and labour, expanding gradually into smiles, and forgetting those miseries which I had before foolishly deemed insupportable." Clearly the reader is meant to follow the example of Goldsmith's "fellow creatures"—and of Goldsmith himself—in "forgetting those miseries" that, on the face of it, seem insupportable and in replacing a troubled countenance with a look of gaiety.

No such act of forgetting and no such look are possible when we read Swift's accounts of the conditions prevailing in the Irish countryside. His depictions work in an opposite manner from Goldsmith's: They move away from satisfied acceptance and reconciliation, toward a deepening sense of outrage and urgency. They are designed precisely to provoke and disturb the reader, to destroy all traces of complacency. In Swift's writings the Irish peasants never metamorphose into happy, innocent country folk blessed with "riches" that are, by implication, far better than material ones. Devoid of the trappings of sentimentality and romance, the Irish farmers as portrayed by Swift remain members of an oppressed class "who pay great Rents, living in Filth and Nastiness upon Butter-milk and Potatoes, without a Shoe or Stocking to their Feet . . . " (PW, 12:10). The pitifully meager fare mentioned here is the same as that described in Goldsmith's essay, but in Swift's description the reader is compelled to contemplate the "Butter-milk and Potatoes" in all their stark inadequacy, as incontrovertible facts of life inimical to the very notion of a hospitable community or a festive gathering. Swift follows this depiction with a bitterly ironic comment: "These, indeed, may be comfortable Sights to an *English* Spectator; who comes for a short Time, only *to learn the Language,* and returns back to his own Country, whither he finds all our Wealth transmitted" (10-11). Goldsmith's "English Gentleman," who takes a brief trip through the Irish countryside "resolved to observe the manners of the inhabitants," could easily qualify as Swift's "*English* Spectator," and is therefore subject to the same kind of implicit criticism. In making this caustic remark, Swift is pointing to the way in which foreign observers habitually ignore the testimony of their eyes by glossing over, and thereby making "comfortable," the sights they encounter. Confronted with these same sights, Swift does not, like Goldsmith, interpret the realities of the peasants' life as only superficially insupportable, but on the contrary, persists in seeing them as utterly and profoundly so; hence his response to the situation comes much closer to the Modest Proposer's than to the typical English spectator's: "I confess myself to be touched with a very sensible pleasure, when I hear of a mortality in any country-parish or village, where the wretches are forced to pay for a filthy cabin and two ridges of potatoes treble the worth, brought up to steal or beg, for want of work, to whom death would be the best thing to be wished for, on account both of themselves and the public" (136).

We find nothing in Swift's writings that corresponds to Goldsmith's picture of the country people's faces, initially "wrinkled with fatigue and labour" but "expanding gradually into smiles." Indeed, Swift makes a point of remarking upon the general absence of happy facial expressions in Ireland. In a letter to Dean Brandreth, for example, he poses the rhetorical question, "Did you ever see one cheerful countenance among our country vulgar? unless once a year at a fair, or on a holiday, where some poor rogue happened to get drunk, and starved the whole week after" (C, 4:34). Swift shows himself to be particularly attentive to the "faces" of both the land and its inhabitants, which invariably mirror Ireland's plight. In his *Short View of the State of Ireland,* he urges "the worthy *Commissioners* who come from *England,* [to] ride round the Kingdom, and ob-

serve the Face of Nature, or the Faces of the Natives" (PW, 12:10);
judging from the account that follows, they will find anything but smiling
countenances. What they are likely to see instead are the same things
Swift encountered in his own travels through Ireland: "a bare face of
nature . . . [and] miserable, tattered, half-starved creatures, scarce in
human shape" (C, 4:34).

The somber, gloomy visage of Swift's landscape contrasts with
the contented looks reflected in the pastoral world, where the earth itself
traditionally wears a cheerful aspect. In Milton's Paradise, the "Silvan
Lodge" of Adam and Eve " . . . like *Pomona's* Arbor smil'd/With flow'rets
deck't. . ." (Book V, 377-79), and in *The Deserted Village,* Goldsmith
refers to "yonder copse, where once the garden smil'd" (137) in the
Edenic time before enclosure. The image of the smiling earth, via a slight
shift in emphasis, could be used as well in a more explicitly political context, as a visual affirmation of the status quo—a comforting testimonial to
the idea that all is well in the prevailing state of things. Interestingly (and
somewhat ironically), a contemporary critic commenting upon *The Deserted Village* found Goldsmith's landscape to possess an excessively and
unjustifiably glum countenance, since "England wears now a more smiling
aspect than she ever did; and few ruined villages are to be met with except
on poetical ground."[50] Swift knew only too well that the situation was
otherwise, at least insofar as Ireland was concerned, and so neither the
land nor its inhabitants ever have occasion to smile in the world he delin-
eates throughout his writings. The mournful features of this world refute
arcadian myths and political propaganda alike.

vi

One final feature of Swift's antipastoral landscape as it functioned
on the levels of both history and historical commentary, of both external
topography and mental perception, was its sparseness of trees, and the
sorry state of those which did exist. Trees, as Curtius notes, have always
been a central feature of the *locus amoenus,* and the Edenic realms portrayed in literature throughout the ages have prominently included a
variety of sacred groves, shady arbors, and well-stocked orchards, such as
the "blissful Bower" in Milton's Paradise (Book IV, 690-95) and the
"lofty Woods" of "tow'ring Oaks" in Pope's *Windsor-Forest* (220-22).
Swift's Ireland, on the other hand, was for the most part denuded of
trees. Ireland had not always suffered from a dearth of foliage; indeed, as
W.E.H. Lecky observes, "When the English first established themselves in
Ireland no country in Europe was more abundantly wooded."[51] The disappearance of Ireland's trees, like the depopulation of her countryside,
was the result not of natural causes but of man-made policies, and it too

constitutes a dismal tale of human greed and exploitation. The seventeenth-century author of a *Natural History of Ireland* explains the phenomenon in the following way:

> In ancient times, as long as the land was in full possession of the Irish themselves, all Ireland was very full of woods on every side. . . . But the English having settled themselves in the land, did by degrees greatly diminish the woods in all the places where they were masters, partly to deprive the thieves of their refuge and partly to gain greater scope of profitable lands. . . . Since the subduing of the last great rebellion before this, under the conduct of the Earl of Tirone . . . the remaining woods have been very much diminished, and in sundry places quite destroyed, partly for the reason last mentioned, and partly for the wood and timber itself . . . and for the making of charcoal for the iron works.[52]

Lecky, noting that the English "had none of the associations which attached the Irish to the trees that had sheltered their childhood and which their forefathers had planted," describes the process whereby "they speedily cut down and sold the woods, and thus inflicted an almost irreparable injury on the country." He cites the testimony of contemporary witnesses to this wholesale devastation, such as the observer who noted in 1697 that the country's finest and most venerable timber was already "destroyed to such a degree that in twenty years there will hardly be left in all probability an oak in Ireland."[53]

A particularly revealing case in point was the sad fate of the once magnificent forests of Munster during the first half of the seventeenth century, under the governance of Richard Boyle, known as the "Great" Earl of Cork. Succeeding to Sir Walter Raleigh's seigniory of Youghal in the county of Cork, Boyle transformed the war-scarred town into a bustling and prosperous seaport, a center for trade with England. An energetic businessman who was adept at the art of economically exploiting his natural environment, Boyle developed a number of commercial enterprises that enriched the town's prominent residents while simultaneously impoverishing the land, such as the manufacture of pipestaves for export to England, which, as Dorothea Townshend notes, "was carried on so recklessly that the forests which had been the pride of Munster disappeared rapidly."[54] Compounding the problem were the royal woodcutters sent over to select oak trees for building the king's ships, who proved to be "even more reckless than the settlers."[55] The history of seventeenth-century Munster highlights the tragic consequences to the Irish soil produced by the combined forces of colonialist appropriation and capitalist expansion.

Eighteenth- and early nineteenth-century travelers to Ireland were confronted by the visual results of these earlier destructive policies. Bush,

in his *Hibernia Curiosa,* asserted: "Woods you meet with but very few of
in this country, though a soil, by nature, capable of producing very fine.—I
make no doubt there is as much wood and timber growing in the county
of Kent as in the whole kingdom of Ireland."[56] Forty years later, in
1806, Richard Colt Hoare made similar observations while touring Ireland:
"I could wish that more attention were paid to one important class of
rural improvement, namely, *Planting;* the more important, as the whole
island is so peculiarly destitute of wood." The few trees he did see were
unevenly and inequitably distributed: " . . . but I complain of the general
want of hedge rows, woods, and timber trees. These are at present confined to the immediate neighbourhood of gentlemen's seats, and the banks
of rivers."[57] Within the primitive democracy of the pastoral world, the
humblest shepherd is surrounded by nature's plenitude and is openly invited to partake of her botanical and arboreal riches, but in eighteenth-
century Ireland access to nature's treasures was restricted to the wealthy,
the impoverished bulk of the rural population having to make do with
Swift's "bare face of nature." A strain of nostalgia pervades Hoare's
Journal—a wistful looking backward to a time when the Irish landscape
abounded in vegetative life, especially in rich forests. Hoare notes, for example, that "the numerous fragments of roots of trees, and timber dug out
of the bog, prove that in former times, the surface of this country bore a
very different appearance."[58] At various points Hoare seems embarked on a
journey through the fallen world, intent upon recovering the faint traces
of a once flourishing and verdurous but now largely denuded paradise.

     Swift likewise testifies to the vestiges of a vanished world once
marked by arboreal plenitude, although characteristically his focus is
upon not the former ideal but the present reality. Discussing the parcels
of land King James I designated "for the augmentation of poor Bishop-
ricks," he observes: "These lands, when they were granted by King
James, consisted mostly of woody ground, wherewith those parts of this
Island were then overrun. This is well known, universally allowed, and by
some in part remembered; the roots being, in some places not stubbed out
to this day" (PW, 12:183–84). Implicitly contrasting this formerly verdurous landscape with Scotland's "bleak barren Highlands," Swift goes on to
describe the massive influx into Ireland of Scotch colonists, "who came
hither . . . as it were into a Paradise." The promise of a re-created Eden
was, however, soon enough shattered by a series of "wars and desola-
tions," which resulted in "the woods being rooted up" (184). Referring
to this and subsequent events in Irish history, Swift as the Drapier tells
Parliament that "there is not another Example in *Europe,* of such a prodigious Quantity of excellent Timber cut down, in so short a Time, with
so little Advantage to the Country, either in *Shipping* or *Building*" (PW,
10:139). The systematic hewing down of Ireland's trees so impressed

itself upon Swift's consciousness that it became for him an emblem of his fellow countrymen's overall plight. Noting, for example, the ruined state of Ireland's trade and economy, the Drapier warns that "now [that] the *Branches* are all cut off, [Wood] stands ready with his *Ax* at the *Root*" (129). The Dean from his pulpit expressed a similar perception: " . . . but now the axe is laid to the root of the tree, and nothing but a firm union among us can prevent our utter undoing" (PW, 9:239). Although Swift entertained hopes of improving the situation and promoted efforts to cultivate the woodlands, his observations about the Irish countryside remained basically pessimistic: " . . . as to the effects of these laws [for encouraging plantations of forest trees], I have not seen the least, in many hundred miles riding, except about a very few gentlemens houses, and even those with very little skill or success" (PW, 12:88).

Swift's perceptions concerning this matter help explain the largely treeless environs described in his mock-pastoral verses. The landscape inhabited by Sheelah and Dermot comprises only grotesquely robust weeds whose monstrous growth makes them seem like parodic substitutions for trees (*A Pastoral Dialogue,* 13-15). *On Cutting Down the Old Thorn at Market-Hill* depicts, in satiric form, the process whereby a once verdurous isle, here referred to as "the fruitful Plain" (10), turns into a desolate terrain—like Ireland, fallen victim to the ax. The thorn tree of the title, which had "stood for many a hundred Years" (3), was the center of a former world traditionally pastoral in its inclusion of an arboreal retreat (5-8). A "Hatchet" serves as Swift's parodic substitute for the conquerors' ax; both are used "To hack [the] hallow'd Timber down" (84). Nora Crow Jaffe notes that "in Ireland (and in most of Scotland) few acts were more sacrilegious in the popular mind or more likely to bring on continued bad luck than the cutting of a thorn tree"[59]—an interesting point in that it underscores Swift's familiarity with native Irish folklore and popular traditions. But, as I have been suggesting, the poem may well also reflect Swift's pained awareness of native Irish history and topography.

Counterparts of Market-Hill's "sickly [and] sapless Thorn" appear in other of Swift's versified landscapes as well. The yew trees into which Baucis and Philemon metamorphose encounter a fate that parodically suggests the fate of most trees planted on Irish soil:

Here *Baucis,* there *Philemon* grew.
Till once, a Parson of our Town,
To mend his Barn, cut *Baucis* down;
At which, 'tis hard to be believ'd,
How much the other Tree was griev'd,
Grew Scrubby, dy'd a-top, was stunted:
So, the next Parson stub'd and burnt it.

(*Baucis and Philemon,* 172-78)

Swift's portrayal differs strikingly from the Ovidian myth on which it is modeled, where the pious couple were transformed into durable, stately trees decorated by the narrator himself, which stood as emblems of spiritual renewal as well as artistic permanence. According to Arthur Golding's sixteenth-century translation of Book VIII of the *Metamorphoses*, mortal decay is suddenly checked by renewed growth as "Philemon old and poore/Saw Baucis floorish greene with leaves, and Baucis saw likewyse/ Philemon braunching out in boughes and twigs before hir eyes" (896-98). The trees, moreover, continue to live and thrive, so that "The Phrygians in that park/Doo at this present day still shew the trees that shaped were/ Of theyr two bodies, growing yit togither joyntly there" (902-4).[60] Dryden follows Golding's example in stressing the ennobling and eternizing aspects of the myth. He describes Old Baucis "Sprouting with sudden Leaves of spritely green" (182) while Philemon's "lengthen'd Arms [became] a sprouting Wood" (184) and concludes the tale with the assurance, "Ev'n yet, an ancient *Tyanaean* shows/A spreading Oak, that near a Linden grows" (191-92).[61] Swift's substitution of a scrubby, dying tree for a green and flourishing one grows out of a mental outlook and a physical terrain that combine to subvert Ovid's vision (as well as that of his subsequent translators) of a verdurous immortality.

It is fitting that, toward the end of his life, when he came upon an elm tree "which in its uppermost branches was much withered, and decayed" while walking with several companions, Swift declared to them, "I shall be like that tree, I shall die at [the] top," thereby symbolically transforming himself, just as he had earlier transformed Baucis and Philemon, into a human embodiment of the rotting Irish landscape.[62] In this remark we can see most clearly the full magnitude of Swift's antipastoral vision, which mirrored an outer landscape even as it reflected a state of mind—even more, an entire sense of being (or rather, dying) in a world in which all traces of paradise had been irrevocably destroyed.

CHAPTER • 4

The Subversion of the Country House Ideal

Although the country house ideal is in many ways closely linked to the pastoral vision, sharing as it does an assumption about man's close relationship to nature within the context of a harmonious rural community, it is nevertheless a subject that demands separate consideration since it adds a very special historical and architectural dimension to Swift's antipastoral perspective. The country house ideal, as exemplified by poems like Jonson's *To Penshurst,* Carew's *To Saxham,* and Marvell's *Upon Appleton House,* constitutes an entire ideology in the sense in which Louis Althusser broadly defines the term, as "a system (with its own logic and rigour) of representations (images, myths, ideas or concepts, depending on the case) endowed with a historical existence and role within a given society." He goes on to point out that this system is "distinguished from science in that in it the practico-social function is more important than the theoretical function (function as knowledge)."[1] The "system of representations" connected with the country house ideal is centered upon the concrete image of the landed estate, which comes to be imbued with a complex matrix of moral, political, and economic values that are closely identified with the interests of a particular group in society. The nature of this group is clear, not only from the dominant role played by its ideology, but also from the fact that, as Mark Girouard succinctly puts it, country houses (at least before the twentieth century) were "power houses—the houses of a ruling class."[2]

In Swift's writings we find a continuing, often incisive critique of the country house ideal insofar as it was described in other contemporary works as a historical reality, representing the highest standards of social intercourse and ethical behavior among members of a clearly defined rural community. Swift's closest approximation to this ideal, Lord Munodi's

estate as described in *Gulliver's Travels*, is, significantly, shown to be
a rare exception to the existing rule; the estate, moreover, is on the
brink of destruction as a result of pressures to conform to the "present
Mode" and "modern Usage" (PW, 11:176). Whereas contemporary writers
used the image of a flourishing, well-ordered estate to celebrate their
country's moral and economic health, Swift characteristically delineated
the existing historical situation via the image of a decaying estate: "Suppose a gentleman's estate of 200*l.* a year should sink to one hundred, by
some accident, whether by an earthquake or inundation it matters not,
and suppose the said gentleman utterly hopeless and unqualified ever to
retrieve the loss; how is he otherwise to proceed in his future oeconomy,
than by reducing it on every article to one half less, unless he will be content to fly his country, or rot in jail? This is a representation of Ireland's
condition, only with one fault, that it is a little too favourable" (PW, 12:
123). Passages like this in Swift's writings generally serve a dual function,
in effect commenting both on prevailing historical circumstances and on
the ideological representations through which these circumstances were
regularly mediated. As poet, polemicist, and satirist, Swift challenged the
country house ideal in a variety of ways: by dramatizing its obsolescence
or irrelevance to contemporary society; by demonstrating its falsification
of empirically verifiable conditions as well as of the actual relationships
existing among groups in society; and by exposing its mythic, at times
explicitly propagandistic status as part of an imaginary construct functioning simultaneously to misrepresent and to rationalize the status quo.

i

In describing the poetic depictions of the country house ideal from
Jonson onward, G. R. Hibbard emphasizes their "constant references to
architecture," their "deep concern with the social function of the great
house in the life of the community," and their "understanding of the
reciprocal interplay of man and nature in the creation of a good life."[3]
Howard Erskine-Hill, discussing the ideal primarily as it relates to Pope,
notes that "above all the use of the house for generous and friendly hospitality is stressed"—a fact that assumes particular significance in light of
Swift's observation that "The old hospitality is quite extinguished by
Poverty and the Oppressions of England" (C, 4:555). Erskine-Hill also
stresses the importance accorded to the house's functionality and its
ability to fill the needs of both its own inhabitants and the denizens of
the surrounding terrain.[4] Critics like Alistair M. Duckworth remind us
that the literary country house is an aspect of eighteenth- and early
nineteenth-century fiction as well as poetry, playing a prominent role
in the novels of Fielding, Smollett, and Austen (among others) as a

repository of venerable customs and normative values.[5] Vita Sackville-West's twentieth-century tribute to the historic English country house reflects the fundamental impulse and vision behind this ideal. Lamenting the possibility that these houses might be turned into museums, she urges their continuation as living things: "But if [the house] keeps its life it means that the kitchen still provides food for the inhabitants. . . . but there is the outside life too; the life in which the landlord is a good landlord, assisting his farmers, keeping his cottages in good repair, adding modern labour-saving improvements, remitting a rent in a case of hardship, employing woodmen to cut trees for his own hearth and theirs. The system was, and is, a curious mixture of the feudal and the communal, and survives in England to-day. One wonders for how long?"[6]

Pope's *Epistle to Burlington* presents an idealized vision of the country house way of life, similarly predicated upon "a curious mixture of the feudal and the communal" and stressing the concept of functionality:

> Who then shall grace, or who improve the Soil?
> Who plants like BATHURST, or who builds like BOYLE.
> 'Tis Use alone that sanctifies Expence,
> And Splendor borrows all her rays from Sense.
>   His Father's Acres who enjoys in peace,
> Or makes his Neighbours glad, if he encrease;
> Whose chearful Tenants bless their yearly toil,
> Yet to their Lord owe more than to the soil. . . .
>
> (177–84)

And again like Sackville-West's depiction, the *Epistle to Burlington,* for all its triumphant affirmation of Burlington's Palladian arts and its anticipations of a future age when "laughing Ceres [will] re-assume the land" (176), exalts Roman antiquity, when ". . . pompous buildings once were things of Use" (24), and implicitly queries how long it will last, in light of a degenerate age typified by men like Villario and Timon. This complex outlook, often combining a sense of loss with an affirmation of the possibilities still available in the present for maintaining a traditional way of life, is exemplified as well in Pope's *Imitations of Horace.* In *Satire II, ii,* for example, a statement of decline—"My lands are sold, my Father's house is gone" (155)—is tempered by assurances that traditional country house hospitality can still survive, on however limited a scale: "But ancient friends, (tho' poor, or out of play)/That touch my Bell, I cannot turn away./'Tis true, no Turbots dignify my boards,/But gudgeons, flounders, what my Thames affords" (139–42).

That both Pope in the 1730s and Sackville-West in the 1940s could view the country house way of life as a yet viable and concretely embodied but imperiled or vanishing ideal underscores the truth of Raymond

Williams's observation that each age tends to see itself as a watershed in history, the critical point at which, for example, the rural values and "organic community" of "Old England," represented by an age immediately preceding it, are disappearing. Williams's historical escalator, whose steps are "the apparent resting places, the successive Old Englands to which we are confidently referred but which then start to move and recede," continues backward without a stop until it arrives at "that well-remembered garden," Eden.[7] Williams claims that these ideal constructs "have some actual significance, when they are looked at in their own terms"; nevertheless, a clear implication of his analysis is that these successive visions of an organic rural community represent an inevitable distortion of historical realities, a mystification of the present as well as of the past. Indeed, Sackville-West's country house depends for its maintenance and functioning not on the traditional "lord of the manor," but on the good, civic-minded but anonymous bureaucrats of the National Trust.

   Similarly, Pope's ideal country house bore only the faintest resemblance to contemporary historical reality. For one thing, as Girouard points out, "although poets like Jonson, Marvell or Pope and moralists like Addison constantly urged landowners to live on their estates, and praised and glamorized the lives of those who did, from the sixteenth century onwards the upper classes were spending more and more time in London—or the area round London in which the court rotated. . . . Even when landowners were in the country they were often longing to get out of it."[8] In addition, the increased appetite for privacy among members of the gentry (which according to Girouard reached its height in the early eighteenth century), combined with the growing separation, in both social and architectural terms, between "the polite world of the gentry and the impolite world of servants, farmers and smallholders," resulted in a marked decline in traditional country house hospitality, with its intermingling of different classes and its communal participation in social rituals.[9] Although Hibbard acknowledges that "the kind of society that Pope approves of was already no more than a ghost when he wrote his poem,"[10] he shows no inclination to question the basic truthfulness, in moral and visionary terms at least, of Pope's outlook. Erskine-Hill likewise displays a strong sympathetic attachment to the kind of vision embodied in the *Epistle to Burlington*. He vindicates the "truth" of such a vision through a deliberately equivocal formulation, supported by numerous qualifying phrases and dominated by the subjunctive tense, which has the effect of muddying the distinction between actuality and possibility, between fact and fancy. In discussing country house poems like those exalting Penshurst and Wrest, he says:

Their art of praise certainly asserts an ideal; the extent to which it also describes a practice must remain in doubt until more historical evidence is brought forward. . . . What does seem clear historically is the dominance of the noble household over the greater part of provincial England; the poems do thus, in a broad sense, describe a real social structure, while (to a greater or lesser extent) idealizing its operation. The network of such families and houses, spread over the face of England, might well be thought to represent the greater part of English society, and each could potentially, if it did not actually, approximate to the role panegyrically expressed by Jonson and Carew.[11]

The problem with this discussion is that it avoids coming to grips with the profoundly ideological character of the country house ideal. So too does Hibbard's argument against the view that Pope's idea of virtue, as set forth in the *Epistle to Burlington,* is a class concept: " . . . I do not believe that Pope thought in terms of class antagonism any more than Jonson did. For both of them their thinking about social issues is controlled by the idea of the co-operative, interdependent society."[12] Neither critic, in short, explores the country house ideal insofar as it functions as a mythic justification of a particular social and economic order.

For example, although Pope's poetry recognizes the contemporary economic forces that are changing the face of the land, creating a situation whereby "Hemsley once proud Buckingham's delight,/Slides to a Scriv'ner or a City Knight" (*Imitations of Horace, Satire II, ii,* 177–78), his images of an agrarian capitalism fundamentally opposed to a traditional country house existence are finally incorporated into a larger vision that affirms the invulnerability of his own "rural" retreat to all threatening forces from without and heralds the ultimate triumph of those "Who plan[t] like BATHURST, or who buil[d] like BOYLE." The actual relationship between a capitalist landowner like Burlington and his property is redefined in light of the imagined relationship between a deity and his creation, which also produces an idealized version of the relationship between an imperialist and his conquered territory: "Bid the broad Arch the dang'rous Flood contain,/The Mole projected break the roaring Main;/Back to his bounds their subject Sea command,/And roll obedient Rivers thro' the Land. . ." (199-202). Similarly, Burlington's treatment of his tenants is depicted as the behavior of a benevolent father toward his deserving children. It is such an example that Karl Mannheim has in mind when he cites, as an instance of "ideological distortion," the situation of a "landed proprietor, whose estate has already become a capitalistic undertaking, but who still attempts to explain his relations to his labourers and his own function in the undertaking by means of categories reminiscent of the patriarchal order."[13] To be sure, Hibbard is probably quite correct when he contends that "Pope [did not think] in terms of class antagonism any more than Jonson did." The error lies in assuming that such antagonism was therefore nonexistent, or that Pope's outlook was therefore unaffected by it. As Althusser points out, ideology is "profoundly *unconscious*," functioning through structures that rarely attain the level of awareness.[14] Pope's depiction of "chearful Tenants" whose greatest debt is "to their Lord," like Jonson's picture of the "rout of rural folk" who "come thronging in" to their master's house, where "Freedom doth with degree dispense" (*To Sir Robert Wroth*, 53–54, 58),[15] tacitly acknowledges class distinctions at the same time that it conveniently glosses over the inequities and conflicts inevitably created by these distinctions.

ii

Swift, in contrast to Pope and Jonson, repeatedly exposes the fictive nature of the country house ideal, especially its yearning for a perfect harmony irreconcilable with the disjunctions and the antagonisms that are part of the historical process. In saying this, I do not mean to suggest that Swift's outlook, in contrast to Pope's, was free of all ideological bias or that it exactly mirrored objective reality: To do so would be to fall into the same kind of mystification I argued against in the preceding section. Nevertheless, I *am* saying something more than that Pope and Swift each convey a different subjective interpretation of the social and economic conditions surrounding them. For as Terry Eagleton reminds us, ideological constructs do not (or at least need not) merely reflect a "false consciousness" that prevents clear historical perception; rather, "by inserting individuals into history in a variety of ways, [ideology] allows of multiple kinds and degrees of access to that history. . . . the truth [is] that some ideologies, and levels of ideology, are more false than others."[16] Although Swift no more than Pope was capable of magically transcending the limits of a mortal and historically determined consciousness, he nonetheless displayed a far clearer insight into the fictive status as well as the rationalizing function of the precepts and ideals of the dominant Augustan world view.

In dealing with aspects of country house living, not only did Swift acknowledge the divisions existing among groups in society, he also explored the often bitter conflicts these divisions produce. That these explorations at times appear in a humorous context, in the form of burlesque or satire, in no way diminishes either the seriousness or the historical validity of Swift's perceptions in this matter. Temperamentally indisposed to embracing easy resolutions of any kind, Swift, in his treatment of the country house ideal, was also strongly influenced by the evidence of empirical reality. Swift's writings continually remind us that the economic relations existing between landlord and tenant in eighteenth-century Ireland are more accurately expressed through images of class warfare than through images of a communal dance or other festive ritual in which all levels of society participate equally. A spirit of perverted individualism is shown to prevail everywhere, profoundly affecting almost all interactions between those who own the land and those who lease and tend it. Insofar as Swift, in his position as Anglican churchman, was himself dependent upon the revenues from leased church lands for his own support, he was quite capable of portraying the problem from the standpoint of an injured landlord:

> Now all the Doctor's Money's spent,
> His Tenants wrong him in his Rent;
> The Farmers, spightfully combin'd,
> Force him to take his Tythes in kind. . . .
>
> *(Part of the Seventh Epistle of the*
> *First Book of Horace, Imitated,* 107-10)

Periodically throughout his correspondence, Swift expressed resentment or vexation concerning the state of his finances as a result of unpaid or underpaid rents. He complained to Lord Orrery, for example, "I am fretting at universall publick Mismanagement; I believe my Estate is near Cork; for my Tenants will not pay me" (C, 5:23). Swift also directed a good deal of his wrath against his agents, especially one named Parvisol, a "Knave" to whose mismanagement Swift attributed his "rotten Affairs," which included "large Arrears upon Laracor" and nonpayment by the farmer-tenants of the deanery (C, 2:48, 30).

But if Swift on occasion attributed his sorry state of affairs to neglectful tenants and conniving managers, he tended far more frequently to lay the blame on the landlord class, whose members showed themselves loath to pay their tithes and whose exploitative practices rendered tenants incapable of fulfilling their obligations; thus "bad payment of rents" is only to be expected "from such miserable creatures as most of the tenants in *Ireland* are" (C, 3:134). The landlord's practices are conceived to be not only inequitable, but vicious and sadistic as well: "The Rise of our Rents is squeezed out of the very Blood, and Vitals, and Cloaths, and Dwellings of the Tenants; who live worse than *English* Beggars" (PW, 12:11). Even in tracts ostensibly dealing with other issues entirely, we find emphatic statements about the callous and mercenary actions of landowners. In *A Proposal for the Universal Use of Irish Manufacture,* for example, Swift declares:

I would now expostulate a little with our Country Landlords; who, by unmeasurable *screwing* and *racking* their Tenants all over the Kingdom, have already reduced the miserable *People* to a *worse Condition* than the *Peasants* in *France,* or the *Vassals* in *Germany* and *Poland;* so that the whole *Species* of what we call *Substantial Farmers,* will, in a very few Years, be utterly at an End. It was pleasant to observe these Gentlemen, *labouring* with all their *Might,* for preventing the *Bishops* from letting their Revenues at a moderate half Value. . . at the very Instant, when they were every where *canting* their own Lands upon short Leases, and sacrificing their *oldest Tenants for a Penny an Acre advance.* (PW, 9:21)

Swift sums up the situation in a particularly bitter letter written to the Earl of Peterborough during his 1726 visit to England. Noting that the Irish gentry, because of their second-class status vis-à-vis those born in England, have been rendered "utterly destitute of all means to make provision for their younger sons," he forcefully calls attention to the way in which a social class will turn its own oppression against others even lower down on the ladder: "All [the gentry] have left is, at the expiration of leases, to rack their tenants; which they have done to such a degree, that there is not one farmer in a hundred through the kingdom who can afford shoes or stockings to his children, or to eat flesh, or drink anything better than sour milk or water, twice in a year. . ." (C, 3:133).

Swift on various occasions presents the landlord as a general type, an emblem of society's corruption, such as the one mentioned in his *Intelligencer, No. IX,* who "grows rich by Avarice, Injustice, Oppression . . . [and] is a Tyrant in the Neighbourhood over Slaves and Beggars, whom he calleth his Tenants" (PW, 12:53). More often, however, we find references to specific, actually existing landlords whose actions are concretely delineated in empirically verifiable detail, having at times directly affected Swift's own life. The behavior of the Percival family is a case in point, exemplifying only too well the debased practices of landed individuals in contemporary Ireland. John Percival of Knightsbrook was a particularly obnoxious neighbor of Swift's in the parish of Laracor—it is to him that Swift refers when he complains to Bolingbroke, shortly after his return to Ireland in 1714, that "a spiteful neighbour has seized on six feet of ground, carried off my trees, and spoiled my grove" (C, 2:130). Percival's eldest son, Robert, apparently carried on the dubious tradition of his father, judging from several letters Swift wrote to him some fifteen years later. In the first, Swift was responding to Robert Percival's continued refusal to pay his tithes: "This odd way of dealing among you folks of great estates in Land and money, although I have been used to, I cannot well reconcile myself with. . . . If your Tenants payd your Rents as you pay your Tyths, you would have cause to complain terribly" (C, 3:366).

Swift's second letter to Percival recounts the minute particulars of Percival's behavior with regard to Swift, in the process transforming Percival into a symbol of the whole Irish squire class:

> ...I told [a worthy friend] the subject of the difference between us: That your Tythes being generally worth 5 or 6ll a year, and by the terror of your Squireship frighting my Agent, to take what you graciously thought fit to give, you wronged me of half my due every year .. That having held from your father an Island worth three pence a year, which I planted, and payd two Shillings annually for, and being out of possession of the sd Island seven or eight years, there could not possibly be above 4s due to you; for which you have thought fit to stop 3 or 4 years of Tyth at your own rate of 2^{ll} - 5^s a year (as I remember) and still continue to stop it, on pretence that the sd Island was not surrendered to you in form; although you have cutt down more Plantations of Willow and Abeilles than would purchase a dozen such Islands. . . . from the prerogative of a good estate the practice of lording over a few Irish wretches, and from the naturall want of better thinking, I was sure your answer would be extremely rude and stupid, full of very bad language in all senses. . . . One thing I desire you will be set right in; I do not despise All Squires. It is true I despise the bulk of them. But, pray take notice, that a Squire must have some merit before I shall honor him with my contempt. For, I do not despise a Fly, a Maggot, or a Mite. (C, 3:366–68)

Swift's opinion of the most affluent and powerful member of the Irish squirearchy, William Conolly, was no better. Rising rapidly from humble beginnings, Conolly became a member of Parliament in 1692 and was unanimously elected Speaker of the Irish House of Commons in 1715. He continued in this capacity until shortly before his death in 1729, serving simultaneously as Lord Justice on ten separate occasions. He began to amass his fortune through the purchase of forfeited estates after the Battle of the Boyne, and at his death owned extensive property throughout ten counties, having become generally recognized as the wealthiest man in Ireland.[17] Swift's estimation of the speaker (which, needless to say, was not enhanced by the latter's allegiance to Walpole and his support of Wood's patent) is conveyed in a letter written two years after Conolly's death: "There was a fellow in Ireland called Conolly, who from a shoeboy grew to be several times one of the chief Governors, wholly illiterate, & with hardly common sence. . ." (C, 3:493). The abundance of Conolly's income (estimated by Swift later in the letter to be £16,000 a year)[18] is seen to be counterbalanced by the paucity of his understanding and the narrowness of his vision.

Conolly is perhaps best known as the owner-builder of Castletown House, a magnificent Palladian mansion that, according to Craig, "is not only the largest but also the most beautiful of the great houses of Ireland."[19] Because of its architectural innovations and its imposing scale, it "became the prototype and source of inspiration for many houses throughout the country, though none would rival its pristine elegance."[20] Swift would have had personal knowledge of this structure, since it was in the process of being built in Celbridge (a small town twelve miles west of Dublin) during the period (1719 and the years immediately following) in which he was making regular trips there to visit Vanessa at Celbridge Manor. Swift, however, chose to remain essentially silent about this renowned embodiment of country house splendor; indeed, his pointed reference, in the *Short View of the State of Ireland* (1727), to "The old Seats of the Nobility and Gentry all in Ruins, and no new ones in their Stead" (PW, 12:10) seems almost a deliberate attempt to consign Castletown House to oblivion, or at least to deny it the status of a traditional country house. One oblique reference to it occurs in Letter I of *The Drapier's Letters*, in a passage projecting the consequences of the circulation of Wood's halfpence: "They say SQUIRE CONOLLY has *Sixteen Thousand Pounds a Year;* now if he sends for his *Rent* to Town, *as it is likely he does*, he must have *Two Hundred and Fifty Horses* to bring up his *Half Year's Rent*, and two or three great *Cellars* in his House for Stowage" (PW, 10:7). Obviously the main thrust of the passage is to dramatize the drastically deflated value of Wood's halfpence, but on another level, the passage points to the grotesquely and ludicrously swelling accumulation of money, ironically culminating in the cancerous proliferation of worthless coins, to which Conolly's considerable energies were dedicated. Whereas many contemporaries, as well as subsequent social commentators, viewed Castletown House as the very pinnacle of elegant country house living, Swift perceived it merely as a giant warehouse for Conolly's ever-increasing monetary possessions—as a testimonial not to traditional values, but to the indulgence of private pleasures and to the new age's acquisitive appetites.

At the other end of the economic spectrum there were those like Swift's friend Thomas Sheridan, a tenant victimized by the inequities of the prevailing system, whose legal and financial entanglements Swift described on a number of occasions. Well aware of Sheridan's improvident nature, Swift counseled his friend at great length concerning the proper management of his church livings (e.g., C, 3:67). But the best advice in the world could not save Sheridan from becoming embroiled in a protracted struggle involving property rights, as Swift painstakingly recorded in *The History of the Second Solomon*, a brief biographical sketch of his friend:

> Solomon [Sheridan] is under-tenant to a Bishop's lease: he is bound by articles to his Lordship to renew and pay a fine, whenever the Bishop renews with his landlord, and to raise his rent as the landlord shall raise it to the Bishop. Seven years expire: Solomon's landlord

demands a fine, which he readily pays; then asks for a lease: The landlord says, he may have it at any time. He never gets it. Another seven years elapse: Solomon's landlord demands another fine, and an additional rent; Solomon pays both; asks to have his lease renewed: The steward answers, he will speak to his master. Seventeen years are elapsed: The landlord sends Solomon word that his lease is forfeited, because he hath not renewed and paid his fines according to articles: and now they are at law upon this admirable case. (PW, 5:224)

Swift's lifelong familiarity with cases such as Sheridan's helps explain his recurring role as forceful advocate of tenants' rights. When, for example, one Mr. Loyd from Coleraine, a town in Londonderry belonging to the London Society, entreated Swift's assistance in obtaining financial relief for the town's oppressed tenants, Swift promptly responded with a strong letter of protest to John Barber, alderman of the society:

It seems, your society hath raised the Rents of that Town; and your Lands adjoining, about three years ago, to four times the value of what they formerly payd; which is beyond all I have ever heard even among the worst screwing Landlords of this impoverished Kingdom; and the consequence hath already been, that many of your Tenants in the said Town and Lands are preparing for their Removal to the Plantations in America. . . . My dear Friend, you are to consider that, no Society can, or ought in prudence or Justice let their Lands at so high a Rate, as a Squire who lives upon his own Estate, and is able to distrain in an hours warning. All Bodyes corporate must give easy Bargains, that they may depend upon recciving their Rents. . . . Although my own Lands as Dean be let for four fifths under their Value, I have not raised them a sixth part in twenty three years, and took very moderate fines. . . .
   I am told, that one Condition in your Charter obligeth you to plant a Colony of English in those Parts; if that be so, you are too wise to make it a Colony of Irish Beggars. Some ill consequences have already happened by your prodigious increase of the Rent. Many of your old Tenants have quitted their Houses in Coleraine: others are not able to repair their habitations, which are daily going to Ruin and many of those who live on your Lands in the Country, ow great Arrears, which they will never be in a Condition to pay. (C, 5:18-20)[21]

In this particular case, a rare one indeed, Swift's appeal was successful, judging from a letter written subsequently by Barber that states that the society's members "have resolved to relieve their tenants in *Coleraine* from their hard bargains" (50). Far more frequently, however, Swift's endeavors met with frustration and failure, thus reinforcing his conviction, expressed in the preceding letter, that "this wretched oppressed Country must of necessity decline every year." Swift's abiding preoccupa-

tion (as well as sense of identification) with the plight of tenants, perennially struggling to survive in habitations "daily going to Ruin," resulted in
the latter's becoming for him a comprehensive metaphor both for Ireland's general state of affairs and for his own precarious existence: "The
public is an old tattered house, but may last as long as my lease in it, and
therefore like a true Irish tenant I shall consider no further" (C, 3:248).

iii

One cannot fully understand Swift's attitude toward the propertied
class in general without examining his view specifically of Ireland's absentee landlords, that " ... Mongril Breed,/Who from [Ireland] sprung,
yet on [her] Vitals feed" (*Verses occasioned by the sudden drying up of
St. Patrick's Well,* 95–96). Swift's antipathy toward this class is conveyed
in his diatribes against "those absentees, who take away almost one half
of the Kingdoms Revenues" (PW, 12:77) and who are deemed a major
cause of such evils as "the depopulating of the Kingdom, the leaving so
many Parts of it wild and uncultivated, the Ruin of so many Country-
Seats and Plantations, [and] the cutting down all the Woods to supply
Expences in England" (PW, 10:130). As he bitterly noted to Pope, "It
is thought there are not two hundred thousand pounds of species in the
whole island; for we return thrice as much to our Absentees, as we get by
trade, and so are all inevitably undone" (C, 3:355).[22]

The absentee system possesses a very special relevance to the country
house ideal—or rather, to the destruction of this ideal. Traditional country
house existence presupposes an intimate bond between the estate owner
and the soil. Rooted in a vision of warmth, closeness, and community, it
assumes a physical propinquity (indeed, actual and continuing physical
contact) between the landowner and his ancestral property. It is precisely
this overwhelming sense as well as literal fact of *presence* (specifically a
benignly paternal presence) that helps define Jonson's picture of an estate
"Where comes no guest but is allowed to eat/Without his fear, and of thy
[Penshurst's] lord's own meat" (*To Penshurst,* 61–62) and that informs
Herrick's portrayal of a country house lord who " ... know'st to lead/A
House-dance neatly, and can'st truly show,/How farre a Figure ought to
go" (*A Panegyrick to Sir Lewis Pemberton,* 90–92).

In contrast, the system of absentee landlordism, as the name itself
would suggest, was founded upon *absence,* not presence; upon *distance,*
not propinquity. Under this system the relationship between men and
their territorial possessions was above all a mediated one; it was characterized by a bureaucratic remoteness and impersonality inimical to the
country house code of hospitality and direct participation in all aspects of
the domestic economy. Arthur Young's discussion of the adverse effects

of absenteeism in the second half of the eighteenth century underscores the system's inherent opposition to the country house ideal: "[The problem] is not the simple amount of the rental being remitted into another country, but the damp on all sorts of improvements, and the total want of countenance and encouragement which the lower tenantry labour under. The landlord at such a great distance is out of the way of all complaints, or, which is the same thing, of examining into, or remedying evils; miseries of which he can see nothing, and probably hear as little of, can make no impression."[23] Instead of personally overseeing the daily activities of their tenants like the traditional lord of the manor, the absentee landlords *overlooked* them in every way possible. Swift, for his part, underscores the inherently unnatural and potentially lethal effects of a relationship thus founded upon remote control when he asserts that Irishmen "are in the Condition of Patients, who have Physick sent them by Doctors at a Distance, Strangers to their Constitution, and the Nature of their Disease" (PW, 12:8).

But if absentee landlordism per se meant physical absence and withdrawal, it simultaneously, and paradoxically, spawned a class of subordinate landlords, or middlemen, defined by an all-too-palpable *presence*, an outrageous familiarity that in effect grotesquely parodied the genuine intimacy and benign paternalism of the traditionally conceived manorial lord. Young refers to this group as "the little country gentlemen, or rather vermin of the kingdom," whose "oppressive conduct" weighed down "very heavy on the poor people." His description of these middlemen and his description of the absentee landlords form a highly ironic balance. Working in conjunction with the total "hands-off" policy of the latter we have the emphatic "hands-on" policy of the former, which included severe beatings of laborers and cottars with a cane or horsewhip for "disrespect or anything tending towards sauciness" and the sexual exploitation of cottars' wives and daughters.[24] Lecky, likewise stressing the pernicious effects of this system of middlemen, observes: "The tenants were therefore under the immediate control of men of a wholly inferior stamp, who . . . having no permanent interest in the soil, were usually the most grasping of tyrants. As the demand for land increased, or the profits of land rose, the head tenant followed the example of his landlord. He often became an absentee. He abandoned all serious industry. He in his turn sublet his tenancy at an increased rate, and the process continued till there were three, four, or even five persons between the landlord and the cultivator of the soil."[25] The estate owners described here, who are separated from their lands not only by a body of water but also by a whole network of intermediaries to whom they yield territorial control, represent alienation with a vengeance: a total disconnectedness from the soil.

Swift too exposed the perversely mediated nature of the relationships governing land ownership and usage, typified for him by the situation in which "... immediate Tenants [of a Bishop], generally speaking, have others under them, and so a Third and Fourth in Subordination, till it comes to the *Welder* (as they call him) who sits at a Rack Rent, and lives as miserably as an *Irish* farmer upon a new Lease from a Lay Landlord" (PW, 9:54). He vividly dramatizes the pernicious consequences of the absentee system in his political parable, *The Story of the Injured Lady,* in which the "Lady" of the title, who represents Ireland, is first seduced, and then both abandoned and cruelly exploited, by a "Gentleman in the Neighbourhood," representing England.[26] The sequence of events that ensues upon the lady's seduction may be seen as an enactment of the gradual death of the country house norm. The story records a continuing process of degeneration manifested, in aesthetic terms, by a movement from beauty to plainness; in moral terms, by a movement from health to sickliness; and in economic terms, by the metamorphosis of a flourishing estate into an impoverished one.

The Story of the Injured Lady describes the degeneration of traditional country life by revealing a combination of icy withdrawal and oppressively pervasive presence similar to that found in Young's account. The seduction of the lady comes to symbolize territorial and economic as well as sexual penetration. Not only her body but her entire household and domestic economy are usurped by the gentleman: "When he had once got Possession, he soon began to play the usual Part of a too fortunate Lover, affecting on all Occasions to shew his Authority, and to act like a Conqueror" (PW, 9:5). But at the same time that the seducer's domination establishes itself with dramatic physical immediacy, it becomes a mediated domination, enforced through a network of agents who, acting as surrogate masters, allow the real master to remain at several removes from his slave:

> I consented that his Steward should govern my House, and have Liberty to employ an Under-Steward, who should receive his Directions. My Lover proceeded further, turning away several old Servants and Tenants, and supplying me with others from his own House. These grew so domineering and unreasonable, that there was no Quiet, and I heard of nothing but perpetual Quarrels. . . . upon every Falling-out, [my Lover] still turned away more of my People, and supplied me in their Stead with a Number of Fellows and Dependents of his own, whom he had no other Way to provide for. (PW, 9:5)

Worse is yet to come. As all pretensions to formal country house existence are discarded, traditional restraints upon the gentleman's actions disappear and he begins "neglecting by Degrees all common Civility in his Behaviour" (5–6). A world of bureaucratic legalism takes the place of paternalistic relationships and communal ritual. Thus the gentleman delivers to the lady a set of commandments that formally institute a rule of law even as they reflect an officially sanctioned state of lawlessness:

> That from henceforward he expected his Word should be a Law to me in all Things: That I must maintain a Parish-watch against Thieves and Robbers, and give Salaries to an Overseer, a Constable, and Others, all of his own chusing, whom he would send from Time to Time to be Spies upon me: That, to enable me the better in supporting these Expences, my Tenants shall be obliged to carry all their Goods cross the River to his Town-market, and pay Toll on both Sides, and then sell them at half Value. . . . And because a Company of Rogues usually plied on the River between us, who often robbed my Tenants of their Goods and Boats, he ordered a Waterman of his to guard them, whose Manner was to be out of the Way until the poor Wretches were plundered; then to overtake the Thieves, and seize all as lawful Prize to his Master and himself. (PW, 9:6)

The debasement of traditional values depicted here is mirrored in the lady's drastic decline in status, from a prosperous estate owner to the "Sempstress to [the gentleman's] Grooms and Footmen" (8), a hierarchic inversion producing "such Confusion and Uncertainty, that my Servants know not when to obey me, and my Tenants, although many of them be very well inclined, seem quite at a Loss" (8–9). The resulting situation dramatically underscores the antithesis between official country house ideology and the empirical realities of the land situation with regard to England and Ireland:

> All this hath rendered me so very insignificant and contemptible at Home, that some Servants to whom I pay the greatest Wages, and many Tenants who have the most beneficial Leases, are gone over to live with him; yet I am bound to continue their Wages, and pay their Rents; by which Means one Third Part of my whole Income is spent on his Estate, and above another Third by his Tolls and Markets; and my poor Tenants are so sunk and impoverished, that, instead of maintaining me suitable to my Quality, they can hardly find me Cloaths to keep me warm, or provide the common Necessaries of Life for themselves. (PW, 9:7)

The fact that this tract was written in 1707, long before the period normally designated by critics as the phase of Swift's Irish nationalism, suggests the extent to which Ireland's oppression at the hands of England was a deeply rooted and abiding preoccupation of Swift's throughout his lifetime, however much it may have assumed more explicit and urgent form in the twenty-five years before his death.

In this connection, it is revealing to consider the light in which Swift viewed Richard Boyle. To Pope, as we have seen, Boyle was the revered third Earl of Burlington, a magnanimous patron who could serve as the perfect model for the good lord of the manor, the kindly protector of his tenants depicted in the *Fourth Moral Essay*. To Swift, however, Boyle was the neglectful and haughty fourth Earl of Cork, one of the largest and wealthiest of Ireland's absentee landlords.[27] Swift would have known exactly who constituted the membership of this group (he refers in one tract to the list of absentees drawn up by Thomas Prior in 1729[28]) and in Letter IV of *The Drapier's Letters,* protesting that "there are so few Employments to be disposed of [among the native Irish population] in this Kingdom," he blames the problem on the prevalence of what might aptly be termed "absentee officeholders" (a logical counterpart to the absentee landlords, and often the same individuals), among whom he expressly includes "the Earl of *Burlington* Lord High Treasurer of *Ireland* by Inheritance" (PW, 10:58). Swift's contempt for men in Burlington's position is evident in the spiteful glee (albeit accompanied by a note of playfulness) with which he reports to Bathurst: "I saw Ld Orrery to day, he is come over [to Ireland] on the knavery of a [steward or agent]. May all Irish absentees have the same fate! . . . God be praised, for the condition you [Englishmen] are in [is justly brought] upon you by your tyranny and oppression to this kingdom. . . " (C, 3:475).

It is interesting that Swift, in his correspondence with Gay, alludes to Burlington as the latter's "Landlord"—an increasingly "richer" one at that (C, 2:443). This is obviously a reference to Burlington's role as patron to the poet, but perhaps also, less obviously, it is implicitly associating his performance in this role with his role as Irish estate owner. And indeed, Boyle's support of Gay appears to have manifested itself through a rather erratic and neglectful (an "absentee," if you will) form of patronage. As James Lees-Milne observes: "By the middle of the 1720s Lord and Lady Burlington had become rather bored by [Gay's] presence and his everlasting escapades and scrapes. They were tending to neglect him, even when he was ill. Gay's friends were critical of the Burlingtons for not giving him enough to eat; and Dr. Arbuthnot declared that he found him one day in bed with a swollen face, eating his poultice for hunger."[29] Even allowing for the exaggerations of overly solicitous friends, it seems clear that Gay's position in his patron's house represented a far cry from the position ideally occupied by the poet according to traditional country house ideology. In Jonson's Penshurst, for example, there is no question of the poet's being deprived in any way by his host, for it is a house "Where the same beer and bread and self-same wine/That is his lordship's shall be also mine" (63–64). Remarks exchanged between Swift and Gay in their correspondence suggest a very different patron-poet relationship. In one letter Gay notes, "I lodge at present in Burlington house, and

have receivd many Civilitys from many great men, but very few real bene-
fits. They wonder at each other for not providing for me, and I wonder at
'em all" (C, 2:439). Indirectly responding to this comment, Swift observed: "I am extremely glad [Pope] is not in your Case of Needing great
Mens favor, and could heartily wish that you were in his" (442). In Gay's
declaration, made after he declined an appointment as gentleman-usher to
the Princess Louisa, that "now all my expectations are vanish'd; and I
have no prospect, but in depending wholly upon my self, and my own
conduct" (C, 3:246), we see articulated an ideal, not of communal sharing
and mutual support, but quite the contrary, of individual survival and
painfully acquired self-reliance. It is an ideal that Swift himself repeatedly
endorsed as a necessary alternative to abject dependence upon capricious
patrons and fickle courts alike.

There was yet another, more personal matter that profoundly influenced Swift's opinion of the earl. The matter concerned the rather
grandiose monument erected in St. Patrick's Cathedral by Burlington's
ancestor, the first (or "Great") Earl of Cork, in memory of his second
wife. (The monument stands there to this day, at the western end of the
cathedral.) By the time Swift took over as Dean of St. Patrick's, the memorial had fallen into a state of disrepair, requiring money for both its
immediate restoration and its future upkeep. Thus, when Swift visited England in 1726 and 1727, he talked to Burlington about the necessity of
repairing the sculpture, as a tribute to his distinguished ancestry. Burlington apparently agreed verbally to Swift's requests "that he would order
the Monument to be repair'd," at a cost of 50£, and that "he would bestow a bit of Land not exceeding 5ll a year to repair it for ever" (C,
3:361). Accordingly, a formal order of the Chapter of St. Patrick's was
sent to the earl in May 1729, accompanied by a personal letter from Swift
reminding Burlington of his promise (334). But neither the chapter's
order nor Swift's missive ever received a response from Burlington. Swift's
smoldering anger at this neglect kept flaring up in his subsequent correspondence. Writing to Gay after six months of Boyle's silence, he expostu-
lated: "I cannot be angry enough with My Lord Burlington. I sent him an
Order of the Chapter of St Patrick's desiring the Dean would write to his
Lordship about his Ancestor's Monument in my Cathedrall. The Gentlemen are all Persons of Dignity and Consequence, of Birth and Fortune,
not like those of your hedge Chapters in England; and it became him to
send an answer to such a Body on an Occasion where onely the Honor of
his Family is concerned" (361). Although Swift's anger clearly stemmed
in part from personal pique, it also expressed a more general disappointment with Burlington's failure to act in a manner consonant with his
exalted rank. Not unlike the "Gentleman" portrayed in *The Story of the*

Injured Lady, Burlington stood guilty in Swift's eyes of "neglecting ... all common Civility in his Behaviour." Indeed, in another letter to Gay he is specifically accused of failing to show "civility" (419).

Reverence for one's ancestral past, along with a commitment to celebrate it with artistic tributes and a life of good works, is central to the values traditionally associated with a landed aristocracy and embodied in its estates. These values were, for example, concretized in the architectural features of Lord Digby's estate, Sherborne, which included carefully restored ruins. As Pope explained to Martha Blount, "What should induce my Lord D. the rather to cultivate these ruins and do honour to them, is that they do no small honour to his Family; that Castle, which was very ancient, being demolishd in the Civil wars after it was nobly defended by one of his Ancestors in the cause of the King. I would sett up at the Entrance of 'em an Obelisk, with an inscription of the Fact: which would be a Monument erected to the very Ruins. . . ."[30] Pope's account makes it clear that the act of restoring ancestral ruins and erecting monuments to the past would have been considered an integral part of country house ideology. In the *Epistle to Burlington*, Pope makes a similar point by emphasizing the restorative as well as the creative aspects of the earl's artistic endeavors: "You too proceed! make falling Arts your care,/Erect new wonders, and the old repair,/Jones and Palladio to themselves restore,/ And be whate'er Vitruvius was before" (191–94). To Swift there must have appeared a particularly bitter irony in the exalted portrait of Burlington as a restorer of "falling Arts" and a repairer of the "old."

Swift's contempt for the earl's behavior may be gleaned from a subsequent letter to Gay, in which he declares: " . . . he that would not sacrifice twenty acres out of two hundred thousand to the honor of his family may live to see them not return him two hundred thousand pence, towards which I believe he [Burlington] feels enough already" (C, 3:419). Swift subsequently noted tersely: "There's a Lord for you [Burlington] wholly out of my favor whom I will use as I did Schomberg's Heiresses" (C, 4:17). The meaning of this allusion is explained by a lengthy passage in an earlier letter to Carteret concerning the failure of Lady Holderness to send a small sum for a monument to her grandfather, the Duke of Schomberg, who was buried under the altar in St. Patrick's Cathedral. Laying the blame for this neglect mainly on her husband, Lord Fitzwalter, Swift comments acerbically:

> I desire you will tell Lord F[itzwalter] that if he will not send fifty pounds to make a monument for the old Duke, I and the chapter will erect a small one of ourselves for ten pounds, wherein it shall be expressed, That the posterity of the Duke, naming particularly Lady Holderness and Mr. Mildmay, not having the generosity to erect a monument, we have done it of ourselves. And if, for an excuse, they

pretend they will send for his body, let them know it is mine; and rather than send it, I will take up the bones, and make of it a skeleton, and put it in my registry-office, to be a memorial of their baseness to all posterity. (C, 3:390)

This rather grotesque image of Schomberg's disinterred skeleton sitting in Swift's registry office as a "memorial" to posterity may be seen as a fitting *memento mori*, signifying the death of a traditional aristocratic code of behavior based on values like patriarchal benevolence, close family ties, and reverence for the past.

Pope, aware of Swift's animosity toward Burlington, predictably attempted to gloss over the conflict to prevent any open rupture between the two men. Thus when Swift remarked in a letter to Pope, "I have not writ to Lord Burlington, but will soon with a vengeance, unless you prevent it" (C, 3:375), Pope's response was immediate and emphatic: "As to your writing to Lord Burl. I would by no means have you, 'twill tend to no good, and only anger, not amend. You are both of you Positive men" (387). Swift subsequently gave Pope assurances that he would refrain from wreaking epistolary "vengeance" on the earl, but we have to think that he derived some degree of malicious satisfaction, and felt a sense of personal vindication, upon reading the news, sent him some years later by John Barber, that "My lord *Burlington* is now selling, in one article, 9000*l.* a year in *Ireland*, for 2,000,000*l.* which won't pay his debts" (C, 5:98). Although this event was not quite a fulfillment of the prophecy made to Gay a decade earlier, it must have seemed to Swift something very like a judgment from Heaven that the man who would not relinquish twenty acres for the honor of his family should find himself in dire financial straits demanding the sacrifice of many times that number.

iv

To be sure, Swift's opinion of men like Percival and Burlington was not the only opinion he expressed concerning the landowning class. Another view may be found in his writings through 1714. As Mr. Examiner during the brief reign of the Tory ministry, Swift produced a body of essays generally affirming the values of the "Country Party," supporting among other things "that noble Bill of *Qualification*," designed to ensure "that future Parliaments should be composed of Landed Men... (PW, 3: 119). But it is wrong to interpret this allegiance as the dominant aspect of Swift's ideological outlook, as critics have customarily done by identifying him exclusively with conservative Tory or Harringtonian principles.[31] Even in his attitude toward those landed noblemen with whom he was friendly, we often find hints of skeptical or comic undercutting, a subtle strain of irony that suggests Swift's equivocal view of their position.

There is, for example, a faintly satirical undertone to Swift's description of Bolingbroke at Bucklebury, the viscount's country estate in Berkshire, which presents him as "a perfect country gentleman": for he "smoakt tobacco with one or two neighbors; he enquired after the wheat in such a field; he went to visit his hounds; and knew all their names" (JS, 1:326). We find a similar hint of a leisurely, indolent existence extraneous to the actual daily operations of a life and economy rooted in the land in a letter Swift wrote to Bolingbroke after his return to Ireland (C, 2:129–30).

The *Examiner* essays do contain recurring expressions of a country house ideology, but in a revealingly limited form that points up Swift's detached attitude toward this ideology and that contains the seeds of his later, increasing dissociation from it. Since concreteness and stability in the face of both temporal and economic fluctuations are among the values most consistently exalted in the *Examiner* essays, it would be reasonable to expect frequent and sustained metaphorical argument based on the image of the traditional country house. But the closest we come to this kind of argument is Swift's occasional use of figurative language related to architecture. For example, he claims that the Tories must protect the state from the assaults of its enemies, whose perverted zeal threatens "to break in Pieces the whole Frame of the best instituted Governments" (PW, 3: 65), and that the new ministry, although it may *"disturb the Neighbourhood* awhile," is nevertheless performing the necessary task of sweeping and mending "a House . . . going to *Ruin"* (168). We look in vain in these essays for any extended or detailed image of a sturdily constructed, flourishing country estate—one that would stand as a triumphant counterpart to the vivid images of a deteriorated estate that appear throughout Swift's later tracts.

For purposes of comparison we might recall the way in which Edmund Burke upholds the interests of the landed aristocracy by using majestic images of castles and country houses as well as stately metaphors derived from that most gentlemanly of eighteenth-century preoccupations, landscape gardening.[32] Burke's language in general reflects an identification with the privileged class, who own the land and create the structures standing on it. Even in his earliest, quite progressive political writings Burke conveys a vision profoundly touched by the ideal of a society founded upon the country house way of life. His *Essay No. 7* of the *Reformer,* for example, which is filled with the frustrated idealism and moral outrage of youth (he was eighteen when he wrote it), is a scathing attack on the oppressions and injustices stemming from the avaricious behavior of the Irish gentry, which has contributed to producing "such Poverty, as few Nations in *Europe* can equal." Burke singles out the representatives of the landed interest as those most responsible for the fact that "one part of the Nation is starved, and the other deserted." And yet the essay concludes with a lengthy and fervent invocation of the country house ideal—specifically, with the extended image of a well-regulated estate clearly intended to serve as the model for a rationally conceived, just society capable of satisfying the needs of all its citizens:

> The Evil is easier seen than remedied; but perhaps the Example of a Gentleman of Fortune, whom I know, may be useful. He came early to the Possession of an Estate valued 2000*l. per Ann.* but set to a vast Number of Tenants at a very high rent: As usual in such cases, nothing could be in a worse Condition than his Estate; his Rents ill paid, the Land out of Heart, and not a Bush, not a tolerable Enclosure, much less Habitation, to be seen. He found his Leases out, but he did not study, with the Greediness of a young Heir, how to raise the price nor Value of his Lands, nor turn out all his poor Tenants to make room for two or three rich. He retained all those to whose honest Industry he had been Witness, and lowered his Rents very considerably: he bound them to plant certain Quantities of Trees, and make other Improvements. Thus in a few years Things had another Face, his Rent was well paid, his Tenants grew rich, and his Estate increased daily in Beauty and Value. . . .
>
> Had many of our Gentlemen the same just Way of thinking, we should no doubt see this Nation in a short time in the most flourishing Condition, notwithstanding all the Disadvantages we labour under.[33]

A similar model of the ideal society and a like body of values presumably lie behind Swift's exaltation of the landed nobility in the *Examiner* essays (as well as in other pieces written during the same period), but we find in them nothing resembling the carefully articulated and lovingly elaborated vision presented by Burke. Even in the rare instance where Swift describes a nonexploitative landlord, the latter appears in the context not of Burke's prosperous and flourishing rural community but, quite the contrary, of an increasingly impoverished and desolate countryside. The landlord's actions prove futile if well meaning, incapable of reversing the trend toward degeneration. Thus the fictive speaker of the *Intelligencer, No. XIX,* himself a solicitous but hapless landlord to "above two Hundred Tenants," offers the example of a fellow estate owner, whose fair dealings with tenants have gone for naught in the face of large-scale emigration to America resulting in widespread abandonment of Irish lands (PW, 12:54, 59). The impossibility of maintaining country house traditions, even if "Landlords should by a miracle become less inhuman" (79), is underscored by Swift's lament elsewhere that even "Gentlemen of no contemptible Estates," because of Ireland's desperate economic plight, "are forced to retrench in every article . . . without being able to shew any bounty to the Poor" (81). Although Swift was reaffirming as late as 1721 the maxim "That the possessors of the soil are the best judges of what is for the advantage of the kingdom" (PW, 9:32), the declaration, here even more than in his earlier writings, remains a terse statement of abstract principle, neither rhetorically nor metaphorically substantiated, in the context of a document whose basic thrust (apart from self-vindication) is to dramatize the corruption of the social and judicial order.

The conclusion we are led to draw from these instances is not that Swift's espousal of "Country Party" norms lacked sincerity or relevance to his outlook, but rather that the country house ideal, however much it may have played a role *conceptually* in Swift's espousal of the landed interests, failed to become an integral part of the way he perceived and interpreted the world—failed to assume the status of a living, meaningful reality in his consciousness. It is not difficult to understand why this should have been so, for the moment he moved from abstract principle to empirical fact, he found that the actual "possessors of the soil" were, when not simply ineffectual, on the whole the *poorest* of judges (not to mention the most culpable of actors) concerning "what is for the advantage of the kingdom," whether they belonged to the "Mongril Breed" of absentees, the "abominable Race" of graziers, or the class of voracious country squires. In the *Examiner* essays, Swift therefore assumed a stance that was even then, but that became increasingly so with the passage of time, riddled with contradictions, at variance with empirical realities, and untenable, given a world filled with Robert Percivals and Lord Burlingtons (as Swift and not Pope perceived them) instead of Lord Munodis.

v

A substantial number of Swift's poems present a continuing commentary on the country house ideal—more specifically, on the ways it has been variously corrupted and undermined. By examining this group of poems we derive a much clearer understanding of the intricately reciprocal link between temperamental predilection and ideological outlook as the two jointly influenced Swift's treatment of this ideal. We also obtain additional insight into Swift's characteristic modes of literary demystification and subversion. Swift's country house poems (or rather, his anti-country-house poems) are at all times firmly grounded in empirical details and historical particularities, unlike their typical counterpart, whose primary allegiance is to an unchanging vision of mythic order and harmony. Nevertheless, they do reveal a process of selection—hence of interpretation—at work, and in the final analysis, one might well conclude that they mirror the mind of their creator as much as they mirror the world of concrete temporal reality.

That Swift was well aware of the English country house poem and capable of consciously playing with its conventions, even directly echoing specific passages from one such poem, is evident from his verses on Vanbrugh's house (though this was technically an urban rather than a rural structure), particularly the final version, probably written in 1708 and entitled *Vanbrug's House, Built from the Ruins of White-Hall that was Burnt.* (Two earlier versions date from 1703 and 1706.) Referring to the private residence Vanbrugh built for himself on the site of what used to be Whitehall Palace, which had been almost entirely destroyed by fire a decade earlier, Swift satirizes the builder's absurd pretensions and overweening pride: "Great *Jove*, he cry'd, the Art restore/To build by Verse as heretofore,/And make my Muse the Architect;/What Palaces shall we erect!" (43–46). The absurdity of Vanbrugh's ambition is underscored by the striking disparity between the splendor and magnitude of his architectural vision on the one hand, and the diminutiveness of the actual structure on the other. Thus when his fellow poets sail along the Thames in search of "its gilded Spires," a surprise awaits them: "At length they in the Rubbish spy/A Thing resembling a Goose Py" (103–4).

Proper proportion is of course central to the country house tradition, assuming a special emphasis by virtue of the eighteenth-century concern with Palladian symmetries. The residence in question is usually extolled for its modest dimensions and its design according to an eminently human scale, which often makes the house an emblem of its owner: "Now, Penshurst, they that will proportion thee/With other edifices, when they see/Those proud, ambitious heaps, and nothing else,/May say, their lords have built, but thy lord dwells" (*To Penshurst*, 99–102). A passage more directly relevant to, because it is consciously echoed by, Swift's poem occurs in *Upon Appleton House,* the first eight stanzas of which are largely devoted to affirming the harmony between dweller and dwelling:

> Why should of all things Man unrul'd
> Such unproportion'd dwellings build?
> The Beasts are by their Denns exprest:
> And Birds contrive an equal Nest;
> The low roof'd Tortoises do dwell
> In cases fit of Tortoise-shell:
> No Creature loves an empty space;
> Their Bodies measure out their Place.
>
> (9–16)

Obviously alluding to these lines by playing upon Marvell's analogy between the tortoise in its shell and the estate owner in his house, Swift suggests a parodically reciprocal bond between Vanbrugh and his newly built residence:

> Thrice happy Poet, who may trail
> Thy House about thee like a Snail;
> Or Harness'd to a Nag, at ease
> Take Journies in it like a Chaise;
> Or in a Boat when e're thou wilt
> Canst make it serve thee for a Tilt.
>
> (109–14)

All parts of the idealized country house harmonize with one another as well as with their immediate surroundings, in direct contrast to Vanbrugh's house, whose builder "... from the motly mingled Style/Proceeded to erect his Pile:/So, Men of old, to gain Renown, did/Build *Babel* with their Tongues confounded" (63–66).

It would seem reasonable enough to conclude from the preceding observations that Swift's verses on Vanbrugh's house are rather orthodox examples of Augustan satire in the vein of Pope's lines on the estates of Timon and Villario, in which a particular building is satirized through its implied contrast with other buildings that embody a set of normative values. That, in any case, is the conclusion arrived at by recent commentators on Swift's poetry. John Irwin Fischer, for example, notes a "process of simultaneous affirmation and qualification" operating in the poem, with Swift using Vanbrugh's negative example ultimately to "affir[m] his faith in the enduring capacity of human art to participate in that harmony which Amphion knew." Since Vanbrugh's house "partially embodies a noble ideal, but embodies it badly," the poem, in Fischer's view, can criticize Vanbrugh's false creation while simultaneously exalting the "noble ideal" concretized by country houses like Penshurst and Appleton House.[34]

But this interpretation of Swift's verse is, in the final analysis, based more on certain a priori assumptions about the techniques of Augustan satire in general than on the specifics of the particular poem in question. Whereas Pope's satiric deflations of ill-contrived houses are balanced against descriptions, within the same poem, of harmoniously designed, normative structures (e.g., the juxtaposition of Timon's estate and Burlington's in the *Fourth Moral Essay*), Swift's ridicule of Vanbrugh's house stands by itself, within a context devoid of references to laudable contemporary structures. Indeed, Vanbrugh's house comes to represent all manifestations of contemporary art, literary as well as architectural, without exception: "A Type of *Modern* Wit and Style,/*The Rubbish of an Antient Pile*" (125–26). Vanbrugh's act of building out of Whitehall's ashes thus constitutes a model for all would-be creative enterprises in the present age: "So *Modern* Rimers wisely *Blast*/The Poetry of Ages past,/Which after they have overthrown,/They from its Ruins build their own" (131–34). If the verse is here ridiculing the Moderns in the spirit of *Battle of the*

Books, it presents us with no existing Ancients capable of countering the harm perpetrated by them.

True, conventional country house poems are to some extent "present" in Swift's poem by virtue of its allusiveness. Nevertheless, when Fischer speaks of "the modesty of Penshurst [which] exists within the context of a life that is larger than itself and informs its modesty with meaning," identifying it as a foil for the absurd and empty pretensions of Vanbrugh's house, he is not referring to anything expressed or even hinted at in the poem, but rather to his own preconceptions about how a typical Augustan would interpret the country house ideal.[35] On the basis of *Vanbrug's House,* we might just as easily conclude that Swift was not only ridiculing a particular Modern's dwelling but also poking fun at the traditional country house as commemorated in verse, which after all reflected its own brand of narcissism and self-aggrandizement, quite explicit once its ideological trappings were stripped away. If, as Ronald Paulson suggests, the architecture of the eighteenth-century country house may be considered a sign system, with the structure itself as the signifier and its inhabitants as the signified, so that "the facts of the house's make-up and decoration both express function and define the owner-inhabitant,"[36] Swift's image of the "Thrice happy Poet, who may trail/[His] House about [him] like a Snail" is as applicable to the traditional country house as it is to Vanbrugh's parodic dwelling. Indeed, Marvell's own words concerning the "Beasts [who] are by their Denns exprest" can be seen as lending support to Swift's image in their yoking together of inner and outer, of signifier and signified, to create an image that officially denotes humility and correct proportion but that, considered from a slightly different angle, points to a self-enclosed, solipsistic world: a closed system in which the unity of signifier and signified is so great that it seems on the verge of turning into cosmic tautology—an absorption of all manifestations of Other into an all-consuming Self. Swift's treatment of the merging of signifier and signified, of word and thing, in Part III of *Gulliver's Travels* might suggest that he would have been particularly sensitive to the satiric potential inherent in the union of dweller and dwelling, whether in terms of the inextricable connection between tortoise and shell or in terms of the self-reflexive bond between the aristocrat and his habitation. Whatever Swift's view was in this instance, the fact remains that although *Vanbrug's House* focuses upon the deflation of a specific creative act by a specific builder, in broader terms it depicts a world in which neither traditional country houses nor the poems that traditionally commemorate them can any longer be created except in burlesque form.

Vanbrug's House was not Swift's first poem having to do with the country house ideal. His *Ode to Sir William Temple,* written more than a decade earlier while he was employed as Temple's secretary at Moor Park, can perhaps best be thought of as a country house poem manqué. It ostensibly exalts the values of the country house poem, but the focus and emphasis are shifted sufficiently to produce a very different kind of verse. In this instance, as in so many subsequent ones, Swift was presented with a situation providing him with material that could have lent itself very well to a traditional, exalted depiction of country estate life but that he chose to use for other purposes. Moor Park, then known as Compton Hall, located one and one-half miles from Farnham, in Surrey, was bought by Temple in 1686 from Sir Francis Clarke's family for the sum of £2,000.[37] There Temple retired, after having become disillusioned by the duplicitous foreign policy of King Charles (which undercut his own efforts as ambassador to the Hague), in order to indulge his passion for gardening and to execute the duties of an improving landowner, leaving his larger, more elaborate, but also less secluded, estate at Sheen (Richmond) in the hands of his son and daughter-in-law. Temple renamed his new residence Moor Park after the famous estate owned by the Countess of Bedford, where he had spent his honeymoon many years earlier.

No doubt because he deemed Bedford's Moor Park "the perfectest figure of a garden I ever saw" as well as the kind "most proper for our country and climate," he wrote an extended description of its setting and arrangement, detailed enough to serve as a blueprint for contemporary landscape designers. For our purposes, the description is significant in that it highlights certain physical manifestations of the country house ideal:

> The length of the house, where the best rooms and of most use and pleasure are, lies upon the breadth of the garden, the great parlour opens into the middle of a terras gravel-walk that lies even with it . . . the border [is] set with standard laurels, and at large distances, which have the beauty of orange-trees, out of flower and fruit: from this walk are three descents by many stone-steps, in the middle and at each end, into a very large parterre. . . .
>
> From the middle of the parterre is a descent by many steps flying on each side of a grotto that lyes between them (covered with lead, and flat) into the lower garden, which is all fruit-trees ranged about the several quarters of a wilderness which is very shady; the walks here are all green, the grotto embellished with figures of shell-rock-work, fountains, and water-works.[38]

The relative smallness of the estate's grounds (like Pope's villa, the grounds encompassed only five acres), consonant with Temple's conviction that "four or five to seven or eight acres is as much as any Gentleman need desire and . . . any Nobleman will have occasion to use in his family," proved especially compatible with those aspects of country house ideology that stressed functionality and humility.

Temple, it is true, emphasized the idea of individual retirement over the concept of a rural community and urged the necessity for private meditation and solitude, thereby suggesting a style of life that was somewhat at odds with the basically social and sociable norms connected with the traditional country house ideal. As he explains his retirement from public life at the end of his *Memoirs:* "And so I take leave of all those airy visions which have so long busied my head about mending the world; and at the same time, of all those shining toys or follies that employ the thoughts of busy men: and shall turn mine wholly to mend myself."[39] Yet we should keep in mind Erskine-Hill's point that "these two traditions [of Stoic retirement and the country house ideal] are not mutually exclusive" since "the Horatian tradition is a powerful presence in the relevant English [country house] writings."[40] Moreover, the fact is that Temple's life at Moor Park was not nearly as isolated and private as his statements would suggest. For one thing, the new household encompassed a little society of its own, including in its membership Temple's wife, Dorothy, his sister Lady Giffard, Esther Johnson, Rebecca Dingley, and, following his son's suicide in 1689, his daughter-in-law, her mother, and his two grandchildren—and, of course, Swift himself.[41] In addition, there was continuing contact with other country house dwellers such as the Duke of Somerset, owner of the more ostentatiously magnificent estate, Petworth, in nearby West Sussex. Finally, Moor Park was by no means devoid of links to the public world beyond it. It maintained important connections with the highest levels of that world. King William, who (as William of Orange) had developed a close relationship with Temple during the latter's ministerial tenure at the Hague, periodically visited the Surrey estate, even on occasion soliciting his old friend's advice on particular public issues. Temple, in turn, paid occasional visits to the king at Windsor and Richmond. In these ways, the mode of existence at Moor Park incorporated the more communal and public aspects of the country house ideal. It also included the exercise of hospitality one associates with this ideal, judging from the account of a Swiss traveler, Béat de Muralt, written in 1694 as part of his *Lettres sur les Anglais.* On a visit to Moor Park he "received every sort of courtesy" and "saw the ideal of a pleasant retreat . . . the air wholesome, the soil good, the view limited but pretty, a little stream which runs near making the only sound to be heard; the house small, convenient, and appropriately furnished; the garden in proportion to the house, and cultivated by the master himself."[42]

Thus Swift, during his first stay in England, came in contact with a way of life that would have been most suitable for a traditional country house depiction. But Swift's earliest poems, his panegyric verses written while he was living at Moor Park, although ostensibly affirming the virtues of country living, neither exemplify this genre nor present a conventional

Horatian statement concerning the joys of retreat. In examining his *Ode to Sir William Temple,* we find a depiction of disturbing, unresolved tensions that cannot be contained within the neatly defined contrast between city and country life, or between the public and the private spheres. Peter J. Schakel, in suggesting that this verse is seriously flawed, argues: "Although emotion, power, and elevation appear in some passages of the ode to Temple, the work as a whole lacks the emotional force to unify the variety of topics it takes up: virtue, learning, peace, designing politicians, pastoral retreat, and the tyranny of the muse."[43] The lack of unity noted by Schakel certainly exists—it is, indeed, one of the strongest impressions conveyed by the poem—but it is not the result of a deficient "emotional force," nor the reflection of any one particular formal weakness, so much as it is the expression of profound discontinuities that Swift experienced during his troubled stay at Moor Park. Things like "virtue, learning, peace, designing politicians, pastoral retreat, and the tyranny of the muse" were not so much "topics" as they were seemingly insoluble problems for the young Swift, who was just beginning to confront the fact that prescribed literary forms and conventions did not work for him in the same way as they did for others: to smooth out rough edges, resolve contradictions, unify disparate elements, and convert the angularities of human existence into the symmetries of art. In other hands, the theme of pastoral retreat might well have served to unite the ode's diverse concerns, thereby presenting an aesthetic solution within the poem much as it proved an existential solution in Temple's own life. Swift would have found examples of this in the poems of Abraham Cowley, which Swift loosely used as models for his own Pindaric odes. Cowley could even have shown Swift how to combine the Horatian and the country house traditions within a single work of panegyric, as he did in the verses concluding his essay, "Of Solitude."[44]

But for Swift, the idea of pastoral retreat was itself so fraught with contradiction and ambiguity that it emerges as but one more problematical strain in his *Ode to Sir William Temple.* The note of panegyric is at various points overwhelmed by passages of condemnation, and the positive is continually either being or threatening to be engulfed by the negative in this poem, which opens with an image of the disintegration of virtue into discordant fragments and an allusion to Man's Fall (1-7), and which continues with successive attacks on philosophy (21-27), academic learning and pedantry (39-49), war (76-80), and politics (92-106). It is not until stanza IX that the muse is invoked to "Sing . . . the Pleasures of Retreat" (135) and to "Go publish o'er the Plain/How mighty a Proselyte you gain!" (139-40). But even here the focus rapidly shifts away from the virtuous country gentleman and his pastoral environs to the idiosyncratic, unruly muse, acting like a Pegasus who "Runs violently o'er his usual Course" (149). Stanza X is the only stanza in the entire ode devoted to Horatian panegyric—the only one unmarked by the venom of Swift's pen. It opens with praise of "this new happy Scene" (159) and terminates with an implied analogy between Temple and a redeemed Adam: "You strove to cultivate a barren Court in vain,/Your Garden's better worth your noble Pain,/Hence Mankind fell, and here must rise again" (175–77).

But, as Kathleen Williams observes, " . . . the poem on the whole does not show Temple's garden of retirement as a Paradise, an ordered epitome of existence like Nunappleton."[45] Indeed, the only mention of "Paradises" appears amidst suggestions of airy illusion and fantasy— juxtaposed, for example, with the image of the muse "soar[ing] clear out of sight" (144). Despite the meticulously cultivated and well-publicized features of Moor Park's landscape, created by one who was recognized both in England and abroad as an authority on gardens, Swift's portrayal of Temple's environs in the ode is strangely abstract and disembodied, containing no mention at all of the terraces, parterres, carefully arranged fruit trees, and grotto that were central features of Temple's surroundings. The setting of Moor Park, as presented in the ode, seems to derive its exalted character more from its contrast with "the hated Court and Town" (157) than from its own independent merits. It beckons above all as an escape from the corruptions of the public world (the "wily Shafts of State" [92]) and from the "Serpent" that "Still lurks in Palaces and Courts" (116–17). If it is made to serve as an emblem of innocence, it simultaneously stands as a constant reminder of human failure and futility; thus Temple vainly strives to accomplish his worldly goals, "Till at last tir'd with loss of Time and Ease,/[He] Resolv'd to give himself, as well as Country Peace" (133–34). We can already see, even in this supposed hymn to "the Pleasures of Retreat," hints of a theme that will become increasingly pervasive in Swift's later works: the land as a place of embittered exile rather than as man's physical and spiritual home.

This sense of estrangement is greatly magnified by Swift's portrayal of himself in the final two stanzas, where he presents the figure of an outsider, dislocated amidst surroundings in which he does not really belong. To the extent that Swift exalts (in his own idiosyncratic and equivocal manner) the rural aristocratic way of life prevailing at Moor Park, he emphasizes his own remoteness from it; it is a type of existence permanently beyond his grasp because it is essentially alien to his own worldly position. In a universe defined by preordained social and economic inequalities, Swift numbers among the disinherited younger sons:

Why then does Nature so unjustly share
Among her Elder Sons the whole Estate?

> And all her Jewels and her Plate,
> Poor we *Cadets* of Heav'n, not worth her Care,
> Take up at best with Lumber and the Leavings of a Fate. . . .
>
> (180–84)

It is characteristic of Swift that he should mention these inequalities in a tone of complaint and resentment rather than with the kind of serene acceptance and affirmation communicated in, say, Pope's vision of the Great Chain of Being in the *Essay on Man,* where hierarchic distinctions are perceived to be mutually beneficial, individually sustaining, and divinely ordained, hence "right." To Swift's indignant question, "Why then does Nature so unjustly share/Among her Elder Sons the whole Estate?" Pope reassuringly counters, "Know, Nature's children all divide her care" (*Essay on Man,* Epistle III, 43), and observes that while "The rich is happy in the plenty giv'n,/The poor contents him with the care of Heav'n" (Epistle II, 265–66).

The divisions in the social and economic hierarchy depicted by Swift are not harmoniously resolved by the way of life followed at Moor Park, which if anything serves to magnify these differences, underscoring the fundamental irreconcilability among the various levels of society:

> Some she [Nature] binds 'Prentice to the Spade,
> Some to the Drudgery of a Trade,
> Some she does to *Egyptian* Bondage draw,
> Bids us make Bricks, yet sends us to look out for Straw;
> Some she condemns for Life to try
> To dig the leaden Mines of deep Philosophy. . . .
>
> (185–90)

It is revealing that Swift later was to use identical language in enumerating the "Causes of the Wretched Condition of Ireland," in a passage that shifts the blame for certain individuals' harsh fate from "Nature" to society and man-made systems—a change that reflects Swift's movement from a profoundly uneasy and equivocal expression of cosmic Toryism to an outright attack upon its very foundations: "Lastly, a great Cause of this Nation's Misery, is that *Ægyptian* Bondage of cruel, oppressing, covetous Landlords, expecting that all who live under them should *make Bricks without Straw. . .*" (PW, 9:201).

The Swiftian muse reveals itself to be radically, even ontologically different from the lord of the manor: "Shall I believe a Spirit so divine/Was cast in the same Mold with mine?" (178–79). Swift has been bequeathed both a social status and a vocation—defined by a landless, itinerant character—that contrast with Temple's in every respect: "Me [Nature] has to the Muse's Gallies ty'd,/ . . . And when I almost reach the Shore/Strait the Muse turns the Helm, and I launch out again" (191, 194–

95). As a consequence, there is a sense of comic incongruity rather than noble harmony in Swift's relationship to his surroundings. Swift, the irresistibly impelled seafarer, can have no genuine ties to the earthbound Temple. The best Swift can do is to parody Temple by revealing himself, in his role as poet, as an incompetent gardener, a cultivator of weeds and failed crops (208-12).

Given this view of things it is not surprising that Swift soon gave up his role as poetic commemorator of Temple's life at Moor Park and chose to conclude his essays in this genre with an emphatic repudiation of the poetic vision (here portrayed as delusion) underlying his odes. The final lines of this last ode, *Occasioned by Sir William Temple's Late Illness and Recovery,* form an interesting counterbalance to, as well as an ironic reversal of, the parting statement of Temple's *Memoirs,* where Temple bids farewell to "all those airy visions which have so long busied my head about mending the world" and resolves instead to "turn [my thoughts] wholly to mend myself." For Temple, the "airy visions" and "follies" of which he desired to purge himself were directly associated with the world of historical reality, public affairs, and "busy men." The alternative to be sought was a life of private retreat and solitary meditation. For Swift, on the contrary, the airy visions and delusions poisoning his head were connected with his troubled, ambivalent life as aspiring poet at Moor Park; they, along with his poetry, were the weedy outgrowth of his alienated existence in Temple's garden world. The "wild form dependent on the brain" (95) and the pernicious "visionary pow'r" (152) exorcised by the poet are the result precisely of a solitude not sufficiently fertilized by the external world. In renouncing his muse's "visionary pow'r" and declaring an end to "the whole delusion" (154), Swift is not only bidding farewell to the Pindaric ode, he is also in some sense taking his leave of an alien form of life with which he can make no meaningful connection and heralding his movement toward greater involvement in a world of external events: a movement that was to include his assumption of increasingly public roles such as those of Mr. Examiner and M. B., Drapier.

A Pastoral Dialogue between Richmond-Lodge and Marble-Hill, written over three decades after the *Ode to Sir William Temple,* is another poem in which Swift depicts the country house way of life prevailing in eighteenth-century England, again amidst surroundings with which he was personally familiar. If the ode is a country house poem manqué, the *Pastoral Dialogue* may be classified as a burlesque country house poem. Richmond-Lodge was acquired as a summer house by the Prince of Wales in 1722. As Swift describes it in the preface to the poem, "*Richmond* Lodge is a House with a small Park belonging to the Crown: It was usually granted by the Crown for a Lease of Years; the Duke of *Ormonde* was the

last who had it. After his Exile, it was given to the Prince of *Wales,* by the
King. The Prince and Princess usually passed their *Summer* there. It is
within a Mile of *Richmond*" (P, 2:407). A contemporary description of
the house suggests its suitability as the subject for an elegant poetic tribute, particularly (in light of its stately yet modest proportions) in the
country house genre: "It does not appear with the Grandeur of a Royal
Palace, but is very neat and pretty. . . . The gardens are very spacious, and
well kept. There is a fine Terrace towards the River. But above all, the
Wood cut out into Walks with the plenty of Birds singing in it, makes a
most delicious Habitation."[46] Defoe's description of the surrounding landscape in his *Tour through the Whole Island of Great Britain,* published
about two years prior to the composition of Swift's poem, makes a similar
point by emphasizing the wealth and prosperity of the neighborhood, as
well as the close-knit conviviality of its privileged residents.[47] Swift evi-
dently enjoyed the hospitality of Sheen's royal residence, where, as he
tells us in the *Pastoral Dialogue,* he was wont "To spunge a Breakfast
once a Week" and, in his usual role as cranky, dissatisfied guest, "To cry
the Bread was stale, and mutter/Complaints against the Royal Butter"
(51-54).

Marble Hill, the other participant in Swift's *Pastoral Dialogue,* was
a Palladian villa overlooking the Thames, built in the mid-1720s by the
Prince of Wales for his mistress Henrietta Howard, Countess of Suffolk.
In his preface to the poem, Swift describes it in the following way:
"*Marble-Hill* is a House built by Mrs. *Howard,* then of the Bed-chamber,
now Countess of *Suffolk,* and Groom of the Stole to the Queen. It is on
the *Middlesex* Side, near *Twickenham,* where Mr. *Pope* lives, and about
two Miles from *Richmond-Lodge.* Mr. *Pope* was the Contriver of the
Gardens, Lord *Herbert* the Architect, and the Dean of St. *Patrick*'s chief
Butler, and Keeper of the *Ice House*" (P, 2:407). As the description suggests, Swift was on far more familiar terms with this house than with
Richmond Lodge. Looked at from one perspective, Marble Hill could
in various ways be considered an embodiment of country house elegance.
As Lees-Milne rather effusively puts it, "On the sympathetic low-lying
meads of Marble Hill the remaining years of [Mrs. Howard's] long life
were henceforth to drift like the purling waters of the silvery Thames at
the bottom of her garden."[48]

Lord Pembroke (Swift's "Lord *Herbert* the Architect"), a friend of
Mrs. Howard's, designed the house for her in 1723. Along with the services of Pembroke, Mrs. Howard benefited from the expert gardening
skills of a notable quartet: Pope, Lord Bathurst, the Earl of Peterborough,
and the king's gardener, Charles Bridgeman. Morris R. Brownell suggests
that the gardens at both Sherborne and Wilton House may well have
served as models for Pope's landscaping activities at Marble Hill.[49] The

extent of these activities is attested to in Pope's personal correspondence
during this period. In the fall of 1724, for example, he wrote to Fortescue:
"My gardens improve more than my writings; my head is still more
upon Mrs. Hd. and her works [Mrs. Howard and her gardens], than upon
my own." Some months later he playfully told Bathurst that "If he will
not vouchsafe to visit either his Servant [Pope], or his handmaids, let him
(as the Patriarchs anciently did) send flocks of Sheep & Presents in his
stead: For the grass of Marble hill springeth, yea it springeth exceedingly. . . ."[50] When one of Mrs. Howard's cows gave birth to a female calf in
her absence, Pope wrote to her to convey the news and then described the
celebration in honor of the event, in the process underscoring Marble
Hill's role in fulfilling the country house traditions of convivial rituals and
boundless hospitality—a hospitality that specifically included Swift.[51]

And what does Swift make of this festive community of friends
amidst the elegant pastoral surroundings of a fashionable mansion? Basically, he converts it into an image of impending decay and obsolescence.
The tone of his verse is predominantly comic and playful, but the issues
the verse treats are serious enough, having implications that bear directly
upon Swift's continuing exposure of contemporary society. The two
houses that converse in *A Pastoral Dialogue,* by lamenting their present
state of neglect and prophesying their imminent decline, become testa-
ments to a vanishing way of life. Richmond Lodge fears that it "shall be
soon forgot" (18) when its master, the Prince of Wales, succeeds to the
throne and becomes "poor as any *King*" (40). (The poem was written
upon the occasion of the death of King George I in June 1727.) Instead of
recounting the hospitable and convivial gatherings held under its roof,
Richmond Lodge reflects, "You see, when Folks have got their Ends,/
How quickly they neglect their Friends" (19–20). Richmond-Lodge's sole
hope for survival depends upon drastic compromise—upon a demeaning
accommodation to the fashion of the world: "I then will turn a Courtier
too,/And serve the Times as others do" (79–80).

Marble Hill foresees its own fate in even more dramatic and irreparable terms: It will inevitably be "Chang'd for the worse in ev'ry Part"
after "Some *South Sea* Broker from the City" purchases it with the aim
of fitting its gardens to "his Vulgar Taste" (67–71). In a kind of mock
variation on the *ubi sunt* motif, the estate anticipates the disappearance of
those upon whom the survival of the country house ideal depends:

No more the Dean, that grave Divine,
Shall keep the Key of my (no) Wine;
My Ice-house rob as heretofore,
And steal my Artichokes no more;
Poor *Patty Blount* no more be seen
Bedraggled in my Walks so green:

Plump *Johnny Gay* will now elope;
And here no more will dangle *Pope*.

(43–50)

Even before the predicted changes have occurred, Marble Hill is already suffering from indifferent and careless treatment: "Him [Pope] twice a Week I here expect,/To rattle *Moody* [the gardener] for Neglect" (95–96). A tone of playful mockery permeates these lines, but passages like the one envisioning the devastation caused by "Some *South Sea* Broker" link this poem with others that attack the contemporary economic situation growing out of capitalist encroachments upon the land (e.g., *The Bubble* and *The Run upon the Bankers*) and remind us that a serious statement is being made amidst the banter. Against Swift's depicted scene reflecting absence and neglect, as well as presaging imminent ruin, we can juxtapose Thomson's identically located but contrastingly portrayed landscape, surveyed as he and Amanda ". . . turn/To where the silver Thames first rural grows" (*The Seasons*, "Summer," 1415–16):

Slow let us trace the matchless vale of Thames;
Fair-winding up to where the muses haunt
In Twit'nam's bowers, and for their Pope implore
The healing god; to royal Hampton's pile,
To Clermont's terraced height, and Esher's groves,
Where in the sweetest solitude, embraced
By the soft windings of the silent Mole,
From courts and senates Pelham finds repose.
Enchanting vale! beyond whate'er the muse
Has of Achaia or Hesperia sung!
O vale of bliss! O softly-swelling hills!
On which the power of cultivation lies,
And joys to see the wonders of his toil.

(1425–37)[52]

For Swift, the "power of cultivation" as exhibited along the banks of the Thames had a very different meaning, as is evident not only from his references in *A Pastoral Dialogue* to the pernicious activities of South Sea speculators but also from his emphasis upon Mrs. Howard's precarious financial circumstances and the danger of her becoming impoverished as a result of the extravagant expenses paid for building and landscaping projects at Marble Hill:

My House was built but for a Show,
My Lady's empty Pockets know:
And now she will not have a Shilling
To raise the Stairs, or build the Cieling;

For, all the Courtly Madams round,
Now pay four Shillings in the Pound.
'Tis come to what I always thought;
My Dame is hardly worth a Groat.

(23-30)

Swift's preoccupation in this regard puts him at odds with the traditional commemorators of country house living, who never portray finances as a problem, since their idealized outlook in effect presupposes country gentlemen who possess all they need for the practical improvement as well as aesthetic enhancement of their estates, who demonstrate prudence and moderation in their expenditures, and who are generous enough to share their wealth with their less fortunate neighbors, thereby making poverty a nonexistent issue. It is inconceivable, for example, that Pope would question the financial capabilities of a Bathurst or a Burlington in one of his epistles—even though, interestingly enough, both men, for all their vast wealth, found themselves in dire economic straits because they overextended themselves in ambitious architectural and landscaping projects. Burlington, as we have already seen, was forced to sell his Irish estates, while Bathurst was obliged to borrow £2,000 from Pope himself and also found it necessary to sell several estates.[53] Financial difficulties like these were in fact not uncommon among England's landowning class during this period, as we see from a letter written to Swift by John Barber: "Is it not shocking that that noble lord [Edward Harley, Lord Oxford], who has no vices (except buying manuscripts and curiosities may be called so) has not a guinea in his pocket, and is selling a great part of his estate to pay his debts? and that estate of his produces nearly 20,000*l.* a year. I say, is it not shocking! But indeed most of our nobility with great estates are in the same way" (C, 5:98).

Swift was acutely aware of the serious economic problems confronting England's estate owners and of their inevitably adverse effects upon the country house way of life. In the *Pastoral Dialogue,* the predicted decline of Marble Hill is ascribable both to its owner's extravagance ("My House was built but for a Show," which is a direct reversal of the situation approvingly noted by Jonson: "Thou art not, Penshurst, built to envious show . . .") and to the spiral of inflation seriously devaluing the country's currency ("For, all the Courtly Madams round,/Now pay four Shillings in the Pound"). Swift's preoccupation with this latter issue is even more evident in his prose, where he stresses the inextricable links between spiraling inflation and the growing inability to maintain traditional country house existence. Thus, lamenting the fact that "the Value of Money in *England,* and most Parts of *Europe,* is sunk above one Half within the Space of an Hundred Years," he points to the example of "Sir—— *Cockain* of *Darbyshire,* the best House-Keeper of his Quality in the Country [in the Reign of *Philip* and *Mary*]," who was able to carry on the tradition by "allow-[ing] his Lady fifty Pounds a Year for maintaining the Family, one Pound a Year Wages to each Servant, and two Pounds to the Steward," but who clearly would not have been able to accomplish this end had he been living in eighteenth-century England with the same amount of money, for "Now this Sum of fifty Pound, added to the Advantages of a large Domain, might be equal to about five Hundred Pounds a Year at present, or somewhat more than four *Fifths*" (PW, 9:50).

The crisis anticipated by Marble Hill in *A Pastoral Dialogue* thus reflects Swift's dual awareness of England's deteriorating economic situation in general and of the improvident handling of funds by individuals among the English gentry, especially as manifested by their grandiose architectural and landscaping projects. Henrietta Howard, like so many others in her position, had in fact overextended herself in embellishing her Twickenham villa. As Lees-Milne observes, "Her friends had joined together in their efforts to produce for her what amounted inside and out to a rare work of art albeit on a modest scale. Modest it may have been but she was, in consequence, if not exactly ruined, then in serious financial difficulties."[54] The situation was exacerbated by a protracted dispute between Mrs. Howard and the Vernon family, from whom the grounds of Marble Hill were in part purchased, which took the form of extended litigation.[55] Financial and legal entanglements such as these were precisely the sorts of things most likely to be focused upon by Swift and, by the same token, precisely the sorts of things certain to be ignored by orthodox commemorators of country house life.

A Pastoral Dialogue between Richmond-Lodge and Marble-Hill may thus be viewed, on one level, as a triumph of hard realities over literary fictions. Yet the clear-cut contrast between reality and fiction finally proves too reductive, for the empirical circumstances of life at Marble Hill were such that they could actually sustain the illusion (even, within a limited framework, support the partial reality) of the country house way of life. The prognostications of financial ruin in the verse, although grounded in fact as we have seen, were at the same time based on only some of the facts. Existing circumstances could have been used to predict a very different kind of future—as well as to affirm a very different kind of present—for Marble Hill. Indeed, as Lees-Milne observes, "Matters did not however turn out so very badly. Her husband's inheritance of the Suffolk earldom gained Henrietta a higher position at court for a time and a larger income. For the rest of her long life she seemed seldom to be without builders or carpenters in the house. She was forever making improvements. . . ."[56] Defoe, who also refused to overlook mundane matters such as finances for the sake of a transcendent, idealized vision, notes in passing the "catastrophe of innumerable wealthy city families, who after they have thought their houses establish'd, and have built their magnificent country seats, as well as others, have sunk under the misfortunes of business, and the disasters of trade." Nevertheless, in viewing essentially the same scene that confronted Swift on his visits to England, he records not signs of approaching economic ruin but numerous proofs of the country's increasing prosperity: "... so that in short all this variety, this beauty, this glorious show of wealth and plenty, is really a view of the luxuriant age which we live in, and of the overflowing riches of the citizens, who in their abundance make these gay excursions, and live thus deliciously all the summer, retiring within themselves in the winter, the better to lay up for the next summer's expence."[57]

Thus while the *Pastoral Dialogue* underscores Swift's preference for concrete realities over appealing illusions, in the final analysis the poem also reflects his tendency to validate and convey one particular kind of reality over another—to see certain aspects of a situation as more significant, more real, than other aspects. It is in this latter sense that we might legitimately conclude that *A Pastoral Dialogue between Richmond-Lodge and Marble-Hill* represents an expression of Swift's consciousness and re-creative vision as much as it represents prevailing conditions. Maynard Mack, with Pope primarily in mind, poses the following rhetorical question: "Could an eighteenth-century poet and Palladian experience, or imagine that he experienced, in the great salon at Marble Hill... if not so metaphysical an echo [as the music of the spheres], at least an exhilarating access of confidence that all things are One?"[58] Whatever Pope may or may not have experienced, the *Pastoral Dialogue* makes it clear that Swift, standing in the great salon at Marble Hill, discerned not heavenly harmonies but all-too-worldly discord, and experienced a sense not of mystical unity but of earthly conflict and fragmentation. There was nothing in the least bit "metaphysical" about the combined social and economic forces Swift saw radically altering the shape of life and art alike as they spread across the land—across even that presumably hallowed and well-protected land around Twickenham.

Another poem dating from this period, *Dr. Swift to Mr. Pope, While he was writing the "Dunciad,"* was composed in commemoration of Swift's stay at his friend's Twickenham villa in 1727. It has the right setting and situation for a country house poem but manages to avoid any mention whatever of the elegant environs and their emblematic significance for the master gardener who helped shape them. Nor does it, on the basis of Swift's relationship to Pope, affirm the ideals of friendship and hospitality. If anything, the verse subverts these ideals, though in a playfully debunking fashion, by focusing precisely on the failure of communication (hence, by implication, the failure of community) between host and guest:

> *Pope* has the Talent well to speak,
>   But not to reach the Ear;
> His loudest Voice is low and weak,
>   The *Dean* too deaf to hear.
>
> A while they on each other look,
>   Then diff'rent Studies chuse,
> The *Dean* sits plodding on a Book,
>   *Pope* walks, and courts the Muse.

(1–8)

The actual circumstances of Swift's visit, like the poetic depiction of it, serve to underscore the fact that for him the country house way of life was no longer tenable; its ideals of continuous hospitality and sustained intimacy between host and guest were fated to dissolve in the face of empirical realities. Thus, at the onset of one of his recurring spells of deafness while he was staying at Twickenham, Swift abruptly left his friend's house for a London inn, much to the consternation of Pope, whose pride in performing a role like that of the model host, Menelaos, in Homer's *Odyssey* presupposed his ability to care for ailing visitors. Pope communicated his dismay in a letter to Thomas Sheridan: "Upon Pretence of some very unavoidable Occasions, he went to *London* four Days since, where I see him as often as he will let me. I was extreamly concerned at his Opiniatrety in leaving me; but he shall not get rid of the Friend, tho' he may of his House."[59] In a letter written the following month to Swift, who was by this time back in Ireland, Pope expressed disappointment at his guest's "so sudden departure," although he was careful not to sound accusatory, indicating that the disappointment was largely with his own ineffectiveness as host (C, 3:241). Swift's departure "so unexpectedly, and in so clandestine a manner" (244) must have been somewhat of a blow to the man who, only months before, had likened his Twickenham residence to "the house of a Patriarch of old, standing by the highway side and receiving all travellers."[60] Hence, in implicit though gentle criticism of Swift's behavior, Pope promised "if I live, to visit you in Ireland, and act there as much in my own way as you did here in yours. I will not leave your roof, if I am ill" (241).

Swift perceived the matter rather differently; as he explained to Pope in his letter of reply: "Two sick friends never did well together..." (C, 3:242). His extended explanation for his unannounced departure from England is a study in qualification and equivocation; it is actually a string of various different explanations, none of which, taken separately, seems quite adequate for the purpose and all of which, added together, still manage to omit any mention of what surely must have been a major consideration in Swift's return, Stella's illness: "I find it more convenient to be sick here, without the vexation of making my friends uneasy; yet my giddiness alone would not have done, if that unsociable comfortless deafness had not quite tired me: And I believe I should have returned from the Inn [in Aldersgate Street from which the Chester coach started], if I had not feared it was only a short intermission, and the year was late, and my licence expiring. . . . I had another reason for my haste hither, which was changing my Agent, the old one having terribly involved my little affairs. . ." (242-43). In his reference to "that unsociable comfortless deafness," we can detect a hint of Swift's increasing tendency to transform an actual physical ailment into a symbol of the unbridgeable distance between human beings and the essential isolation of the self, whether in the midst of Ireland's most desolate regions or amidst the bustling life of Twickenham's fashionable society. As a circumstance that "utterly disqualifie[d him] for all conversation" (C, 4:476) and forced him to "turn a Speculative Monk" (C, 3:40), the deafness was used with greater and greater frequency during the final two decades of his life as an explanation for his withdrawal from the world, his general unfitness for human society, and his inability to participate in the country house way of life.

Swift's visits to England in 1726 and 1727 undoubtedly included their share of good fellowship and enjoyable reunions with old friends amidst elegant and comfortable settings: Swift not only stayed at Twickenham but also was entertained at Bolingbroke's estate, Dawley, in Uxbridge, as well as at Gay's Whitehall lodgings; he visited Bathurst's Oakley Wood at Cirencester, was taken by his host on tours of the countryside outside London, including Lord Cobham's Stowe and the Royal Gardens at Richmond, and went "rambling" through Cambridge and other areas in England with various friends (C, 3:137). Nevertheless, what is conveyed most strongly in Swift's written accounts of his visits is his chronic discontent and restlessness, his recurring sense of disorientation and persistent feelings of anxiety, which result in a desire either to return "home" or to resume his travels (234). Swift's letters from England are filled with descriptions of a "giddy," "dizzy," and "tottering" state of body that seem to testify to a similar state of mind: a general sense of being out of kilter with one's surroundings. He is, as he reveals to Mrs. Howard, "like a great Minister in a tottering condition" (231). The deafness and giddiness to which he repeatedly refers, while they are symptoms of an actual disease, seem at moments to point even more to a profound state of "dis-ease." He describes his feelings in a letter to Sheridan just prior to his departure: "I am very uneasy here, because so many of our Acquaintance come to see us, and I cannot be seen; besides Mr. *Pope* is too sickly and complaisant; therefore I resolve to go somewhere else. . . . I want to be at home, where I can turn you out, or let you in, as I think best" (229).

Given Swift's striking unsuitability to fulfill the traditional role of the country house guest, it is not surprising that he recorded his stay in England in verses like *A Pastoral Dialogue* and *Dr. Swift to Mr. Pope, While he was writing the "Dunciad"*—verses that, in their own flippant, self-mocking way, undermine or reverse the situations and relationships upon which the country house ideal depends. Nor is it surprising that in later years, when Swift reflected back on his various visits to England, he called to mind not the elegant pastoral surroundings of Twickenham or the stately Palladian mansions that afforded him shelter as well as numerous amenities, but "a dear scurvy London lodging," inadequate for his needs, to which he would never want to return (C, 4:378). Swift therefore resisted all attempts by his friends to lure him back to England, either for another extended visit or for purposes of resettlement. The explanations offered for this resistance at times suggest the same sense of growing separation and incommunicativeness between himself and his friends that we saw comically depicted in *Dr. Swift to Mr. Pope.* Writing to one correspondent, for example, he declares: "My Lord Bolingbroke and Mr Pope press me with many kind Invitations. But, the former is too much a Philosopher; he dines at six in the evening, after studying all the morning till after noon; and when he hath dined; to his Studyes again. . . Mr Pope can neither eat nor drink; loves to be alone, and hath always some poetical Scheme in his head. Thus the two best companions and friends I ever had, have utterly disqualifyed themselves for my conversation, and my way of living" (184).

Pope's letters dealing with Swift's visits to England and with the possibility of his return highlight the differences in the way they reflected upon the past and viewed the future. In a letter written on the threshold of Swift's return to Ireland in August 1726, Pope declared to his departed friend:

> Many a short sigh you cost me the day I left you, and many more you will cost me, till the day you return. I really walk'd about like a man banish'd, and when I came home, found it no home. 'Tis a sensation like that of a limb lopp'd off, one is trying every minute unawares to use it, and finds it is not. . . . Besides my natural memory of you, you have made a local one, which presents you to me in every place I frequent: I shall never more think of Lord Cobham's, the woods of Ciceter, or the pleasing prospect of Byberry, but your Idea must be joyn'd with 'em; nor see one seat in my own garden, or one room in my own house, without a Phantome of you, sitting or walking before me.
>
> (C, 3:156–57)

We see here a mode of perception and description that is as alien to Swift as it is congenial to the country house tradition: an affirmation of abiding friendship and hospitality put in terms of (indeed, actually incarnated in) the shapes and textures of a physical landscape as well as its architectural structures. And countering Swift's pessimism about the possibility of a sustained community of friends residing together, Pope declares that although neighbors and loved ones have departed the scene, "yet my house is enlarg'd, and the gardens extend and flourish, as knowing nothing of the guests they have lost. . . . For God's sake, why should not you . . . e'en give all you have to the Poor of Ireland (for whom you have already done every thing else) so quit the place, and live and die with me?" (C, 4:472).

By contrast, Swift's accounts of the interactions between friends are generally devoid of natural description and seem to take place in a vacuum. Perhaps the most striking aspect of the verse *Dr. Swift to Mr. Pope* is its total lack of local color and physical setting. Remaining wholly unembodied and existing solely as an assumed background, Twickenham is "present" in Swift's poem only by virtue of its conspicuous absence. Given Pope's sense of the connection between human ties and a concrete, abiding environment as conveyed in his letters, we can readily understand how he came to produce poems like the *Epistle to Burlington* and *Satire II, ii* of his *Imitations of Horace*—poems that acknowledge the fact of human loss and mutability in one breath (or couplet), only to transcend it in the next, and that describe a landscape of permanence, plenitude, and community. By the same token, reading Swift's epistolary accounts of his anxiety-ridden visits with friends as well as his denials that these temporary visits could be translated into a lasting reunion, we can understand how Swift came to write verses like *A Pastoral Dialogue between Richmond-Lodge and Marble-Hill* and *Dr. Swift to Mr. Pope*—poems that assert the incontrovertible fact of human transience and loneliness and that reflect a landscape of destructive change on the one hand, of fragmentation and absence on the other.

vi

Swift's verses mocking or subverting the country house ideal as it pertains specifically to Ireland resemble in certain essential ways the verses just examined, but they tend to be more emphatic in their denial of the ideal and more bitter in exposing its fictive nature. Moreover, because of Ireland's direr circumstances and greater poverty, they are more insistent upon the reality of present decay than upon the possibility of future degeneration.

We have already noted in passing the way in which his *Part of the Seventh Epistle of the First Book of Horace, Imitated* undercuts the harmonious vision of the traditional country house poem. Swift is portrayed in this poem as a frequent guest of Lord Harley's at Windsor, to which he grows increasingly attached. He is soon dispatched to Ireland, however, presumably "To live in Plenty, Power and Ease" (92), though the description is more suggestive of a humiliating expatriation: "Poor S——t departs, and, what is worse,/With borrow'd Money in his Purse;/ Travels at least a Hundred Leagues,/And suffers numberless Fatigues" (93-96). Swift does in fact manage to establish a country "Seat" (98)— representing his house and garden at Laracor—but the venture quickly turns sour as Swift finds himself embroiled in financial problems, cheated by tenants and farmers to the point where he winds up "Above a Thousand Pounds in Debt" (115). Naturally his status as an inferior clergyman at the mercy of "The wicked Laity's contriving" (105) makes him even more a parody of the aristocratic estate dweller. It is telling that Swift should have chosen to bypass entirely the first half (lines 1-45) of Horace's own epistle, which evokes a world of blissful rural retirement ("my own delight to-day is not queenly Rome, but quiet Tibur or peaceful Tarentum" [45]), and instead chose to adapt only that portion of Horace's poem which deals with Volteius Mena, who, after being a habitual guest at Philippus's country estate (much like Swift at Windsor), buys his own farm and enthusiastically throws himself into rustic existence, only to have his pastoral dream turn into a nightmare of dead or stolen animals and failed crops.[61]

Swift's *Horace, Lib. 2. Sat. 6, Part of it imitated* offers another perspective on the poet's estrangement from the land. Once again Swift chooses to adapt only a portion of the original verse, thereby eliminating all matter alien to his own idiosyncratic vision and communicating a sense of fragmentation that qualifies not only Horace's literary form but his pastoral ideal as well. Swift's verse begins with a statement of yearning for a rustic retreat, here again modeled on his Laracor residence:

> I Often wish'd, that I had clear
> For Life, six hundred Pounds a Year,
> A handsome House to lodge a Friend,
> A River at my Garden's End,
> A Terras Walk, and half a Rood
> Of Land set out to plant a Wood.
>
> (1-6)

The dream becomes a reality in the next line—"Well, now I have all this and more"—yet Swift (in lines he added to the folio version of 1738, eleven years after its initial publication) hastens to inject a reminder of mortality and impermanence into the scene: "But here a Grievance seems to lie,/All this is mine but till I die" [9-10]. Almost immediately thereafter Swift is summoned to the despised world of the English Court (in an ironic reversal of his enforced departure to Ireland in his *Part of the*

Seventh Epistle of the First Book of Horace, Imitated), where "...in a Sea of Folly tost,/My choicest Hours of Life are lost" (105-6). Although he develops a close friendship with Harley ("Always together, *tête à tête*" [86]) and again becomes a familiar face at Windsor, the picture conveyed is not of a joyous reunion but of a restless exile. At the end of the poem there is no actual return to his estate, only an incessant, seemingly futile longing to be there: "Yet always wishing to retreat;/Oh, could I see my Country Seat" (107-8). (The final eight lines of the poem have occasionally been attributed to Pope. But they appear in Stella's transcript and, as Williams concludes, "they may be accepted as [Swift's]" [P, 1:197].) The verse is governed by the conditional and subjunctive tenses—by a mood that suggests, above all, unfulfilled desire and deprivation.

Pope, in reprinting Swift's partial imitation as a folio in 1738, added almost ninety lines of his own, and in so doing indirectly highlighted the contrast between their respective outlooks. The contrast is explicitly acknowledged in the printed "Advertisement," which declares: "The World may be assured, this Publication is no way meant to interfere with the *Imitations* of *Horace* by Mr. *Pope*: His Manner, and that of Dr. *Swift* are so entirely different, that they can admit of no Invidious Comparison."[62] The despairing subjunctive tone of Swift's partial imitation gives way in Pope's version of the poem to the confidently affirmed, joyous indicative tense, and the picture of the dispossessed poet longing fruitlessly for "sweet oblivion" changes to a scene of conviviality and gratified appetites, with the poet once more delightedly ensconced in his native setting: "O charming Noons! and Nights divine!/Or when I sup, or when I dine,/My Friends above, my Folks below,/Chatting and laughing all-a-row..." (133-36). Pope's verse is as suffused with feelings of comfort and fulfillment as Swift's is fraught with a sense of deprivation.

A more playful undercutting of country house existence occurs in *Stella at Wood-Park,* in connection with Charles Ford's estate, located about eleven miles outside Dublin in the county of Meath, on the road to Trim. The house and landscape at Wood-Park were undoubtedly shaped by Ford's elegant, aristocratic tastes, which took the form of a preference for all things English coupled with a disdain for most things Irish. (Ford eventually resettled in England more or less permanently.) In *Stella at Wood-Park,* the flowery, self-consciously poetic language used to describe the estate's surroundings—"purling Streams and Fountains bubbling" (27)—conveys the picture of an artificial, farcically romantic landscape, one antithetical to the kind of rural environs portrayed by Marvell, "Where ev'ry Thing does answer Use" (*Upon Appleton House,* 62). It is language entirely appropriate for surroundings that belong more to a world of wishful fantasy and imitation than to a world of concrete reality. Ford is here dubbed "Don Carlos," perhaps because of the penchant for praising Italian "Grandeur, Elegance and Wit" ascribed to him in *To Charles Ford Esqr. on his Birth-day* (93); while in one sense he performs the traditional role of magnanimous host ("He entertain'd [Stella] half a Year/With gen'rous Wines and costly Chear" [3-4]), in another sense he parodies this role since his pampering of Stella is done in a joking way, as part of "a merry Spight" (1) designed to make his guest so inured to the luxuries of Wood-Park that she will no longer be able to tolerate her rather meager and squalid lodgings at Ormond Key. In order to facilitate his aim of making Stella into a superior country lady, "Don *Carlos* made her chief Director,/That she might o'er the Servants hector" (5-6). So successful is Ford's stratagem that Stella rapidly acquires delicate and genteel tastes almost too rarefied for Wood-Park's own ambience:

> Now at the Table-Head she sits,
> Presented with the nicest Bits:
> She look'd on Partridges with scorn,
> Except they tasted of the Corn:
> A Haunch of Ven'son made her sweat,
> Unless it had the right *Fumette*.
> Don *Carlos* earnestly would beg,
> Dear Madam, try this Pigeon's Leg;
> Was happy when he could prevail
> To make her only touch a Quail.
>
> (9-18)

We see here a striking reversal of the typical dinner scene depicted in the country house poem, which tends to emphasize natural, homey foods (often the literal fruits of the earth), rather than quaint delicacies designed specifically for gourmet palates, and which is a leveling ritual that negates social divisions rather than a largely solitary, unsociable activity that re-inforces elitist and snobbish attitudes.

After Stella reluctantly returns to her Dublin lodgings, "She [strives] in vain to ape *Wood-Park*" (64), but its elegant furnishings have been re-placed by "The smutty Wainscot full of Cracks,/And half the Chairs with broken Backs" (55-56), and its "lordly Banquet[s] " are counterbalanced by Ormond Key's meager fare: "Two Bottles call'd for, (half her Store;/The Cupboard could contain but four;)/A Supper worthy of her self,/Five *Nothings* in five Plates of *Delph*" (65-68). The situation is comically resolved as Stella ". . . [falls] into her former Scene./Small Beer, a Her-ring, and the D——n" (71-72), and the poem ends on a lighthearted note, as Swift graciously assures Stella, "A Cottage is *Wood-Park* with you" (92). But the verse leaves us with two equally untenable extremes, repre-sented by the shift "From purling Streams and Fountains bubbling,/To

The Subversion of the Country House Ideal   139

Liffy's stinking Tide in *Dublin*" (27–28): country house artificiality and pretentiousness on the one hand, urban squalor and poverty on the other.

The poem *Robin and Harry* is a more explicit, and somewhat more devastating, satire on the country house ideal. Swift describes the respective situations of Robert and Henry Leslie, sons of the noted nonjuror, Charles Leslie. Robert inhabited the family seat at Glaslough, in county Monaghan, while his younger brother, Henry, having lost his commission in the Spanish army, retired with his Spanish wife to an estate at Market-Hill. In Swift's treatment, the two men are transformed into comic emblems of both the age's and the land's degeneration. The elder brother's act of giving alms to the poor, an important part of the manorial lord's function, is here made to reflect irresponsibility and contempt rather than Christian benevolence and charity: "Robin, to beggars, with a curse/ Throws the last shilling in his purse,/ And, when the Coach-man comes for pay,/ The Rogue must call another day" (1–4). Swift's Robin, who "Runs out in tongue, as in estate" (10), epitomizes prodigality. He is a squanderer of words, land, fortune, and inheritance alike, hence merely a parody of the traditional estate owner, who generously spreads his wealth around. Ultimately his seeming liberality reveals itself as selfish and greedy materialism: "Robin, who ne'r his mind could fix/ To live without a coach and six,/ To patch his broken fortunes, found/ A Mistress worth five thousand pound. . ." (29–32). The final stage of Robin's somewhat Hogarthian progress through life takes the form of his reduction to an absurd and implicitly impotent fop—a mere sign of a man:

> Old Robin, all his youth a sloven,
> At fifty two, when he grew loving,
> Clad in a coat of Podesway,
> A flaxen wig, and wast-coat gay,
> Powder'd from shoulder down to flank,
> In courtly style addresses Franck;
> Twice ten years older than his wife
> Is doom'd to be a Beau for life:
> Supplying those defects by dress
> Which I must leave the world to guess.
>
> (45–54)

This portrayal, however comic in tone, echoes Swift's descriptions elsewhere of the degeneration of noble families and their territorial possessions, expressed through similar images of prodigality, impoverishment, and impotency (see, e.g., PW, 12:53).

The younger brother Henry undergoes a similar process of deflation. Having brought his foreign bride back with him to Ireland, he establishes a mock country seat, where he parodically discharges the functions of hospitable host:

> Repairs a cabin gone to ruin,
> Just big enough to shelter two in;
> And, in his house, if any body come,
> Will make them welcome to his modicum:
> Where Goody Julia milks the Cows,
> And boyls Potatoes for her Spouse,
> Or darns his hose, or mends his Breeches,
> While Harry's fencing up his ditches.
>
> (21-28)

Speaking of Henry Leslie in his *Anecdotes,* William King observes that "With an estate, worth about 500*l.* per annum, he made a good figure, kept a very hospitable table, and was universally esteemed by all his neighbours and acquaintance" (P, 3:878, n. 24). In Swift's verse, however, Henry's estate dwindles into a tiny cabin and his "very hospitable table" becomes translated into milk and boiled potatoes—the typical meager fare of Irish peasants. As for making "a good figure," Swift's "Harry" deteriorates in physical appearance as well as in status: "From gold brocade and shining armour,/[He] Was metamorphos'd to a farmer;/His Grazier's coat with dirt besmear'd,/Nor, twice a week will shave his beard" (41–44). From this characteristically Swiftian metamorphosis, the change from a "golden" past to a "besmear'd" present, we can discern a suggestion of the land's and the age's decline.

That *Robin and Harry* was intended primarily as a *jeu d'esprit,* addressed to men with whom Swift was on friendly terms, does not cancel out the serious overtones of the verse. For Swift's literary "trifles" (and at one time or another he characterized most of his poems as such) more often than not were the equivalent of other writers' "heaviest" pieces. One indication of this is the fact that a number of Swift's *jeux d'esprit* were deemed by contemporaries to have transgressed the bounds of amiable amusement and to have the gravest of implications. They also produced serious consequences, on occasion provoking outcries against Swift's alleged abuse of his friends' hospitality. Swift's contemporaries could no doubt discern, in even the most "playful" of his writings, a characteristic cutting edge, a devastating (rather than cherishing) irony, which distinguished them from Sheridan's and Delany's companion pieces and removed them from the category of lighthearted trivia.

The controversial and alienating aspects of Swift's bagatelles are conveyed perhaps most clearly in his verse *The Journal,* yet another piece functioning to subvert the country house ideal, here parodically represented by Gaulstown House, the Westmeath estate of Lord Rochfort, formerly Speaker of the Irish House of Commons and Chief Baron of the Exchequer until the fall of the Tory ministry in 1714. The poem appeared in the Pope-Swift *Miscellanies* of 1732 under the title *The Country Life,* suggesting that it was in some fundamental way intended as a commentary on rural existence. That it was thought to be a rather unorthodox commentary is indicated by the criticisms it incurred. One, appearing in the *Whitehall Journal* as a prefatory letter to the poem and allegedly penned by one "Philoxenus," characterizes it as ". . . the Dean's satire upon the hospitable Baron, and the rest of his friends and messmates, for almost a whole summer," and declares: "The malevolents amongst us cast invidious reflections on the Dean for writing this poem; and say that it was odd in him, after the kindest entertainment for some months together at Mr. Rochford's house, who was Lord Chief Baron in this kingdom, in the last reign, to vanish away one morning *sans ceremonie*; and that it was ungrateful, after having sucked all the sweets of Gaulstown, to leave the following sting behind him."[63] The reference to Swift's abrupt and unceremonious leave-taking may call to mind Swift's similar departure from England in the fall of 1727 when, as Pope and Gay put it, he "went away from [them] so unexpectedly, and in so clandestine a manner" (C, 3:244). It would appear that Swift's mode of leaving his friends' hospitable lodgings was often as idiosyncratic, as potentially offensive and open to misinterpretation, as so many other aspects of his behavior.

Moreover, Dean Percival, another guest of Baron Rochfort during the summer of 1721, who was satirized in Swift's verse ("I might have told how oft *Dean Per——l*/Displays his Pedantry unmerciful,/How haughtily he lifts his Nose,/To tell what ev'ry School Boy knows. . ." [79–82]), responded with an angry poem of his own, called "A Description in Answer to the Journal," which also charges Swift with ingratitude and betrayal of hospitality: "Sometimes to Gallstown he will go,/To spend a month or two, or so,/Admires the baron, George and's spouse,/Lives well, and then lampoons the house."[64] Although Swift did defend himself against these allegations of his misconduct—insisting, for example, that works like *The Journal* were "only amusements in hours of sickness or leisure, or in private families, to divert ourselves and some neighbours, but were never intended for publick view, which is plain from the subjects and the careless ways of handling them" (C, 4:27)—his own words on various other occasions tend to lend at least some substance to the reservations expressed about his behavior as Baron Rochfort's guest. For example, in a letter to fellow guest Reverend Daniel Jackson, written about a week after his departure from Gaulstown, he asserts: "I had no mind to load you with the secret of my going, because you should bear none of the blame. I talk upon a supposition, that Mr. Rochfort had a mind to keep me longer, which I will allow in him and you, but not one of the family besides, who I confess had reason enough to be weary of a man, who entered into none of their tastes, nor pleasures, nor fancies, nor opinions, nor talk" (C, 2:407-8). Swift's implied protest against the Rochfort family's breach of hospitality in desiring the departure of their guest, combined with his tacit confession of his own violation of hospitality by behaving in a contrary, unsociable manner, points to a breakdown in traditional country house relationships, which we also see, ironically, in a letter in which Swift commends his friend Robert Cope (owner of Loughgall, an estate in county Armagh) for the excellence of his hospitality and his unexcelled abilities as host: "I am grown so peevish, that I can bear no other country-place in this kingdom [than Loughgall]; I quarrel everywhere else and sour the people I go to as well as myself. . . . The worst of it is, that if you grow weary of me (and I wonder why you do not), I have no other retreat" (453). Even making allowances for the characteristic Swiftian exaggeration evident here, we can discern in such statements Swift's feelings of disorientation and estrangement amidst the presumably serene, bucolic ambience and elegant surroundings of his friends' country estates.

Although Gaulstown was, at the time of Swift's visit, "old-fashioned" in its adherence to the principles of French formal gardening, it was a flourishing country estate whose owner was continually involved in making improvements. A decade earlier, Samuel Molyneux had described the canal being built on its grounds: "tis ye most noble canal by far I ever saw and cousin Dopping assured us as fine as any he had seen in England. It has three noble large Basons one at each end and one in the middle. Tis twenty one yds broad and 1000 long. A Terras Wall on each side planted with Lime trees. In the furthest Bason from the House stands on an Island a Pretty Summer House which very agreeably Determines your view. . . ."[65] Typically, Swift's verse is devoid of any description of Gaulstown's meticulously designed landscape. The latter is only fleetingly acknowledged, through terse (usually one-word) references to "Bowers" (7), "Ponds" (22), and the like. Instead of the "most noble canal," *The Journal* mentions a "Lake" in which "the *Dean* was drench'd" and where "Valiant *George*" (Baron Rochfort's eldest son) "sav'd his Oar, but lost his Hat" (68-72). These lines refer to incidents that actually occurred, as is evident from remarks Swift made to friends during his Gaulstown visit: ". . . I row or ride every day, in spite of the rain, in spite of a broken shin, or falling into the lakes, and several other trifling accidents" (C, 2:403). Such comments underscore the extent to which the poem's content justifies its title; for, as "Philoxenus" (for all his hostility to the poem) rightly observes, "It is a true and real Irish Journal."[66]

The Journal presents a series of rapidly moving and continually shifting scenarios that suggest a sense of frenetic activity verging on chaos and

that are reinforced through theatrical imagery: "So when this Circle we
have run,/The Curtain falls, and we have done./I might have mention'd
several facts,/Like *Episodes* between the Acts. . ." (59–62). By way of describing life at a country estate as it is shared by the distinguished host,
members of his family, and his select guests, the verse recounts a seemingly endless stream of debunking details and farcical events, a typically
Swiftian catalogue that, through its promiscuous juxtapositions, indirectly
undermines the carefully balanced, hierarchic order inherent in the country house ideal. That majestic and exalted view of life is likewise implicitly
challenged by the poem's persistent recording of trivia and commemoration of the quotidian:

> At Seven, the *Dean* in Night-gown drest,
> Goes round the House to wake the rest:
> At Nine, grave *Nim* and *George* Facetious,
> Go to the *Dean* to read *Lucretius.*
> At Ten, my Lady comes and Hectors,
> And kisses *George,* and ends or Lectures:
> And when she has him by the Neck fast,
> Hawls him, and scolds us down to Breakfast.
> We squander there an Hour or more,
> And then all hands, Boys, to the Oar
> All, Heteroclit *Dan* except,
> Who neither time nor order kept.
> But by peculiar Whimseys drawn,
> Peeps in the Ponds to look for Spawn:
> O'er sees the Work, or *Dragon* rowes,
> Or spoils a Text, or mends his Hose.
> Or—but proceed we in our *Journal* . . . .
>
>   (9–25)

The hour-by-hour account of the day's activities, which emphasizes the
passage of time, functions as a continuing reminder that life at Gaulstown
House is part of a world of transient existence, not a world of enduring
art or myth.

To emphasize this fact, the poem ends with a vision of impermanence
and the promise of imminent, dramatic change—an implicit denial of the
possibility of any solid structural endurance in time. Swift reflects upon
"How transient all things are below:/How prone to change in human life"
(116–17) and portrays the arrival of "*Clem* [Clement Barry, a distant
cousin of the then Lord Santry, who lived near Dublin] and his Wife"
(118) as a "Grand Event" (119) heralding the disruption of what little order previously existed:

> Henceforth expect a different survey,
> This House will soon turn topsy turvey;

> They talk of further Alterations,
> Which causes many Speculations.

(127–30)

Whereas the traditional country house is an emblem of stability and rootedness in the soil, Gaulstown House stands (or rather, threatens to crumble) as an emblem of incessant change.

Aubrey Williams's view of the poem as "a humorous yet telling illustration of the way in which the quite humdrum, and quite autobiographical, events of a manorial day may be turned into an artful and canny comment on the inherent dissatisfactions of mortal life" has validity, but it glosses over the more specific and topical grounds on which the bucolic ideal is undercut.[67] For the characterization we see here, of transience and continual alteration in connection with a country estate, bears resemblances to the treatment of the land's changing and mutable shapes that we find in so many other of Swift's writings, where they reflect particular aspects of the prevailing historical and topographical situation. Moreover, with the introduction of Baron Rochfort into the verse, the focus shifts from the moment-by-moment, trivial actions of private individuals to topical events of a far more public and consequential nature:

> But now, since I have gone so far on,
> A word or two of Lord Chief *Baron;*
> And tell how little weight he sets,
> On all Whig Papers, and Gazets:
> But for the Politicks of Pue,
> Thinks ev'ry Syllable is true;
> And since he owns the King of *Sweden*
> Is dead at last without evading.
> Now all his hopes are in the *Czar,*
> Why *Muscovy* is not so far,
> Down the black Sea, and up the Streights,
> And in a Month he's at your Gates:
> Perhaps from what the Packet brings,
> By *Christmas* we shall see strange things.

(97–110)

The reference in these lines is to the baron's strong Tory allegiances, here depicted as active Jacobite sympathies—indeed, as outright traitorous views since he is characterized as a supporter of Charles XII of Sweden and Peter the Great of Russia, who during the first decades of the eighteenth century posed the greatest threat to continued Hanoverian rule because of their hinted invasions of England. According to the passage just quoted from *The Journal,* Baron Rochfort clung to the desire for such an invasion even after the death of Charles XII in 1718, placing his hopes thereafter in the military capabilities of "*Muscovy.*" This, when we think about it, is really a rather shocking passage, in comparison with which the others allegedly expressing ingratitude or breach of hospitality pale into insignificance.

It is also the passage that best explains Swift's insistence that this poem was intended for private circulation only. For as we know from other writings of Swift's, *The Journal* was written during a period of lingering political hysteria and repression directed against Tory activists and suspected Jacobites; it was a "plot-discovering age" in which "an innocent man" of the wrong political persuasion could be "seized and imprisoned, and forced to lie several months in chains, while the Ministers were not at leisure to hear his petition, until they had prosecuted and hanged the number they proposed" (PW, 9:33). In a letter written less than a year later, in October 1722, to Robert Cope, Swift laments that "every Plot costs *Ireland* more than any Plot can be worth" and declares:

> I escaped hanging very narrowly a month ago; for a letter from *Preston,* directed to me, was opened in the post-office, and sealed again in a very slovenly manner, when *Manley* [the Postmaster] found it only contained a request from a poor curate. This hath determined me against writing treason: however, I am not certain that *this* letter may not be interpreted as comforting his most excellent majesty's enemies, since you have been a state prisoner [in 1715 by order of the Irish House of Commons]. Pray God keep all honest men out of the hands of lions and bears, and uncircumcised Philistines.— I hoped my brother *Orrery* [Charles Boyle, fourth Earl of Orrery] had loved his land too much to hazard it on Revolution principles. (C, 2:434–35)

It would appear that, given the political atmosphere then prevailing, Swift's lines on Baron Rochfort's continuing hopes for England's deliverance through foreign invasion were not only inhospitable and indiscreet, but highly provocative and potentially dangerous as well.

Swift would have been additionally familiar with the risks that an espouser of heterodox political sentiments could incur from the example of his friend Knightley Chetwode, who was also a staunch Tory and a Jacobite—though a good deal more active than Rochfort, for he actually went over to France to join the Duke of Ormonde in the Pretender's cause, returning to Ireland to find his situation so precarious that he had trouble finding somewhere to settle and was offered an empty coach house by Swift for sanctuary (C, 2:293 and n.). The correspondence between Swift and Chetwode during the period from the winter of 1721 through the winter of 1723 indicates the extent of the latter's legal difficulties stemming from government reprisals against him. Continually dodging and only narrowly escaping prosecution, Chetwode was repeatedly urged by Swift to forget about politics (Chetwode's hot temper and indiscreet na-

ture made this especially necessary) and tend to his own affairs, particularly his gardens and landscaping improvements: "Do you find that your
trees thrive and your drained bog gets a new coat? I know nothing so well
worth the enquiry of an honest man, as times run" (449).

Rereading the lines from *The Journal* in light of the preceding remark, we might well be tempted to interpret them as cautionary advice
(paradoxically, in seemingly the most incautious of literary pieces), hint-
ing that if the baron persists in remaining involved with Jacobite politics
and hoping for deliverance by the "*Czar*" instead of minding only his
gardens and landscaping improvements, his world is likely to "turn topsy
turvey." But a further—and substantial—complication to this whole matter arises from the fact that Swift himself was apparently quite an ad-
mirer of Charles XII and even came close on at least one occasion to
numbering himself among the latter's followers.[68] In the fall of 1709,
shortly after Charles's defeat at Pultowa by Peter the Great and his flight
across the Turkish frontier, Swift lamented to Ambrose Philips: "My
Heart is absolutely broke with the Misfortunes of K. of Sweden[;] nothing
pleased me more in the Thoughts of going abroad than some hopes I
had of being sent to that Court" (C, 1:153). Several years later, Pope
claimed that Swift, in the course of conversation, "gave us a Hint as if
he had a Correspondence with the King of Sweden."[69] In a letter to Ford
written about two years before his Gaulstown visit and less than a month
after Charles was killed at Fredrikshald, Swift avers: "I am personally
concerned for the Death of the K of Sweden, because I intended to have
beggd my Bread at His Court, whenever our good Friends in Power
thought fit to put me and my Brethren under the necessity of begging.
Besides I intended him an honor and a Compliment, which I never yet
thought a Crownd head worth, I mean, dedicating a Book [*An Abstract
of the History of England*] to him. Pray can you let me know how I could
write to the Count of Gillenburg" (C, 2:311). The count, as Harold Williams explains in a footnote to this letter, "had been Swedish ambassador
in London from 1710 to 1717 when, on 30 Jan., he was arrested for complicity in the plot to support a new Jacobite rising with 12,000 Swedish
troops." In the summer of that year he was permanently expelled from
England—an occurrence that did not, however, prevent Swift from changing his dedication of the *Abstract* from the deceased Swedish king to the
count: "a curious choice in either instance," as Williams observes (C, 3:63
n.), although it is perhaps not so very curious given Swift's self-confessed
"Infelicity in being so Strongly attached to Traytors (as they call them)
and Exiles, and State Criminalls" (C, 2:464). As late as June 1725, he was
indicating his continued association (or rather, his desire for a renewal of
his association) with Gyllenborg, asking the Continent-bound Reverend
James Stopford to find out if possible the count's address, for "... I

would be glad to know where to write to him, upon an Affair wherein he promised to inform me" (C, 3:63).

Returning once again to the relevant passage in *The Journal,* we can now perhaps arrive at a more accurate interpretation of its significance. To the extent that Swift shared his host's admiration for the Swedish king (though there is no indication he desired Charles's invasion of England) and to the extent that he was willing to ally himself publicly with those suspected of Jacobitism (though he himself continued to insist upon his adherence to the Revolutionary Settlement of 1689), the passage dealing with Baron Rochfort in *The Journal,* followed by the description of turmoil and impending chaos, is not so much an argument for giving up all worldly concerns and cultivating one's garden as a demonstration that such purely private and detached activity is impossible, given the contemporary political situation in Ireland and its inevitable impingement upon personal lives. The poem, in other words, is less a call to retreat to the country than it is a poetic statement in support of Swift's observation to Charles Ford that ". . . as the World is now turned, no Cloyster is retired enough to keep Politicks out" (C, 2:330). The country house ideal is overturned in *The Journal*— quite literally, "turn[ed] topsy turvey"—not because Baron Rochfort failed to heed the lessons of Epicurus, but because (among other reasons) Gaulstown House exists in a world where no private niche is safe from the intrusions of informers, Whiggish persecutors, and assorted plots whether real or fancied.

As though to demonstrate this fact, Swift follows up the passage concerning Baron Rochfort with the calamitous arrival of Clement Barry, which is characterized as a major invasion from the outside world (specifically, from the area around Dublin, the official seat of governmental power) into Gaulstown's not-so-enclosed garden realm. The invasion is described in language having political connotations:

> This Grand Event half broke our Measures,
> Their Reign began with cruel Seizures;
> The *Dean* must with his Quilt supply,
> The Bed in which these Tyrants lie. . . .

> (119–22)

This account of a new "Reign" instituted by "Tyrants" suggests a situation that parodically mirrors the larger public world beyond Rochfort's elegantly designed canal—a world where "cruel Seizures" (of private papers and correspondence, of political dissidents and suspected conspirators, of territorial possessions belonging to the discredited) continually occur.

I am not arguing here that *The Journal* should be construed as a serious political parable—its exuberant and comic tone clearly belies such a view—nor that any literal association is being made between Clement Barry and Whiggish persecutors of suspected Jacobites, but rather that the poem subtly conveys a certain mood and ambience, a sense of turmoil connected with the arbitrary actions of "Tyrants" and magnified by the sudden advent of a "Grand Event" on what moments before had been the small stage of Gaulstown's private theater, which in the political climate of the day would have almost certainly acquired broader dimensions and hinted at serious implications, even when treated in a burlesque manner. Just as, in *A Pastoral Dialogue between Richmond-Lodge and Marble-Hill,* we see the country house vision undermined by the threatened encroachments of South Sea brokers, so here, in *The Journal,* we see that same vision shattered by an actual invasion from without, devoid of explicit political meaning but described in political terms and occurring immediately after talk of the manorial lord's unrepentant desire for the fall of the House of Hanover. Here again we are reminded that the architectural and topographical shapes of a pastoral retreat cannot stand immutable, impervious to the continually changing political realities of the world outside the garden.

Political and economic realities are likewise seen to intrude upon Patrick Delany's would-be garden retreat, Delville, in the poem *An Epistle upon an Epistle,* where Swift manages to turn a description of Delany's elegant villa into a playfully expressed but nonetheless serious comment on the follies of political patronage and the perils of financial improvidence. The eleven-acre estate of Swift's friend was situated in Glasnevin, then a village about two miles beyond the city limits, which in effect represented Ireland's version of Twickenham in that it was picturesquely located along the shore of a river (in this case the Tolka), was both separate from yet close to the capital city, and served as the residence of an intellectual community that included Addison and Thomas Tickell, along with many families of distinction and prominent members of the nouveau riche class.[70] After his friend Richard Helsham relinquished his joint interest in the property, Delany, embarking on a series of ambitious and expensive building projects, leveled the original house then known as the Glen and designed his own villa, planning it as a place to entertain his friends on a rather lavish scale. The carefully landscaped grounds were intended to incorporate features of noted English gardens like Pope's Twickenham, where Delany stayed on several occasions, and Kent's Rousham, a particular favorite of Delany's, where he stayed as guest of Sir Clement Cotterell in 1743.[71] According to J. Cooper Walker, a late-eighteenth-century historian of the development of Hibernian gardening, Delany was the man who introduced into Ireland the "modern" style of gardening: "a style by which Pope, with whom he lived in habits of intimacy, taught him to

soften into a curve the obdurate and straight line of the Dutch; to melt
the terrace into a swelling bank, and to open his walks to catch the vicinal
country."[72]

When Mary Pendarves, a woman with aristocratic connections and
cultivated tastes, visited Ireland in 1731, she enjoyed Delany's hospitality
at Delville and subsequently, as Delany's second wife, she dedicated much
of her time and energies to further, even more extensive improvements of
the estate. From her letters we can get an idea of the infinite care that
went into furnishing and decorating the house: "The drawing-room hung
with tapestry, on each side of the door a japan chest, the curtains and
chairs crimson mohair, between the windows large glasses with gilt frames,
and marble tables under them with gilt frames; the bedchamber within
hung with crimson damask, bed chairs and curtains the same; *the closet
within it is most delightful. . . .*"[73] Her description of Delville's grounds,
moreover, communicates a typically Augustan zeal for landscape gardening and prospects and suggests the extent to which the Delany estate was
designed to satisfy the traditional aesthetic requirements of country
house existence:

> On the left hand of the bowling-green is a terrace-walk that takes in
> a sort of a parterre, that will make the prettiest orangery in the
> world, for it is an oval of green, planted round in double rows of elm-
> trees and flowering shrubs, with little grass walks between them,
> which will give a good shelter to exotics. The terrace . . . is bounded
> at one end by a wall of good fruit, in which there is a door that leads
> to another very large handsome terrace-walk, with double rows of
> large elms, and the walk well gravelled, so that we may walk securely
> in any weather. . . . About half way up the walk there is a path that
> goes up that bank to the remains of an old castle (as it were), from
> whence there is an unbounded prospect all over the country: under
> it is a cave that opens with an arch to the terrace-walk, that will
> make a very pretty grotto. . . .[74]

Mary Delany's own drawings of the Glasnevin landscape indicate
that she had absorbed her optical and aesthetic lessons well in the cultured
English society in which she circulated. One such drawing, suggestive of
a Claude Lorrain painting, is framed by two trees on either side, assumes
an elevated angle of vision, consists of alternating bands of light and dark,
each representing a separate plane at a different distance from the viewer,
and leads the eye from the foreground to the far horizon.[75] This rendering
of landscape would have been consistent with Mrs. Delany's feeling that
Delville afforded an escape from the urban decay she observed spreading
through large areas of Dublin, epitomized by "narrow streets and dirty-
looking houses."[76] Presumably, from the combined vantage and sanctuary
of her Glasnevin villa, she was safe from visual (not to mention olfactory)

assault by Dublin's squalor, yet at the same time she was near enough to enjoy "a most extensive and beautiful prospect of the harbour and town of Dublin,"[77] as well as an unobstructed view of the lovely Wicklow Mountains further south. In her more immediate purview, she would have seen, instead of the cramped, excremental environs of the Liberties, the peaceful brook running from the Tolka River through her property, her stables, her flower and vegetable gardens, the guesthouse surrounded by ripening melons and grapes, and the park beyond furnished with grazing cows and deer, which, in her own words, gave to the scene a "rurality" that was "wonderfully pretty."[78]

Even before Mrs. Delany's tenure as reigning hostess and landscape designer at Delville, visitors to the Glasnevin villa attested to its distinctive topographical and ornamental features, ones with which Swift, as a frequent guest of Delany's, would have been familiar. Letitia Pilkington, for example, recalls an occasion when she "met [Swift and Delany] on a noble terrace whose summit was crowned with a magnificent portico, where painting and sculpture displayed their utmost charms."[79] The verses she composed celebrating Delville's attributes reveal the ways in which the estate lent itself to pastoral encomia and fit in with traditional country house ideology:

Hail, happy *Delville!* blissful seat!
The muse's best belov'd retreat!
With prospects large and unconfined;
Blest emblem of their master's mind!
Where fragrant gardens, painted meads,
Wide-op'ning walks, and twilight shades —
Inspiring scenes! — elate the heart!
Nature improved, and raised by Art,
So Paradise delightful smil'd,
Blooming and beautifully wild.[80]

Such poetic fictions were rooted in the facts surrounding not only Delville's famed gardens but also the Delanys' often grandiose displays of country house hospitality—a hospitality that was, as F. Elrington Ball notes, "unceasing" and that was extended to numerous personal friends as well as eminent literary and political figures of the day.[81] The lavish meals prepared by the Delanys for their dinner guests occasioned much conversation and, one must assume, satisfied the most discerning of palates. One such meal, served to four guests, consisted of "Fish, Beefsteaks, Soup, Rabbits and Onions, Fillet Veal" for the first course, "Turkey Pout, Salmon Grilde, Pick[led] Sal[mon], and Quaills, Little Terrene Peas, Cream, Mushrooms, Terrene, Apple Pye, Crab, Leveret, Cheesecakes" for the second course, and multivarious desserts that included "Blamange,

Cherries, Dutch Cheese, Raspberries and Cream, Sweetmeats and Jelly, Strawberries and Cream, Almond Cream, Currant and Gooseberries, [and] Orange Butter."[82]

Swift's sole poetic record of Delville, *An Epistle upon an Epistle,*[83] predictably enough omits all reference to the beauties and elegancies of the landscape, just as it omits all mention of its owners' renowned hospitality and of the festive gatherings regularly taking place there. It is not that Swift was oblivious to Delville's attractions or to the gracious hospitality it offered. When, for example, he attempted to entice Pope to visit Ireland in the spring of 1730, he was not above using Delville as a drawing card of sorts (C, 3:397), and he observed to John Barber that "Doctor Delany lives very happyly and hospitably, entertain[ing] his old friends..." (C, 4:175-76). Yet when it came to writing his verses on Delville, Swift chose to ignore these praiseworthy qualities of its host and instead focused entirely on the negative and laughable aspects of Delany's country house existence. *An Epistle upon an Epistle* portrays Delany's ambitious architectural undertakings and continual improvements of the land as frenetically pointless activities that result in ludicrous metamorphoses:

> You sprung an Arch, which in a Scurvy
> Humour, you tumbled Topsy Turvy.
> You change a Circle to a Square,
> Then to a Circle, as you were:
> Who can imagine whence the Fund is,
> That you *Quadrata* change *Rotundis?*
>
> (71-76)

There may be an oblique allusion in these lines to *Upon Appleton House,* where the poet, in extolling the modest design of Fairfax's estate, asserts, "Let others vainly strive t'immure/The *Circle* in the *Quadrature!*" (45-46), and proceeds to describe the spiritual rapport between the noble lord and his dwelling: "But where he comes the swelling Hall/Stirs, and the *Square* grows *Spherical*..." (51-52). By contrast, the structural features of Delville do not alter themselves naturally and freely, of their own accord and by an inner mystical movement, in order to accommodate themselves to their master's measurements, but instead are continually being destroyed and rebuilt by him, victimized by his ever-changing whims. Swift's lines also contain echoes of Horace's *Epistle I, i,* where the poet chides himself for his inconsistencies and inner conflicts: "... quid, mea cum pugnat sententia secum,/quod petiit spernit, repetit quod nuper omisit,/aestuat at vitae disconvenit ordine toto,/diruit, aedificat, mutat quadrata rotundis?" ("... what, when my judgement is at strife with itself, scorns what it craved, asks again for what it lately cast aside; when it shifts like a tide, and in the whole system of life is out of joint, pulling down, building up, and changing square to round?" [97-100]).[84]

Like Gaulstown House in *The Journal*, Delville in *An Epistle upon an Epistle* is pervaded by an atmosphere of frantic confusion and seems perennially on the verge of collapse, always about to be turned "Topsy Turvy." Ultimately Delany's villa emerges as part of a fantasy world in which Delany, as a result of his building endeavors, becomes enmeshed in comic delusion:

> To *Fame* a Temple you Erect,
> A *Flora* does the Dome protect;
> Mounts, Walks, on high; and in a Hollow
> You place the *Muses* and *Apollo;*
> There shining 'midst his Train, to Grace
> Your Whimsical, Poetick Place.
>
> These Stories were, of old, design'd
> As Fables: But you have refin'd
> The Poets Mythologick Dreams,
> To real Muses, Gods, and Streams.
> Who wou'd not swear, when you contrive thus,
> That you're *Don Quixote Redivivus?*

(77-88)

Whereas Pope enthusiastically encouraged his friends' architectural and gardening projects, Swift debunks Delany's similar endeavors and admonishes him: "To Your Ambition put an End" (114).

Swift's scornful treatment of Delville in this verse was in all likelihood influenced in part by his perception of the equivocal and schizophrenic role it was being made to play: as a small suburban villa trying to be a traditional country house that could sustain a way of life in the grand style. We have already noted Swift's awareness of the fictions governing the conventional but no longer valid distinction between city and country. An outgrowth of this awareness was his role as perspicacious critic and exposer of suburbia, that bastardized form of existence rooted by its very nature in pretense and delusion, since it was bereft of the hallowed traditions of genuine country existence even though it strove to emulate them, and since it represented a flight from the city while simultaneously reflecting a desire to continue enjoying the amenities of urban life. Inevitably suburban life was characterized by a certain kind of inauthenticity. Although Delany's reason for acquiring Delville was to provide a place to offer old-fashioned hospitality and to hold convivial gatherings of a close-knit intellectual community, the villa was inaccessible to many would-be visitors because of its relative distance from town and its restricted space for accommodating overnight lodgers. Swift makes this clear on various occasions in his correspondence. As he explained to Mary Pendarves after her return to England, ". . . Dr. Delany lives entirely at Delville, the town air will not agree with his lady, and in winter there is no seeing him or dining with him but by those who keep coaches, and they must return the moment after dinner" (C, 4:298).

From Swift's perspective, Delville was thus something of a white elephant; its basic impracticality made it a fitting habitation for a *"Don Quixote Redivivus."* Swift perceived in its owner a basic failure to deal with reality, at least with the specific geographic and economic realities of Irish existence, which included poor roads that were particularly hazardous in cold and rainy weather and coach fares that could easily become a serious drain on already dwindling purses. Concerning the first of these circumstances, it is interesting to recall that Swift, during the period of his association with the Tory ministry, expressed particular appreciation for the ease with which social life in England could be conducted on a regular basis, in contrast to the difficulties that were encountered in Ireland: "That's something charms me mightily about London; that you go dine a dozen miles off in October, stay all day, and return so quickly: you cannot do any thing like this in Dublin"—to which comment Deane Swift appended an explanatory footnote: "When this letter was written there were no turnpike roads in *Ireland*" (JS, 1:38). As for the second difficulty confronting visitors to Delville, the financial one, Swift complained in a letter to Lord Orrery that "Dr Delany costs two *thirteens* [two English shillings] to be visited in wet weather, by which I should be out of pocket nine pence when I dine with Him" (C, 4:367). Repeated petulant entries in the *Journal to Stella* indicate that Swift was acutely conscious of—one might even say obsessive about—the expenditures required for coach fares, and more reluctant than most to accept them as an ordinary and necessary expense.

Clearly, Swift very much felt the loss of Delany from the Dublin scene, which left him in a state of increasing isolation: "All our evening Meetings here have been long broke up, the Grattans are never to be found, [and] Dr Delany is wholly a Countryman at a mile and half distance" (C, 4:397). Underlying Swift's laments was the memory of regular meetings of the Thursday Club, over which Swift himself presided, at Delany's townhouse on Stafford Street, before the move to Glasnevin. Swift's partly amused, partly critical view of Delville is summed up in an observation he made to Mrs. Pendarves: "Dr. Delany hath long ago given up his house in town. His Dublin friends seldom visit him till the swallows come in. He is too far from town for a winter visit, and too near for staying a night in the country manner; neither is his house large enough; it minds me of what I have heard the late Duchess [presumably the Duchess of Somerset] complain, that Sion House was a 'hobbedehoy, neither town nor country' "(456). In light of this perception, it is not surprising that Swift poetically depicted Delany's residence as part of an insubstantial and illusory world of ambiguous, continually changing shapes—a world that was neither this nor that.

The illusoriness of Delville's world in Swift's eyes was also in part caused by Delany's failure to acknowledge the actual state of his own finances. Delany's extravagant ways were an open secret among his contemporaries. His varied architectural and landscaping projects required expenditures that far exceeded his relatively modest income. As Ball bluntly puts it: "Throughout his life Delany displayed an ambition of making a figure in the world, and in order to do so he lived in a style that his means did not justify. At Delville he sought to gain the reputation of an improver, and for many years he indulged there in reckless outlay."[85] Toward the end of 1729, the extremity of his economic circumstances prompted Delany to write "An Epistle to His Excellency John *Lord* Carteret Lord Lieutenant of *Ireland*," which contained an extended complaint about the meagerness of his income and which none too subtly solicited additional preferment to cover his growing expenses: "My Lord, I'd wish—to *pay the Debts I owe,*—/I'd wish besides—to *build,* and to *bestow*" (93–94; P, 2:474). The publication of this epistle was the immediate occasion for Swift's *Epistle upon an Epistle.* Delany's poem has an embarrassingly self-pitying as well as self-justifying tone, which made it ripe for a healthy dose of Swiftian mockery:

> Would my good Lord but cast up the Account,
> And see to what my Revenues amount,
> My Titles ample! but my Gains so small,
> That one good Vicarage is worth 'em all —
> And very wretched, sure, is he, that's double,
> In nothing, but his Titles, and his Trouble.
>
> (39–44; P, 2:472–73)

The situation in which Delany placed himself by writing his epistle furnished Swift with suitable material for the comic treatment of a recurring concern of his—the poet-patron relationship along with its attendant humiliations and frustrations. "You can't, grave Sir, believe it hard,/That you, a low *Hibernian* Bard,/Shou'd cool your Heels a while, and wait/ Unanswer'd at your *Patron*'s Gate" (3–6).

The depiction of Delany as a whining place-seeker, the author of "... Begging, Vain, Familiar Letters" (118), has the effect of comically undercutting his pose as gentleman landowner and lord of the estate. By incorporating allusions to Delany's "Epistle to Lord Carteret" into his own poem, Swift underscores the fact that his friend's pretensions as generous manorial host, as well as his ambitious landscaping projects, are rooted in fantasy—founded on thin air. The vanity, affectation, and self-delusion that characterize these pretensions are highlighted in a passage where Swift interweaves words straight out of Delany's "Epistle" with his own humorous elaboration upon them:

> But you must have Cascades, and all
> *Ierna*'s Lake, for your Canal,
> Your Vistos, Barges, and (A Pox on
> All Pride) our *Speaker* for your Coxon:
> It's Pity that he can't bestow you
> Twelve Commoners in Caps to Row you.
> Thus *Edgar* proud, in Days of Yore,
> Held Monarchs labouring at the Oar;
> And as he pass'd, so swell'd the *Dee*
> Inrag'd, as *Ern* would do at thee.
>
> (37–46)

Delany here emerges as another Belinda, sailing along "*Ierna*'s Lake" (the Lake of Erin, where Sir Ralph Gore, Speaker of the Irish House of Commons, had a villa) like a male Cleopatra in a stance of mute self-worship. The magnitude of Delany's pretensions underscores, through contrast, the modesty of his social and economic status and reinforces the fictionality surrounding the country house myth as it is portrayed here.

Characteristically, and reminiscent of his depiction of Marble Hill, Swift overlooks the existing strengths and positive potential of Delville in order to predict future disaster:

> But you forsooth, your *All* must squander,
> On that poor Spot, call'd *Del-Ville,* yonder:
> And when you've been at vast Expences
> In Whims, Parterres, Canals and Fences:
> Your Assets fail, and Cash is wanting
> For farther Buildings, farther Planting.
>
> (59–64)

As in all of his writings, Swift here insists on the inextricable links between aesthetic and economic matters, refusing to contemplate the beauties and elegancies of the landscape in a vacuum, apart from the money begged, borrowed, or stolen to put them on display for the acquisitive, carefully conditioned Augustan eye.

Considered within the larger context of Swift's canon, the depiction of Delville in *An Epistle upon an Epistle* in many ways represents a comic version of the scornful depictions recurring throughout his prose tracts in which Ireland, revealed as a land of poverty and desolation, is also a land that hides its shame beneath layers of silks and other fineries imported from abroad: a land where a farmer on the verge of starvation will buy expensive imported coats for his wife rather than being satisfied with the cheaper and far more practical, if less fashionable, native woolen goods. Delany's pretensions may be seen on one level as a comic counterpart to "that monstrous Pride and Vanity" Swift discerned and attacked in his countrymen, "who, in the Midst of Poverty, are suffered to run into all Kind of Expence and Extravagance in Dress, and particularly priding themselves to wear nothing but what cometh from Abroad. . . . those, whose Fortunes can hardly support their Families in the Necessaries of Life, will needs vye with the Richest and Greatest amongst us, to the Ruin of themselves and their Posterity" (PW, 9:200). I do not mean to suggest that Swift was consciously drawing a parallel between Delany's activities and those just described, but the fact remains that the same set of assumptions and perceptions underlies both Swift's view of his friend's landscape and his contemplation of the contemporary political and economic scene. The discrepancy between appearance and reality that defines the relationship of Delville's elegant landscape to Delany's empty purse is essentially the same discrepancy that Swift dramatizes in terms of Ireland as a whole, which in its senseless extravagance is like "a man in an embroidered coat begging out of Newgate in an old shoe" (PW, 12:127) and which has stubbornly failed to learn the lesson that "those who possess most Wealth, make the least Parade; which they leave to others, who have nothing else to bear them out. . ." (7). In Delany's variation on the importation of luxuries from abroad, his adoption of the principles of English landscape gardening with its expensive if tasteful mode of conspicuous consumption, we see a comic version (one treated with a cherishing rather than with the more usual devastating irony) of Ireland's self-destructive folly and approaching ruin. We see, in addition, a comic exposure of the reasons why the country house way of life was necessarily anomalous and, for the most part, illusory in the context of eighteenth-century Ireland.

The anomalous nature of the country house way of life is established beyond doubt in Swift's verse description of Sheridan's Cavan residence, *To Quilca, a Country House in no very good Repair:*

> Let me my Properties explain,
> A rotten Cabbin, dropping Rain;
> Chimnies with Scorn rejecting Smoak;
> Stools, Tables, Chairs, and Bed-steds broke. . . .
>
> (1-4)

Quilca, upon which Swift heaped almost obsessive attention, as frequent passages in his poetry, prose pieces, and letters demonstrate, comes to epitomize his somber perceptions of Ireland's terrain and its architectural structures. It emerges in effect as a testament to the death of traditional country house existence in an environment clearly incapable of sustaining it. The surrounding Cavan landscape reflects an absolute negation of *concordia discors,* natural plenitude, and cosmic harmony:

> Here Elements have lost their Uses,
> Air ripens not, nor Earth produces:
> In vain we make poor *Sheelah* toil,
> Fire will not roast, nor Water boil.

(5–8)

Ordinarily the elements are important and active participants in life at a country house, contributing significantly to both its aesthetic and its practical features. Addressing Penshurst, for example, Jonson observes: "Thou joy'st in better marks, of soil, of air,/Of wood, of water; therein thou art fair" (7–8). And at Carew's Saxham, "Water, Earth, Ayre, did all conspire,/To pay their tributes to [its] fire" (29–30).[86] In place of a benevolent and fruitful genius of the place, we have, at Quilca, "Thro' all the Vallies, Hills, and Plains,/The Goddess *Want* [who] in Triumph reigns" (9–10). Quilca in every possible respect reverses the way of life prevailing at a Penshurst or an Appleton House, "Where ev'ry Thing does answer Use" (62). Its basic disfunctionality is demonstrated also by servants who refuse to perform their designated offices and by laborers who no longer fulfill their prescribed tasks: ". . . our Servants eat and drink like the Devil, and pray for Rain, which entertains them at Cards and Sleep, which are much lighter than Spades, Sledges, and Crows. Their maxim is: *Eat like a Turk,/Sleep like a Dormouse;/Be last at Work,/At Victuals foremost"* (C, 3:64).

Ironically reversing the usual portrayal of a country house as a noble, majestic edifice that mirrors the exalted qualities of its inhabitants, Swift depicts the way in which Quilca's architectural disintegration reflects the collapse of strong familial ties and comes to define the interrelationships among the people residing in it, producing domestic dissension between host and hostess, warfare between servant and master, and general discord between friend and friend. The interconnectedness of landscape and human behavior emerges with a vengeance from Swift's descriptions of Cavan: "This is the dirtiest town, and, except some few, the dirtiest people I ever saw, particularly the mistress, daughter, and servants of this house. . . . By the conduct of this family [the Sheridans], I apprehend the day of judgement is approaching; the father against the daughter, the wife against the husband, &c. I battle as well as I can, but in vain, and you shall change my name to Doctor *Shift"* (C, 4:426–27). Both the visitors and the permanent residents become infected by, and thus begin to mirror, the environment, according to *The Blunders, Deficiencies, Distresses, and Misfortunes of Quilca:*

The Ladies and the Dean's Servants growing fast into the Manners and Thieveries of the Natives: The Ladies themselves very much corrupted; the Dean perpetually storming, and in Danger of either losing all his Flesh, or sinking into Barbarity for the Sake of Peace.

Mrs. *Dingley* full of Cares for herself, and Blunders and Negligence for her Friends. Mrs. *Johnson* sick and helpless: The Dean deaf and fretting; the Lady's Maid aukward and clumsy; *Robert* lazy and forgetful; [and] *William* a pragmatical, ignorant and conceited Puppy. (PW, 5:220-21)

Images of convivial feasts and communal dances are replaced by battle terminology: "Mutiny . . . among the Servants" occasioned by inadequate sleeping accommodations; "*Bellum atque faeminam:* Or, a Kitchen war between Nurse and a nasty Crew of both Sexes; she to preserve Order and Cleanliness, they to destroy both; and they generally are Conquerors"; and "*Bellum lactaeum*: Or, the milky Battle, fought between the Dean and the Crew of *Quilca*" in which "the Dean got the Victory; but the Crew of *Quilca* begin to rebel again. . ." (PW, 5:219-21). Despite the comic tone evident here, the descriptions of Swift's visits to Quilca convey a sense of struggle and a spirit of contentiousness that demand to be taken with at least some degree of seriousness.

In contrast to the typical guests at an eighteenth-century country house, who spend their time leisurely contemplating their host's carefully arranged gardens or giving gentlemanly assistance to their host's projects for improving the landscape, Swift and Stella, together with their Dublin entourage, are forced to undertake strenuous labor in order to obtain the most basic creature comforts—indeed, to ensure their very survival. This is not surprising, considering that Quilca was "a little obscure Irish Cabbin" situated in "a very wild country" (C, 3:84, 60), whose inhabitants were reduced to living "among a Million of wants" (89). As a guest of Sheridan, Swift immediately found himself occupying the role not of admiring spectator or innovative designer, but rather of basic handyman and repairman, as well as constant fender against ever-threatening catastrophes:

The Grate in the Ladies Bed-chamber broke, and forced to be removed, by which they were compelled to be without Fire, the Chimney smoking intolerably; and the Dean's great Coat was employed to stop the Wind from coming down the Chimney, without which Expedient they must have been starved to Death. . . .
April 28. This Morning the great Fore-door quite open, dancing Backwards and Forwards with all its Weight upon the lower Hinge, which must have been broke if the Dean had not accidentally come and relieved it. (PW, 5:220)

Swift found himself "levelling mountains and raising stones, and fencing against [the] inconveniencies of a scanty lodging. . ." (C, 3:60). Although he is shown to be capable on occasion of having some limited success in applying temporary expedients and thereby stemming the tide of disaster, his more characteristic pose is that of a person whose exertions are largely futile: "My first attempt was to repair the *Summer House,* and make the way passable to it; whereupon *Boreas* was so angry, that he blew off the roof" (C, 4:427). Even something as basic as lighting a fire for food and warmth—which is automatically taken for granted in country house existence, where both warmth and nourishment are always plentiful—proves to be a major problem amidst the rocky, damp, bog-filled terrain of county Cavan. "The cursed turf is two hours kindling, and two minutes decaying," complains Swift from Quilca, in the midst of a cold winter during which storms are a frequent occurrence (431). Sheridan's "country house," like Swift's "townhouse," was located near a body of water with an unfortunate propensity for flooding, which aggravated the problem: "The Lake is strangely overflown, and we are desperate about Turf, being forced to buy it three Miles off" (C, 3:64). Apparently the purchase of kindling material was not an adequate solution, for in other instances the guests were compelled to look for it and bring it home themselves: "Not a Bit of Turf this cold Weather, and Mrs. *Johnson* and the Dean in Person, with all their Servants forced to assist at the Bog in gathering up the wet Bottoms of old Clamps" (PW, 5:219).

To be sure, there were for Swift other, more positive associations with Quilca, which presumably help to explain his recurring visits to the cabin and his decision to use it as a retreat while completing *Gulliver's Travels.* As he confessed to Chetwode, despite the wild and primitive conditions in Cavan, ". . . there are some agreeablenesses in it, or at least I fancy so" (C, 3:60). And although he complained at times about "want of victuals" (60), he made it clear elsewhere that he was hardly starving: "Wildfowl is cheap, and all very good, except the ducks. . . . It is nothing to have a present of a dozen snipes, teal, woodcock, widgeon, duck and mallard, &c." (C, 4:430-31). In the poem *A Receipt to Restore Stella's Youth,* he treats life at Quilca in a lighthearted, playful manner. Comparing Stella to a starving cow, "Meager and lank with fasting grown" (7), Swift advises that she "Be sent to *Quilca* down to graze;/Where Mirth, and Exercise, and Air,/Will soon [her] Appetite repair" (26-28). For every humorous invitation to Quilca that Swift proffered, however, there were at least two somber admonitions to stay away. Writing to Chetwode in the spring of 1725, he declared in no uncertain terms: "I can give you no encouragement to go out of your way for a visit to this dismal place; where we have hardly room to turn ourselves, and where we send five miles round for a lean sheep. I never thought I could battle with so many inconveniencies, and make use of so many Irish expedients, much less could I invite any friend to share in them" (C, 3:61). His continual complaints about weather "so foul that [he] cannot walk at all" (C, 4:426) and about environs "so perpetually and abominably dirty" that they destroy all desire to be outdoors (430) underscore Quilca's unsuitability for usual country house pastimes and activities.

Swift seems to have had a love-hate relationship with Quilca; he was simultaneously attracted to and repelled by its unadulterated rusticity and primitive conditions, its severe climate, and its harsh, angular beauty. Cavan's strange, unmanageable landscape impressed itself on his mind and suffused his imagination, not unlike the way Monaghan, another cold, northern Irish county similarly characterized by bogs and drumlins, captured the imagination of the twentieth-century poet and novelist Patrick Kavanagh, whose autobiography vividly evokes its shapes and textures and highlights the landscape's dualistic aspects of beauty amidst bleakness and desolation, of cultivated ground bordered by wild, primeval country.

> Around our house there stood little hills all tilled and tame. Yellow flame-blossoms of the whin lit bonfires all over the landscape; the whin was as persistent and as fertile as sin and disease. The sunny side of the hills was good soil and boasted some tall thorn trees, but the black side facing the north was crabbed and poverty-stricken and grew only stunted blackthorns and sorrel plants. There were no trees to speak of except the poplar and the sally; here and there a cranky old elm which had survived the crying of a cold kitchen spread about his trunk and tried to look a forest. From the tops of the little hills there spread a view right back to the days of Saint Patrick and the druids.[87]

Perhaps more than any other place, Cavan became for Swift a country of the mind as well as a physical terrain, which reflected his profoundly ambivalent feelings toward Ireland and his basic insight into the irrelevance of pastoral and country house conceptions for the Irish landscape.

The most sustained poetic subversion of the country house ideal in connection with Ireland appears in Swift's verses related to Market-Hill, the estate owned by Sir Arthur Acheson, Swift's "Gosford Knight," who was a fifth baronet of Scottish descent, married to the daughter of the Right Honorable Philip Savage, Chancellor of the Exchequer in Ireland for many years and a personal friend of Swift's. Swift paid three lengthy visits to Market-Hill, staying for periods ranging from three to eight months: from June 1728 to February 1729; from June 1729 to October 1729; and from the end of June 1730 to the end of September 1730. The Achesons owned a townhouse on Capel Street, in the northern part of Dublin, but resided mainly at Market-Hill, located near the city of Armagh, where, as Harold Williams notes, they "entertained Swift with the most generous and lavish hospitality" (P, 3:847). It was a hospitality clearly appreciated by their guest. As Swift explained in a letter to Sheridan, who was awaiting his friend's overdue visit to Quilca, "yet I would contrive to be pres'd more to stay [at Market-Hill] till *Christmas* . . . . And my Reason of Staying is, to be here the Planting and Pruning Time, &c. I hate *Dublin,* and love the Retirement here, and the Civility of my Hosts" (C, 3:296).

Because of its successful linen trade, Armagh was probably the most prosperous area in Ireland during this period. Swift himself remarked that the county of Armagh, "excepting it's [*sic*] cursed roads, and want of downs to ride on, is the best part I have seen of Ireland" (C, 4:536). Market-Hill itself was "situated in the midst of a fertile country, the extensive demesne and splendid castle of Gosford, the property of Viscount Gosford, adding greatly to its beauty."[88] Acheson's estate would have provided suitable subject matter for a literary tribute to the land, to its noble inhabitants, and to the exalted values it embodies, consistent with the country house tradition. Instead we are presented with the contrary: irreverent, undisciplined verses (fifteen in all), dominated by a tone of burlesque and travesty and filled with images of confusion, collapse, and estrangement. Despite Swift's light-hearted description of his activities as the Achesons' guest, the poems he wrote commemorating his visits— including the "family verses of mirth [written] by way of libels on my Lady" (C, 3:311)—treat serious, potentially ominous matters and can no more be dismissed as mere bagatelles than any of the other seemingly only playful country house verses. In the final analysis, Sir Arthur's estate is made to stand as a witness to the passing away both of a private Augustan community (Swift and the Achesons, who grew increasingly distant after Swift's last visit in 1730) and of the public world necessary to sustain such a community. (The fact that the Achesons themselves separated not long after his visits provides a kind of retroactive support for Swift's vision of dissolution.)

The disintegration of the landscape, along with the human ties it symbolizes, is treated in a broadly burlesque vein in *The Revolution at Market-Hill,* which deals not only with Acheson but also with his Armagh neighbor, Henry Leslie, the "Harry" of the verse *Robin and Harry.* (Swift was a guest of Leslie's also during the summer of 1730.) The poem opens with "An odd Triumvirate of Friends" (2)—Swift, Acheson, and Leslie— who, as "Three [banish't] Suff'rers in a ruin'd Cause" (6-7), come together at Market-Hill. The scene appears to be set for Swift's version of Pope's grotto: a blessed retreat where unpopular and persecuted companions ("Chiefs, out of War, and Statesmen, out of Place" [*Imitations of Horace, Satire II, i,* 126]) can shut out the dissensions of a corrupt public world and form a noble community of their own. The harmony of purpose proves illusive, however, for the prospect of peaceful coexistence dissolves as impending class warfare divides "the Pair of humble Gentry" (17) on the one hand and the "Knight" (20) "in his lordly Castle" (19) on the other. Swift and Leslie, "Condemn'd to live in Service hard" (11) while Acheson "triumphant reigns betwixt" (20), resent the inequities of the social hierarchy: "To be his Slaves [they] must pay him Rent;/ Attend him daily as their *Chief,*/Decant his Wine, and carve his Beef" (22–24). Once again Swift, eschewing the ideological mystifications traditionally used to gloss over disparities in economic status and social rank, exposes these disparities, playfully but not without serious import, as the consequences of an unfair distribution of wealth and power: "O Fortune, 'tis a Scandal for thee/To smile on those who are least worthy./ Weigh but the Merits of the three,/His [Acheson's] Slaves have ten Times more than he" (25–28). Emphatically rejecting the spirit of cosmic Toryism, the poet asserts himself as a determined leader of rebellion:

> Come *Spaniard,* let us from our Farms
> Call forth our Cottagers to Arms;
> Our Forces let us both unite,
> Attack the Foe at Left and Right. . . .

> (43–46)

The poem makes us acutely aware of differences in social rank, as well as the power relationships and the clearly differentiated functions ensuing from them. In the course of the verse narrative we meet *Hannah,* Lady Acheson's waiting maid (67), "valiant *Dennis,*" Sir Arthur's butler (85), *Peggy Dixon,* the Achesons' housekeeper (86), and *Lorimer,* their agent (96). These personages constitute a cast of behind-the-scenes characters who perform services essential to the country house way of life but who rarely if ever appear in traditional country house poems. The master (or mistress)-servant relationship as portrayed by Swift, far from seeming to reflect a natural or divinely ordained hierarchy, points to an arbitrary, hence alterable, set of circumstances that makes it possible to anticipate a role reversal, a total reorganization of the established order:

> Then, (let me see) we'll make the Knight
> Our Clerk, for he can read and write;
> But, must not think, I tell him that,
> Like *Lorimer,* to wear his Hat.
> Yet, when we dine without a Friend,
> We'll place him at the lower End.
> Madam, whose Skill does all in Dress lye,
> May serve to wait on Mrs. *Leslie:*
> But, lest it might not be so proper,
> That her own Maid should overtop her;

To mortify the *Creature* more,
We'll take her Heels five Inches lower.

(93-104)

We are reminded here of Mrs. Pilkington's account of the yearly feast initiated by Swift and several acquaintances, "in imitation of the *Saturnalia* . . . . whereat the servants personated their masters and the masters waited as servants."[89] Swift's assertion, "And soon as we have got Possession,/ We'll act as *other* Conqu'rors do;/[and] Divide the Realm between us two" (90-92), along with his plan "to hang [Hannah] on the Spot" after they "have no [more] need of her," since ". . . all your Politicians wise/Dispatch the Rogues by whom they Rise" (105-10), is a humorous but also cynical reminder that all power structures as well as property rights are determined by brute force and greed, not by providential plan or benevolent human design.

The Grand Question debated, another poem showing the land and its structures in a state of flux, depicts a debate between Sir Arthur and his wife concerning the fate of a bawn—an anglicized form of the Irish *bábhun,* designating "a Place . . . inclosed with Mud or Stone-Walls, to keep the Cattle from being stolen in the Night" (P, 3:863-64)—located on their property. The "Grand Question" to be answered is explained by the poem's subtitle: "Whether *Hamilton's Bawn* should be turned into a *Barrack* or a *Malt-House.*" Sir Arthur inclines toward the latter alternative, largely for compelling economic and political reasons:

If I make it a *Barrack,* the Crown is my Tenant.
My Dear, I have ponder'd again and again on't:
In Poundage and Drawbacks, I lose half my Rent,
Whatever they give me I must be content,
Or join with the Court in ev'ry Debate,
And rather than that, I would lose my Estate.

(19-24)

As a staunch, unrepentant Tory living in a society dominated by Whigs, Acheson must learn the same lesson taught to Baron Rochfort in *The Journal.* He is confronted with the fact that, even in his rural retreat a considerable distance from Dublin, he cannot completely escape from the political circumstances prevailing in the public world beyond the garden. Swift deals with this same matter in a prose piece where, in a tone of scathing irony, he demonstrates the government's "generosity" to Acheson: "It is whispered about, as a certain Truth, that this Gentleman is to have a Grant of a certain Barrack upon his Estate, within two Miles of his own House; for which the Crown is to be his Tenant, at the Rent of sixty Pounds *per Annum;* he being only at the Expence of about *Five Hundred* Pounds, to put the House in Repair, build Stables, and other

Necessaries" (PW, 12:166). Despite these dismal financial prospects, Lady Acheson urges that Hamilton's Bawn be converted into a barrack: "I'm grown a meer Mopus; no Company comes;/But a Rabble of Tenants, and rusty dull Rumms;/. . . But, if you will give us a *Barrack,* my Dear,/The *Captain,* I'm sure, will always come here. . ." (27–28, 31–32). Lady Acheson's words help dispel the myth of idyllic country living by emphasizing the latter's provincial dullness and vacuity. A rural retreat is here seen to be an isolating prison that, for all its remoteness, cannot provide a sanctuary from the outside world's turbulence.

The remainder of Swift's verse consists of Hannah's fanciful scenario of the situations and dialogue that would ensue from the conversion of Hamilton's Bawn into a barrack, after "the Troop is arriv'd" (68). It is a scenario that, like the one in *The Revolution at Market-Hill,* serves to confound social ranks and to topple orthodox hierarchies, partly through satire directed at Swift himself. Hannah's portrayal of the dinner gathering as an occasion characterized by jealousies and antagonism and as a ludicrous spectacle for the servant class overturns the conventional country house motif:

> The *Captain* at Dinner appears in his Glory;
> The *Dean* and the *Doctor* have humbled their Pride,
> For the *Captain*'s entreated to sit by your Side;
> And, because he's their Betters, you carve for him first,
> The *Parsons,* for Envy, are ready to burst:
> The Servants amaz'd, are scarce ever able,
> To keep off their Eyes, as they wait at the Table. . . .
>
> (130–36)

Several verses in the Market-Hill group portray country house life in general, and the rural visitor Swift in particular, through the eyes of a persona representing Lady Acheson. *My Lady's Lamentation and Complaint against the Dean* translates the relationship between the two into a burlesque version of the relationship between host and guest in traditional country house poetry: "Before he came here/To spunge for good cheer,/I sat with delight,/From morning till night. . ." (15–18). The poem goes on to mock Swift's comically futile attempts to adopt a rural way of life and to perform the role of estate visitor. His rambles through the Achesons' grounds, accompanied by his reluctant and disdainful hostess, parody Pope's famed "saunterings" with his friends among "the multiplied scenes" of his garden while contemplating the beauties of artfully-contrived nature and discussing the finer points of philosophy:[90]

> By the worst of all Squires,
> Thro' bogs and thro' briers,
> Where a cow would be startled,

I'm in spite of my heart led:
And, say what I will,
Haul'd up every hill;
'Till, daggled and tatter'd,
My spirit's quite shatter'd,
I return home at night,
And fast out of spite. . . .

                                                              (45-54)

Swift's intimate involvement with his social inferiors creates the image of
a world devoid of rank, a world turned upside down:

He's all the day saunt'ring,
With labourers bant'ring,
Among his colleagues,
A parcel of Teagues,
(Whom he brings in among us
And bribes with mundungus.)
Hail fellow, well met,
All dirty and wet:
Find out, if you can,
Whose master, whose man. . . .

                                                              (159-68)

Swift's endeavors to shape the earth with his own hands and to
create his own modest country seat (of sorts), which provide an additional
subject for Lady Acheson's harangue, constitute a burlesque version of
Augustan landscape gardening:

How proudly he talks
Of zigzacks and walks;
And all the day raves
Of cradles and caves;
And boasts of his feats,
His grottos and seats;
. . . .
A hole where a rabbit
Would scorn to inhabit,
Dug out in an hour,
He calls it a bow'r.

                                               (173-78; 183-86)

Even these most humble undertakings are doomed to failure, as Swift's
hostess gleefully notes as she watches a wild calf ". . . run helter-skelter/
To his arbor for shelter,/Where all goes to ruin/The Dean has been doing"
(191-94).

    Instead of grateful villagers bringing loving tributes to the country
house lord, we see them contemptuously and irreverently tearing apart

the manorial landscape at Market-Hill. The only "tribute" they leave behind is of a far less dignified and delectable—though undoubtedly even
more abundant—nature than the gifts that Jonson's appreciative tenants
bring to Penshurst:

> The girls of the village
> Come flocking for pillage,
> Pull down the fine briers,
> And thorns, to make fires;
> But yet are so kind
> To leave something behind:
> No more need be said on't,
> I smell when I tread on't.
>
> (195–202)

Pseudobuilder and failed gardener, Swift finally becomes a meddling
and unwanted guest. "Oh! that I could but once be rid/Of that insulting
Tyrant Dean," cries out his exasperated hostess in *Lady A——s——n
Weary of the Dean* (43–44). This verse mockingly undercuts the ideal of
country house hospitality, here shown to be violated by a parasitic estate
visitor and, to a lesser extent, by a harried, short-tempered estate dweller.
The financial problems besetting the owner of a country house (a recurring concern of Swift's, as we have seen) here emerge in a new light,
attributed not to the owner's extravagance or irresponsibility, but to the
guest's excessive demands: "The House Accounts are daily rising/So much
[Swift's] Stay do's swell the Bills;/My dearest Life it is surprizing,/How
much he eats, how much he swills. . ." (29–32).

Three particularly significant poems in the Market-Hill sequence relate to "Drapier's Hill," Swift's projected house at Drumlack, to be built
on land purchased from Acheson. Although sharing the ironic perspective
and comic tone of their companion pieces, they focus upon especially
serious matters that lie at the very heart of Swift's lifelong historical and
artistic preoccupations. *Drapier's Hill* and *To Dean Swift; by Sir Arthur
Acheson* (as its title suggests, the latter poem employs Market-Hill's host
rather than its hostess as persona) crystallize Swift's persistent yearning
to escape posterity's neglect by creating a lasting monument against short
time and to achieve redemption from that world of "transient or imaginary" things that Mr. Examiner specifically associates with landless and
unpropertied beings (PW, 3:119). The proposed "Mansion" is to be
Swift's tangible counterpart to the *Verses on the Death of Dr. Swift:* a
means of preserving his name in stone rooted in earth rather than in
fragile, perishable words that can, like *The Drapier's Letters,* be reduced
to mere "waste Paper" (*Drapier's Hill,* 17). Even if they manage to escape
the refuse heap, after all, these *Letters* are inadequate vehicles for ensur-

ing their author's immortality, for they are occasional writings inextricably tied to one unique event, one fleeting moment in history, and are therefore doomed to extinction, or to an anachronistic and largely irrelevant
existence, by the temporality of their nature. But a sturdily constructed
house standing on ancient and solid ground is, presumably, a monument
that can transcend the endless passage of specific occasions and discrete
moments, as well as the obsolescence conferred by historical change.

Thus the Drapier, having risen to momentary prominence as a result
of writings whose very success ironically destroyed their own raison
d'être, looks to the abiding, timeless earth and its architectural structures
for assurances of eternal fame, urged on by his aristocratic and propertied
host:

> Sir *Arthur* too shall have his Will,
> And call the Mansion *Drapier*'s Hill;
> That when a Nation long enslav'd,
> Forgets by whom it once was sav'd;
> When none the DRAPIER'S Praise shall sing;
> His Signs aloft no longer swing;
> His Medals and his Prints forgotten,
> And all his Handkerchiefs are rotten;
> His famous LETTERS made waste Paper;
> This Hill may keep the Name of DRAPIER:
> In Spight of Envy flourish still,
> And DRAPIER'S vye with COOPER'S Hill.

(9–20)

The second poem, in which Acheson—the "landlord to the Drapier" (2)—
is speaker, underscores the momentous significance of this project by
comparing Swift's planned dwelling with another that brought lasting
fame and honor to its inhabitants and its literary commemorator alike:
"But now your name with Penshurst vies,/And wing'd with fame shall
reach the skies" (33–34).

But in the end (and not surprisingly), no mansion rises from atop
Drapier's Hill; indeed, not even the first stone is ever laid. "I will fly
as soon as build," Swift tersely informs Pope in a letter announcing the
scheme's demise. "I have neither years, nor spirits, nor money, nor patience for such amusements. The frolick is gone off, and I am only 100*l.*
the poorer" (C, 3:355). In lieu of a solid, enduring monument we are
left with a scattered pile of jolting, uneven rhymes—specifically, a poem
setting forth "The Dean's Reasons For not Building at Drapier's Hill."
Swift renounces all his designs in connection with Drumlack and with
them, implicitly, his vocation as architect. "I will not build on yonder
mount," his verse emphatically begins. He depicts his original plan as an
absurd and illusory idea, fit only for the "greatest cully of mankind" (12):

"How could I form so wild a vision,/To seek, in deserts, Fields Elysian?/ To live in fear, suspicion, variance,/With Thieves, Fanatics, and Barbarians?" (15–18). Swift is telling us, in effect, that external circumstances have played a grotesque joke on him, making his noblest ambitions into airy nothings worthy only of a self-deluded dreamer and transforming his would-be durable structures into mere castles in the air: "Whate'er I promised or intended,/No fault of mine, the scheme is ended. . ." (5–6). But the defeat of Swift's exalted scheme has as much to do with his own nature as it does with the adverse features of his environment. Temperamentally and ideologically (as well as financially) incapable of creating beauty out of ugliness, of bringing forth order from chaos, he has no alternative except to relinquish all hopes of cultivating "Fields Elysian" in the midst of "deserts."

The true subject of *The Dean's Reasons* goes far beyond the abandonment of one particular architectural project, for it concerns failure and disillusionment in their profoundest ramifications. The comically debased landscape surrounding Market-Hill—"Here poor Pomona sits on thorns:/ And there neglected Flora settles/Her bum upon a bed of nettles" (92–94)—combines with the scornful portrait of Acheson to negate the entire panoply of traditional values and relationships associated with country house existence. Swift presents Acheson as a man who, through his every inclination and action (or, to be more precise, inaction), betrays this way of life:

> The neighbours wonder why the Knight
> Should in a country life delight,
> Who not one pleasure entertains
> To chear the solitary scenes:
> His guests are few, his visits rare,
> Nor uses time, nor time will spare;
> Nor rides, nor walks, nor hunts, nor fowls,
> Nor plays at cards, or dice, or bowls. . . .
>
> (81–88)

The reciprocity between man and nature is doomed by the perverse disposition of a landlord who "Despises exercise and air" and who thus "His rural walks . . . ne'er adorns" (90–91).

The most vivid passages in *The Dean's Reasons* show the breaking up of a collective, social vision into private, fragmented perspectives. The poem abounds in images of solipsism and isolation, both stemming from and reinforcing an absolute cessation of all human contact. Acheson exists in a world of his own, "Still rapt in speculations deep,/His outward senses fast asleep" (45–46). His solitary contemplation signifies an "avarice of mind" typical of those who "Their knowledge, to themselves confin[e] " (37–38). The inevitable result is a total absence of rapport between host and guest: "Where friendship is by Fate design'd,/It forms an union in the mind:/But, here I differ from the Knight/In every point, like black and white. . ." (69–72). Swift's attempts at dialogue inevitably turn into monologue, for Acheson ". . . while I talk, a song will hum,/Or, with his fingers, beat the drum;/Beyond the skies transports his mind,/And leaves a lifeless corpse behind" (47–50). Here we are suddenly in the world of *Tristram Shandy:* a similarly fragmented and solipsistic world where Walter Shandy earnestly holds forth on his favorite theory while Uncle Toby whistles *Lillabullero.* It is, moreover, a world similarly characterized by unfinished structures, by schemes of the intellect and the imagination that will never be completed.

Swift quite appropriately ends his poem with an invocation to the forces of anarchy and destruction, with an implicit statement of Market-Hill's vulnerability and transience:

> Let ev'ry cottager conspire
> To cut his hedges down for fire;
> The naughty boys about the village
> His crabs and sloes may freely pillage:
> He still may keep a pack of knaves
> To spoil his work, and work by halves. . . .
>
> (105–10)

The rending of the landscape serves as an image of all-encompassing human, social, and geographical fragmentation. As in other, related verses, most notably *The Revolution at Market-Hill,* Swift emerges not as a singer of noble tribute and preserver of immortal memory, but as a self-styled—and not-so-benign—lord of misrule and resolute consigner to oblivion.

However much the poem deliberately exaggerates Sir Arthur's antisocial tendencies and the resulting gulf between host and guest, it undoubtedly reflects important aspects of the actual situation. As Harold Williams puts it, "Reading between the lines we may guess that by 1730 Sir Arthur and his lady had begun to weary of a difficult guest; and, perhaps, took no great pains to conceal the fact" (P, 3:874). Although Swift saw Sir Arthur at least once after his 1730 visit to Market-Hill, upon the baronet's return from London (C, 4:90–91), it is clear that some form of estrangement occurred between them. After the fall of 1730 Swift made no more visits to the Armagh estate, and the few references to the Achesons that appear in his correspondence indicate an increasingly critical attitude toward them. Noting that Lady Acheson is even guiltier of neglecting her health than is his friend Charles Ford (known for his intemperate eating and drinking habits), Swift tells the latter, "She is an absolute Dublin rake, sits up late, loses her money, and goes to bed sick, and resolves like

you never to mend" (92). The description here makes Lady Acheson
sound like the woman satirically portrayed in *The Journal of a Modern
Lady,* who "By Nature turn'd to play the Rake-well" (36) and ". . . sat
all Night up at *Quadrill*" (41), to the detriment of both her morals and
her health. In a letter written several years later to the Reverend John
Towers, Swift pronounces a much harsher judgment on the family: "How,
a wonder, came young Acheson [Archibald, Sir Arthur's eldest son] to
be among you? I believe neither his father nor mother know any thing
of him; his mother is at Grange with Mrs. Acheson, her mother, and, I
hear, is very ill of her asthma and other disorders, got by cards, and
laziness, and keeping ill hours. Ten thousand sackfuls of such knights and
such sons are, in my mind, neither worth rearing nor preserving. I count
upon it that the boy is good for nothing" (C, 4:375). The Achesons are
here in effect numbered among those noble families attacked elsewhere
by Swift, who are "coming to an End by the Sloth, Luxury, and abandoned Lusts, which enervated their Breed through every Succession"
(PW, 12:53). It is no wonder that the Market-Hill poems convey the picture of a disintegrating way of life.

Increasingly during the final fifteen years of his life, Swift eschewed
visits to friends' rural residences and remained confined to his Dublin
environs. A major reason was his deteriorating health, which made journeys of even moderate length both painful and risky. While repeatedly
citing this explanation to his correspondents, however, Swift also often
took the opportunity to suggest a far broader range of factors militating
against his continuance of the customs associated with traditional country
house hospitality. Responding to an invitation from William Richardson
to visit Richardson's estate in county Londonderry, near Coleraine, for
example, Swift commented:

> Your Invitation is very generous and friendly, and what I would
> be glad to accept if it were possible; But, Sr I have not an ounce of
> Flesh about me, and can not ride above a dozen miles in a day with-
> out being sore, and bruised and spent. My head is every day more or
> less disordered by a Giddyness: Yet I ride the Strand here constantly
> when fair weather invites me. But if I live till Spring next, and have
> any Remainders of Health I determine to venture, allthough I have
> some Objections; I do not doubt your good Chear and welcome, but
> you brag too much of the Prospects and Scituations. . . . I own you en-
> gage for the Roads from hence to your house; but, where am I to ride
> after rainy weather, here I have always a Strand, or a turnpike for
> four or five miles. Your being a Batchelor pleaseth me well; and
> as to Neighbours, considering the Race of Squires in Ireland, I had

rather be without them. If you have Books in large print, or an honest Parson with common Sense, I desire no more ... But here is an Interval of above six Months, and in the mean time, God knows what will become of me and perhaps of the Kingdom, for, I think we are going to ruin as fast as it is possible. . . . (C, 4:536)

As this letter makes clear, the country house way of life, with its exchange of sociable visits and noble courtesies, is dependent for its sustenance upon a number of personal, geographical, and, in the broadest sense, political conditions: good health, good roads, suitably attractive terrain, and, perhaps above all, a basic faith in the survival of both self and world—in the ability of one's country as well as one's individual being to weather fate's vicissitudes by means of enduring social institutions and structures. In a world infected by the "Race of Squires" and filled with fatigued old men who are too "sore, and bruised and spent" to travel, whose illnesses mirror the infirmities of an entire kingdom likewise facing imminent extinction, even the most generous and friendly offer of hospitality must prove ineffectual. The country house ideal as presented in this letter has already become a diminished thing: It is an essentially private and solitary vision, devoid of both familial and communal harmony, in which the fact of bachelorhood is extolled—contrary to Herrick's more traditional view that what ". . . most makes sweet [a] country life,/Is, the fruition of a wife" (A Country Life: To his Brother, Master Thomas Herrick, 31-32)—and in which the absence of neighbors, rather than community with them, is cited for approbation. But not even this shrunken version of the ideal has much chance of surviving when the whole of Ireland, as well as individual members of its population, is ". . . going to ruin as fast as it is possible."

Swift never did avail himself of Richardson's offer of hospitality. The untraversed distance between Dublin and his friend's Coleraine estate may be seen to symbolize the increasing fragmentation and disintegration of country house existence. Both the psychological feeling and the geographical fact of distance played an ever-increasing role in Swift's life and came to permeate his language as well as to govern his actions—to define his perception of all human transactions and relationships. Writing to Pope in the winter of 1735-1736, for example, he remarked, "I look upon you as an estate from which I receive my best annual rents, although I am never to see it" (C, 4:457). We may well suspect that Swift could not have been oblivious to the irony of depicting himself, in effect, as an absentee landlord, even if one who has presumably treated his property with a good deal more love and care than his typical contemporary counterpart. The primary significance of the comment is that, even when considered in the most positive light, the relationship between friend and friend, be-

tween host and guest, between the manorial lord and his estate, could be
described by Swift only in terms of absence, only as a wistfully evoked,
permanent separation.

Pope's use of similar terminology to characterize his relationship
with Swift conveys, not surprisingly, a very different body of associations.
Writing to Swift shortly after the latter's departure from Twickenham in
the summer of 1726, Pope expresses the hope that his friend will find all
things as he would wish them back in Ireland, "so that your visit to us
may have no other effect, than the progress of a rich man to a remote
estate, which he finds greater than he expected; which knowledge only
serves to make him live happier where he is, with no disagreeable prospect
if ever he should chuse to remove" (C, 3:157). It is typical of Pope that
he should employ metaphoric language that reconciles potential contradictions and glosses over the fact of disjunctiveness. While acknowledging
the separation between Swift and himself through the analogy of the
distance between a rich man and his estate, Pope's comment celebrates the
overcoming of this distance in the immediate past and allows for the
possibility of continued contact in the future. The estate, however "remote," can be visited whenever one desires and returned to in a final act
of homecoming. Thus a situation suggestive of absentee landlordism is
harmonized with a vision of traditional country house existence, of the
unseverable bond between the estate dweller and his land. Swift's remote
estate, on the contrary, no matter how high its annual yield, is doomed to
remain permanently out of sight and reach; its existence is felt primarily
in terms of absence and loss. Swift's metaphorical estate, like many of the
actual ones mentioned throughout his writings, retains just enough links
to the country house ideal to serve as a painful reminder of the latter's
obsolescence.

C H A P T E R · 5

The Spectator in the Landscape

i

In the spectator society of eighteenth-century Britain, certain ways of seeing—and certain types of seers—were automatically exalted above others. Joseph Addison's "Man of a Polite Imagination," for example, who is ". . . let into a great many Pleasures that the Vulgar are not capable of receiving," enjoys a very special perception of the world, one shared only by a small elite. He ". . . feels a greater Satisfaction in the Prospect of Fields and Meadows, than another does in the Possession. It gives him, indeed, a kind of Property in every thing he sees, and makes the most rude uncultivated Parts of Nature, administer to his Pleasures. . . ."[1] His vision, in short, is a form of power that makes the phenomenal world his personal property, subordinate to both his eye and his will. Addison's singling out of a prospect to exemplify this privileged vision is most appropriate,[2] since prospects were among the most coveted ingredients in his contemporaries' visual diet.

Throughout her correspondence, Mrs. Delany underscores the premium placed upon prospects by the privileged classes of eighteenth-century England and Ireland, enthusiastically describing to her sister the "pleasant meadows, bounded by mountains of various shapes, with little villages and country-seats interspersed . . . ," as well as "a most extensive and beautiful prospect of the harbour and town of Dublin" visible from Delville's position overlooking the bay.[3] Indeed, not content to have these prospects readily accessible to her the moment she walked outside, into the gardens surrounding Delville, Mrs. Delany devoted a good deal of time and money to devising ways of bringing them into her house. As she explains to her sister, "My bed-chamber is very large, comfortable, with pleasant views

173

and the bow closet! I have now completed it by two looking-glasses that
fill the side panels of the bow window, and reflect all the prospects. You
would say indeed I am greedy of prospect were you to see it, *not to be
contented* without those reflectors. . . ."[4]

It is not surprising, therefore, that modern critics, deeming Swift
exemplary of traditionally defined Augustan tastes and values, should
identify him with the stance of the typical Augustan landscape observer,
especially the prospect viewer. One scenario, for example, reconstructs
Swift's periodic visits to Howth Castle, located ten miles north of the
deanery, overlooking Dublin Bay: "In the garden round the castle walls he
would wander along beech *allees* from which he would gaze over the sea
to the romantic St Nessan's Island (Ireland's Eye). Or if he continued his
ride through the St Lawrence demesne up the rocky bridleways of the
hill of Howth he would look over Dublin Bay whose shores were dotted
with historic castles, or north to the pale mountains of Mourne on the
horizon."[5] In a similar vein, Constantia Maxwell pictures Swift at Delville's temple, ". . . admiring the view of Dublin and its harbour with the
long range of mountains beyond."[6] But in point of fact, throughout his
writings Swift shows an indifference toward or a contempt of prospects.
Nowhere does he claim membership in an elite defined by its superior
visual powers or reveal himself in the typical stance of the Augustan
spectator, allowing his eye to expatiate over the distant terrain and
enjoying the panoramas thus exposed to his view. The word "prospect"
appears only twice in Swift's poetry, and in neither case does it refer to
visual expanse or beautiful scenery (see *Ode to Dr. William Sancroft,*
207, and *A Panegyric on the Reverend D——n S——t,* 179). It is somehow
quite appropriate, symbolically "right," that in a rare instance in which
he seeks to obtain such a view, during his enforced stay in Holyhead
while awaiting passage to Ireland, he is prevented from doing so by a
veil of fog: "Wat [his manservant] and I walked up the monstrous mountain properly called Holy head or Sacrum promontorium by Ptolemy, 2
miles from this town. . . . I looked from the top to see the wicklow
hills, but the day was too hazy. . ." (PW, 5:206).

Some of the reasons behind Swift's failure to indulge in this kind
of landscape observation may be inferred from his comment in *A Short
View of the State of Ireland,* that "The conveniency of Ports and Havens,
which Nature hath bestowed so liberally on this Kingdom, is of no more
Use to us, than a beautiful Prospect to a Man shut up in a Dungeon"
(PW, 12:8). This statement, appearing as it does in a tract exposing Ireland's wretched conditions, goes a long way toward explaining why
Swift's writings are devoid of typically Augustan descriptions of prospects. We might compare Swift's comment with one of Addison's:
". . . by this Faculty [man's imaginative power as it operates upon sense-

derived images] a Man in a Dungeon is capable of entertaining himself with Scenes and Landskips more beautiful than any that can be found in the whole Compass of Nature."[7] It is characteristic that Swift, in opposition to any such implication that the pleasures of the visual imagination can adequately compensate for a man's loss of freedom, should insist upon the intractable reality of physical confinement and suggest that a prisoner has desires and needs more pressing than the enjoyment of pretty landscape scenes. As a self-described "poisoned rat in a hole" (C, 3:383) and a politically suspect individual alternately confronting "a Dagger . . . at my Throat, a halter about my Neck, or Chains at my Feet" (C, 2:465), Swift, like the hypothetical "Man shut up in a Dungeon," would have found little use for "a beautiful Prospect," even had it spread itself ostentatiously before his eyes (and we know from contemporary descriptions by visitors that Dublin and its environs afforded a number of such views to the carefully trained eye "greedy of prospect"[8]). For Swift, the act of seeing was inevitably an expression of the spectator's position in every sense—his standing both in a physical landscape and in society. Swift would therefore have found it pointless to speak of a situation in which the eye can freely range abroad while the body itself remains behind bars. Beautiful prospects should be left to the typical *"English* Spectator" referred to elsewhere in the *Short View,* who "comes for a short Time" and then "returns back to his own Country" (PW, 12:10-11); they should be left, in other words, to those who have the freedom and money to devour choice sights, turn away from others that might prove too unpleasant, and leave when their visual appetites have been satisfied. For those deprived beings who are trapped in their surroundings, detached aesthetic contemplation is at best laughable, a sign of self-delusion and blindness rather than superior perception or visual discernment.

The absurdity of such a situation is made clear in those instances where Gulliver, as satiric butt, imitates the actions of a typical eighteenth-century Mr. Spectator by exclaiming upon the beauties of a prospect while he is literally imprisoned—chained like a mastiff or caged like a pet canary. In Part I, for example, Swift juxtaposes the account of Gulliver's confinement ("The Chains that held my left Leg . . . being fixed within four Inches of the Gate, allowed me to creep in, and lie at my full Length in the Temple") with Gulliver's exalted contemplation of his environs: "When I found myself on my Feet, I looked about me, and must confess I never beheld a more entertaining Prospect. The Country round appeared like a continued Garden; and the inclosed Fields . . . resembled so many Beds of Flowers" (PW, 11:28-29). An eighteenth-century Irishman, forced into a like position of abjectness by the petty but vicious tyrannies of England, would presumably subject himself to similar ridicule if he chose to affect the stance of a detached gentleman spectator. The point is reiterated when Gulliver travels through Brobdingnag in an elaborate box constructed by the queen's cabinetmaker. It is through the small, wired windows of this box that the captive's progress through the countryside, in a mock version of the eighteenth-century gentleman's Grand Tour, is measured in terms of scenic views and vistas: "In Journeys, when I was weary of the Coach, a Servant on Horseback would buckle my Box, and place it on a Cushion before him; and there I had a full Prospect of the Country on three Sides from my three Windows" (113). The satiric fictions of *Gulliver's Travels* demonstrate that the state of oppression or subjugation, however cushioned, makes the stance of detached aesthetic contemplation laughable, at best.

ii

The absence of visual prospects from Swift's writings is intimately connected with his lack of prospects in other senses as well. The word itself can function on several different though related levels, as indicated by a passage from Johnson's *Rambler No. 2:* "This quality of looking forward into futurity seems the unavoidable condition of a being, whose motions are gradual, and whose life is progressive . . . ; as, by continual advances from his first stage of existence, he is perpetually varying the horizon of his prospects, he must always discover new motives of action, new excitements of fear, and allurements of desire."[9] The "horizon of [a man's] prospects" may be conceived of in concretely visual terms even as it is part of a mental landscape shaped by temporal hopes and expectations. Johnson's entry for the word "prospect" in his *Dictionary* makes its dual significance explicit, both by assigning separate temporal and spatial meanings to individual definitions and by yoking the two within the same definition, as in his second one, "Place which affords an extended view," which is glossed with the Miltonic quotation, "Him God beholding from his *prospect* high,/Wherein past, present, future he beholds,/Thus spake. . . ."[10] Both the temporal and the spatial meanings of the term were often simultaneously invoked by eighteenth-century poets in particular. Ralph Cohen, discussing *The Seasons,* points to Thomson's "method of placing the country estates as look-out points from which one sees the world extending from immediate surroundings to infinity. In this way the estate becomes an ideal point from which to conceive of a future eternity."[11] The result is a resoundingly optimistic and forward-looking statement in every respect—an expression of satisfaction and confidence in what lies in front of the poet, in terms of both the geographical expanse spreading before his eyes and the hopes of an expanding future.

That Swift remained a stranger to sweeping panoramas of the kind described in *The Seasons* is, we might accordingly conjecture, linked to the fact that he was a man obsessed with visions of approaching doom for his native land, as well as a man devoid of expectations for his own worldly advancement. In the poem *To Janus On New Year's Day. Written in the Year 1729,* although there is no explicit mention of prospects, temporal expanse is described in visual terms. Janus, looking both backward and forward, surveys a temporal landscape in much the same way that an estate dweller might oversee the topographical landscape surrounding his demesne, but the connotations of "forward Sight" in this instance are decidedly negative:

> God of Time, if you be wise,
> Look not with your future Eyes:
> What imports thy forward Sight?
> Well, if you could lose it quite.
> Can you take Delight in viewing
> This poor Isle's approaching Ruin?
> When thy Retrospection vast
> Sees the glorious Ages past.
>
> Happy Nation were we blind,
> Or, had only Eyes behind.—

(9-18)

The verse continues in a playful, lightly mocking vein, with an unidentified female (meant to represent Lady Acheson) rebutting the poet's advice, but the passage just cited remains on one level a serious statement of Ireland's increasingly wretched situation and the latter's inevitable consequence in terms of rendering futile any act of looking ahead, whether at a spatial expanse or at a temporal continuum. Swift makes a similar point through his use of the word "prospect" in his prose tracts and correspondence, where it invariably signifies bleak anticipations of pitiful dearth, growing enslavement, and imminent ruin. We read, for example, how his attitude has been "sowered" alternately "by personal ill treatment, or by melancholy prospects for the publick" (PW, 9:34). Elsewhere, discussing the problem of widespread Irish emigration to other countries, Swift concludes: "From whence it is manifest, that our present miserable condition and the dismal prospect of worse, with other reasons above assigned are sufficient to put men upon trying this desperate experiment of changing the scene they are in although Landlords should by a miracle become less inhuman" (PW, 12:79). Here the temporal prospect directly and concretely affects the geographical one. The lack of expectations, of faith in the future, results in a physical change of "scene"—a thoroughgoing alteration of one's existential landscape.

Because Swift felt himself to be a man of thwarted expectations whose early hopes for career preferment remained unfulfilled, dismal or

nonexistent prospects had a very special relevance for him, quite apart
from Ireland's wretched state of affairs. One may recall the sense of disappointment and frustration permeating his autobiographical fragment,
which ends with an insistence upon the cruel betrayal of his worldly prospects at the hands of those in power: King William, who made "a Promise . . . to Sr W[illiam] T[emple] that he would give Mr Swift a Prebend
of Canterbury or Westminster"—a promise never realized; the Earl of
Romney, "who professed much friendship for [Swift and] promised to
second his Petition" to the king, but "said not a word" to the latter; and
the Earl of Berkeley, who encouraged Swift's hopes of becoming the earl's
secretary but then "after a poor Apology gave that Office to [another]"
(PW, 5:195). Throughout these vicissitudes of fortune, we view Swift as
a youthful aspirant wasting precious time in "long attendance in vain"
upon the great. The fragment's final terse statement, "The Excuse pre-
tended was his being too young, although he were then 30 years old,"
underscores Swift's pained awareness that the rapid passage of time had
culminated in fading prospects for an aging place-seeker.

Swift's depiction of Eugenio in the *Intelligencer, Nos. V and VII,*
provides another example of a youth unjustly robbed of prospects. Obviously patterned in many ways upon Swift himself, Eugenio also must
confront the bitter reality of a world devoid of prospects. His experience,
like his creator's, is largely made up of defeated hopes and thwarted expectations: "He was a thousand Times recommended by his poetical
Friends to great Persons . . . and received a thousand Promises: But his
Modesty, and a generous Spirit, which disdained the Slavery of continual
Application and Attendance, always disappointed him; making room for
vigilant Dunces, who were sure to be never out of Sight" (PW, 12:45).
The ending to this tale crystallizes Swift's own situation and thus supplies
a further insight into both his standing in the landscape and his angle of
vision:

> Wearied with weak Hopes, and weaker Pursuits, he accepted a Curacy
> in *Derbyshire,* of thirty Pounds a Year; and when he was five and
> forty, had the great Felicity to be preferred by a Friend of his
> Father's, to a Vicaridge worth annually sixty Pounds, in the most
> desert Parts of *Lincolnshire;* where, his Spirit quite sunk with those
> Reflections that Solitude and Disappointments bring; he married a
> Farmer's Widow, and is still alive, utterly undistinguished and for-
> gotten; only some of the Neighbours have accidentally heard, *that
> he had been a* notable Man *in his Youth.* (PW, 12:45)

Eugenio winds up a prospectless man in every sense. Consigned to an
isolated vicarage in the barren northlands as a minor clergyman "utterly
undistinguished and forgotten," he must reconcile himself to living in a

geographical wasteland devoid of prospects as well as to a life without a future. The general *lowness* of Eugenio's situation, the fact that he occupies an inferior post without the possibility of rising any further and that his "Spirit [is] quite sunk," reinforces his prospectless state, since prospects require a position of elevation. Swift characterizes himself also as being in a "sunken" state, which would render lofty prospects inaccessible to him. In the autobiographical fragment he observes that "... by the ill Treatment of his nearest Relations, he was so discouraged and sunk in his Spirits, that he too much neglected his Academical Studyes" (PW, 5:192), and in the same letter to Pope in which he mentions the "melancholy prospects for the publick," he suggests that his own "genius and spirit [are] sunk by encreasing years" (PW, 9:34).

iii

The necessary connection between prospects and an elevated stance suggested in the preceding paragraph is of crucial significance; this position of ascendancy, although primarily a physical fact, has a number of symbolic overtones as well. The spectator is always very conscious of his lofty position vis-à-vis the objects he is surveying, as is evident from John Bush's description of his view of the lakes of Killarney from a nearby mountain peak:

> From the lofty shaggy top of this rocky mountain [known as the *Turc*] is seen a prospect the most fertile of aqueous, rural, and romantic beauties within the extent of half a dozen miles on either hand, that any hill, perhaps, in the world affords, within the same extent. The extremities of your view, from this eminence, present the out-lines of the several lakes, with the surrounding verdant mountains, rocks and precipices; a general view, likewise, of the deep and most irriguous valley and straight that leads from the upper down to the lower lake, and which, in any other situation is seen but very partially ... with a view of the town of Kilarny, and the several seats and villas in the neighbourhood of the lake; and *below,* in a literal sense, indeed, from the lofty eminence it is taken from, you have a prospect of the lakes. ...[12]

The spectator, as a man of "eminence," towers over the surrounding landscape. Looking down upon the scenery *"below,"* he can display his superior visual powers by seeing things that "in any other situation [are] seen but very partially." He is, in short, a man of comprehensive as well as heightened vision.

The prospect viewer's exalted standing has important ideological implications. An elevated position is particularly appropriate for members of a political and economic elite, who from such a vantage point can lit-

erally as well as figuratively look down upon those on the lower rungs of
the social hierarchy as well as the countryside spreading beneath their
feet. Hilltops, mountain peaks, and other promontories are therefore
central features of an aristocratic landscape. From such heights the
eighteenth-century spectator, like a lord overseeing his creation, was able
to "command" a view of the landscape and thereby to exert control over
it in much the same way that the aristocratic class ruled over those below
them in society. In many instances the word "command" retained the
force of its military associations, as in Cowper's assertion, "Now roves the
eye,/And posted on this speculative height,/Exults in its command" (*The
Task*, Book I, 288-90).[13] Even where the word's martial connotations are
not consciously evoked, as in Bush's description of "a situation that commands the most extensive prospect of the several lakes [of Killarney] and
country adjacent,"[14] the spectator is shown to exert a very real power
over the landscape as a result of the "superior" views his lofty position
affords him.

Swift shows his awareness of the combined symbolic and ideological
significance of height, on occasion using imagistic contrasts between exalted and lowly stature as a way of reflecting, among other things, social
class. In a letter to Lord Orrery, for example, he playfully chides the
latter for his frequent and lengthy absences from Ireland: "For, a Star
of the first magnitude, wholly out of sight, or at too great a distance, is
a very useless part of Gods works to those who grovel upon the Earth"
(C, 4:145). Similarly, in *The Birth of Manly Virtue, from Callimachus*,
Swift portrays Lord Carteret through images of ascent and apotheosis:
"Now change the Scene; a nobler Care/Demands him in an higher
Sphere. . . " (111-12). In contrast to the Orrerys and Carterets of the
world, Swift tends to characterize himself as a creature whose stature is as
low as the earth grovelers'. In one satiric piece, for example, he describes
how a large mastiff who was being persecuted by a horde of Tories ". . . ran,
without Thinking, between my Legs, as I was coming up *Fishamble-
street;* and, as I am of low Stature, with very short Legs, bore me riding
backwards down the Hill, for above Two Hundred Yards. . ." (PW,
12:221). Like the instance in which Swift vainly tried to attain a view of
the Wicklow hills, the situation depicted here, in which the Swiftian
persona is prevented from completing his ascent, conveys a symbolic
truth about Swift's position in the landscape. So too does the depiction
of him as one "of low Stature," a creature for whom any position of
eminence would be manifestly incongruous.

Elevated stance possessed an added political and symbolic significance in Swift's Ireland, shaped as it was by the policies, perceptions,
and language of the Protestant Ascendancy. Edmund Burke, speaking in
this instance as the embittered half-Catholic Irish exile outraged by the

treatment his countrymen had to endure, underscores the full force of "ascendancy" as word and concept as well as fact in a letter in which he commends his son Richard for engaging like himself "in the relief of an oppressed people," namely the Roman Catholics in Ireland. After demonstrating that the traditional, legitimate meanings of the term no longer apply to its contemporary usage, Burke explains:

> New *ascendency* is the old mastership. It is neither more nor less than the resolution of one set of people in Ireland to consider themselves as the sole citizens in the commonwealth; and to keep a dominion over the rest by reducing them to absolute slavery under a military power. . . .
> The poor word ascendency, so soft and melodious in its sound, so lenitive and emollient in its first usage, is now employed to cover to the world the most rigid, and perhaps not the most wise, of all plans of policy. The word is large enough in its comprehension. I cannot conceive what mode of oppression in civil life, or what mode of religious persecution, may not come within the methods of preserving an *ascendency*. In plain old English, as they apply it, it signifies *pride and dominion* on the one part of the relation, and on the other *subserviency and contempt*—and it signifies nothing else.[15]

In the process of demystifying the word "ascendancy" by exposing it as a pleasing euphemism designed to conceal a harsh reality, Burke reveals how its implications of height translate into the contrast between a loftiness and a lowness that is at once symbolic and concretely political.

Swift, himself technically part of this "ascendant" group, was acutely sensitive to the full implications of the elevated status its members occupied in society. His suggestion of the words *Fastigia despicit urbis* ("Height or rank looks down on the city") as an inscription for the temple at Delville demonstrates that he could on occasion comment playfully upon the exalted position of the ascendant class and their attitude of *looking down*, both literally and figuratively, from a high elevation. The word *despicit*, while describing the temple's geographical location atop a hill overlooking Dublin harbor, conveys at the same time its tropological meaning, "to look down upon, to despise, disdain."[16] The temple's stance of "looking down upon" and "disdaining" the lower levels of terrain mirrors Mrs. Delany's stance toward the "narrow streets and dirty-looking houses" representative of Dublin's lower-class ambience and urban squalor. It was an attitude well suited to Delville's fashionable, sophisticated hostess—to one who was a notable member of the Protestant Ascendancy in Ireland.

In other instances, Swift views the consequences of "ascendancy" in a more serious light. He shows how even the lowest, most paltry Englishman, when transplanted to Ireland, undergoes a sudden and dramatic elevation in status, as exemplified by the *"Corrector* of a Hedge-Press, in some *Blind-Alley* about *Little-Britain,"* who upon his arrival in Ireland proceeds to *". . . erect* himself up into an *Orator* and *Politician,* and lead a *Kingdom* after him" (PW, 9:20). The members of the ruling class, like the *"Corrector* of a Hedge-Press" only on a much grander scale, are shown to have falsely set themselves up as lofty authority figures. Noting the *"contemptuous* Treatment of *Ireland* in some chief *Governors,"* reflected in "that high Style of several Speeches from the *Throne,"* Swift mentions a speech given by Lord Wharton and concludes: "From whence it is clear, that some *Ministers* in those Times [during the two last reigns], were apt, from their *high* Elevation, to look *down* upon this Kingdom, as if it had been one of their *Colonies* of *Out-casts* in *America"* (20–21). Thus the English colonialists and their representatives in Ireland's Protestant Ascendancy occupy a position similar to Lord Lyttelton's as he "gain[s] the height" of Hagley's hill ("Spring," 950). The "high elevation" of both places them automatically in a position of command, whether over a subjugated people or over a "verdant field" (953) spread out below.

Along with its dependence upon elevation, the prospect presupposes the act of seeing from a distance. John Dunton, in his account of his tour through Ireland, suggests the significance of viewing portions of the landscape from afar when he comments on Athenry: "A mile or two from you it makes a great figure, but like most other ill things it shows best at a distance, for when you are in it 'tis a poor, pitiful miserable place."[17] Distance, in other words, makes a scene appear lovelier by enhancing its most pleasing aspect while concealing the topographical scars and warts. Sir John Clerk sums up the matter in his description of the kind of landscape that should surround a "Country Seat":

> So there are Pictures done with utmost art,
> Which must at proper Distances be seen:
> For when their bold rough Strokes are brought too nigh,
> They lose their Beauty and offend the Eye.
> . . .
> Lakes from afar will charm the Eye and seem
> Huge Silver Mirrors set in verdant frames.
> But come we nearer, feeble nature shrinks
> To find them hideous Gulphs with perilous Banks.[18]

As the passage just quoted suggests, there is a security to be found in distance: a protection from the potentially frightening concreteness and immediacy of reality—a defense against assaults upon the eye and the body alike.

It is no wonder, then, that the majority of eighteenth-century visitors to Dublin automatically sought out vantage points from which they could survey the city from a safe distance and thereby blot out the numerous eyesores, as well as the more palpable dangers, accompanying so much poverty and deprivation. That they were often successful in their visual manipulations is evident from one such visitor's bird's-eye view of Dublin, obtained as he "sauntered over the Hill of Killiney" and saw a "choice of admirable prospects" and ". . . the most pleasing images, notwithstanding the miseries that brood upon the land."[19] If, in other words, the spectator stationed himself at a sufficient distance from the objects of his scrutiny, he could convert even the most wretched circumstances into "pleasing images" and thereby render invisible those "hideous and depressing spectacles" that Irvin Ehrenpreis associates with the eighteenth-century poor, who, as he succinctly notes, "did not invite pleasurable scrutiny."[20] A traveler through other, more rural parts of Ireland was likewise confronted with the problem of positioning himself in such a way that the beauties of the landscape revealed themselves to his sight while the ugliness remained hidden from view, held at a sufficient arm's (or rather, eye's) distance. When it became no longer possible to keep these eyesores at a safe remove, the resourceful spectator found ways of incorporating them into a larger picture of aesthetic contrasts that had the effect of greatly minimizing their existence. John Bush, for example, having ecstatically described the magnificent view attainable while riding through an area known as the Glyn of the Mountains, continues:

> From these lofty and sublime curiosities of nature, you must now make a descent with me into the dreggs of Ireland, down into the very bogs, with which this island abounds, and some of them to an extent of many miles. However unpromising the prospect, yet, perhaps, it may not be altogether infertile of entertainment: it may serve, at least, as a contrast to, and give a higher relish for, the more pleasing subjects which will afterwards occur. However, I will carry you over them as safe and with as much expedition as I can; staying no longer on them than just to let you know what ground you are upon, and will conduct you again to prospects more inviting and fertile of entertainment.[21]

Bush's Dantesque journey into Ireland's nether regions is a symbolic enactment of what happens when the landscape viewer leaves his eminence and comes closer to the ground and nearer to the objects in his field of vision.

Thus prospects determined both how and what one saw, as well as what one chose *not* to see. It is important to emphasize this aspect of not seeing, since a prospect is customarily thought to be synonymous with breadth and comprehensiveness of vision. Yet if we examine, say, Thomson's description of Hagley's prospect, we discover a view that is admitted-

ly sweeping, but that nevertheless reveals a partialness and circumscription
of vision, a very special kind of selectivity at work:

> Meantime you gain the height, from whose fair brow
> The bursting prospect spreads immense around;
> And, snatched o'er hill and dale, and wood and lawn,
> And verdant field, and darkening heath between,
> And villages embosomed soft in trees,
> And spiry towns by surging columns marked
> Of household smoke, your eye excursive roams—
> Wide-stretching from the Hall in whose kind haunt
> The hospitable Genius lingers still,
> To where the broken landscape, by degrees
> Ascending, roughens into rigid hills
> O'er which the Cambrian mountains, like far clouds
> That skirt the blue horizon, dusky rise.
>
> ("Spring," 950–62)

Much scholarship has been devoted to descriptions and analyses of what
Thomson sees from atop Hagley's hill,[22] but what interests me is what
Thomson and Lyttelton do *not* see as they look out over the Worcestershire environs—or at least what it is they see only so remotely and peri-
pherally that it cannot truly be said to exist in their world. The mention
of ". . . villages embosomed soft in trees,/And spiry towns by surging
columns marked" suggests that people—ordinary people who till the
soil and inhabit the farmlands of Worcestershire—occupy the part of the
landscape that presents itself to Thomson's survey; yet the passage offers
no particulars about these inhabitants or their way of life, no appreciation
of their importance to the land, no real recognition even of their existence.
We find no indication here that these "villages" and "spiry towns" enjoy
any independent status apart from the role they occupy in the perception
of the Hagley spectator, nor is there any suggestion that they are more
than momentary resting places for the voracious eyes of Lyttelton's guests
as the latter feast upon the surrounding vistas. Because of the distance
maintained by the spectator, specific topographical and architectural
details that might provide insights into prevailing social and economic conditions become lost in the larger picture and give way to idealized abstractions that have little to do with the actual state of things. Throughout *The
Seasons,* the physically constituted, empirically functioning eye is subordi-
nated to the "imagination's vivid eye" ("Spring," 459), the "mind's
creative eye" ("Autumn," 1016), and the "philosophic eye" ("Autumn,"
1133)—all suggesting modes of perception that are superior to "mere"
physical sight but in fact signifying modes of perception that can avoid
seeing by "transcending" what actually exists in the landscape.
     Overlooked by this kind of perception are not only certain aspects of

the landscape but also their significance for human beings. For example, in the context in which Thomson's fleeting reference to "household smoke" appears, the smoke merely adds to the passage's pictorial emphasis. But what specific consequences does the smoke have for the villagers' everyday existence? We might reasonably suppose it is intended as a sign of well-being in the sense that it implies warmth, as well as fire for preparing food. Yet household smoke could have very different implications, for in many eighteenth-century accounts of tours through Ireland, it is presented as a virtual symbol, as well as palpable proof, of the peasants' hardships. Arthur Young, for example, attributed the unusually high rate of blindness in Ireland to household smoke, arguing that the smoke trapped in the peasants' "miserable looking hovels" is, due to an absence of chimneys, "as injurious to their eyes as it is to the complexions of the women, which in general in the cabbins of Ireland has a near resemblance to that of a smoaked ham."[23] A century earlier, John Dunton had cited the prevalence of lice and smoke in the Irish cabins as the reason for his reluctance to venture into them.[24] Even if the habitations in Worcestershire were not characterized by the squalor of their Irish counterparts, the "household smoke" that was for Thomson a conveniently placed detail in an attractive scene might well have been a source of ugliness or profound discomfort when encountered close at hand. The point is made even more dramatically by the inclusion of smoke (the urban, industrial variety) in the "goodly prospect" described in "Summer," which affords views of the Thames Valley, with London in the background. Thomson's image of "The stretching landskip [decaying] into smoke" (1441) becomes part of an idealized picture of the English cityscape and the way of life it supports: "Full are thy cities with the sons of art;/And trade and joy, in every busy street,/Mingling are heard. . ." (1457-59). Again the empirical realities of the environment are overlooked—specifically, industrial as well as domestic coal-burning, which was even then beginning to produce the ugly and unhealthy pall of smoke that daily hovered over London and that was continually commented upon with amazement and disapproval by foreign visitors later in the century.[25]

We might well be tempted to conclude that Thomson's well-ordered, harmonious, aesthetically satisfying universe is based not so much on a comprehensive or ideal vision as on a carefully cultivated *blindness* to a whole body of prevailing conditions in the environment, which is reinforced by the distance maintained between viewer and viewed objects. As John Barrell insightfully observes in his discussion of the quintessential eighteenth-century elitist view of landscape, "those who held this attitude towards landscape, in short, were able to do so because they were not involved in the landscapes they met with: their eye 'looked over' them, and manipulated the objects in them, simply according to the rules and structures sanctioned by a pure and abstract vision, and without any reference to what the function of those objects might be, what their use might be to the people who lived among them."[26] The act of "looking over" the objects in one's field of vision often meant overlooking them in the fullest sense. These objects were quite literally eliminated from the spectator's view, at least partly because they proved inconceivable or unacceptable from his standpoint.

iv

In contrast to these prospects or "long views," Swift's characteristic mode of observation is a close-up view, which, although it can produce grotesque distortions (as in his minute descriptions of the female body), can also result in a visual clarity that makes possible a more truthful, because more detailed and intense, perception of landscape. Throughout his writings we find evidence of his awareness that distance has a profound effect on one's perception. In advising Celia, "Delude at once and Bless our Sight,/When you are seen, be seen from far" (*The Progress of Beauty,* 70--71), he is (however facetiously) making a point akin to the one reiterated in descriptions of landscape, where a distant vantage point is recommended to ensure an attractive view. Observing anything too closely is likely to result in visual discomfort or revulsion, as when Gulliver is filled with "Horror and Disgust" upon seeing the Brobdingnagian maids' naked bodies at close range (PW, 11:119) and when, the situation reversed, a Lilliputian friend informs Gulliver "... that my Face appeared much fairer and smoother when he looked on me from the Ground, than it did upon a nearer View when I took him up in my Hand, and brought him close; which he confessed was at first a very shocking Sight" (92). Similarly "shocking Sight[s]" are revealed when Swift examines his physical surroundings close at hand. For example, he counters a correspondent's apparently idealized conception of the Irish countryside with his own detailed account of what he saw during his trip through county Tipperary: "... filthy cabins, miserable, tattered, half-starved creatures, scarce in human shape; one insolent ignorant oppressive squire to be found in twenty miles riding; a parish church to be found only in a summer-day's journey, in comparison of which, an English farmer's barn is a cathedral; a bog of fifteen miles round; every meadow a slough, and every hill a mixture of rock, heath, and marsh" (C, 4:34).

The very title of Swift's tract, *A Short View of the State of Ireland,* suggests his mode of observation, the word "short" not only literally characterizing a brief polemic only a few pages in length but also denoting a close-up, eye-level view. The body of the tract deals directly with the differences between accurate and distorted ways of seeing; Swift instructs "the worthy *Commissioners* who come from *England*" how to view the Irish landscape clearly and thus rid themselves of prior misconceptions as well as potential misperceptions. His advice to "... ride round the Kingdom, and observe the Face of Nature, or the Faces of the Natives" (PW, 12:10) calls for a close scrutiny inconsistent with the sweeping, lofty gaze of the prospect viewer. The "faces" Swift recommends for observation have little in common with "Earth's universal face" mentioned in *The Seasons* ("Winter," 238) or "... the face/Of universal nature" depicted by Cowper (*The Task,* Book IV, 324-25), for in the former case the concern is with particularity, not universality—with unique characteristics that aid in making distinctions, not with general qualities that presumably create a harmonious whole. Swift's "rider" will inevitably see sights that are shielded from the eyes of the typical English spectator: "The miserable Dress, and Dyet, and Dwelling of the People. The general Desolation in most Parts of the Kingdom. The old Seats of the Nobility and Gentry all in Ruins, and no new ones in their Stead. The Families of Farmers, who pay great Rents, living in Filth and Nastiness upon Butter-milk and Potatoes, without a Shoe or Stocking to their Feet; or a House so convenient as an *English* Hog-sty, to receive them" (PW, 12:10).

Swift's scornful reference to the "*English* Spectator," who can afford if he wishes to transform these horrors into "comfortable Sights," and who "comes for a short Time, only *to learn the Language,* and returns back to his own Country, whither he finds all our Wealth transmitted" (PW, 12:10–11), indicates that he perceived the close connection between visual and economic exploitation. The portrayal of the activities of the typical English spectator in the *Short View* suggests how the well-bred English gentleman can plunder with his eyes and his hands alike as he feasts his gaze on desirable scenery while fattening his pocketbook on profits obtained from Ireland's natural resources. The tract makes clear Swift's abiding sense of Ireland's total vulnerability, to perceptual distortion as well as to economic abuse and political oppression. This distortion results in grossly inaccurate reports about the state of the country: "... because there may be a Dozen Families in this Town, able to entertain their *English* Friends in a generous Manner at their Tables [,] their Guests, upon their Return to *England,* shall report, that we wallow in Riches and Luxury" (12). These "Guests," who carefully limit their social activities to the "safe" realm occupied by the well-to-do Protestant gentry in Dublin and thereby banish all signs of urban poverty from their purview, have something in common with those "strangers from other Countries" who completely refrain from visiting Ireland, "... where they can expect to see nothing, but Scenes of Misery and Desolation" (9). Swift's comment that another pamphleteer, responsible for erroneous accounts of Ireland's state of affairs, "appear[s] to write as a Stranger"

(23), points to the kind of vision that Swift often condemned, deeming it instrumental in reinforcing the country's wretched conditions. To write about or view Ireland "as a Stranger" is to survey the country with a remote and alien vision. A stranger's act of perception presupposes a distance similar to the one separating the Irish, as ailing "Patients," and the English, as "Doctors at a Distance, Strangers to their Constitution, and the Nature of their Disease" (8), whose prescribed "Physick" is aggravating rather than helping to cure the illness.

Another "short view" of Ireland, similar to Swift's, appears in an account written for the periodical the *Reformer* by the eighteen-year-old Trinity College student, Edmund Burke. His essay, like Swift's, demonstrates the inextricable links between perceptual and ideological stance, between one's position as either close or remote observer of the landscape and one's insight into the nature of society. Burke too shows that an accurate view of prevailing conditions depends on which parts of the landscape one chooses to look *at,* as opposed to which parts one can afford to look *over:*

> In this City [Dublin] Things have the best Face; but still, as you leave the Town, the Scene grows worse, and presents you with the utmost Penury in the Midst of a rich Soil. . . . [The people's] Cloaths [are] so ragged, that they rather publish than conceal the Wretchedness it was meant to hide; nay, it is no uncommon Sight to see half a dozen Children run quite naked out of a Cabin, scarcely distinguishable from a Dunghill. . . . Let any one take a Survey of their Cabins, and then say, whether such a Residence be worthy any thing that challenges the Title of a human Creature.[27]

Burke goes on to note that the cabins' furnishings are "much fitter to be lamented than described," thus in effect agreeing with Dunton's point, made a half-century earlier, that the habitations of the Irish peasants "are so very wretched things that perhaps the pen . . . would be very defective in describing them."[28] Such descriptions of Ireland represent an ironic reversal of the literary convention, particularly evident in eighteenth-century poetry, according to which words are deemed inadequate for conveying the ineffable beauties of the landscape. Thomson, for example, reflects upon ". . . hues on hues [that] expression cannot paint" ("Spring," 554) and, acknowledging art's inferiority to nature (. . . But who can paint/Like Nature? . . ." [468–69]), he laments, ". . . If fancy then/ Unequal fails beneath the pleasing task,/Ah, what shall language do? ah, where find words/Tinged with so many colours. . ." (473–76). In eighteenth-century Ireland, it was more often than not the *wretchedness* that defied description. The best a writer could do was to focus his attention wholly upon the concrete details unfolding before his view, to marry word

and thing as closely as possible, for "things"—that is, the harsh, empirically verifiable realities of the Irish countryside—spoke for themselves, with
their own form of nonrhetorical eloquence.

We see this meticulous allegiance to observed detail throughout
Burke's portrayal of the Irish countryside: "You enter [a cabin], or rather
creep in, at a Door of Hurdles plaistered with Dirt, of which the Inhabitant is generally the Fabricator; within-side you see (if the Smoke will
permit you) the Men, Women, Children, Dogs, and Swine lying promis-
cuously; for their Opulence is such that they cannot have a separate
House for their Cattle, as it would take too much from the Garden, whose
produce is their only Support. . . . I Appeal to any one, who knows the
Country, for the Justness of the Picture."[29] This passage reflects a mode
of vision predicated on impassioned immediacy rather than Olympian detachment. The writer, far from being the typical aloof spectator like
Thomson atop Hagley's hill, is an involved actor in the scene, who has
emphatically rejected the visual refuge offered by geographical distance.
That Burke invokes the testimony specifically of one "who knows the
Country" suggests that he, like Swift, recognized the distortions likely
to result from viewing the landscape as a "stranger."

The "Picture" Burke presents in the *Reformer* essay is not the
kind that would ever have adorned the walls of a Houghton or a Twickenham villa. For Burke's "Picture" derives its meaning precisely from what
lies *beyond,* because inherently alien to, the Augustan frame of reference
and framework of values. Its subversive implications with regard to them
may be gleaned from the extent to which it approximates a class analysis
of society. Following his minutely detailed account of the country's rural
poverty, for example, Burke declares:

> Who, after having seen this, comes to Town and beholds [the gen-
> try's] sumptuous and expensive Equipages, their Treats and Diver-
> sions, can contain the highest indignation? . . . I fancy, many of our
> fine Gentlemen's Pageantry would be greatly tarnished, were their
> gilt coaches to be preceded and followed by the miserable Wretches,
> whose Labour supports them . . . that among Creatures of the same
> Kind there should be such a Disproportion in their manner of living;
> it is a kind of Blasphemy on Providence.[30]

The linguistic placing of the "gilt coaches" next to "the miserable Wretches,
whose labour supports them" grows out of a manner of perception that
has inescapable ideological implications, for through it the contemplation
of visual contrasts in the landscape becomes the simultaneous perception
of economic disparities in society, accompanied by the dismaying revelation of massive inequities in all aspects of contemporary life.

Similarly in Swift's writings, a careful scrutiny of existing conditions exposes the inequities of a class society. In the *Short View* we see Irish tenants "who live worse than *English* Beggars" juxtaposed against "those worthy Gentlemen the BANKERS; who . . . [with a few exceptions] are the only thriving People among us. . ." (PW, 12:11). Elsewhere Swift deals with this matter in a less direct but no less forceful manner by dramatizing the fallacies inherent in any mode of vision based upon generalization and abstraction, which is therefore incapable of distinguishing among different landscapes, living conditions, and classes within society. His tract entitled *Maxims Controlled in Ireland,* for example, was written to challenge the supposedly universal validity of ". . . certain Maxims of State, founded upon long observation and experience, drawn from the constant practice of the wisest nations, and from the very principles of government, nor ever controlled [refuted] by any writer upon politics" (131). The "long observation and experience" mentioned here, like the Augustan "long view" with regard to landscape, proves to be in direct conflict with the kind of close observation and day-to-day experience necessary for an accurate understanding of a particular set of circumstances. (Tellingly, those whose reasoning is "founded upon long observation and experience" become identified with "short thinkers" later in the tract.) The tract shows that the words "observation" and "experience" are paradoxically often put to the most unempirical of ends, made to serve the cause of general precepts or theories rather than actual circumstances. The reliance upon "long observation," whether by prospect viewers or political analysts, is likely to result in short-sightedness, in a vision as restricted from one point of view as it is comprehensive from another.

The insistence upon clear, accurate perception is a continuing note throughout Swift's Irish tracts, which repeatedly exhort readers to take off their blinders and open their eyes to both the environmental and the political conditions confronting them: "If I tell you there is a Precipice under you, and that if you go forwards you will certainly break your Necks: If I point to it before your Eyes, must I be at the Trouble of repeating it every Morning? Are our People's *Hearts waxed gross?* Are *their Ears dull of hearing,* and have *they closed their Eyes?*" (PW, 10:22). Swift's role as combined pamphleteer and political activist is to *un*close the people's senses by *dis*closing the facts and precise details of the prevailing situation: "Give me Leave to do what the *Drapier* hath done more than once before me; which is, to relate the naked Fact, as it stands in the View of the World" (105). The blindness of the average Irishman, unlike the carefully cultivated "blindness" of the Augustan spectator, is created by others, imposed from without (though reinforced from within, by his own gullibility), for purposes of political deception rather than aesthetic delectation. As Swift explains it (with the scheme for coining Wood's halfpence in mind), even "the most ruinous project" can be rendered acceptable to the Irish natives:

For the poor ignorant people, allured by the appearing convenience in their small dealings, did not discover the serpent in the brass, but were ready, like the Israelites, to offer incense to it; neither could the wisdom of the nation convince them, until some, of good intentions, made the cheat so plain to their sight, that those who run may read. And thus the design was to treat us, in every point, as the Philistines treated Samson, (I mean when he was betrayed by Dalilah) first to put out our eyes, and then bind us with fetters of brass. (PW, 9:238)

The association made here between blindness and captivity is of particular significance for Swift's writings, which are intended to clarify as well as to focus his countrymen's perception—to direct their gaze to the most important objects and issues confronting them, as a means not only of heightening their consciousness, but also of freeing them in a very literal sense.

The perceptual distortion that appears throughout Swift's early odes, with their imagistic emphasis upon optical illusions, blindness, and visual as well as moral and physical errancy, tends to become translated into more specifically political terms in his later writings. Instead of "the *deluding Muse*" who "... blinds [the poet] to her Ways" (*Ode to the Athenian Society*, 234), we have a deluding colonialist power that tries to blind an entire nation to its practices. The people's "prostituted sight," produced by their "deflower'd eye," which cannot "face the naked light" (*Ode to Dr. William Sancroft*, 221–22), is later understood as a visual affliction perpetrated on them by the ruling class (though unwittingly intensified by their own folly). Swift's subsequent role as political pamphleteer, opener of his compatriots' eyes, is foreshadowed in the *Ode to Sir William Temple*, where he "expose[s] the Scene" behind the curtains of "The wily Shafts of State, those Juggler's Tricks" (97, 92) and "Down the ill-organ'd Engines fall;/Off fly the Vizards and discover all,/How plain I see thro' the Deceit!/How shallow! and how gross the Cheat!" (98–101). Temple's young amanuensis, who could pierce the façade in order to expose the "Cheat" within, later becomes the Drapier-Dean, capable of "ma[king] the cheat so plain to [his countrymen's] sight." Again and again, Swift's writings urge the pursuit of clear-sightedness, a form of vision that in virtually every case calls for close scrutiny and thus rejects the "long views" prescribed by conventional Augustan wisdom.

v

The extent to which Swift's stance as spectator differed from the typical stance of his contemporaries is apparent in an exchange of letters between himself and Bolingbroke in the summer of 1729. In part responding to an epistle addressed jointly to himself and to Pope several months earlier, in which Swift complained that "I never wake without finding

life a more insignificant thing than it was the day before" (C, 3:329),
Bolingbroke writes in a spirit of philosophic detachment, assuring Swift
that "if you will come to a certain farm in Middlesex, you shall find that
I can live frugally without growling att the world" (348) and advising him
to adopt a more stoical attitude toward life, which requires that Swift
change his mode of viewing the world:

> you say you are no Philosopher, and I think you are in the right to
> dislike a word which is so often abused, but I am sure you like to
> follow Reason, not custom, which is sometimes the Reason & oftner
> the Caprice of others, of the Mob of the world. now to be sure of
> doing this, you must wear your philosophical Spectacles as constant-
> ly as the Spaniards used to wear theirs. you must make them part of
> your dress, and sooner part with your broad brimmed Beaver, your
> Gown, your Scarf, or even that emblematical vestment your Surplice,
> thro' this medium you will see few things to be vexed att, few per-
> sons to be angry att. (C, 3:349)

Bolingbroke is here proposing a presumably superior mode of perception
that is actually a call for selective blindness to "the Mob of the world"
as well as to the existential conditions connected with it—to the very world
of poverty, disease, and starvation that Swift was agitatedly describing in
ever greater detail in his correspondence and pamphlets. Indeed, in a letter
written only two weeks before Bolingbroke counseled use of the "philosophical Spectacles," Swift was telling Pope about the "three terrible
years dearth of corn" in Ireland and concluding somberly, "These evils
operate more every day, and the kingdom is absolutely undone, as I have
been telling it often in print these ten years past" (C, 3:341).

Given Swift's preoccupations during this period and his sense of
urgency about the contemporary situation, it is not surprising that he
found Bolingbroke's advice inappropriate as well as uncongenial to his
own way of looking at the world. He makes this clear in his response to
the viscount two months later: "I renounce your whole Philosophy, because it is not your practice by the figure of Living. . . . I wish you could
learn Arithmetick, that 3 and 2 make 5, and will never make more. My
Philosophical Spectacles which you advise me to, will tell me that I can live
on 50^{ll} a Year (Wine excepted which my bad health forces me to) . . ." (C,
3:354-55). Swift characteristically gets down to brass tacks and everyday
realities. While Bolingbroke waxes eloquent upon the lofty detachment
enjoyed by the wise man, affirming that he himself finds "little Regret
when I look backwards, little apprehension when I look forwards" (348),
Swift is insisting in a letter to Pope that ". . . we wise men must think of
nothing but getting a little ready money" (355), thereby typically shifting
the basis of wisdom from an otherworldly transcendence to a clear, unob-

structed look at the concerns of *this* world. In a situation where "there are not two hundred thousand pounds of species in the whole island . . . and so are all inevitably undone" (355), the act of contemplating one's surroundings through "philosophical Spectacles" makes no more sense than the act of admiring beautiful prospects through the barred windows of a dungeon. The uselessness of Bolingbroke's "philosophical Spectacles" is indirectly underscored in Swift's poem *The Bubble*, which makes the point that concrete realities will not conveniently disappear or change into something more palatable simply because one uses an artificial, presumably superior medium through which to observe them:

> But as a Guinnea will not pass
> At Market for a Farthing more
> Shewn through a multiplying Glass
> Than what it allways did before;
>
> So cast it in the *Southern* Seas,
> And view it through a *Jobber*'s Bill,
> Put on what Spectacles You please,
> Your Guinnea's but a Guinnea still.
>
> (117–24)

Undoubtedly one can, through a variety of visual manipulations, "see few things to be vexed att, few persons to be angry att," but for Swift there is a heavy price to pay for this "luxury": condemning oneself to a world of fantasy and self-deception. As he explains the matter in a letter countering Dean Brandreth's "philosophical" perception of the country in Tipperary, "I have not said all this [concerning the poverty and desolation of the Tipperary landscape] out of any malicious intention, to put you out of conceit with the scene where you are, but merely for your credit; because it is better to know you are miserable, than to betray an ill taste. . ." (C, 4:34). Swift is in effect telling Brandreth to *remove* his "philosophical Spectacles" so that he can view his surroundings accurately, without comforting illusion.[31] It is characteristic of Swift that he associates Brandreth's unrealistically rosy picture with the stance of "an excellent philosopher," for throughout his writings he uses the term "philosopher" in alternately ambiguous, mocking, or ironic ways, to denote attitudes fundamentally inimical to his own temperament and mode of perception. The pejorative associations of the word are epitomized in Swift's versified comment addressed to Lady Acheson:

> You, like some acute Philosopher,
> Ev'ry Fault have drawn a Gloss over:
> Placing in the strongest Light,
> All your Virtues to my Sight.
>
> (*An Epistle to a Lady,* 95–98)

The philosopher's mode of perception, far from being disinterested and objective, is here defined as manipulative, hence deliberately deceptive and self-serving. Systematically "Gloss[ing] over" an entire body of earthly realities in the process of magnifying another, it results in a "cosmetic" vision, designed to beautify through selective concealment and appealing distortion. The philosopher's mode of perception is ironically akin to the warped perspective expressed by the Tale-teller in the "Digression on Madness": "How fade and insipid do all Objects accost us that are not convey'd in the Vehicle of *Delusion?* How shrunk is every Thing, as it appears in the Glass of Nature? So, that if it were not for the Assistance of Artificial *Mediums,* false Lights, refracted Angles, Varnish, and Tinsel; there would be a mighty Level in the Felicity and Enjoyments of Mortal Men" (TT, 172).

The insistence upon intractable realities, stubbornly resistant to all forms of visual rearrangement, optical illusion, and wishful thinking, is central to Swift's outlook and writings. It is an aspect that can be too easily overlooked in our understandable preoccupation with Swift's multiple ironies and with the complex ambiguities that make us feel as though we are walking on shifting sands when we read much of his work. There was an important side of Swift, however, that enabled him to cut through layers of confusion, delusion, and illusion as did no other eighteenth-century writer, in order to reveal the unalterable, often visible and tactile reality beneath. For all of Swift's acute awareness of shifting perspectives and how they affect the way in which external reality is interpreted, he remained throughout his life a firm believer in the latter's unequivocal existence and its susceptibility to being clearly defined and objectively verified. By the same token, although there was a side of Swift that could very well understand the appeal of that "sublime and refined Point of Felicity, called, *the Possession of being well deceived . . .*" (TT, 174)—a side that indulged the yearning for pleasing appearances since, as the Tale-teller puts it, ". . . in most Corporeal Beings, which have fallen under my Cognizance, the *Outside* hath been infinitely preferable to the *In . . .*" (173)[32]—we should keep in mind that the major thrust of Swift's writings was directed *against* the state of being "well deceived," and reflected his commitment to seeing things clearly, as they really are.

Thus, in a verse written on the occasion of Stella's birthday, Swift exults in the deterioration of his eyesight, which allows him to indulge in both mental and optical illusion, even as he simultaneously acknowledges the irrevocable fact of advancing age and indirectly confirms the very realities that his faulty vision negates:

> But, *Stella* say, what evil Tongue
> Reports you are no longer young?

That *Time* sits with his Scythe to mow
Where erst sate *Cupid* with his Bow;
That half your Locks are turn'd to Grey;
I'll ne'er believe a Word they say.
'Tis true, but let it not be known,
My Eyes are somewhat dimmish grown;
For Nature, always in the Right,
To your Decays adapts my Sight,
And Wrinkles undistinguish'd pass,
For I'm asham'd to use a Glass;
And till I see them with these Eyes,
Whoever says you have them, lyes.

                    (*Stella's Birth-Day* [1725], 35–48)

The poem, with its opening simile reminding us of the inevitable passage of time ("As when a beauteous Nymph decays/We say, she's past her Dancing Days") and its frank recognition of the toll this passage has taken on praiser and praised alike, is finally less a tribute to the "sublime and refined Point of Felicity, called, *the Possession of being well deceived*" than it is an affirmation of man's ability to see things as they really are despite the ever-present temptation of, and periodic flirtations with, comforting illusion. Swift, as one "asham'd to use a Glass," refuses to look at the world, or his beloved friend, through any kind of spectacles, philosophical or otherwise, and consequently he sees things in their natural state even though he can playfully pretend to see them otherwise.[33]

Significantly, Swift, in playfully commenting upon Bolingbroke's spectacles, implies a link between his friend's mode of perception and his class affiliation, his "station" in life. It is not coincidental that in the same letter in which he rejects Bolingbroke's use of "philosophical Spectacles," Swift alludes to the vast discrepancy in social and economic status between the two men: "My Lord I writ to Mr Pope, and not to you. My Birth although from a Family not undistinguished in its time is many degrees inferior to Yours, all my pretensions from Persons and parts infinitely so; I a Younger Son of younger Sons, You born to a great Fortune" (C, 3:354). The characterization of himself as "a Younger Son," although factually inaccurate, serves to dramatize his sense of identification with a class of estateless, disinherited beings who must struggle for their survival in a world controlled by others. Swift's comment immediately following ("Yet I see you with all your advantages Sunk to a degree that could never have been so without them. But yet I see you as much esteemed, as much beloved, as much dreaded, & perhaps more . . . than e'er you were in your highest exaltation . . .") develops further the imagistic contrast between height and lowness. Although Bolingbroke's fortune has "Sunk," he remains to all intents and purposes in a position of "highest exaltation," while Swift, "many degrees inferior," occupies a place much lower down in the social order. This difference in elevation corresponds to a difference in angle of vision.

Despite Bolingbroke's protestations that he must resign himself to lean times and increasing economic hardships (C, 3:348), Swift indicates that he is very well aware of the wide gap between Bolingbroke's romanticized notions about accepting "forced Retrenchments" in order to live a simpler, more frugal existence and the realities of his situation as a lord "born to a great Fortune": ". . . can you, could you, come over and live with Mr Pope and Me at the Deanery when you are undone. I could almost wish the Experiment were tryed.—No—God forbid, that ever such a Scoundrel as *want* should date [*sic*] to approach you. But in the meantime do not brag; Retrenchments are not your Talent. . ." (354). In a letter written to Pope some fifteen months earlier, Swift underscored even more emphatically the unbreachable gulf between the viscount and himself:

> By the way, I must observe, that my Lord Bolingbroke (from the effects of his kindness to me) argues most sophistically: The fall from a million to an hundred-thousand pounds is not so great, as from eight hundred pounds a year to one: Besides, he is a controller of Fortune, and Poverty dares not look a great Minister in the face, under his lowest declension. I never knew him live so great and expensively as he hath done since his return from Exile; such mortals have resources that others are not able to comprehend. (C, 3:294)

Here Bolingbroke is perceived not merely as a man "born to a great Fortune" but as the master of his fate and ruler over his environs. He can enjoy his philosophic flights atop a lofty peak remote from the "Mob of the world" precisely because he has sufficient wealth and "resources"— because he can *afford* to do so in every sense. Swift, on the contrary, condemned to remain a "slave" in Ireland, cannot afford to become a philosopher or to view his surroundings through "philosophical Spectacles," struggling as he must with the mundane issues of human survival.

vi

As Swift's comments suggest, Bolingbroke belonged to a very special group in society for whom philosophical spectacles were the appropriate instruments to attain refined perception: a group whom we may think of as the "spectator class," whose members automatically defined themselves as viewers rather than viewed objects, as surveyors (not to mention creators) of the landscape rather than features of the landscape that were subject to being surveyed (and re-created) by others. John Berger indirect-

ly points to the profound ideological ramifications of this role in his discussion of certain perceptual aspects of post-Renaissance European art:
"The convention of perspective . . . centres everything on the eye of the
beholder. It is like a beam from a lighthouse—only instead of light travelling outwards, appearances travel in. The conventions called those appearances *reality*. Perspective makes the single eye the centre of the visible
world. Everything converges on to the eye as to the vanishing point of
infinity. The visible world is arranged for the spectator as the universe
was once thought to be arranged for God."[34] Berger's wording emphasizes
the enormous power implicit in the role of spectator, a power emphasized
also by Denis Donoghue in his phrase, "The Eye as Benevolent Despot."[35]
Both characterizations are particularly applicable to eighteenth-century
aesthetics and ideology as reflected in the period's literature.

It is not accidental that Pope's eye is accorded particular attention
and plays a crucial role in his verse, occupying as it does the center of his
poetic world in much the same way that the all-seeing eye of Bishop Berkeley's God is at the center of the divinely created world. In both uni-
verses, perception is a very concrete and awesome power: the power to
define and constitute essence, to validate (or, as the case may be, to *in*-
validate) one's very being. The two worlds function similarly on the
Berkeleian principle that "everything is as it is perceived," so that the
inhabitants of each must depend upon an observer's steady, reaffirming
gaze in order to escape extinction. Throughout Pope's poetry, the relationship between perceiver and perceived is implicitly hierarchic in nature,
analogous to the distinction between controller and controlled, between
creator and created. We see this most clearly exemplified in the relationship between the poet and his satiric butts: objects minutely scrutinized
and placed on perpetual display, at times explicitly converted into *objets
d'art* that are shown off in Pope's picture gallery, like the portraits of
women in his *Epistle To a Lady*. Such objects are rendered impotent as
a result of their exposure to the poet's withering glance and to the gaze
of other onlookers whom he summons forth as a viewing audience. We
may recall the depiction of Silia's sudden rages: "All eyes may see from
what the change arose,/All eyes may see—a Pimple on her nose" (*Second
Moral Essay: To a Lady*, 35-36). On another level, Pope's seemingly
God-like vision comprehends the entire world in one sweeping glance.
In the *Essay on Man,* for example, Pope helps us scan the universe (or,
more accurately, scans the universe for us), substituting for the divine fiat
his own version of a divine stare, which at once "visualizes things into existence" and confirms their position in the Great Chain of Being. The
authority Pope exercises as our tour guide through the universe derives
from his appropriation of the all-seeing eye of God, defined precisely as
"He, who thro' vast immensity can pierce,/See worlds on worlds compose

one universe,/ [and] Observe how system into system runs. . ." (Epistle I,
23–25). The broad sweep and superior detachment of Pope's survey,
achieved with what he elsewhere describes as "philosophic eyes" that can
". . . view this dreadful All without a fear" (*Imitations of Horace, Epistle
I, vi,* 7, 10), in effect proclaims him master of the visible world spread
before him and of all those enclosed within its boundaries.[36]

Swift had little to do with the exalted status and efficacy of this
kind of God-like spectator. His writings indicate that he tended to identify not so much with the perceivers as with the objects of perception (or,
as the case may be, of *non*perception, since those with the power to see
could also exercise their prerogative of *not* seeing, of turning their gaze
elsewhere). Swift, in much of his verse, portrays himself as a figure *in,*
rather than overlooking, the landscape, often as someone on alien turf,
either being watched and laughed at or ostentatiously ignored by others
in his milieu.

In *Gulliver's Travels,* although the persona-protagonist regularly
performs the role of observer and recorder of his surroundings, recurring
passages, some of which are among the most memorable in the work, depict him as the viewed object rather than the viewer. By the very fiction
of the work he is a highly conspicuous creature amidst alien surroundings.
In Lilliput, Gulliver is subjected to the intensely curious scrutiny of
virtually the entire native population: "It was reckoned that above an
hundred thousand Inhabitants came out of the Town . . . [to have an Opportunity of viewing me] ; and in spight of my Guards, I believe there
could not be fewer than ten thousand, at several Times, who mounted
upon my Body by the Help of Ladders" (PW, 11:28). In Brobdingnag,
Gulliver is looked upon by the farmer who discovers him "as a Curiosity" requiring minute visual inspection (88). Later he is made an object
of display, exposed to the gaze of "Thirty People at a Time" at the Green
Eagle Inn (97), and soon after becomes a one-man traveling freak show,
performing "ten Times a Day to the Wonder and Satisfaction of all
People" (99). At the Brobdingnagian Court he continues to be a creature
on display. The King of Brobdingnag has three wise men examine Gulliver
carefully in order to determine his exact nature: "They observed by my
Teeth, which they viewed with great Exactness, that I was a carnivorous
Animal. . . . One of them seemed to think that I might be an Embrio, or
abortive Birth. But this Opinion was rejected by the other two, who observed my Limbs to be perfect and finished; and that I had lived several
Years, as it was manifested from my Beard; the Stumps whereof they
plainly discovered through a Magnifying-Glass" (103–4). This scenario
is repeated almost exactly in the fourth voyage, where the perplexed
Houyhnhnms examine Gulliver in order to ascertain what he is: "The two

Horses came up close to me, looking with great Earnestness upon my Face and Hands" (225).

The sense communicated in these instances of being the observed rather than the observer, the victim rather than the master of perception, reflects an important aspect of Swift's own feelings about himself and his relationship to others in his society. As a friend of and propagandist for the Tory ministry in London during the years 1710-1714, he often found himself in a situation not wholly unlike Gulliver's: an outsider and a subordinate being watched by those in power. Entries in the *Journal to Stella* point to Swift's awareness of being in such a position. In one entry, for example, he reports: "There was a drawing-room to-day at Court; but so few company, that the queen sent for us into her bed-chamber, where we made our bows, and stood about twenty of us round the room, while she looked at us round with her fan in her mouth, and once a minute said about three words to some that were nearest her, and then she was told dinner was ready, and went out" (JS, 1:328). In the world of English royalty and politics, someone in Swift's position could be made into a spectacle, an object on display for the diversion of his betters, almost as readily as Gulliver in Lilliput. His presence could be demanded at any time, much as Gulliver in Brobdingnag, whose queen "became so fond of [his] Company, that she could not dine without [him]" (PW, 11:105).

The account of the "diversions" at the Lilliputian Court similarly shows the way in which those in power can reduce others to mere spectacles. Subjects trying to curry favor with the emperor and empress must continually entertain; their entire life turns into an endless performance, as exemplified by the "Rope-Dancers, [who] performed upon a slender white Thread, extended about two Foot, and twelve Inches from the Ground," and by those who "undergo a Tryal of Dexterity" by *"leaping* and *creeping"* over and under a stick held by the Emperor (PW, 11:38-39). Although Gulliver is initially included among the spectators, he inevitably becomes part of the show, assisting in various military exercises for the horses of the royal stable (40). Gulliver's creator, befriended by the leaders of the Tory ministry, was also permitted at least partial entrance into the ruling spectatorial class even as he remained—and felt himself to be—on the outside, subject at any moment to being ushered before them and relegated to the status of spectacle: "Mr. Examiner" turned into the object of examination.

The other side of the coin holds true for Swift as well: He could abruptly be relegated to invisibility by being *dis*regarded—quite literally, in the sense that someone's "regard" was suddenly taken away from him. Those in power had the option of refusing to see him. Throughout the *Journal to Stella,* we find expressions of his resentment at not having been allowed access to Harley or Bolingbroke—at having to return to his lodg-ings without "being seen": "I went to the secretary in the morning, and he was gone to Windsor. . . . This toad of a secretary is come from Windsor, and I can't find him; and he goes back on Sunday, and I can't see him to-morrow" (JS, 1:309, 312). Swift's bitter memory of the ne-glect he suffered at the hands of Godolphin and other Whig ministers in 1710 made him especially sensitive to even the slightest hint of indiffer-ence or disregard shown toward him by the great: "I have been used barbarously by the late ministry; I am a little piqued in honour to let people see I am not to be despised" (233). Swift's hypersensitivity in this matter was exacerbated by memories of the treatment he received at Moor Park:

> . . . one thing I warned him [Bolingbroke] of, Never to appear cold to me, for I would not be treated like a school-boy; that I had felt too much of that in my life already (meaning from sir William Temp-le); that I expected every great minister, who honoured me with his acquaintance, if he heard or saw any thing to my disadvantage, would let me know it in plain words, and not put me in pain to guess by the change or coldness of his countenance or behaviour; for it was what I would hardly bear from a crowned head, and I thought no subject's favour was worth it. (JS, 1:230)

Swift's writings, verse and prose alike, attest to his continuing strug-gle to steer a course between the Scylla of being made the center of atten-tion, viewed with scorn and/or amusement as an anomalous figure in the landscape, usually (but not necessarily) by his betters, and the Charybdis of not being seen at all, of being consigned to oblivion because the eyes of the powerful have turned elsewhere. Throughout his life Swift both yearned to be seen, to be recognized and regarded in his own person (as he noted in one letter, "I never loved to make a visit, or be seen walk-ing with my betters, because they get all the eyes and civilities from me" [C, 3:331]) and dreaded being seen, in the way and to the extent that those in the lower social and political ranks were "seen" by those in power, surveyed with aloof disdain, mild curiosity, or scornful amusement. We may recall that Swift, in listing "The Blessings of a Country Life," included "not [being] seen by our Betters" (P, 3:1036). Subconsciously Swift might well have sensed that Bolingbroke's method of observing his surroundings through "philosophical Spectacles" usually meant *overlook-ing* men in Swift's station, both in the sense of "look[ing] down upon; . . . survey[ing] from above, or from a higher position" and of "look[ing] over and beyond and thus not see[ing] ; . . . leav[ing] out of consideration, disregard[ing], and ignor[ing] " (see *Oxford English Dictionary,* 1933 ed., meanings 4 and 2).

The two horns of this epistemological dilemma are given humorous treatment in a number of Swift's verses, such as *Part of the Seventh Epistle of the First Book of Horace, Imitated,* where Swift first appears as a viewed figure in the landscape, seen through the eyes of Harley. As the latter is "Returning home one Day from Court," he

> Observ'd a *Parson* near *Whitehall,*
> Cheapning old Authors on a Stall.
> The Priest was pretty well in case,
> And shew'd some Humour in his Face;
> Look'd with an easie, careless Mien,
> A perfect Stranger to the Spleen;
> Of Size that might a Pulpit fill,
> But more inclining to sit still.
>
> (5-12)

Like Gulliver, Swift is a curiosity piece—a specimen to be examined with alternating wonder and amusement. Significantly, Harley spies the pedestrian, Swift, while riding in his coach; his view, therefore, clearly reflects the hierarchic distinction between them. The next time the two men find themselves in the same place, Swift is once more a part of the urban scene unfurling before the eyes of carriage riders: "Some few Days after *HAR-LEY* spies/The Doctor fasten'd by the Eyes,/At *Charing-Cross,* among the Rout,/Where painted Monsters are hung out" (57-60). As Swift watches the grotesque spectacle in Charing-Cross, he himself becomes part of it. He is wholly exposed to view—like Gulliver, subject to the whims and commands of the beholders: "He [Harley] pull'd the String, and stopt his Coach,/Beck'ning the Doctor to approach./S——t, who could neither fly nor hide,/Came sneaking to the Chariot-side..." (61-64). The poem follows Swift as he moves (or rather, is moved) from one landscape to another, from the squalid cityscape where he mingles with "the Rout" to the affluent environs of Windsor, which proves yet more tasty bait: "S——t much admires the Place and Air,/And longs to be a *Canon* there" (83-84).

It is at this moment, when he has cleverly lured the fish into the net ("In short, the Gudgeon took the Bait" [80]), that Harley starts to lose interest in the sport and begins moving his eyes away from Swift, who is now no longer the object of regard but the victim of *dis*regard. On a manifestly false pretext, Harley in effect "exiles" Swift to Ireland, which is also to say that he banishes Swift from his sight. Later, when a very bedraggled, long-suffering Swift returns to Harley after a disastrous experience in Ireland, having lost all of his money and "Above a Thousand Pounds in Debt" (115), he is almost denied renewed access to Harley's sight: "He soon arrives at *HARLEY*'s Gate;/But was so dirty, pale and thin,/Old *Read* would hardly let him in" (118-20). Balancing the outset

of the poem, the ending allows us to view Swift once again through Harley's eyes:

> Said *HARLEY*, Welcome Rev'rend Dean!
> What makes your Worship look so lean?
> Why sure you won't appear in Town,
> In that old Wig and rusty Gown!
> I doubt your Heart is set on Pelf
> So much, that you neglect your Self.

(121-26)

Once more captured and defined (in this case, grossly misinterpreted) by
Harley's aloof gaze, Swift can only plead to be left alone and returned to
the landscape he occupied before he was moved about at the whim of
those more powerful: "Then since you now have done your worst,/Pray
leave me where you found me first" (137-38). Considering the fate Swift
incurs as a result of having been placed in the spotlight, it is hardly surprising that he should prefer a state of anonymity and invisibility.

Yet this state brings with it its own set of frustrations and humiliations. We are reminded of Eugenio in the *Intelligencer, Nos. V* and *VII*,
whose worldly fortunes suffer because he disdains slavish attendance upon
the great, thereby leaving the field open to "vigilant Dunces, who were
sure to be never out of Sight" (PW, 12:45). Remaining in the "sight" of
one's betters is conceived of here as a form of "slavery," but at the same
time it is deemed the necessary means to advancement and success in the
eyes of the world. Eugenio's deliberate withdrawal from the "sight" of
great persons eventually culminates in his removal from the "sight" of the
entire world—his retreat into "the most desert Parts of *Lincolnshire*"
where he lives out the remainder of his life as a forgotten piece of an un-
visited and unviewed landscape.

Swift's lifelong dread of encountering a similar fate may be inferred
from passages in his writings that express his desire to be seen and regarded
—to be admired by all including (indeed, especially) the great. In a letter
addressed jointly to Pope and to Bolingbroke, for example, he confesses,
"I hate a crowd where I have not an easy place to see and be seen. A great
Library always maketh me melancholy, where the best Author is as much
squeezed, and as obscure, as a Porter at a Coronation" (C, 3:330). This
image is peculiarly appropriate for Swift; the obscurity of "a Porter at
a Coronation" was precisely the condition Swift strove to avoid throughout his life, perhaps because he was particularly vulnerable to it as a
relatively poor and obscure Irishman regularly thrust into privileged
surroundings, where he found himself in the company of the well-born
and the powerful. Whether at Whitehall, Windsor, or Moor Park, Swift
participated in important functions of state while never actually shedding

his status as an inferior and a servant. As he notes to Stella in a journal entry: "They [members of the Tory ministry] call me nothing but Jonathan;
and I said, I believed they would leave me Jonathan as they found me" (JS,
1:193-94). In his warning to Bolingbroke that he "would not be treated
like a school-boy," a form of behavior he "would hardly bear from a
crowned head" let alone a fellow subject, we are in a sense hearing the
peeved and rebellious voice of the "Porter at a Coronation," refusing to
accept his condition in life as a "much squeezed" and "obscure" flunky
for the great, demanding to be regarded at all times.

Above all a man of concrete, visual imagination, Swift was acutely
conscious of the necessity to cut a certain kind of figure in the world so
as to be seen in the first place, and in the second, to be seen in a desirable
light. He expresses this need in a self-mocking manner in *The Author upon
Himself*: "The Waiters stand in Ranks; the Yeomen cry,/*Make Room*; as
if a Duke were passing by" (35-36). Swift realized only too well that in
order to gain acceptance into the inner circles of English political and
social life, he would not only have to possess exceptional qualities of
mind and soul, but would also have to make these qualities *visible* to the
well-born, influential "spectators" of the age: ". . . all my endeavours
from a boy to distinguish my self, were only for want of a great Title and
Fortune, that I might be used like a Lord by those who have an opinion
of my parts . . . and so the reputation of wit or great learning does the office of a blue riband, or of a coach and six horses" (C, 3:330-31). In the
absence of "great Title and Fortune," Swift had to make his wit and learning conspicuous so that others would easily recognize and respond to
them as they would to the visible marks of social distinction and worldly
power.

Swift's dilemma was never satisfactorily resolved, of course, given the
political and historical realities of the world he inhabited. His life was
marked by the profound, continued struggle that inevitably characterizes
members of a class dependent upon a higher class for its status and legitimacy, in a sense for its very definition. His writings record this struggle,
but they also celebrate a kind of triumph and success impossible to achieve
in the actual world. Through a variety of rhetorical, particularly satiric
means, Swift again and again turns the tables—or, to be more precise, the
eyes—on his beholders/oppressors and subjects them to the same imperious and humiliating scrutiny he himself had to endure as part of his daily
existence. We see repeated instances of this tactic in *Gulliver's Travels*,
where Gulliver, the minutely examined object, suddenly takes over as the
observer and reduces his captors to an absurd spectacle. In Brobdingnag,
for example, the Queen makes Gulliver the staple of her regular dinner-
time entertainment: "Her Majesty used to put a Bit of Meat upon one of
my Dishes, out of which I carved for my self; and her Diversion was to see

me eat in Miniature." Whereupon Gulliver, taking his cue from the Queen's actions, reduces *her* to grotesque visual display: "For the Queen . . . took up at one Mouthful, as much as a dozen *English* Farmers could eat at a Meal, which to me was for some time a very nauseous Sight. She would craunch the Wing of a Lark, Bones and all, between her Teeth, although it were nine Times as large as that of a full grown Turkey; and put a Bit of Bread in her Mouth, as big as two twelve-penny Loaves" (PW, 11:106). Similarly, when the Maids of Honour ask Glumdalclitch to bring Gulliver to their apartments for their voyeuristic pleasure ("They would often strip me naked from Top to Toe, and lay me at full Length in their Bosoms" [118]), *they* rather than Gulliver turn into the main objects on display: "Their skins appeared so coarse and uneven, so variously coloured when I saw them near, with a Mole here and there as broad as a Trencher, and Hairs hanging from it thicker than Pack-threads. . ." (119). This strategy of perceptual reversal is epitomized in the passage where a friend comes to visit the Brobdingnagian farmer in order to inspect Gulliver with his own eyes, and himself winds up the comic spectacle under the pressure of Gulliver's mischievous gaze: "This Man, who was old and dim-sighted, put on his Spectacles to behold me better, at which I could not forbear laughing very heartily; for his Eyes appeared like the Full-Moon shining into a Chamber at two Windows. Our People, who discovered the Cause of my Mirth, bore me Company in Laughing; at which the old Fellow was Fool enough to be angry and out of Countenance" (96).

Swift's verse is likewise filled with instances where the denigrated object becomes the exulting subject—where Swift the comic spectacle wreaks his revenge upon his amused, condescending audience, whose members suddenly find themselves center stage, gawked at and ridiculed by their inferiors turned tormentors. *An Apology to the Lady C*[a]*r*[tere]*t*, for example, dramatizes Swift's vulnerability as a member of an alternately scrutinized and disregarded class, but it ultimately suggests an "out" for him through his assumption of the role of spectator and comic delineator. The "Lady" of the title has sent an invitation to Swift to dine with her at Dublin Castle. His response and subsequent preparations for the dinner exemplify a broadly comic but at the same time painful self-consciousness, an awareness of all eyes being upon him:

> His Beaver brush'd, his Shoes, and Gown,
> Away he trudges into Town;
> Passes the Lower Castle Yard,
> And now advancing to the Guard,
> He trembles at the Thoughts of State;
> For, conscious of his Sheepish Gait,
> His Spirits of a sudden fail'd him,
> He stop'd, and cou'd not tell what ail'd him.

(27–34)

The passage is above all humorous, of course, yet it does point to something important about Swift's sense of place (or rather, lack of place) in the world. Swift's self-portrayal reflects the radical anxieties and insecurities of the class under observation, not the easy self-confidence and certainty about worldly position displayed by the "spectator" class.

This distinction would have been particularly relevant to the situation presented in *An Apology,* where Swift, a Dubliner of relatively obscure origins, finds himself at the palatial residence of the English nobleman Lord Carteret, who had shortly before commenced his tenure as lord lieutenant of Ireland. The distinction was intensified at this time because Swift, in his role as Drapier, was in the act of waging battle against Wood's patent and its supporter, the Walpole ministry, whose interests Carteret had come to Ireland to represent. Although Swift and Carteret had always been on friendly terms in the past, Swift's correspondence during this period indicates the deepening strain between the two men as a result of their divergent political positions. It likewise reflects the division between the observers and the observed, for as lord lieutenant, Carteret performed the function of overseer of Irish affairs, while the political activist Swift was very definitely a man under careful observation, a man whose every word and deed were subjected to minute scrutiny by England's watchdogs in Ireland. His writings abundantly attest to his acute awareness of being looked upon by those in power with suspicious and hostile eyes, of being under constant surveillance.

In its depiction of Swift parading himself in the full view of both the great and their lackeys on the grounds of Dublin Castle, symbol of English authority, *An Apology to the Lady C[a]r[tere]t* presents a comic version of Swift's exposed and conspicuous position in the context of contemporary Irish affairs. It also interestingly serves to confirm the validity of Addison's differentiation between Englishmen and Irishmen as manifested by their respective forms of impudence: "Impudence in an *Englishman,* is sullen and insolent; . . . in an *Irishman* absurd and fawning: As the Course of the World now runs, the impudent *Englishman* behaves like a surly Landlord, . . . and the *Irishman* like a Stranger who knows he is not welcome. There is seldom any thing entertaining either in the Impudence of a *South* or *North Briton;* but that of an *Irishman* is always Comick."[37] In the *Apology* the Irish dean simultaneously displays and mocks his own "absurd and fawning" behavior at Dublin Castle, where his every gesture suggests his sense of being "a Stranger who knows he is not welcome"—one who entertains an impromptu audience with his own unique brand of comic self-assertion.

This exposure to view, with its attendant humiliations, is stressed throughout the poem. Swift, discovering that Lady Carteret is not at home, assumes that a joke has been played upon him and returns to the deanery without waiting. When his hostess reappears after what has been only a brief stroll, she is shocked to learn of Swift's abrupt departure and, resolving to "...Try his Manners once again" (68), sends another invitation for the following morning, whereupon the burlesque progress from the deanery to Dublin Castle is repeated (75–78). Lady Carteret agrees to forgive Swift's earlier offense provided he write a verse explaining his behavior. In composing the promised lines, Swift underscores the dual problem for him of being seen as a comic spectacle on the one hand, and of not being seen at all on the other—the no-win situation in which he is faced with either the wrong kind of regard or utter disregard:

> Consider what it is to bear
> The powder'd Courtier's witty Sneer;
> To see th' important Men of Dress,
> Scoffing my College Aukwardness.
> To be the strutting Cornet's Sport,
> To run the Gauntlet of the Court;
> Winning my Way by slow Approaches,
> Thro' Crowds of Coxcombs & of Coaches;
> From the first fierce cockaded Centry,
> Quite thro' the Tribe of waiting Gentry;
> To pass to many crowded Stages,
> And stand the Staring of your Pages;
> And after all, to crown my Spleen,
> Be told—*You are not to be seen*. . . .

(145–58)

The humiliation of learning that he is *"not to be seen"* by his hostess, especially after having endured the scornful gaze of her servants, is linguistically balanced against the terrifying consequences of *being seen* by her: "Or, if you are [seen], be forc'd to bear/The Awe of your Majestick Air?/ ... is he criminal that flies/The living Lusture [*sic*] of your Eyes?" (159–60, 165–66). Here playful courtly praise combines with comic apology to suggest Swift's continuing predicament as the awkward, self-conscious Irish churchman who throughout his lifetime fretted about cutting the right kind of figure in public while periodically retiring in disgust to some remote place where he could escape into invisibility.

But the poem is more than an exercise in self-mockery and self-exposure, for ultimately Swift does succeed in asserting his own form of control over the situation. As poet he gets his revenge even though, as Dean and Drapier, he remains vulnerable to the powers that be. Swift exchanges his role of captive guest for that of host, performing a partly serious, partly parodic version of a country house lord for the visiting Lady Carteret, whereupon she is captured within the gaze and the song of the onlooking Swift, who watches with a hint of malicious glee as she battles the elements in the deanery garden, a landscape as alien and hostile to her as her regal environs are to Swift. Thus the "gracious Dame"

... tho' seeming pleas'd, can't bear
The scorching Sun, or chilling Air;
Frighted alike at both Extremes,
If he displays, or hides his Beams;
Tho' seeming pleas'd at all she sees,
Starts at the Rust'ling of the Trees;
Can scarsely speak for want of Breath,
In half a Walk fatigu'd to Death.

(121-28)

In the verses he writes "To vindicate his late Offence" (130), Swift subjects his noble guest once again to his penetrating, gently mocking gaze and underscores her ineptitude amidst alien surroundings:

If long confin'd to Fires and Screens,
You dread the waving of these Greens;
If you, who long have breath'd the Fumes
Of City Fogs and crowded Rooms,
Do now solicitiously shun
The cooler Air, and dazzling Sun;
If his Majestick Eye you flee,
Learn hence t'excuse and pity me.

(137-44)

The cool composure and air of authority that Lady Carteret displays in the familiar environs of Dublin Castle turns into anxiety, bewilderment, and disorientation the moment she is transported to the deanery, just as the ironic detachment and air of mastery Swift manifests as host at St. Patrick's turns into painful self-consciousness and uncertainty when he is transferred to the grounds of Dublin Castle. As a result of this change of scene, Lady Carteret must flee the sun's "Majestick Eye" just as Swift earlier felt the need to escape "The living Lusture of [Lady Carteret's] Eyes."

The reversal of roles and the resulting relativity of perception depicted in the *Apology* are characteristic of Swift's poetic method. Many of his verses are rooted in a similar two-way vision whereby Swift the comic spectacle is allowed to turn the tables and assert himself as spectator, hence delineator and controller, of the scene. We may be reminded particularly of the Market-Hill poems, where Swift and Lady Acheson take turns at playing opposite roles: satirist and satirized, master and hapless victim of their environment. In *My Lady's Lamentation and Complaint against the Dean,* for example, Swift is, as the title itself suggests, subjected to the withering scrutiny and accompanying commentary of his exasperated hostess: "He's all the day saunt'ring,/With labourers bant'ring,/... Hail fellow, well met,/All dirty and wet" (159-60, 165-66). But the poem also sets up a mechanism that allows Swift to get back

at his scornful detractor—to have his own perception and his own say in
the matter despite the fact that he is not the poem's speaker. Thus Lady
Acheson, in explaining the reasons for her "Lamentation and Complaint,"
recounts the Dean's verbal assaults upon her and in the process unwittingly turns herself into the object of Swift's ridiculing gaze:

> He takes me to pieces.
> From shoulder to flank
> I'm lean and am lank;
> My nose, long and thin,
> Grows down to my chin;
> My chin will not stay,
> But meets it half way;
> My fingers, prolix,
> Are ten crooked sticks:
> He swears my el——bows
> Are two iron crows. . . .
>
> (70–80)

The victimized hostess gets her revenge in turn by reassuming her role as
observer and reducing Swift to a comic spectacle in surroundings that
finally prove beyond his ability to control: "But, Oh, how we laugh,/
To see a wild calf/Come, driven by heat,/And foul [his] green seat. . ."
(187–90).

The poem's continually shifting perspective, by means of which we
alternately see Lady Acheson through Swift's eyes and Swift through
Lady Acheson's, differs significantly from the typical Augustan poem
where the poet, standing on sure ground and able to control his surroundings with his eye as well as his pen, establishes a fixed point of view with
himself at its center, from which we the readers view the landscape exactly as he charts it out. Berger, in his discussion of the spectator's deified
position vis-à-vis the visible world, notes that "according to the convention of perspective, there is no visual reciprocity. There is no need for God
to situate himself in relation to others: he is himself the situation."[38]
It is precisely this "visual reciprocity," along with a recognition of the
need "to situate himself in relation to others," that characterizes Swift's
outlook and writings. Acutely aware of his inferior social status and precarious political position, Swift was unable to assume the deified stance
of the typical Augustan spectator, for whom (in Berger's words, quoted
earlier in this chapter) the visible world was "arranged . . . as the universe
was once thought to be arranged for God." Instead, he continually
jockeyed for position in his landscape; he fought for an angle of vision
from which to observe clearly while he struggled to be seen by certain of
his superiors and safely hidden from others.

One result is the multiple perspectives and changing roles that we generally explain as aspects of Swift's satiric strategy. But although they do have connections with his satire, they also have a profounder bearing upon Swift's perceptions of himself and his station in the world, which were necessarily as tentative and shifting, as marked by complexities and ambiguities, as the bewildering variety of literary personae and real-life personas that Swift chose alternately to adopt and to put aside. By exploiting a number of literary, specifically satiric techniques, Swift, a man born into a class of overlooked beings, turns his humiliating invisibility into a desirable, because protective, anonymity and emerges as his own uniquely restless, self-ironic, highly unorthodox spectator in the landscape.

CHAPTER • 6

The Drapier-Dean in His Landscape

A Stranger in a Strange Land

i

As the preceding chapters have shown, Swift's landscape was a peculiarly and uniquely Irish one, for reasons and with manifestations that go far deeper than the simple fact that he was born in Dublin and spent the greater part of his life there. At the same time, his relationship to Ireland was a profoundly ambivalent, often tortured one. In a letter to Pope he characterized himself as "a stranger in a strange land" (C, 3:341), and to another correspondent he described himself as "an obscure exile in a most obscure and enslaved country" (C, 4:468)—a statement that gains special significance from his assertion to Pope, recorded in Spence's *Anecdotes*, that he was born in Leicester, England, which Harold Williams terms "a curious fault of memory" (C, 4:229, n. 3), but which probably was intended not so much to convey a literal fact as to dramatize Swift's sense of being an exile in his own land.[1] Other statements in his letters likewise communicate strong feelings of alienation and estrangement even when they do not deny his Irish birth. In a letter addressed to the Earl of Oxford (Robert Harley's son) he declares: "I loved My Lord Your father better than any other Man in the World, although I had no obligation to him on the Score of Preferment, having been driven to this wretched Kingdom (to which I was almost a Stranger) by his want of power to keep me in what I ought to call my own Country; though I happened to be dropped here, and was a Year old before I left it, and to my Sorrow did not dye before I came back to it again" (C, 5:46–47).

Swift's epithet, "a stranger in a strange land," echoes Moses' words referring to Israel's wanderings and captivity in Egypt (*Exod.* 2:22, King James Version). The phrase, however, rather than functioning primarily as a biblical allusion, has a very personal and existential significance in connection with Swift. While it has obvious relevance to his feelings about his extended "exile" in Ireland, it serves in various ways to characterize his relationship with almost *all* the places he visited or inhabited during his lifetime. Invariably he felt himself to be a "stranger" and an "exile"— a wayfarer far from home. Temporarily laid up in Holyhead, he writes "as a passenger who is in a scurvy unprovided comfortless place without one companion, and who therefore wants to be at home . . ." (PW, 5:204). Swift was perennially "in passage," as his recurring navigational imagery emphasizes—perennially "launch[ing] out again" after futile attempts to "reach the Shore" (*Ode to Sir William Temple,* 194-95).

The significance of Swift's images in this respect can be understood more clearly if we compare them with the journey metaphors used by his English friends. In their writings, the images tend to be employed in rather conventional ways, often taking on traditional Christian associations such as those connected with *homo viator.* Bolingbroke, for example, writes to Swift, ". . . even you men of this world have nothing else to do, but to let the ship drive till she is cast away, or till the storm is over. for my own part I am neither an owner, an officer, nor a foremast man. I am but a Passenger, said my Lord Carbury" (C, 3:490). Bolingbroke's itinerancy coexists with a feeling of being at home in the world, of being settled and comfortable even in alien surroundings. In his letter-journal to Swift written during his trip back to England from the Continent, he serenely notes from Ostend, "Since I am likely to wait here for a wind, I shall have leisure to talk with you more than you will like perhaps. . . ," and follows this with an extended reflection upon the nature of fame and immortality (349). In Calais, he once again embarks on a leisurely contemplation of worldly fame while waiting for passage. He opens the concluding paragraph of his letter with the notation, "From my farm [Dawley] . . . I am here . . ." (350), which confidently affirms the fact of a homecoming. Images of transience are tempered by the sense of stability and steadfastness conveyed by natural imagery: "I am in my farm, and here I shoot strong and tenacious roots: I have caught hold of the earth, (to use a Gardener's phrase) and neither my enemies nor my friends will find it an easy matter to transplant me again" (264).

We see another combined journey and homecoming that contrasts strikingly with Swift's sense of earthly passage in Mrs. Delany's return trip to Ireland after a visit to England in the winter of 1746-1747. Starting out across the Irish Sea not from Holyhead but Parkgate, a small seaport located twelve miles west of Chester, she too is confronted with a lengthy delay caused by contrary winds, whereupon she writes to her sister: "'Tis cruel my dearest sister to have lost so many precious hours; for *here we are still,* and *may be some days longer.* . . ." Having expressed these feelings of impatience over the enforced wait, however, Mrs. Delany proceeds to make the best of the situation and to transform an unforeseen obstacle into an occasion for indulging in leisurely pastimes and reflection:

> . . . we keep up our spirits as well as our present disagreeable circum-
> stances will allow. . . . We walk out twice or thrice a-day. . . . A few
> ships lie before us, and continually people passing and repassing,
> which is some amusement. . . .
>
> In our walks this morning we were much amused in finding a
> variety of fine caterpillars. . . . Another great pleasure to us, was
> hearing and watching the lark singing, as he soared, hovering, waver-
> ing, and fluttering from side to side as he varied his strains, and
> at last dropped down to the grass to meet his mate. How many
> natural and exquisite delights daily poured down on us from heaven,
> are daily lost upon us for want of a leisure moment to attend to
> them. . . .[2]

Writing a week later from Delville, Mrs. Delany assures her sister, ". . . we have had (I thank God) a very good journey and safe voyage, and are arrived at our own dear villa. . . ."[3] Having weathered temporary traveling difficulties and frustrations, she, like Bolingbroke, arrives "home."

The basic attitude conveyed by both Bolingbroke and Mrs. Delany toward their respective travel delays differs dramatically from Swift's response upon being similarly delayed by contrary winds at Holyhead. Whereas Bolingbroke's enforced wait becomes an occasion for philosophic reflection, and Mrs. Delany's, for a leisurely contemplation of nature, Swift's is immediately converted into an emblem of imprisonment, aliena-tion, and loneliness:

> . . . I am in the worst part of wales under the very worst circum-
> stances; afraid of a relapse; in utmost solitude; impatient for the
> condition of our friend [Stella]; not a soul to converse with, hinderd
> from exercise by rain, cooped up in a room not half so large as one
> of the Deanry Closets. . . . But the worst part is my half hourly long-
> ing, and hopes and vain expectations of a wind; so that I live in sus-
> pense, which is the worst circumstance of human nature. . . . Forsan
> et haec olim is a damned lye, for I shall always fret at the remem-
> brance of this imprisonment. (PW, 5:207, 205)

Swift's tempestuous journeys, whether actual or metaphorical (or, as is often the case, a combination of both), are never satisfactorily con-cluded, either by means of Christian archetypes or by the actual attainment of a specific destination. They convey at all times an existential reality, accompanied by a sense of urgency and peril. Swift's account in the *Holy-*

head Journal of the initial, ill-fated voyage across the Channel functions at once as empirical description and symbolic statement; it is a record both of one particular autobiographical event and of Swift's precarious, continually thwarted passage through life: "You will now know something of what it is to be at sea. We had not been half an hour in the ship till a fierce wind rose directly against us. We tryed a good while, but the storm still continued: so we turned back, and it was 8 at night, dark and rainy before the ship got back, and at anchor" (PW, 5:208). Rough seas and adverse winds were a common occurrence for the traveler attempting to cross the sea between Ireland and Wales. John Bush describes a voyage marked by "40 hours rolling and traversing the boisterous Irish sea, for 20 leagues only, with the wind, as the sailors say, *right in our teeth.*"[4] What is characteristically Swiftian in the *Holyhead* account is therefore not its emphasis upon the difficulties encountered at sea, but the fact that these difficulties in effect constitute the final word. The account ends on a note of failure, with the traveler shown to be frustrated in his attempt to reach his destination and without any immediate prospect of future success: ". . . the other passengers went back in a boat to Holyhead: but to prevent accidents and broken shins I lay all night on board, and came back this morning at 8: am now in my Chamber, where I must stay, and get in a new stock of patience." By contrast, Mrs. Delany, after also experiencing fickle winds and rough seas on another of her return trips from Parkgate to Dublin, concludes her account with the reappearance of "good weather" and the "fair prospect of landing soon."[5] It is precisely a "fair prospect of landing soon" that is invariably absent from Swift's journeys, which at every moment threaten to lose their direction or abruptly change course and thereby elude their destination (assuming they had one to begin with). The account in the *Holyhead Journal* is representative in this respect. One can say of the packet that conveyed Swift on his aborted voyage what Swift says about himself in the *Ode to Sir William Temple* concerning his inability to reach the shore despite repeated launchings out.

To the extent that a conception of "home" appears in Swift's writings, it is often identified as the place he is furthest away from at the moment, or the place he has just left behind; hence the impression he repeatedly conveys of moving through alien space in his various scenes of "banishment." Living in London while working for the Tory ministry, he seems frequently to have felt no less "a stranger in a strange land" than he did after his return to Dublin, as is evident not only from his remarks at the time but also from retrospective comments recalling his stay in England not as the Golden Age postulated by critics, but as a period of hardship when he was compelled to ". . . make shifts and lie rough, and be undone by starving in scanty lodgings, without horses, servants, or conveniences" (C, 4:257) and when he was forced to make do with "a dear scurvy London lodging" (378). Such wording suggests that London in the years 1710-1714, like Holyhead in the fall of 1727, represented yet one more "scurvy unprovided comfortless place" encountered in his earthly travels.

Repeatedly expressing discontent with his environs, Swift was continually moving from one set of London accommodations to another, never quite able to settle himself comfortably in any one place (see JS, 1:142-43, n. 16). His attitude toward these various accommodations is epitomized by his complaints concerning his St. Martin's Street lodgings in Leicester Fields, where he stayed for little more than a month in the fall of 1711: "Last Saturday night I came home, and the drab had just washed my room and my bed-chamber was all wet, and I was forced to go to bed in my own defence, and no fire: I was sick on Sunday, and now have got a swinging cold" (JS, 2:411). Proclaiming himself alternately tired of and disillusioned with London life, Swift expressed a recurring nostalgia for Ireland: "I'm weary of courts, and want my journies to Laracor; they did me more good than all the ministries these twenty years. . . . Oh, that we were at Laracor this fine day! the willows begin to peep, and the quicks to bud" (JS, 2:413; 1:220). Once having returned to Ireland, however, Swift discovered not a rich array of willows and buds, but gardens and groves that were all "sadly desolate" (C, 2:193), and a strange, primitive country transformed beyond recognition by its impoverished circumstances, making the rare visitor to it think he was traveling in "*Lapland,* or *Ysland*" (PW, 12:10). Swift's acute sense of being an exile in a land isolated from the rest of the world contributed to his characterization of himself as a recluse who is "as meer a Monk as any in Spain" (C, 4:4) and as one "wholly out of [the world]" (C, 2:330). His friends in England picked up on this sense of isolation and estrangement, so that Pope, for example, refrained from ever visiting Swift in Ireland and confessed, "I look upon a friend in Ireland as upon a friend in the other world" (C, 2:211).

ii

Paradoxically, Swift's characterization of himself as "a stranger in a strange land" underscores his *affinities* with his fellow countrymen rather than his separation from them, for in a very fundamental way the Irish as a nation were "strangers in a strange land," raised in a country of refugees, migrants, and dispossessed people who were forced to wander from place to place for their daily survival and often compelled by economic circumstances to emigrate to distant regions in Europe or America. W.E.H. Lecky presents a detailed picture of the extensive exile and itinerancy forced upon all levels of Irish society in the eighteenth century, which took the form of both a flight to foreign lands and a transient existence within Ireland's own borders. With regard to the manifestations of such itinerancy at the lowest levels, Lecky explains: "Over a great part of Ireland the cottiers were driven for the most part to the mountains, where they obtained little plots of potato ground, too small, however, to support them during the year. They eked out their subsistence by migrating from place to place during the summer and autumn in search of work."[6] According to the contemporary testimony of Arthur Dobbs, during the summer months great numbers of farmers "shut their houses, and with their whole families . . . [went] begging till harvest time." He computed the number of strolling beggars in an average year to be 34,000.[7] Dobbs's account lends credence to the scene presented at the outset of *A Modest Proposal*, which shows "the *Streets*, the *Roads*, and *Cabbin-doors* crowded with *Beggars* of the Female Sex" who are "forced to employ all their Time in stroling to beg Sustenance for their *helpless Infants*" (PW, 12:109).

Lecky goes on to discuss the unsettled, peripatetic lives of even those at the higher levels of Irish society, who along with their less fortunate brethren often found it necessary to flee to other lands:

> . . . It would be difficult indeed to conceive a national condition less favourable than that of Ireland to a man of energy and ambition. If he were a Catholic, he found himself excluded by his creed from every position of trust and power, and from almost every means of acquiring wealth, degraded by a social stigma, deprived of every vestige of political weight. If he were a Presbyterian, he was subject to the disabilities of the Test Act. If he were a member of the Established Church, he was even then compelled to see all the highest posts in Church and State monopolised by Englishmen. If he were a landlord, he found himself in a country where the law had produced such a social state that his position as a resident was nearly intolerable. If his ambition lay in the paths of manufacture or commerce, he was almost compelled to emigrate, for industrial and commercial enterprise had been deliberately crushed.
>
> The result was that a steady tide of emigration set in, carrying away all those classes who were most essential to the development of the nation. . . . All the miserable scenes of wholesale ejections, of the disruption of family ties, of the forced exile of men who were passionately attached to their country, were enacted.[8]

It was this general situation that prompted Dr. Johnson to excuse the alleged absence of orchards in Ireland by pointing to the "unsettled state of life, and the instability of property" in the country[9] (an explanation, incidentally, that might shed light on the reasons why, when one particular Irishman *did* undertake to plant an orchard, he called attention to its tenuous status and precarious title by naming it Naboth's Vineyard).

Inveterate wanderers in foreign lands, eighteenth-century Irishmen carried a sense of homelessness and rootlessness with them wherever they went. It is this sense, in part, that underlies the emigré Burke's statement in *A Letter to a Noble Lord:* "At every step of my progress in life, (for in every step was I traversed and opposed,) and at every turnpike I met, I was obliged to show my passport, and again and again to prove my sole title to the honour of being useful to my country. . . ."[10] This state of being a perennial outsider who invites the suspicions and distrust of those around him is one that Swift would have understood only too well.

Acutely conscious that he was residing in a land of exiles and outcasts, Swift continually alluded in his various tracts to the pervasive phenomenon of Irish emigration, declaring in the *Intelligencer,* for example, through the persona of "a Country Gentleman in the North of Ireland":

> It must needs be a very comfortable Circumstance, in the present Juncture, that some Thousand Families are gone, or going, or preparing to go from hence, and settle themselves in *America.* The poorer Sort, for want of Work; the Farmers whose beneficial Bargains are now become a Rack-Rent too hard to be born. And those who have any *ready Money,* or can purchase any, by the Sale of their Goods or Leases; because they find their Fortunes hourly decaying, that their Goods will bear no Price, and that few or none have any *Money* to buy the very Necessaries of Life, are hastening to follow their departed Neighbours. (PW, 12:58-59)

In the process of emigrating, the families described by Swift's "Country Gentleman" encounter enormous physical hardships and deprivations, discovering too late that in their frantic attempt to escape "the extremest Degree of Misery and Want" they end up flying ". . . to the first Appearance of Relief, let it be ever so vain or visionary" (PW, 12:61). The "Country Gentleman" depicts the journey to America as "so tedious and hazardous a Voyage, in all Seasons of the Year; and so ill accommodated in their Ships, that many of [the emigrating families] have died miserably in their Passage," with those who have the dubious fortune of having survived the trip finding, upon their arrival in the New World, that they are to be settled in designated areas of harsh, wild land "as a Screen against the Assaults of the *Savages,*" while at the same time they are forced into slave labor for the rest of their mercifully short lives (60).

That this assessment of the situation reflects historical fact rather than Swiftian satiric exaggeration is demonstrated by an abundance of contemporary documentation. According to Samuel Madden, writing in 1738, at least one-third of the Irish emigrants to the West Indies died either at sea or by contracting disease during the first weeks after their arrival.[11] Nine years earlier, the Irish Privy Council, lamenting "the numbers of Protestant inhabitants who have been seduced out of this kingdom in hopes of obtaining advantageous settlements in America," noted that "many of these poor people have perished at sea by the fraud of the masters of ships, who have been paid beforehand for their passage. . . ," a situation confirmed by a parliamentary committee report of 1735 that found one Thomas Cumming ". . . guilty of great barbarities and violence towards many Protestant passengers, seduced and taken by him on board the ship called the 'George of Dublin,' bound for North Carolina," which, however, judging from its scant provisions, was apparently "never intended to have carried such passengers thither."[12] That the vast majority of these emigrants were Ulster Presbyterians, who went to America to escape not only debilitating economic conditions but also the necessity of paying tithes to Anglican clergymen, adds a special significance to Swift's depiction.[13] So great was his outrage against the circumstances that provoked the emigration that it succeeded in overcoming his deep-seated antipathy to the Dissenters and his usual utter lack of sympathy for their situation.

Swift knew about his countrymen's miserable plight as oppressed exiles from firsthand observation, and he felt a very personal involvement as well as identification with these outcasts, who were forced to wander through strange lands. The extent of his empathy may be inferred from an exchange of letters between himself and Charles Wogan, a descendant of an old Irish family who led a picaresque existence of a typically Irish cast as an escapee from Newgate Prison, an adventurer who offered his services to various powers abroad, and a soldier who became a brigadier general in the Spanish army and ultimately wound up governor of La Mancha. The peculiar nature of Wogan's fate as an alienated, dispossessed person, which is also to say as an eighteenth-century Irishman, is suggested by his comment concerning Swift's literary friends in England: ". . . they are fitter for the Augustan age than for this. They are at home, and endeavour to give the world a sense of its follies with great humour and gaiety. The cheerfulness of my temper, is, in a great measure sunk under a long and hopeless exile, which has given it a serious, or, if you will, a supercilious turn. I lash the world with indignation and grief, in the strain of Jeremy" (C, 4:113). The contrast Wogan notes here between men like Pope and Gay and himself has an interesting, not to mention uncanny, relevance for Swift's own temperamental and literary differences from his English counterparts. Swift, for his part, addresses Wogan as "an Exile, a Soldier, and a Native of *Ireland*" and insists, "Although I have no great Regard for your Trade, from the Judgment I make of those who profess it in these Kingdoms, yet I cannot but highly esteem those Gentlemen of *Ireland*, who, with all the Disadvantages of being Exiles and Strangers, have been able to distinguish themselves by their Valour and Conduct in so many Parts of *Europe*" (51). It was in a letter written to Wogan that

Swift characterized himself as "an obscure exile" (468), thus calling special attention to the common bond he felt with that homeless soldier of fortune and fugitive from a sham justice.

Swift's admiration for and at least partial identification with such "Exiles and Strangers," who constituted so large a proportion of his fellow countrymen, expressed itself as well in his creation of that archetypal "stranger in a strange land," Gulliver, and in his collaboration in the *Memoirs of Captain Creichton,* an account of the adventures of an aged soldier whom Swift met while visiting the Achesons at Market-Hill. Like so many contemporary Irishmen, Creichton was forced to leave his native shores at an early age in search of his fortune, thereupon embarking on a life of picaresque wanderings. Born at Castle-Fin in the county of Donegal, Creichton fell into the common fate of his country's poor, prospectless natives—having made an improvident marriage at the age of eighteen, he found it necessary to support an ever-growing number of offspring and was unable to "think of [any] other Course to advance [his] Fortune, than by getting into the Army" (PW, 5:129). After going off to fight the rebels in the wilds of Scotland, Creichton continually had to confront the harsh realities of being an alien. The word "stranger" recurs throughout the *Memoirs,* conveying the captain's abiding sense of disorientation and displacement; for example, he laments his fate as "a poor *Stranger,* born in *Ireland*" (172). Like Wogan and Swift in their respective ways, Creichton's status as "a stranger in a strange land" is inextricably bound up with his birthright as an eighteenth-century Irishman, even as it simultaneously reflects the fate of a rugged individualist.

iii

However different, however seemingly more established and stable Swift's life was in comparison with Wogan's or Creichton's, Swift chose to view it in similar terms. About to be uprooted once again after the collapse of the Tory ministry, he told Dr. Arbuthnot, "I am a vexed unsettled Vagabond" (C, 2:46), and as if to prove his claim to this title, he traveled through the Irish and Welsh countryside "in Rags," having prematurely sent off his luggage, containing all of his clothing and linens, to Ireland (90, 99). The sense of being an "unsettled Vagabond" remained with Swift even after he took up residence in the deanery. He suggested his affinities with an itinerant existence when he told Charles Ford, "I like Mr. L——s [the Welsh-born Erasmus Lewis's] manner of Life, strolling thro the Kingdom, better than any amongst you" (331). Swift's actual travels, although restricted to the British Isles and to those periods of his life when his fragile health permitted, likewise had a certain picaresque quality, revealing him alternately as a solitary wanderer forced to overcome major obstacles at each stage of his journey and as a fellow traveler thrown together with individuals and classes living marginal existences on the fringes of organized society. These peregrinations included Swift's various journeys from London to Holyhead on horseback, often under the most trying and primitive conditions, along stretches of wild, unpopulated land. Swift speaks in one letter of "fourty miles riding over Welch mountains" (131), a reference to the rugged, often dangerous terrain between Chester and Holyhead, consisting of almost ninety miles of "very rough roads" (C, 1:366, n. 1).

The detailed account of one such journey through northern Wales in the *Holyhead Journal* reveals the picaresque aspects of Swift's style of travel, which was at the very least unorthodox for a man of his station:

> Friday, at 11 in the morning I left Chester. It was Sept. 22d, 1727.
> I bated at a blind ale-house 7 miles from Chester. I thence rode to Ridland; in all 22 miles. I lay there, had bad meat, and tolerable wine. I left Ridland a quarter after 4 morn. on Saturday, stopt on Penmenmawr, examined about my sign verses: the Inn is to be on t' other side, therefore the verses to be changed. I baited at Conway, the Guide going to anothr Inn, the Maid of the old Inn saw me in the Street, and said that was my House, she knew me; there I dined, and send for Ned Holland, a Squire famous for being mentioned in Mr Lyndsay's verses to Davy Morice. . . . I came to Bangor, and crossed the Ferry a mile from it, where there is an Inn, which if it be well kept will break Bangor. There I lay—it was 22 miles from Holyhead. I was on horseback at 4 in the morning, resolving to be at Church at Holyhead, but to shew Wat [his servant] Owen Tudor's Tomb at Penmany. We passt the place (being a little out of the way) by the Guides knavery, who had no mind to stay. I was now so weary with riding, that I was forced to stop at Langueveny, 7 miles from the Ferry, and rest 2 hours. Then I went on very weary, but in a few miles more Watt's Horse lost his two fore-shoes, so the Horse was forced to limp after us. The Guide was less concerned than I. In a few miles more, my Horse lost a fore-shoe; and could not go on the rocky ways. I walked above two miles to spare him. It was Sunday, and no Smith to be got. At last there was a Smith in the way; we left the Guide to shoe the horses, and walked to a hedge Inn 3 miles from Holyhead; There I stayd an hour, with no ale to be drunk. a Boat offered, and I went by Sea and Sayl in it to Holyhead. The guide came about the same time. I dined with an old Inkeeper, Mrs. Welch, about 3, on a Loyn of mutton, very good, but the worst ale in the world, and no wine, for the day before I came here, a vast number went to Ireld after having drank out all the wine. There was Stale beer, and I tryed a receit of Oyster shells, which I got powderd on

purpose; but it was good for nothing. I walked on the rocks in the
evening, and then went to bed, and dreamt (he) I had got 20 falls
from my Horse. (PW, 5:201-3)

The idiosyncratic nature of Swift's travels is also made clear in journal
entries to Stella written during the final days of his extended stay in
England, which recorded Swift's deliberate rejection of the amenities normally available to, and taken for granted by, men of his rank while on the
road: "I can ly somewhere after I land, & I care not where nor how. . . .
therefore take no lodgings for me, to pay in my absence, the poor Dean
can't afford it" (JS, 2:669, 671).

The preceding account from the *Holyhead Journal* provides support
for a description of Swift's style of travel by Lord Orrery, who was in
most respects hardly a reliable authority on Swift but who here conveys
a central truth about the latter's temperamental proclivities as they revealed
themselves in his peregrinations: "He often went in a waggon, but more
frequently walked from *Holyhead* to *Leicester, London,* or any other part
of *England.* He generally chose to dine with waggoners, hostlers, and persons of that rank; and he used to lye at night in houses where he found written over the door *Lodgings for a penny.* He delighted in scenes of low life.
The vulgar dialect was not only a fund of humour for him, but I verily
believe was acceptable to his nature. . . ."[14] A popular contemporary
anecdote states that "Swift in his journies on foot from Dublin to London,
was accustomed to stop for refreshment or rest at the neat little ale-houses
on the road's sides" (P, 2:403). Swift's connection with common ale-
houses likely to be filled with "scenes of low life" is commemorated by
a series of verses he wrote on the windows of inns he passed or frequented
in his travels through the English and Welsh countryside in 1726 (400-5).

Orrery's description is consistent with a remark Swift made to Wogan,
which suggests the type of people Swift tended to converse with in his
passage through unfamiliar landscapes: "I do assert that from several
Experiments in travelling over both Kingdoms [Ireland and England], I
have found the poor Cottagers here, who could speak our Language, to
have much better natural Taste for good Sense, Humour, and Raillery,
than ever I observed among People of the like Sort in *England*" (C, 4:51).
Swift's curiosity about local customs and the distinctive character of the
common folk in each region of the country is demonstrated by his remarks
to Stella after she had journeyed to southeastern Ireland: "Pray observe
the inhabitants about Wexford; they are old English; see what they have
particular in their manners, names, and language. . . . Write your travels . . ."
(JS, 1:311).

In his own way manifesting the same restless energy and "insatiable
Desire of seeing foreign Countries" displayed by Gulliver (PW, 11:80),

Swift early in his career entertained hopes of going off to Germany and Vienna as a member of Lord Berkeley's staff (C, 1:108, 126), confessed plans for fleeing to Sweden if the political situation in Ireland worsened (C, 2:311), and on several occasions expressed his desire to travel to France (C, 3:140, 234). When in London in 1727, he was strongly advised not to go to France because of possible danger (207), but he persisted in his plans to travel abroad, and at one point was actually about to embark on the journey when prevented by external circumstances. Even after this set-back, Swift assured a correspondent, "I will go to France if my health will permit me, to forget my self" (238). In virtually all of these instances, political or health considerations combine with an innate restlessness and thirst for adventure to reveal Swift as an eager, if at times also somewhat apprehensive and ambivalent, wanderer.

Swift's "insatiable Desire" to explore unfamiliar territory was also evident from his activities within Ireland's borders. In the spring of 1715, he expressed a wish to travel "to Connaught and half round Ireland" (C, 2:161) (namely, to those desolate, sparsely populated, and rarely visited regions in the northwest) and four years later he announced, "I have bought a Horse at a great Price, and am resolved to ramble about this Scurvy Country this Summer" (322)—an undertaking very different from the Delanys' periodic trips through the Irish countryside. Preparing to set out for county Down in the summer of 1744, for example, Mrs. Delany wrote to her sister:

> The roads are excellent, the weather very good for travelling, and I hope the journey will be pleasant; the seeing of new places is enter-taining, and we are going into such a hospitable country, that we shall not lie at an inn all the way. To-morrow we lie at Dunleer, which is twenty-five miles from hence, at Mr. Hamilton's. . . . There I believe we shall rest a day. We are to take up our residence for the time we stay in the North, at Dr. Mathews's a clergyman of a very singular good character, a most hospitable generous man: his house is near Down; and Mr. Forde, Mrs. F.'s eldest son, lives in that neighbourhood. If I could be reconciled to leaving Delville I should be very well pleased with this little pilgrimage. . . .[15]

Belonging to a privileged class that represented an extremely small propor-tion of Ireland's population, Mrs. Delany could afford to travel in high style, assured of all the conveniences and amenities that elegant country hospitality could offer.

The extent to which Swift's journeys differed from Mrs. Delany's country tours is particularly evident from two extended trips on horse-back he took in the spring of 1722 and the summer of 1723, respectively. In the first of these, he apparently traversed a large part of the province of

Ulster and saw, among other things, "the longest Lake in Ireland," Lough
Erne (C, 2:431). He too visited friends along the way (Bishop Stearne at
Clogher, Robert Cope at Loughgall, and Sheridan at Quilca), but his
epistolary comments about the trip suggest that it was a far cry from Mrs.
Delany's "pleasant" travels into a most "hospitable country." Swift's
correspondence emphasizes the difficulties encountered in traversing long
distances in at least partially desolate, uncultivated terrain "where Polite-
ness is as much a Stranger as Cleanlyness" (433); it depicts the arduous,
at times perilous movement through unfamiliar, eminently inhospitable
space:

> I have not rode in all above poor 400 Miles since I saw you [Vanessa],
> nor do I believe I shall ride above 200 more till I see you again, but
> I desire you will not venture to shake me by the Hand, for I am in
> mortal fear of the Itch and have no hope left, but that some ugly
> vermin called Ticks have got into my Skin, of which I have pulled
> out some, and must scratch out the rest; Is not this enough to give
> one the Spleen? for I doubt no Christian Family will receive me. And
> this is all a man gets by a Northern Journy. (C, 2:433)

Swift's description of his wanderings through Ulster conveys a sense of
hardship and danger combined with a sense of adventure about confronting the unknown: "Yesterday I rode 28 Miles without being weary. . . .
Here I leave this Letter to travel one way while I go another, but where I
do not know, nor what Cabbins or Bogs are in my Way" (C, 2:433).

The second journey the following summer was through southern Ireland, with Swift traveling as far as Schull in the southwest corner of county
Cork before swinging north to Clonfert to pay Bishop Bolton a visit.
Swift's remarks to Cope concerning the anticipated trip inevitably bring to
mind that subsequent one recorded by "a passenger . . . in a scurvy unprovided comfortless place": "I will tell you that for some years I have intended
a Southern journey; and this summer is fixed for it, and I hope to set out
in ten days. I never was in those parts, nor am acquainted with one Christian among them, so that *I shall be little more than a passenger. . . .* I go
where I was never before, *without one companion,* and *among people
where I know no creature . . .*" (C, 2:453, 456). (Italics mine.) The few
letters written during this southern journey, like those written during the
trip north a year earlier, record one man's struggles against adversity and
the difficulties encountered in getting from one place to another. Writing
to Sheridan from Clonfert, in county Galway, he declares: "No, I cannot
possibly be with you so soon, there are too many Rivers, Bogs, and Mountains between. . . . [*Quilca*] is about a hundred Miles from *Clonfert;* and I
am half weary with the four hundred I have rode" (463-64). While exploring the rugged cliffs near Schull (poetically commemorated as the Carbery

Rocks), Swift came close to having an accident that might well have proven fatal.[16]

When not roaming the Irish countryside, Swift was likely to find himself in the position of an uneasy captive in the deanery, prevented from moving through space by a variety of problems: the difficulty of procuring a horse in good condition or mishaps that befell a horse already in his possession, prolonged spells of miserable weather, irresponsible or incompetent grooms, and physical disabilities that made a trip on horseback too painful. Complaints about "the want of a Horse" began at least as early as 1710, while he was still at Laracor (C, 1:162), and grew in both frequency and stridency in the following decades. Some nine years later he lamented to Ford that ". . . this whole Kingdom will not afford me the medicine of an unfoundred trotting Horse" (C, 2:311). In later years Swift's difficulties in traversing the landscape were attributable less to the unavailability or ill condition of his mounts and more to the poor state of his own health. He repeatedly alludes in his correspondence to a persistent lameness in his legs and to the problems it creates for his mobility, explaining on one occasion, "I ride often, but not above ten miles a day at most, and I ride in Gambadoes, if you ever have heard of such implements . . the advantage is that my foot as I ride stands even as upon a floor for I cannot yet bear the least stretch of the great sinew above my left heel, and God knows when I shall" (C, 4:37). (Harold Williams defines "Gambadoes" as "large boots fastened to the saddle to protect the rider's feet and legs" [35, n. 2]). Predictably displaying an inability to appreciate the reality of these hardships, Bolingbroke flippantly remarked that "to talk of being able to ride with stirrups is trifling. get on Pegasus, bestride the Hipogryph, or mount the white Nag in the Revelation" (45).

iv

It is no wonder that Bolingbroke should have conceived of movement through one's environs as easy and unimpeded, given the fact that country estates like Dawley Farm represented womblike enclosures specifically designed to allay the anxieties and satisfy the needs and desires (whether aesthetic, spiritual, or sensual) of their privileged owners, who were thus assured protection from the harsh, unpredictable world outside the garden and allowed to enjoy an environment shaped exactly according to their specifications and completely under their control. The grounds of a gentleman's estate well exemplified what Jay Appleton terms the prospect-refuge theory of landscape, fulfilling the dual need for a lookout onto the world and for a sanctuary from it.[17] Moving through the spaces of these man-re-created environments was an eminently felicitous and pleasurable experience. In Thomson's portrayal of Hagley Park, for example, the feminized landscape opens herself up completely to the visual and perambulatory penetrations of both estate owner and poet, readily yielding up all of her treasures to the eye and other senses.[18] As Thomson strolls through the park, ". . . she spreads/Unbounded beauty to the roving eye" ("Spring," 506-507). When he wanders through the "mingled wilderness of flowers," his senses are overwhelmed by all manner of stimuli and delights as "Fair-handed Spring unbosoms every grace" (528-29). Nature's abundant favors are of course similarly available to Hagley's host. When he tires in his straying through the park he can rest in ". . . the shade/Of solemn oaks . . ." and feel beneath him ". . . the swelling mounts/Thrown graceful round by Nature's careless hand" ("Spring," 914-16). In Hagley's protective, comforting, both maternal and erotic landscape, Thomson's needs and desires can be satisfied on a magnificent scale. Artfully regulated nature yields to his wishes in a way that "Amanda" (his beloved Elizabeth Young, who terminated their eight-year courtship by marrying another) never did.

Those familiar with the ambience of Augustan estates would therefore have had little comprehension of what it felt like to be a stranger in a strange land, accustomed as they were to the warm, acquiescent parts of nature's body and her eager invitation to them to penetrate further her interior regions. The stroller was on intimate terms with the terrain, received by it as both a lover and a master. When Thomson and Amanda take their country stroll, it is clear that there is no chance of their encountering any danger or discomfort: "Oh, come! and, while the rosy-footed May/Steals blushing on, together let us tread/The morning dews. . . ./Nor is the mead unworthy of thy foot,/Full of fresh verdure and unnumbered flowers . . ." ("Spring," 489-91; 503-4). When the poet looks downward, it is to view some object of beauty at his feet; there is no compulsion or anxiety in the gesture, for there is no chance of falling into a ditch or getting lost in dense foliage.

The world beyond the gentleman's carefully regulated and protected garden presented of course a very different environment, filled with all the unpredictable and hazardous elements that had been rigorously fenced out of the garden. Contemporary travel journals attest to the often profound difficulties and discomforts the traveler was likely to encounter on his worldly peregrinations to distant, unfamiliar places. Nevertheless, the typical traveler went abroad armed not only with his diary and walking stick but also with comforting assumptions about his relationship to the land he was about to explore—assumptions about his ability to render even its most remote, exotic regions familiar to his touch and subject to his control. John Bush, for example, journeying into the more inaccessible regions of eighteenth-century Ireland, looked around him and saw a landscape passively displaying its attractions before him, like an acquiescent mistress in a harem:

> For as a *Turk* of the greatest sensibility would have his taste and choice confounded amidst a seraglio of surrounding beauties, and till he had separated them, could neither be so sensible of their particular charms, nor have that exquisite joy and satisfaction that each, in a more distinct and less interrupted situation, would be capable of giving; so here, on the *Lake* of *Kilarny*, the best plan for obtaining the highest entertainment, should seem to be the sailing from one beauty to another, from variety to variety.[19]

When Bush does, as he inevitably must, encounter obstacles in his path or expanses of inhospitable terrain, he treats them as minor, temporary ills that serve as nature's indirect way of intensifying the traveler's appreciation of the more agreeable aspects of his surroundings. Noting, for example, a length of unnavigable water at the entrance to one of the lakes that the traveler is "ill prepared" to meet with, he assures the reader: "Yet nature, ever provident for her faithful votaries, has happily thrown it in his way. . . . by eracing, in some degree, the impressions on his mind from the enchanting scene he has just passed through, [the obstruction] prepares him for the more perfect injoyment of the new and opening variety that presents itself in his navigation above the shallow."[20] In ways such as this, Bush transforms his position as a stranger in a strange land into alternately that of a pampered guest, a revered master, and an intimate standing on warmly receptive ground.

By contrast, journeying through Swift's landscape is a profoundly unsettling and disorienting experience, and often a rather hazardous one as well. Instead of the lush, sexually generous, ever-compliant landscape spread like a sumptuous feast before the eyes of Augustan poets and their aristocratic patrons, we see through Swift's eyes a sullen, hostile, niggardly landscape, itself undernourished and refusing to nourish others. Not only does it fail to display its charms for the aesthetic and sensual delight of the traveler, but it is also loath to provide him with even his most basic necessities, such as fuel for a fire during cold weather (PW, 5: 219). Whereas Ireland's bogs are for Bush a temporary inconvenience, to be examined as a topographical curiosity and then left well behind in favor of more congenial and aesthetically pleasing terrain,[21] for Swift they remain a central and inescapable feature of the Irish landscape, characteristic of its indifference to human needs. The continuously yielding mistress who readily "unbosoms every grace" for the delectation of the Lytteltons and the Burlingtons or who services her "faithful votaries" as though she were one of the beauties in a Turk's seraglio suddenly turns into a frigid, nay-saying lady, steadfast in her unreadiness and unwillingness to please.

Along with feelings of rejection and deprivation, Swift's landscape communicates a recurring sense of man's helplessness vis-à-vis his environment. The image of Swift battling an onslaught of ticks in bleak northern country or leading a lame horse on foot through the mountainous terrain along the Welsh coastline is the very image of vulnerability, a testimonial to the earthly traveler's lack of protection against all forms of external encroachment upon his immediate space and person, whether by natural adversities or human aggression. Even in Dublin Swift remained in an exposed position, open to threats of political reprisal as well as personal attack, and helpless against the severities of the climate. In contrast to the womblike sanctuary provided by the typical Augustan landscaped garden, Naboth's Vineyard left its owner out in the cold, vulnerable to all the natural and man-made disasters regularly occurring in the outside world. Despite the wall Swift committed considerable amounts of money to constructing, the vineyard remained subject to the onslaughts of northeast winds, the periodic flooding of the Poddle, and the larceny of neighbors eager to take possession of its fruit. No part of Swift's environs afforded protection from the chaos of the outside world. London, as seen through Swift's eyes, could at any moment turn into an urban jungle. We read in the *Journal to Stella* about the terror created for innocent town walkers—and for Swift in particular—by a gang of thugs known as the Mohocks: "Did I tell you of a race of Rakes calld the Mohacks that play the devil about this Town every Night, slitt peoples noses, & beat them &c. . . . My Man tells me, tht one of the Lodgers heard in a Coffee-house publickly, tht one design of the Mohocks was upon me, if [the]y could catch me. . . . I walkt this evenig in the Park, & mett Prior, who made me go home with him, where I staid till past 12, and could not get a Coach, and was alone, and was afraid enough of the Mohocks. . ." (JS, 2:508-9, 511, 516).

Nocturnal strollers through Dublin were likely to encounter similar perils, judging from Swift's insistence upon the need to reduce the city's transient population so that "Our Shop-Doors will be no longer crouded with so many Thieves and Pick-pockets, in Beggars Habits, nor our Streets so dangerous to those who are forced to walk in the Night" (PW, 9:208). However much Swift may have championed the value of physical exercise and urged his friends to use their legs more, a walk through his landscapes was a most precarious undertaking. External circumstances necessitated that he continually look down at the ground, to discover what potential disaster he might be walking into next, and above his head, to see what new object might be threatening to fall on it. I am speaking quite literally here; as Swift noted to the Earl of Oxford, "It is dangerous to walk the Streets [of Dublin] for fear of Houses falling on our heads, and it is the same in every City and Town through the Island" (C, 4:249). When he visited Sheridan in Cavan, his head was once more threatened by onslaughts from above. His attempt "to repair the *Summer House*" proved futile, for "*Boreas* was so angry, that he blew off the roof" (427). Swift subsequently noted that the "back and fore door [are] always left open, which, in a storm (our constant companion) threatens the fall of the whole edifice" (441). His head was also vulnerable to sudden downpours since Quilca was "A rotten Cabbin, dropping Rain" (*To Quilca,* 2). In *Gulliver's Travels* we are presented with a comic version of this danger from above. As Gulliver walked under an apple tree in Brobdingnag, the court dwarf, angered by one of his wisecracks, "shook it directly over my Head, by which a dozen Apples, each of them near as large as a *Bristol* Barrel, came tumbling about my Ears; one of them hit me on the Back as I chanced to stoop, and knocked me down flat on my Face. . ." (PW, 11:116).

Counterbalancing the hazards above were the threats of danger or discomfort from below. Interestingly, in the same chapter that Gulliver gets clobbered on the head with apples, he also gets "filthily bemired" in excrement: "There was a Cow-dung in the Path, and I must needs try my Activity by attempting to leap over it. I took a Run, but unfortunately jumped short, and found my self just in the Middle up to my Knees" (PW, 11:124). These, it would seem, are two recurring poles in Swift's experience with the landscape. Although he was capable of converting either into comic or symbolic statement, both remained concrete aspects of his empirical world. In Cavan, for example, when he was not watching the roof to see if it was about to fall, he was looking down at the ground and complaining about the layers of mud and dirt that impeded his progress on foot: "Our kitchen is a hundred yards from the house; but the way is soft, and so fond of our shoes, that it covers them with its favours. . . . I have no other temptation to ride or walk except that of health; our house, and shoes, and streets, are so perpetually and abominably dirty" (C, 4:427, 430). Sheridan responded by observing to one of their mutual correspondents, ". . . I can assure you that the dirt of our streets is not quite over his shoes, so that he can walk dry. If he would wear goloshes, as I do, he would have no cause of complaint" (416). But inevitably we feel that galoshes would not have done Swift any good since sliding about in the mud with wet shoes was simply one aspect of his idiosyncratic mode of moving through his environment. Indeed, Sheridan elsewhere seems to suggest as much when he tells the same correspondent: "The Dean may talk of the dirtiness of this town; but I can assure you, that he had more upon his shoes yesterday than is at the worst in our corporation, wherever he got it. As for my part, I am tired of him, for I can never get him out of the dirt. . ." (427).

The image of Swift sliding about on Cavan's ground has its own special aptness since Swift lived, after all, in a very slippery world, both literally and figuratively. In a letter written at Cavan he indicates that he understood the way in which empirical reality and symbolic act combined in his life to simultaneously dramatize and burlesque his position in the world: "My leg is so well, that I have been twice riding, and walk in the town, that is to say in the dirt, every day. We have now a fine frost, and walk safe from the dirt; but it is like a life at court, very slippery" (C, 4:446). Moving through Swift's landscape was indeed, from at least one perspective, very much like being at court. Both created precarious existences and entailed continual maneuvering for position in order to retain one's standing; and both seemed ruled more by the fickle fingers of fate than by the guiding hand of Providence. In both, moreover, the risks were high and one was faced with the continual threat of suffering either decapitation or a resounding fall. Swift, as a stranger in a strange land, continually had to battle against the ever-present danger of losing either his bearings or his footing, whether he was on political or natural terrain—whether he was alternately left out in the cold and led astray by the inner circle of those in power, or lost amongst the bogs in Ulster and hanging onto Carbery's rocks for dear life.

At Home as "Absolute Monarch in the *Liberties*"

i

Although Swift, as we have seen, conveyed in both his life and his writings the sense of being a stranger in a strange land, he never became a man without a country. On the contrary, he showed a strong attachment to his native land in both word and action, often expressing it in language that affirmed the existence of blood ties between himself and Ireland, and it was on this basis that he finally came to be a man in significant ways at home in his world. When he wrote to the Duke of Chandos requesting the return of certain ancient records relating to Ireland, he pointed out that "they are only valuable in the place of their birth, like the rest of our natives" (C, 4:251). In *An Humble Address to Both Houses of Parliament,* the final document signed by the Drapier, he offers vivid testimony in support of this proposition. Alluding to Ireland's *"perpetual Absentees,"* Swift observes:

> I knew many of them well enough, during several Years, when I resided in *England*. . . . And I used to wonder, how a Man of Birth and Spirit, could endure to be wholly insignificant and obscure in a *foreign* Country, when he might live with Lustre in *his own;* and even

at less than half that Expence, which he *strains* himself to make, without obtaining any *one* End; except that which happened to the *Frog* when he would needs contend for Size with the *Ox*. . . . But to be *preceded* by *Thousands,* and *neglected* by *Millions;* to be wholly without *Power, Figure, Influence, Honour, Credit,* or *Distinction,* is not, in my poor Opinion, a very *amiable Situation* of Life, to a Person of *Title,* or *Wealth,* who can so cheaply and easily *shine* in his native Country. (PW, 10:130)

Swift puts the matter more succinctly, as well as more bitterly, when he denounces ". . . the Folly, the Vanity, and Ingratitude of those vast Numbers, who think themselves too good to live in the Country which gave them Birth, and still gives them Bread; and rather chuse to pass their Days, and consume their Wealth, and draw out the very Vitals of their Mother Kingdom, among those who heartily despise them" (PW, 9:200).

Ingratitude was a particular anathema to Swift, who attacked it with uncompromising fervor at every opportunity. Not surprisingly, he was especially quick to discern its manifestations when it was directed against himself, but he was also sensitive to its adverse consequences for others. He was particularly angered when ingratitude assumed the form of indifference to, or denial of, obligations growing out of blood ties. When the granddaughter of the Duke of Schomberg, a war hero killed in the Battle of the Boyne, refused to contribute any money to help erect a monument to his memory in St. Patrick's Cathedral, where he was buried, Swift placed a black slab over the duke's remains bearing a Latin inscription that stated in part: *Plus potuit fama virtutis apud alienos/Quam sanguinis proximitas apud suos* ("So much could the admiration of his virtues avail with strangers more than the nearest ties of blood with his own relations") (see C, 3:457 and n., 468 and n.).[22]

The kind of behavior Swift denounced when it was displayed toward individuals he found even more reprehensible when directed against one's country. His sermon *Doing Good* is an impassioned condemnation of this ingratitude, in which he powerfully develops the imagery of matricide:

> Lastly, all offences against our own country have this aggravation, that they are ungrateful and unnatural. It is to our country we owe those laws which protect us in our lives, our liberties, our properties, and our religion. Our country produced us into the world, and continues to nourish us so, that it is usually called our mother; and there have been examples of great magistrates, who have put their own children to death for endeavouring to betray their country, as if they had attempted the life of their natural parent. (PW, 9:239)

Matricide becomes for Swift a dramatic emblem of all those unforgivable sins of ingratitude and betrayal committed by men (specifically, Irish and

Anglo-Irish men) against one who has faithfully provided them with life and nourishment. Patriotism for Swift is, above all, a son's unwavering loyalty to, and commitment to protect the life of, his mother. As the Drapier explains to Viscount Molesworth, "It is a known Story of the Dumb Boy, whose Tongue forced a Passage for Speech by the Horror of seeing a Dagger at his Father's Throat. This may lessen the Wonder, that a Tradesman hid in Privacy and Silence should *cry out* when the Life and Being of his Political *Mother* are attempted before his Face. . ." (PW, 10:89).

The Drapier's description of Ireland as ". . . a Country, where *Loyalty is woven into the very Hearts of the People*" (PW, 10:92) is at once rhetorical strategy, wishful thinking, and a sincere conviction of his countrymen's potential for patriotic commitment and action.[23] If this potential has been only sporadically and partially realized, the blame must be laid not only on the greed, misguided ambition, and self-delusion of individuals, but also, perhaps even more, on external circumstances beyond the Irish people's control, which have often left them no choice but to commit acts of faithlessness and self-betrayal: "A People long used to Hardships, lose by Degrees the very Notions of *Liberty;* they look upon themselves as Creatures at Mercy. . . . Hence proceed that *Poverty* and *Lowness of Spirit,* to which a *Kingdom* may be subject, as well as a *particular Person.* And when *Esau* came fainting from the Field, at the Point to die, it is no Wonder that he sold his *Birth-Right for a Mess of Pottage*" (53). The real pathos and tragedy of Ireland's situation lies in the fact that its natives have been reduced by political and economic oppression to being strangers in their own land, forced to relinquish their rightful inheritance and their most precious (in many cases, their only) possession, their birthright.

Although Swift at various points in his life indulged in self-denial (in the most literal sense), in the final analysis he emerged as a patriot with strongly affirmed ties to his homeland: an anti-Esau figure who insisted that the love of country is ". . . a duty to which we are more strictly obliged than even that of loving ourselves" (PW, 9:233). Despite repeated invitations proffered by English friends in his later years and other enticements to resettle in or near London, and despite his persistent complaints about life in Ireland, Swift chose to remain in Dublin—in a position where he could protect "the Life and Being of his Political *Mother*" against constant assaults from both within and without. It is significant that during his visit to England in 1726, he wrote to Sheridan about "the fairest Offer made me of a Settlement here that one can imagine . . . within twelve Miles of *London,* and in the midst of my Friends," but for reasons never made clear he announced his decision to reject the offer, affirming instead his intention to return very shortly to Ireland, "a Place good enough to die in." As usual he stressed the necessity of his doing so, but we come to realize, in reading his explanation, that the "necessity" must have been founded as much upon inner compulsion as upon external circumstance: "This is the first time I was ever weary of *England,* and longed to be in *Ireland,* but it is because go I must. . ." (C, 3:140).

And go he did. Moreover, he not only returned but *stayed*—on and on, until he became a legend in his time, a living, seemingly indestructible monument that threatened to outlast even the dozens of signposts commemorating the Drapier throughout the country that were rapidly becoming "worn out" (C, 4:54), ironically survived by the man whose memory they were intended to perpetuate. He stayed on while others—Addison, Ford, Delany, Carteret—came and went, using Ireland merely as a stepping-stone to preferment elsewhere. As he once drily observed to Gay, "Here I will define Ireland a Region of good eating and drinking, of tolerable Company, where a Man from England may sojourn some years with Pleasure, make a Fortune, and then return home, with the spoyls he has got by doing us all the Mischeif [*sic*] he can, and by that make a Merit at Court" (C, 3:359-60). When Thomas Tickell, employed as secretary in Dublin Castle, appeared to be on the verge of receiving promotion to England, Swift wrote him: "I have often thought it a monstrous Folly in us who [are] tyed [to] this Kingdom, to have any Friendship with vous autres who are Birds of Passage, while we are sure to be forsaken like young Wenches who are seduced by Soldiers that quarter among them for a few Months" (77). As in *The Story of the Injured Lady,* the situation of the Irish is here conceived of as female vulnerability to outside male assertiveness and subsequent abandonment. The phrase "Birds of Passage" reappears elsewhere in Swift's writings (usually in a far less humorous context) as part of an attack on those opportunists who ". . . thrive and fatten here [in Ireland], and fly off when their *Credit* and *Employments* are at an End" (PW, 10:132; see also PW, 12:11). But Swift's most impassioned protests were directed against native Irishmen who opted to fly from their homeland instead of being "content to *live at home,*" thereby becoming part of the mass exodus that had dire consequences for their country (PW, 10:130). Despite Swift's rambling, restless nature, he was far more a homing pigeon than a "bird of passage." In this respect he exemplified another crucial aspect of Swiftian patriotism: continuous contact with a particular geographical location, that is, abiding links to a specific landscape.

The verse *To Charles Ford Esqr. on his Birth-day* reflects another stage in the process of defining patriotism in terms of one's allegiance to a particular landscape. Ford's perspective as an Anglophile, as a man increasingly disposed to spending lengthy periods in England, is contrasted with the outlook reflected by members of Swift's "fav'rite Clan" (79), the Grattans and the Jacksons, "Fellows of modest Worth and Parts,/With

chearfull Looks, and honest Hearts" (81-82)—men who spent their entire
lives in Ireland, content to serve their native land in such capacities as a
vicar (the Reverend John Jackson), a Dublin physician (James Grattan), a
prebendary in St. Patrick's Cathedral (Robert Grattan), and the master of
a school in the north of Ireland (Charles Grattan) (see C, 2:294, n. 1; and
152, n. 4). The descendants of these men, moreover (e.g., Henry Grattan,
Ireland's illustrious native son), were to become famous for their political
activism motivated by love of country.

> Can you [Ford] on Dublin look with Scorn?
> Yet here were You and Ormonde born
> Oh, were but You and I so wise
> To look with Robin Grattan's Eyes:
> Robin adores that Spot of Earth,
> That litt'rall Spot which gave him Birth,
> And swears, Cushogue is to his Tast,
> As fine as Hampton-court at least.
>
> (83-90)

Although Swift himself was known on many occasions to view Dublin "with Scorn," and although it is difficult to imagine him ever adoring
"That litt'rall Spot which gave him Birth," a significant part of Swift's
unique perception consisted precisely in being able "To look with Robin
Grattan's Eyes" at his surroundings. This meant being able both to observe
his immediate physical environs and to view the world at large from the
perspective of a native Irishman willing to accept his birthright, together
with all it implied in terms of a concrete place to stand and a distinctive
angle of vision. Hence we must reject J. C. Beckett's contention that
"there can be no doubt at all that [Swift] regarded himself, and wanted
others to regard him, as an Englishman."[24] Swift's love-hate relationship
with Ireland can yield superficial support for such a claim, but a more
careful consideration of Swift's posture in this respect indicates quite the
contrary. His remark to Francis Grant that "I am a Teague, or an Irishman, or what people please" (C, 4:229) is a flippant and self-mocking
version of something Swift declared over and over again, in many different
ways, often with the utmost seriousness of intent even if characteristically
tinged with Swiftian irony. These varied statements merge into a coherent
if somewhat elusive definition of both a "homeland" and a "home"—one
well suited to a perennial stranger and unsettled vagabond who was nevertheless intent upon letting both contemporaries and posterity know of
his firm ties to a particular plot of ground with a special history and
character of its own.

Swift's pride in this history (we may recall St. Patrick's impassioned
outcry, "*Britain*, with Shame confess, this Land of mine/First taught thee

human Knowledge and divine. . ." [*Verses occasioned by the sudden drying up of St. Patrick's Well*, 27-28]), coupled with his pained awareness of Ireland's tragic past, caused in part by its vulnerability to outside encroachments, informed Swift's stance as patriot, which combined profound sympathy for his country's plight and outrage against those who would continue to wreak destruction on Ireland:

> Weary and Sea-sick when in thee confin'd,
> Now, for thy Safety Cares distract my Mind,
> As those who long have stood the Storms of State,
> Retire, yet still bemoan their Country's Fate.
> Beware, and when you hear the Surges roar,
> Avoid the Rocks on *Britain*'s angry Shore:
> They lye, alas, too easy to be found,
> For thee alone they lye the Island round.
>
> (*Horace, Book I, Ode XIV,*
> *Paraphrased and inscribed to Ir——d*, 57-64)

To be sure, Swift's patriotism was not unqualified by feelings of anger and disgust directed against the Irish themselves, which reflected his critical view of an enslaved as well as an enslaving mentality. Nor did Swift's fervent support of Ireland's interests signify an unawareness of the profoundly frustrating, often thankless task confronting those who assume the role of patriot. Throughout his Irish tracts he stresses the futility of his endeavors on behalf of his oppressed countrymen (e.g., PW, 12:66, 75). The bitterness of the unheeded patriot-prophet is most clearly evident in *An Answer to a Paper, called "A Memorial,"* where, after examining the miserable conditions of the Irish farmers, Swift declares: "If so wretched a State of Things would allow it, methinks I could have a malicious Pleasure, after all the Warning I have in vain given the Publick, at my own Peril, for several Years past; to see the Consequences and Events answering in every Particular. . ." (22). Yet for all Swift's complaints about the kind of response that greeted his actions as a patriot, he continued to perform this role with unrelenting vigor, exhorting others to follow his example rather than become unwitting accomplices in Ireland's undoing by selling both themselves and their country "for nought" (a recurring phrase throughout Swift's writings). In his verse *On the Irish-Club*, Swift counsels his fellow Hibernians:

> Defend your liberties and laws.
> Be sometimes to your country true,
> Have once the public good in view:
> Bravely despise Champagne at Court,
> And chuse to dine at home with Port:
> Let Pr[elate]s, by their good behaviour,

Convince us they believe a Saviour;
Nor sell what they so dearly bought,
This country, now their own, for nought.

(16–24)

These examples make it clear that the "stranger in a strange land," despite
periodic cynical disclaimers, had in fact come to recognize—even more, to
embrace—a "homeland."

ii

In the broadest sense this "homeland" was the whole of Ireland—
that *"Poor floating Isle, tost on ill Fortune's Waves"* (*Horace, Book I,
Ode XIV,* 1). But in more specific terms, and on a more intimate level,
"home" for Swift was Dublin: first, the tall Jacobean house in Hoey's
Court next to St. Werburgh's Church, owned by his uncle Godwin Swift
and made available to his parents upon their emigration from England,
where he was born and which in subsequent years he "frequently mentioned, and pointed out," we can only conjecture with what mixture of
pride and scorn;[25] and later the deanery, "a large House, convenient
enough for my unrefined taste" (C, 4:504), from which he could exit
directly into the streets of the Liberties, and where he exploited his combined official position as Dean of St. Patrick's and unofficial status as
popular folk hero to assert himself, in his own words, as "absolute monarch in the *Liberties,* and King of the Mob."[26]

Shortly after his return to Ireland following the collapse of the
Tory ministry, Swift had explained to Ford, "I stay here out [of] a
Publick Spirit . . . And I stay here to forget England and make this Place
supportable by Practice" (C, 2:132), and a good part of the years after
1714 were devoted precisely to making his Irish environs (first Laracor,
then the deanery) "supportable by Practice"—to changing an initially
hostile, threatening environment into familiar and even generally friendly turf. A footnote to the *Verses on the Death of Dr. Swift* attests to the
antagonistic atmosphere Swift encountered immediately upon his return
to Dublin: "Upon the Queen's Death, the Dean returned to live in *Dublin,*
at his Deanry-House: Numberless Libels were writ against him in *England,*
as a Jacobite; he was insulted in the Street, and at Nights was forced to be
attended by his Servants armed" (P, 2:568, n. 3). Within a relatively short
time, however, the situation had completely changed, with Swift becoming a welcome and respected figure on the scene. As Bishop Wyse Jackson
observes, "[Swift] was to find that Dublin in general, and the Liberties
in particular, suited his temperament well, and he grew into them."[27]

The two-way process whereby Swift gradually but inexorably "grew

into" his deanery environs while the latter increasingly accommodated itself to his dominant presence is implicitly attested to in a number of letters Swift wrote in the early and mid-1730s, turning down invitations to
visit or resettle in England and stressing the virtues of his Dublin abode,
where he could feel "at home" (C, 4:212). In a letter to Arbuthnot, he
explains some of the advantages of living at the deanery (although he complains of the drastic reduction of his revenues) and conveys the sense of
being on friendly territory: "I have here a large convenient house; I live
at two thirds cheaper than I could there [in England], I drink a bottle of
French wine my self every day . . . I ride every fair day a dozen miles, on
a large Strand, or Turnpike roads; You in London have no such Advantages" (268-69). A letter Swift wrote to Pope in the summer of 1733
makes even clearer why Dublin and not London became "home" for Swift:

> . . . I hate the thoughts of London, where I am not rich enough to
> live otherwise than by shifting: which is now too late. Neither can I
> have conveniences in the Country for three Horses and two servants,
> & many others which I have here at hand. I am one of the Governors
> of all the Hackney Coaches, Carts, & carriages, round this town, who
> dare not insult me, like your rascally waggoners or Coachmen, but
> give me the way. nor is there here one Lord or Squire for a hundred
> of yours to turn me out of the road, or run over me with their
> Coaches & six. Thus I make some advantage of the publick poverty,
> & to give you the reasons for what I once writ, why I chuse to be a
> freeman among slaves, rather than a slave among freemen. Then I
> walk the streets in peace, without being justled, nor ever without a
> thousand blessings from my friends the Vulgar. I am Lord Mayor of
> 120 houses, I am absolute Lord of the greatest Cathedral in the King-
> dom: am at peace with the neighboring Princes, the Lord Mayor of
> the City, and the A. Bp. [Archbishop] of Dublin, only the latter,
> like the K. of France sometimes attempts encroachments on my
> Dominions, as old Lewis did upon Lorrain. In the midst of this
> railery, I can tell you with Seriousness, that these advantages con-
> tribute to my ease, & therefore I value them. (C, 4:171)

His Dublin environs contributed to a landscape Swift could comfortably inhabit because, among other things, it permitted him the fluidity of
roles that was so central an aspect of his nature (not to mention of his
writings).[28] Within its boundaries, as this letter to Pope indicates, he was
able to occupy a position of power and privilege—as a "Governor," a
"Lord Mayor," and an "absolute Lord"—but in a characteristically parodic manner; it was a position ironically qualified by his implicit identification with "[his] friends the Vulgar" and his mocking portrayal of other
authority figures as "neighboring Princes" and as figures reminiscent of
King Louis XIV. We may recall his comment elsewhere to Lord Castle-

Durrow: "I often reflect on my present life as the exact Burlesque of my middle age, which passed among Ministers. . . . I am now acting the same things in Miniature, but in a higher Station, as a first Minister, nay sometimes as a Prince; in which last quality, My House-keeper, a grave elderly woman, is called at home and in the Neighborhood Sr Robert [Walpole]" (C, 4:555). This self-mocking assertion of authority, tacitly affirming a relativistic hierarchy of shifting power relationships and roles, defines a major aspect of Swift's satiric writings and of his domestic landscape as well.

In contrast to Pope's "pensive Grott," an exclusive retreat safely removed from the world's "distant Din," protected from the rabble and the barbarian hordes outside, Swift's urban habitation remained open to the flow of all forms of human traffic—to the continual comings and goings of "the Vulgar" and to the problems of the impoverished residents within the Liberty of St. Patrick's. We cannot truly understand either Swift's landscape or his writings if we fail to appreciate the extent of his daily, often intimate participation in the life of the working-class community surrounding St. Patrick's, exemplified by, but not limited to, his exertions on behalf of the unemployed weavers and his noted displays of charity to the poor. His identification with the members of this community is clear from his assertion to one correspondent, "I am only a favourite of my old friends the rabble; and I return their love, because I know none else who deserve it" (C, 4:537), and his declaration to another, "My Lord, you are entirely mistaken about the politicks of this Country, where I have no friends but Citizens and the rabble" (409)—statements reinforced by the Drapier's reference to "my faithful Friends the common People" (PW, 10:88).

Swift's close association with "the common People" was reinforced by his manner of traversing his environs. An inveterate walker, Swift covered almost every inch of the Liberties and their surroundings on foot as often as his health and the weather would permit. The importance of this fact in determining the kind of people and situations he met with, as well as his perspective toward them, is suggested by a contemporary while specifically commenting on Swift's penchant for "walking the streets so constantly as he did": ". . . this gave him an opportunity of examining into the condition of every poor person he met. Which he did, with so well-practiced a sagacity, as could seldom be imposed upon. And every man that follows his example, will soon find, that this practice will lead him into the exercise of more charity, than is possible to be practised in carriages of any kind; all which hurries you beyond the object you would relieve, before you can possibly consider his case."[29] The profound implications of using one's feet rather than some other mode of conveyance are similarly noted by the anonymous translator of the French emigrant

Latocnaye's *Rambles through Ireland:* "Our countryman Goldsmith somewhere says, that a man who travels through Europe on foot, forms a very different idea of things from him who is whirled through it in a post-chaise."[30]

When Swift was not traveling on foot (or, as we saw in the preceding chapter, on horseback), he had recourse to public conveyances that, like his ambulatory habits, put him in close contact with the common people. In one letter to Vanessa, written shortly after his arrival at Gaulstown, he notes that he "... had a weary Journy in an Irish Stage Coach" (C, 2:393), an observation that F. Elrington Ball glosses with the following footnote: "It was probably of most primitive construction. The allusion is the earliest which I know to the use in Ireland of a public conveyance by a man of Swift's rank."[31] Although there is no evidence of his regular employment of such vehicles, Swift consistently eschewed the private carriages appropriate to one of his social position. His friend Delany, for example, who was another Anglican dean of comparable status, regularly traveled through the Irish countryside in a chaise, followed by a coach-and-four with the cook, housemaid, and other servants, and a car for carrying the luggage.[32] But although Swift had recourse to coaches while living in London during the years 1710-1714, he often (and increasingly as he grew older) displayed a contemptuous attitude toward them and all they represented. This attitude is evident in his comment to Bishop Stearne—"It is happy for me that I know the persons of very few bishops, and it is my constant rule, never to look into a coach; by which I avoid the terror that such a sight would strike me with" (C, 4:183)—and in his remark to Lord Orrery concerning the difficulties preventing him from paying a visit: "For your Coach I utterly renounce, being not used to that vehicle for many years" (145). Swift's negative view of coaches was undoubtedly shaped in part by experiences like his encounter with Lord Blayney, a member of the House of Lords, while riding on horseback along the Strand one night between Dublin and Howth. The nobleman drove his carriage "in so violent a manner" that Swift's servant "who rode behind him was forced to give way with the utmost peril of his life," while Swift himself was nearly overthrown and threatened with a loaded pistol (PW, 5:199-200). The *Dean of St. Patricks Petition to the H. of Lords, Against the Lord Blaney* indirectly underscores the opposition on every level (in terms of social class, power, and outlook) between travelers in private coaches and journeyers on horseback. Whether mounted or on foot, Swift regularly moved through his environs in such a way as to confirm his affinities and his sense of identification with his "old friends the rabble."

We need not accept without reservation Maurice Craig's oversimplified view that "after 1714 the only political allies in whom [Swift] trusted were the common people of Dublin"[33] (even less, J. A. Preu's far more misleading claim that, throughout his political writings, Swift "affirmed a staunch confidence in the common man"[34]) in order to recognize that Craig's view at least conveys a truer picture than the more orthodox arguments asserting Swift's continued unswerving allegiance to an aristocratic class of politically disinherited English Tories, contemptuous of the lower classes who were made to bear much of the blame for the ills of contemporary society. There was a time in his life when Swift certainly shared many of these attitudes, but increasingly he moved away from them as both his standing in a specific landscape and his angle of vision changed. The extent of this shift in sympathies and point of view may be inferred from a letter to Swift written by Bolingbroke, responding in part to news that "those men of eminent gratitude & integrity, the Weavers & the Judges," had given Swift's printer, Waters, a sound drubbing. Bolingbroke expresses the hope that "instead of tossing you in the person of yr Proxy" they will "toss you in yr proper person, the next time you offend by going about to talk sense or to do good to the Rabble. is it possible that one of yr age & profession should be ignorant that this monstrous Beast has passions to be mov'd, but no reason to be appeal'd to. . . . Dear Jon: since you cannot resolve to write as you preach, what publick authority allows . . . leave off instructing the Citizens of Dublin" (C, 2:394–95).

Swift, of course, continued to "talk sense [and] to do good to the Rabble," as well as to "instruc[t] the Citizens of Dublin." Among the many things he learned in his daily contact with them was that the passions Bolingbroke so contemptuously ascribes here to the "Beast" included deep affection, gratitude, and a childlike loyalty to one they considered their champion. It was such passions that prompted the common people of the Liberties to rally to Swift's aid when the satirized "Booby" Bettesworth threatened to harm Swift. Their deep expressions of concern and unqualified offer of protection are preserved in a paper they delivered to Swift on January 8, 1733–1734, in which they affirmed their "great Love and Respect to the said Dean, to whom the whole Kingdom hath so many Obligations," and promised "to defend the Life and Limbs of the said Dean against the said Man, and all his Ruffians and Murderers, as far as the Law will allow, if he or any of them presume to come into the said Liberty with any wicked or malicious Intent, against the House, or Family, or Person, or Goods of the said Dean" (PW, 5:341–42). Swift's response to this declaration, written as he lay extremely ill, is a moving tribute to the affection he felt for his neighbors in the Liberties:

I Receive, with great Thankfulness these many kind Expressions of your Concern for my Safety, as well as your declared Resolutions to

defend me. . . . as long as [my life] continues I shall ever bear a
grateful Memory for this Favour you have shown, beyond my Ex-
pectation, and almost exceeding my Wishes.

The Inhabitants of the Liberty, as well as those of the Neighbourhood, have lived with me in great Amity for near Twenty Years;
which I am confident will never diminish during my Life. I am
chiefly sorry, that by two cruel Disorders of Deafness and Giddiness, which have pursued me for four Months, I am not in a Condition either to hear, or to receive you, much less to return my most
sincere Acknowledgments, which in Justice and Gratitude I ought
to do. May God bless you and your Families in this World, and
make you for ever happy in the next. (PW, 5:342-43)

Traditional approaches to Swift do not allow us to explore his growing sense of distance—psychological, emotional, and ideological as well as
geographic—from former friends in England, which coincided with a growing closeness (again, on a more than geographic level) to the ordinary
"Citizens" and the "Rabble" who constituted a large part of his circle of
acquaintances in Dublin and who provided him with an emotional nourishment and support that he was unable to get elsewhere. It is revealing
that in the same letter in which he assures his correspondent that "as to
[Ireland], I am only a favourite of my old friends the rabble; and I return
their love, because I know none else who deserve it"—indeed, in the
very sentence immediately preceding this statement—he observes, "My
English friends are all either dead or in exile, or, by a prudent oblivion,
have utterly dropped me; *having loved this present world*" (C, 4:537).
Swift thus establishes a clear-cut distinction between Irish presence and
English absence, between a sense of intimacy and a sense of remoteness:
a contrast between a living, constantly reaffirmed friendship and one that
has dissolved into death or oblivion.

A similar structure of feeling governs the *Verses on the Death of Dr.
Swift,* which is rooted in a process of temporal distancing that contrasts
not only the assorted passions and prejudices of the immediate moment
with the detached, "objective" perspective produced by an extended passage of time, but also a specifically London ambience and existence with
an emphatically Irish one. Whereas the former fades into a remote past
and is in the process reduced to meaningless prattle on the one hand,
idealized memories on the other, Swift's life and actions as an Irish patriot
emerge clearly in the forefront, both temporally and spatially, and come
to constitute the final word in his epitaph, as well as the concrete grounds
for his enduring fame.[35]

The eulogist, although (or perhaps, precisely because) his claims to
impartiality are in various ways undercut (especially, as Peter J. Schakel
has noted, by his ideological allegiance to the Tory Opposition[36]), suc-

ceeds admirably as a mouthpiece for relegating Swift's tenure in England
in support of the Bolingbroke-Harley ministry to the realm of romantic
mythification:

> And, oh! how short are human Schemes!
> Here ended all our golden Dreams.
> What ST. JOHN'S skill in State Affairs,
> What ORMOND'S *Valour,* OXFORD'S Cares,
> To save their sinking Country lent,
> Was all destroy'd by one Event.
> Too soon that precious Life was ended,
> On which alone, our Weal depended.
>
> (371–78)

At the same time that he is burying Swift's English past in a shroud of
idealized and apocalyptic memories, the eulogist is unwittingly heightening Swift's Irish present (the historical present beyond the poem, and,
within the poem's fiction, that part of Swift's past closest to the speaker's
present), making it live through specific deeds that have produced concrete results and through projects that will continue into the future (e.g.,
the construction of an insane asylum).

Although presumably one of the premises of the eulogy is that
Swift's life in Ireland after the ministry's collapse was characterized by
tragic loss and diminution, by an "Exile" in which "He spent his Life's
declining Part;/Where, Folly, Pride, and Faction sway" (432–33), the
speaker unwittingly demonstrates that Swift's years in Ireland were in
many ways the most fruitful and significant of his career, standing in
sharp contrast to his brief tenure in England, which was marked on the
whole by failure and frustration, by a sense of hopelessness even before
the actual fall of the Tory ministry: "He labour'd many a fruitless Hour/
To reconcile his Friends in Power;/. . . But, finding vain was all his Care,/
He left the Court in meer Despair" (365–66, 369–70). Whereas he was
reduced to being a passive and helpless spectator in England—"With Horror, Grief, Despair the Dean/Beheld the dire destructive Scene:/His
Friends in Exile, or the Tower,/Himself within the Frown of Power"
(391–94)—Swift, after his return to Ireland, becomes an effective and
powerful political activist who virtually single-handedly saves his country
from destruction:

> The Dean did by his Pen defeat
> An infamous destructive Cheat.
> Taught Fools their Int'rest how to know;
> And gave them Arms to ward the Blow.
> Envy hath own'd it was his doing,
> To save that helpless Land from Ruin. . . .
>
> (407–12)

Moreover, although the speaker wishes to portray him in the role of lone martyr—"By Innocence and Resolution,/He bore continual Persecution" (399-400)—he shows, in recounting details of the Dean's public activities in Ireland, that Swift was far from being the isolated and victimized figure implicit in the eulogy's official myth; thus during the Drapier affair "The grateful People stand his Friends" and refuse to allow the force of the law to be brought down on his head (425-30).

Despite the eulogist's emotional and ideological allegiance to pre-1714 England, when the Tory party was in its ascendance, the primary focus of his narrative is on post-1714 Ireland, which is seen to provide much the better stage for Swift's political abilities and for the expression of his personality. Whereas his life in England dissolves into Grub Street scribbles (165-68), idle discourse (179-218), hypocritical pronouncements interspersed with parlor games (225-42), and finally merciful oblivion (245-48), his activities in Ireland assume a vivid and detailed reality. As Dublin Dean and Drapier, Swift is shown to have lived a life not of "golden dreams" but of potent words and effective actions; a tangible monument ("a House for Fools and Mad") attests, however parodically, to its builder's well-deserved fame. Schakel is right to point out the ironic discrepancy between the eulogist's supposed status as one "indiff'rent in the Cause" and his politically partisan statements, but the even greater and more interesting irony is that the eulogist, for all his idealization of the period in England under the Tory ministry, locates Swift's true moment of glory and acme of power not in his association with Harley and Bolingbroke in London, but in his role as Irish patriot through the long years following his flight to Dublin. The *Verses on the Death* chronicles the decisive movement of Swift's life from an English to an Irish setting and homeland.

iii

Other poems attest in more explicit and emphatic ways to Swift's shift in perceptual focus and allegiance to a uniquely Irish landscape. This group includes the poems that contain specific topographical descriptions of, or allusions to, his Irish surroundings, as well as topical verses such as those on Wood's halfpence (P, 1:331-54) and others cited earlier in this chapter, which present Swift in the role of Irish patriot. Regarding these Irish verses, which have been largely ignored even by the few critics who have bothered to examine Swift's poetry at all, it is unfortunate that Schakel, in his chapter on "The Poems on Ireland," talks mostly about the Bible, Horace, and Virgil and very little about the contemporary Irish milieu.[37] He thus calls special attention to the topical verses, only to rob them of their topicality, a result in part of his zeal to show that through

Swift's mastery of allusive techniques, ". . . an initially local or personal situation or incident [can be expanded] into a significant statement on art and morality."[38] In this respect Schakel is perpetuating the tendency of Swift criticism to remove Swift's writings from their most immediate context as well as from their native soil and to place them instead within a traditionally defined Augustan frame of reference—a tendency exemplified by the most authoritative modern editor of Swift's poems, Harold Williams, who, although arguing that "the poems of Jonathan Swift have been undeservedly overshadowed," goes on to declare that "nevertheless it must be recognized that his standing was within the circle of the Augustan poets. . . . In verse Pope was his superior. . . . Gay and Prior had a more lyrical gift" (P, 1:xv).

Nora Crow Jaffe provides a necessary corrective for Schakel's and Williams's views when she clearly differentiates between Pope's and Swift's poetry, concluding that ". . . without a new perspective and altered methods [with regard to poetic analysis], the same scholarly intelligence that battens on Pope will starve on Swift."[39] Yet Jaffe's discussion of "The Poet Swift" virtually ignores most of Swift's political broadsides and poems on Ireland and thus fails to deal with the profound links between Swift's poetry and a specifically, distinctively Irish landscape. Contemporary English compilers and editors of Swift had their own way of minimizing or even denying these links, as we can see from an early London reprinting of Swift's broadside, *Helter Skelter,* in which "Dublin" is changed to "London" in the verse's final line ("Hey for Dublin Town agen!" [56]) (see P, 2:574 and n.), and as is evident likewise from the extensive cuts poems like the *Verses on the Death* suffered at the hands of their English printers.

The contrast between Pope's and Swift's poetry may in part be understood in terms of the distinction between a learned or formal and a popular satiric tradition. A large number of Swift's poems follow directly in the line of satirists like Butler and Rochester, while his political broadsides rely upon popular ballads and look back to the seventeenth-century *Poems on Affairs of State.*[40] Swift as poet frequently made use of local folk tunes and ballads—for example, *An Excellent new Song on a seditious Pamphlet,* "To the Tune of *Packington's Pound,*" and *Dingley, and Brent. A song,* "To the Tune of *Ye Commons and Peers.*" Swift's verses record the sounds and smells of Dublin life, along with the dialects and special vocabulary of its inhabitants. His instinctive attraction to street people and their mode of existence is commemorated in his street cries, *Verses made for Women who cry Apples, &c.,* which capture a sense of local place and color. Swift's interest in, as well as keen sense of observation and hearing with regard to, urban street life was of course also displayed during his stays in London, as we see from various entries in the *Journal* to *Stella* and verses like *A Description of a City Shower* and *A Description of the Morning.* But whereas the latter two are among the most frequently discussed of his poems, others, grounded in Dublin rather than London life, go wholly unnoticed.

One such example is *The Yahoo's Overthrow; or, The Kevan Bayl's New Ballad, upon Serjeant Kite's insulting the Dean,* "To the Tune of *Derry down*," which opens by addressing the "Jolly boys of St. Kevans, St. Patrick's, Donore,/And Smithfield...." (St. Kevans was the parish in which St. Patrick's was located; the other names signify areas of the Liberties. The "Kevan Bayl" of the title refers to the Liberty of the deanery and cathedral.) This poem might be devoid of the minute physical detail of the London poems, but it nonetheless succeeds in evoking the rough and raucous atmosphere of the Liberties, the area's constant potential for violent eruptions, and its reliance upon private forms of "justice":

> Tho' he [Booby Bettesworth] cring'd to his
>   Deanship in very low strains,
> To others he boasted of knocking out brains,
> And slitting of noses, and cropping of ears,
> While his own ass's Zaggs were more fit for the shears.
>   *Knock him down, down, down, knock him down.*
>
> On this Worrier of Deans whene'er we can hit,
> We'll show him the way how to crop and to slit;
> We'll teach him some better address to afford
> To the Dean of all Deans, tho' he wears not a sword.
>   *Knock him down, down, down, knock him down.*
>
> We'll colt him thro' Kevan, St. Patrick's, Donore,
> And Smithfield, as Rap was ne'er colted before;
> We'll oil him with kennel, and powd'r him with grains,
> A modus right fit for insulters of Deans.
>   *Knock him down, down, down, knock him down.*
>
>   (46–60)

Behind this comic view of Dublin street justice, in which Swift characteristically implicates himself in the satiric scene as an agitator of the lawless actions that the verse exposes, was an empirical situation marked by widespread violence and an absence of effective institutional law enforcement. As Peter Somerville-Large notes, "Proper policing of the city was still disorganized and the various means of ensuring civil law and order were ineffective.... Most policing was done by patrolling watchmen who got their jobs as the result of charitable efforts by different parishes. As a result they were often old and feeble."[41] Bitter vendettas between both individuals and groups (Lecky speaks of the "savage feuds between the Ormond and the Liberty boys, between the students of the University and the butchers around St. Patrick, between the butchers and the weavers, and between the butchers and the soldiers"[42]) were a common part of everyday life in eighteenth-century Dublin.

Contemporary newspaper accounts attested to the prevalence of the kind of unofficial street justice and mob action implied in Swift's ballad and microcosmically reflected in the contention between himself and "Booby" Bettesworth. (The fact that the latter, an irascible bully who threatened to cut off Swift's ears, was himself a serjeant-at-law and member of Parliament serves of course to highlight the emptiness of officially sanctioned legal and judicial forms.) The economically oppressed weavers, for example, were involved in frequent street actions. One contemporary report, dating from the spring of 1734, describes how

> a mob of weavers of the Liberty rose in order to rifle the several shops in this city for English manufactures, and stopped at the houses of Messrs. Eustace and Lindsay, woollen drapers on High Street. . . . They forced off the hinges of Mr Eustace's shop windows with hammers and chisels, but were prevented doing further mischief by the timely assistance of the sheriff and his bailiffs, whom the mob attacked. They then attacked several other shops of woollen drapers . . . . Several were made prisoners in one house they broke into, and were sent to Newgate. They retired in a body to the Liberty, and threatened to pull down several houses if their associates who had been captured were not released. At length the army had to be brought against them. . . .[43]

Accounts such as this give a very special relevance and force to Swift's self-described role as "King of the Mob," a role proudly flaunted in another of his verses, *Ay and No. A Tale from Dublin,* in which Archbishop Boulter of Armagh uneasily notes that "The mob is grown bold" (3) in reaction against the lowering of the gold standard in 1737, which he himself helped bring about, while Swift, an opponent of the measure, coolly reflects, "It's a pity a Prelate should die without law;/But if I say the word—take care of *Armagh!*" (17–18). The context of this rather shocking statement, which represents a not-so-implicit threat against the limbs if not the life of the archbishop, and which makes him, together with Bettesworth, an appropriate object for the Dean-led mob to punish, is clarified in a letter written by Lord George Sackville to his father, the Duke of Dorset, in the fall of 1737: "The other day at the Lord Mayor's feast the Dean before all the company talked against lowring the gold, and told the Primate that had it not been for him he would have been torn to pieces by the mob, and that if he held up his finger he could make them do it that instant" (P, 3:842). This sense of being "absolute monarch in the *Liberties,* and King of the Mob," rooted in a feeling of genuine pride and actual power in the world, however much it may be accompanied on various occasions by a tone of self-mocking deflation, permeates many of Swift's political broadsides, investing them with a geographical specificity as well as topicality.

The Yahoo's Overthrow reflects the poet Swift's links to a uniquely Irish landscape in other ways as well. The choice of words in the poem indicates Swift's familiarity with local colloquialisms and regional dialects, his interest in language other than King's English, which reveals the social class and background of the speaker. Examples include the description of the plan to "colt" Bettesworth and to "oil him with kennel, and powd'r him with grains"—to beat him with "a piece of rope knotted or weighted at one end," then to "drag him in the gutter and cover him with the dry straw and refuse of the street" (P, 3:817 and n.)—and the use of the word "skip" in the seventh line, signifying a footman or manservant. As Williams notes, "The word was in use at Trinity College, Dublin" (814 n.). Terms like "Bonny-Clabber" and "Sowins" (Mad Mullinix and Timothy, 260; An Answer to the Ballyspellin Ballad, 33; A Pastoral Dialogue, 51), signifying types of food indigenous to Ireland and constituting a major part of the Irish peasants' diet, are sprinkled throughout Swift's verse and reinforce its regional flavor. In a "Preface to the English Edition" of The Grand Question debated, the editor George Faulkner carefully situates the poem in the "North of Ireland" and observes: "Some Expressions being peculiar to Ireland, I have prevailed on a Gentleman of that Kingdom to explain them, and I have put the several Explanations in their proper Places" (P, 3:866). One expression thus glossed is "Rumms" ("I'm grown a meer Mopus; no Company comes;/ But a Rabble of Tenants, and rusty dull Rumms" [27–28]), which Faulkner defines as "A cant Word in Ireland for a poor Country Clergyman" (P, 3:868 and n.).

Swift goes beyond using cant English words that reflect a regional bias. In A Ballad (beginning "Patrick astore, what news upon the town?"), written to protest the lowering of the gold standard in 1737, he employs words that are distinctly Gaelic in sound and origin (the term "astore" means literally "O treasure," and is the equivalent of "darling"):

> Musha! Why Parliament wouldn't you maul,
> Those *carters*, and paviours, and footmen and all;
> Those rascally paviours who did us undermine,
> Och ma ceade millia mollighart, on the feeders of swine!
>   Sing och, och, hoh, hoh.
>
>   (16–20)

Line 19 (the first part of which means "A hundred thousand curses on thee") would seem to suggest Swift's at least limited familiarity with the

native language, an inference corroborated by verses from Sheridan's
"Appendix to the Trifles," addressed "To the Dean of St Patricks":

> Oxford & Ormond he supplies
> In ev'ry Irish Teague he spies;
> So far forgetting his old Station
> He seems to like their Conversation.
> Conforming to the tatter'd Rabble
> He learns their Irish Tongue to gabble. . . .
>
> (27–32; P, 3:1040)

The reference to Swift's "learn[ing] their Irish Tongue to gabble"
is perfectly plausible as a statement of fact, given the bonds of friendship
he felt with his "old friends the rabble" and his interest in conversing with
the common people in both Dublin and the remoter regions of the island.
Swift's remark that "it would be a noble achievement to abolish the Irish
language in this kingdom" (PW, 12:89) is regularly quoted out of context
and erroneously used to identify him with an arrogantly colonialist outlook. Not only does Swift significantly qualify the remark so that it reflects not a blanket statement of policy but considerations of a practical
nature limited to occasions of business, but there is also an unmistakable
note of irony in Swift's seconding of this scheme—one of a number sent
him by various modest and not-so-modest proposers, a group of would-
be experts on Ireland's problems usually having little familiarity with
the country's actual state of affairs, whose misplaced priorities (how
urgent and crucial, after all, was a scheme to abolish the Irish language
in a country suffering from a "miserable dearth of money" [89] and a
widespread famine threatening to drive away half the inhabitants of
Ireland and to starve the rest [22]?) Swift contemptuously exposed in
other tracts written during the same period (e.g., *An Answer to a Paper,
called "A Memorial"*).[44] I am by no means claiming that Swift ever achieved
any real proficiency in the Irish language, nor even that he necessarily
acquired anything more than the most superficial knowledge of it. My
point, rather, is that Swift's interest in the vernacular, as shown by his
occasional poetic employment of Irish words, indicates a receptiveness
to the native culture and to a popular "street" literature whose structural,
linguistic, and implicitly ideological character contrasts with the formal
Augustan literary tradition in England and helps account for the unorthodox features of Swift's verse as well.

It is this basic perspective that also explains Swift's ballad *The
Description of an Irish-Feast, translated almost literally out of the Original Irish*. The original poem, *Pléaraca na Ruarcach*, composed during the
first decade of the eighteenth century and attributed to Hugh MacGauran,
was set to music by the renowned Irish bard, O'Carolan (better known

simply as Carolan), an almost legendary figure celebrated by Oliver Gold-smith in his essay, "The History of Carolan, the Last Irish Bard."[45] Carolan served for a time as a paid harpist for his patron, Swift's friend Patrick Delany, who subsequently helped print an edition of Carolan's songs after the bard's death in 1738.[46] According to popular tradition, the noted blind harpist and the famous Dean of St. Patrick's met face to face—an encounter that, although probably fictitious, in a sense ought to have occurred, given the two men's common roles as popular folk heroes and patriotic actors on behalf of their country's interests (while the Drapier distributed his *Letters,* Carolan composed a song about Wood's halfpence), and given the joint tribute to both that stands to this very day on Swift's home territory: A memorial to Carolan erected by Lady Morgan faces a monument to Swift across the nave of St. Patrick's Cathedral. The following anecdote describes one of the purported meetings:

> The Dean admired Carolan's genius, had him frequently at the Deanery House in Dublin, and used to hear him play and sing the pléaraca. He was particularly struck with the happy and singular onomatopoeia in several passages of the original, particularly that which represented the sound of the wet in the dancers' shoes, '*glug-glug i n-a mbrbg.*' This was thought to be inimitable by English words, till Carolan bade him send his servant to walk over shoes in a pool of water and then dance before him. This coincided with the Dean's own whimsical fancy. The experiment was made, and the Dean caught the sound and expressed it by
> Splish, splash in their pumps. . . .[47]

There are similar stories about a personal meeting between Swift and the poet MacGauran, who is himself supposed to have furnished Swift with a literal translation of *Pléaraca na Ruarcach* on that occasion, a claim less improbable than the one concerning the meeting with Carolan. As Williams notes, "The evidence for this story is slight, but it need not be dismissed as impossible" (P, 1:244).

Swift's translation, representing lines 1-40 and 45-72 of the complete Irish text, which consists of 96 lines, is a spirited verse that serves to underscore Swift's aesthetic affinities with the native bardic tradition in Ireland:

> *OROURK's* noble Fare
>   Will ne'er be forgot,
> By those who were there,
>   Or those who were not.
> His Revels to keep,
>   We sup and we dine,
> On seven Score Sheep,
>   Fat Bullocks and Swine.

Usquebagh to our Feast
    In Pails was brought up,
An Hundred at least,
    And a Madder our Cup.
O there is the Sport,
    We rise with the Light,
In disorderly Sort,
    From snoring all Night.

                                                        (1-16)

Reminiscent of the boisterous, coarse, and lively drinking and swiving
songs of Rochester, Etherege, and other Restoration libertines, Swift's
ballad nevertheless calls attention to its uniquely Irish character by
retaining a number of Gaelic words ("*Usquebagh*" [9], from the Irish
"uisge-beatha," signifying water of life, or whisky; "Madder" [12], from
the Irish "meadar," a square wooden drinking vessel; and "*Yean*" [56],
which Faulkner glosses as "another *Irish* Name for a Woman" [P, 1:
244-46]). Moreover, it is sprinkled with place names that clearly indicate
its regional nature (74-76) as well as similarly identifiable human appella-
tions (46, 48, 77), and it features the indispensable figure of the Irish
harper (25). The portrayal of the feast's degeneration into complete
mayhem and chaos seems peculiarly appropriate to Swift's sensibilities
and rhetorical constructions alike, exemplifying, together with works
like *Helter Skelter* and *The Revolution at Market-Hill*, the destructuring
effects of much of his verse:

Good Lord, what a Sight,
    After all their good Cheer,
For People to fight
    In the Midst of their Beer:
They rise from their Feast,
    And hot are their Brains,
A Cubit at least
    The Length of their Skeans.
What Stabs and what Cuts,
    What clatt'ring of Sticks,
What Strokes on Guts,
    What Bastings and Kicks!

                                                        (57-68)

Poems like *The Yahoo's Overthrow, A Ballad,* and *The Description
of an Irish-Feast* are not unique in Swift's poetic canon; rather, they make
more than usually explicit certain of its characteristic features and techniques. Such verses suggest that the term "Swift and his Irish circle,"
which Williams uses to denote the group of friends, including Delany,
Sheridan, and the Rochforts, who exchanged riddles, pasquinades, and

poetic trifles for diversion (P, 3:965), may in fact have a broader applica-
tion for much of Swift's poetry. This view is in effect argued by Maurice
Craig. Noting the existence, during Swift's lifetime, of "a small school of
Irish poets with a flavour peculiar to Ireland," he declares that "[Matthew
Concanen's] anthology *Miscellaneous Poems Original and Translated*
(1724) represents the whole school: Swift, Parnell, Delany, Brown, Ward,
Sterling and others, including Irish low-life pastorals by Brown and
Ward. . . ."[48] We may well balk at the inclusion of Swift in a clearly defined Irish "school" and the easy, unqualified identification of him with
the poets enumerated (one is reminded, after all, of Swift's less than
admiring comment about Concanen in *On Poetry: A Rapsody* [397–
98]), but this association nevertheless serves as a much-needed antidote to
the continual associations of Swift with poets like Pope and Gay and helps
to dramatize the extent of his links to an Irish culture and soil. So too
does Vivian Mercier's discussion of Swift's important links to what he
defines as "the Gaelic Tradition."[49] Like Craig's view, Mercier's requires
some fairly serious qualification; but again like Craig's, his interpretation
allows us to see Swift's poetry in a new and potentially fruitful context.

iv

It is the role of the Drapier that most clearly illuminates Swift's
profound ties to Ireland and best explains how he could combine a sense
of being an outsider with his self-assertion as a loyal native son, a patriotic
activist dedicated to fostering a sense of community among his fellow
countrymen. Although from one perspective M. B., Drapier was a temporary identity assumed for a particular occasion, from another perspective
he embodied essential characteristics of Swift himself and bore important
resemblances to other of Swift's less temporally defined literary creations.
As C. J. Rawson observes, "The Drapier is much more directly and consistently a spokesman for Swift's own views than the *Tale*'s 'author' or
Gulliver, or the Modest Proposer, but he has many features in common
with them."[50] Because of the Drapier's fundamental connection with his
own creator as well as with other Swiftian personae, it is wrong to view
him, as William Ewald does, as simply a convenient mask that Swift brief-
ly put on and then completely discarded, since he ". . . never used any
mask a second time, after it had done the work for which he created it."[51]
On the contrary, however much he was tied to a fleeting moment in history and to a body of writings whose very success destroyed their raison
d'être, hence ensured their own extinction, M. B., Drapier lived on for a
long time in the context of Dublin affairs, making tactical reappearances
when the political situation warranted, as well as being immortalized on
tavern signs and banners throughout the country. The house on "Drapier's

Hill" may never have been built, but the memory—even more, the living essence— of the Drapier survived nonetheless. It survived, indeed, in geographical surroundings and an architectural ambience far more appropriate to his class affiliation and style of existence.

The Drapier shared Swift's own environment. As the proprietor of a shop in St. Francis Street (PW, 10:94) (a street located west of St. Patrick's between the Coombe and St. Thomas Street, in the heart of the weavers' and woolen manufacturers' district[52]), he, like his creator, was a resident of the Liberties, a man who inhabited the same urban landscape and who was surrounded by the same socioeconomic conditions as the Dean. The Drapier's agitations against Wood's halfpence were supplemented and paralleled by Swift's own agitations in the same cause, so that the St. Francis Street linen shop and St. Patrick's Cathedral, along with John Harding's shop in Molesworth's Court in Fishamble Street, where *The Drapier's Letters* were printed, became the primary centers of political protest, where the pamphlet war and various unofficial street actions designed to topple the proposed coinage scheme were coordinated. While the Drapier was ostensibly writing his *Letters* in one part of the Liberties and having them printed up in another, his creator was preaching against Wood's halfpence to his congregation in yet another part and coordinating, if not actually organizing, protest demonstrations there, which included the collecting and publishing of numerous petitions from tradesmen throughout the country (see PW, 10:xvi).

The links between creator and persona, which reflect the intimate bond that always existed for Swift between words and deeds, assume a variety of forms. M. B.'s "little Account of [him] self" to Viscount Molesworth suggests the nature as well as the range of these links:

> I was bred at a Free-School, where I acquired some little Knowledge in the *Latin Tongue*. I served my Apprenticeship in *London*, and there set up for my self with good Success; until by the *Death of some Friends, and the Misfortunes of others*, I returned into this Kingdom; and began to employ my Thoughts in cultivating the *Woollen-Manufacture* through all its Branches; wherein I met with great Discouragement, and powerful Opposers; whose Objections appeared to me very strange and singular. They argued, that the People of *England* would be offended, if our Manufactures were brought to equal theirs: And even some of the *Weaving*-Trade were my Enemies; which I could not but look upon as *absurd* and *unnatural.* (PW, 10:82)

Like the Drapier, Swift acquired a knowledge of Latin (though presumably a deeper and more extensive one than the shopkeeper's); served an "apprenticeship" of sorts in England, first in Surrey under the tutelage

of Sir William Temple and later in London under the direction of Harley
and Bolingbroke; and, "by the *Death of some Friends*"—Temple in 1699
and Queen Anne (though a "friend" only symbolically speaking) in
1714—and "*the Misfortunes of others*" (the confinement of Harley to the
Tower and the exile of Bolingbroke after the Tory ministry's fall), was
forced to return to Ireland, where he too "met with great Discouragement, and powerful Opposers." While the Drapier devoted his energies to
cultivating the native woolen manufacture as a means of providing protective garments "*. . . to defend [the lower and poorer Sort of People]
against cold Easterly Winds; which then blew very fierce and blasting
for a long Time together*"(PW, 10:82), and indirectly as a way of helping
Ireland become economically independent of England, the Dean wrote
pamphlets suggesting a parliamentary resolution "against wearing any
Cloath or Stuff in their Families, which were not of the Growth and Manufacture of this Kingdom" and urging his fellow countrymen "never to
appear with one single *Shred* that comes from *England*" (PW, 9:16). The
Drapier's combined anger and bewilderment that "even some of the
Weaving-Trade were [his] enemies" echoes Swift's own frequently expressed amazement and contempt at the way large segments of the Irish
population persisted in going against their own best interests by supporting England. Moreover, the Drapier's ability to make different kinds of
cloth (hence also, by metaphoric association, to write different kinds of
tracts) to suit each separate class in Irish society—"*plain, strong, coarse
Stuff*" for the "*lower and poorer Sort of People,*" "*a second* and a *third*
Kind of *Stuffs* for the *Gentry,*" and "a *fourth* Piece, made of the best
Irish Wool [he] could get," which was "grave and rich enough to be worn
by the best *Lord* or *Judge* of the Land" (PW, 10:82-83)—reflects that
very special "language of accommodation" practiced with consummate
skill by his creator in the latter's masterful playing of roles, which included speaking in different voices and dialects to disparate audiences on
a variety of occasions. The Drapier, like the Dean, has mastered the art
of moving in and out of different social and economic worlds, as well
as addressing himself to their respective (often conflicting) interests.

   In a sense, Swift in *The Drapier's Letters* resolves the conflict presented in *A Tale of a Tub* between a suit of clothing whose features are
fixed for all time according to written commandment, and one continually subject to the changing fashions of the world. The Drapier, in his role as
master tailor, deftly combines the absolutism of the Ancients and the relativity of the Moderns by making garments of a definite, unchanging
quality that nevertheless allow for the varying tastes and needs of individuals in different social classes. Equally capable of fashioning garments
for the purpose of basic survival (for the poor) and aesthetic adornment
(for the wealthy), the Drapier himself confronts the world in symbolic

nakedness, going into battle against an opponent who is top-heavy with his cumbersome armor: "I was in the Case of *David,* who *could not move in the Armour of* Saul; and therefore I rather chose to attack this *uncircumcised Philistine* (*Wood* I mean) *with a Sling and a Stone.* And I may say for *Wood's* Honour, as well as my own, that he resembles *Goliah* in many Circumstances, very applicable to the present Purpose: For *Goliah* had *a Helmet of* BRASS *upon his Head, and he was armed with a Coat of Mail.* . . . In short, he was like Mr. *Wood,* all over BRASS. . ." (PW, 10:48). To the extent that the garments made by the Drapier represent his writings, the *Letters* are a more (though by no means wholly) secular version of the father's will in the *Tale;* they combine universal authority with individual interpretation, reconciling the unity of God's Truth with the multiplicity of human perspectives and intellectual capacities. The Drapier, a middle-class tradesman with a classical education, knowledgeable about both finances and the Scriptures, shows himself to be capable of functioning equally well in the worlds of both the Ancients and the Moderns. In this respect he is similar to his creator, who many years earlier had been drawn by his patron, Temple, into a battle whose clear-cut lines of opposition were basically uncongenial to his nature, given the fact that his allegiances to the Ancients were even then inextricably bound up with a decidedly Modernist sensibility. The battle lines drawn in the conflict over Wood's halfpence were far better suited to Swift's outlook and peculiar brand of militancy.

The protean nature of the Drapier's position in society, which permits close contact with those both above and below him in the social hierarchy, is underscored in *A Letter to Mr. Harding the Printer,* where the Drapier asserts: "I am no inconsiderable Shop-keeper in this Town, I have discoursed with several of my own, and other Trades; with many Gentlemen both of City and Country; and also, with great Numbers of Farmers, Cottagers, and Labourers. . ." (PW, 10:16). In this respect the Drapier resembles other Swiftian personae such as A. North, the "Country Gentleman" from the county of Down who, although he belongs to a privileged class as a member of Parliament and an estate owner with "above two Hundred Tenants," displays an intimate knowledge of "the Sufferings . . . the meaner Sort undergo" as well as a personal involvement in the plight of the whole range of other social classes: ". . . the *Buyers* and *Sellers,* at *Fairs* and *Markets;* the *Shopkeepers* in every *Town;* the *Farmers* in general; all those who travel with *Fish, Poultry, Pedlary-ware,* and other Conveniences to sell: But more especially *Handycrafts-men,* who work . . . by the Day; and common Labourers. . ." (PW, 12:54-55). The Drapier too reveals an intimate acquaintance with the conditions of the lower classes—"the poorer Sort of *Tradesmen*" he addresses in Letter I (PW, 10:11)—and manifests his sympathy for their plight by giving up his own profits for distribution among his dyers and pressers (83), an action that brings to mind the Dean of St. Patrick's, who regularly walked the streets of the Liberties giving alms to the poor. In his social mobility and his interest in the lower classes, the Drapier likewise resembles the "real" Swift who confessed his inclination to converse with "poor Cottagers" during his "several Experiments in travelling" through both Ireland and England (C, 4:51), and who could assume the diverse roles of "... Thatcher, Ditcher, Gard'ner, [and] Baily" as well as Dean and country house guest (*A Panegyrick on the D——n, in the Person of a Lady in the North,* 156).

The Drapier who discourses with members of his own and other trades, with city and country gentlemen, with farmers and laborers, like the socially promiscuous Dean himself, emerges as a man for all classes if not all seasons: one capable of appealing so effectively to the collective reason and emotions of his countrymen that "the People of all Ranks, Parties, and Denominations" do indeed become "convinced to a Man, that the utter undoing of themselves and their Posterity for ever, will be dated from the Admission of that execrable Coin [Wood's halfpence]" (PW, 10:60). It is thus inaccurate to view Swift's position in *The Drapier's Letters* as representative of the special interests of a ruling minority, as critics have by and large done. J. C. Beckett, for example, maintains that "'the whole people of Ireland,' to whom [Swift] addressed the fourth of his *Drapier's Letters* and whose cause he so vigorously championed, meant for him the narrow circle of the established church," while W. A. Speck implicitly questions Swift's reputation as Irish patriot by arguing that "he stood not for the liberty of all Irishmen so much as for the independence of the Anglican élite."[53] Roger McHugh comes far closer to the mark when he observes that "*The Drapier's Letters* were important not only in defeating a gross political piece of jobbery but in establishing a basis of psychological unity between the colonists and the native Irish."[54]

The fallacy of views such as Beckett's or Speck's is suggested by a letter Swift wrote to the Earl of Oxford in November 1724: "There is a Fellow in London, one Wood, who got a Patent for coyning Halfpence for this Kingdom, which hath so terrifyed us, that if it were not for some Pamphlets against these Halfpence, we must have submitted. Against these Pamphlets the Lieutenant hath put out a Proclamation: and is acting the most unpopular Part I ever knew. . . . This is just of as much Consequence to your Lordship, as the news of a Skirmish between two petty States in Greece was to Alexander while he was conquering Persia, But even a Knot of Beggars, are of Importance among themselves" (C, 3:41). In its broadest implications, Swift's reference to the Irish resisters against Wood's project as "a Knot of Beggars" goes beyond emphasizing the fact that, from the point of view of the haughty English, even the elite members of the Protestant Ascendancy in Ireland seem as lowly and inconsequential as penniless vagabonds. Even more, he is suggesting that in a very real sense, given a situation in which "... the whole Nation [of Ireland] itself is almost reduced to Beggary by the Disadvantages we lye under, and the Hardships we are forced to bear" (PW, 9:209), the Anglican "elite" in Ireland *were* in fact little more than beggars enduring hardships and oppressions in common with their only relatively more disadvantaged compatriots. Under the circumstances, anyone who chose to speak for, and act in the interests of, "a Knot of Beggars" was inevitably representing, on one level or other, the entire spectrum of Irish society. Denis Donoghue is therefore right when, in alluding to this letter, he observes that it "... corresponds to the tone of the fourth [Drapier's] Letter; the identity is secure, the unity unmistakable. The knot of beggars is the whole nation, and Swift is its voice."[55]

Yet it is important to recognize that the unity Swift represents here does not grow out of any facile assumptions about the "natural" wholeness of the social order, and is very different from the picture of social and cosmic harmony posited in the *Essay on Man.* The Drapier is a man for all classes in a genuine sense, for the unity he helps to achieve, reflected by the "universal Opposition to Mr. *Wood*" (PW, 10:61), is grounded not in a romanticized notion of a classless society but in the altogether realistic view of a society whose members, for all their profound social conflicts and economic divisions, can, at least for one brief moment in history, given sufficient external provocation, come together in recognition of a mutually shared interest to defeat a common enemy. On the most obvious level, the enemy is that "*poor, private, obscure Mechanick*" William Wood (41); but it is also the man standing behind him, the patent-giver, Walpole, who intends to "*cram his Brass down our Throats*" (67); and finally, in the broadest sense, it is that same avaricious country that, according to the Modest Proposer, "*would be glad to eat up our whole Nation...*" (PW, 12:117). Faced with this blatant arrogance of power, members of the Anglo-Irish gentry in Dublin can without compunction acknowledge a common bond of oppression with the shopkeepers in the Liberties, and even the butchers and the cloth merchants—two groups with a history of conflict between them—unite on this one occasion (PW, 10:7), under the banner of M. B.'s emotionally persuasive and rhetorically effective campaign.

Whereas the Dean, in various of his other literary roles, tends to *accentuate* class warfare while in the very act of organizing concerted political action (e.g., as a disgruntled and rebellious "Slave" to an oppressive "Knight" in *The Revolution at Market-Hill,* he asserts himself as a forceful inciter to riot [43-46]), the Drapier is enabled by the historical situation, specifically by the enormity of the outside threat to Ireland, momentarily to rise above class conflict and to create a unified community consisting of all segments of the Irish population. As he states in his *Letter to the Whole People of Ireland,* "...*Money,* the great *Divider* of the World, hath, by a strange Revolution, been the great *Uniter* of a most *divided* People" (PW, 10:61). The Dean, preaching to his congregation "On the Occasion of WOOD'S Project," also extols the spirit of national unity produced by Wood's coinage scheme at the same time that he implicitly underscores its tentative and provisional nature resulting from the deep-rooted conflicts in Irish society: "And God be praised for his infinite goodness, in raising such a spirit of union among us, at least in this point, in the midst of all our former divisions; which union, if it continue, will, in all probability, defeat the pernicious design of this pestilent enemy to the nation" (PW, 9:236).

The ability both to foment rebellion among the lower classes and to create a tightly knit constituency whereby conflicts can be at least temporarily reconciled depends upon the Dean's and the Drapier's shared position as "middlemen": figures without a clearly fixed position in society who can therefore assume—and later discard—a wide variety of social roles, establishing ties with one class or another as the occasion demands. The Drapier and the Dean represent a different kind of "middleman" from (although they belong to the the same world as) the one Ronald Paulson associates with the typical subject of a Swiftian satire: "He is a middleman in the sense that he is a hack writer, a popularizer of other men's ideas, and, to Swift's thinking, a relatively new species (literary, political, economic, moral): the man who accrues his own profit by peddling the products of other people who are more clearly defined in terms of good and evil."[56] Paulson emphasizes the negative side of the middleman's activities and the unsavory aspects of his role, but in Swift's world middlemen could also represent certain *positive* forces in the contemporary milieu that managed to avoid potentially destructive forms of absoluteness (in political terms, translatable into tyranny), steering between reductive extremes in their embodiment of a liberating openness and assuming diverse manifestations or, in literary terms, personae. Of *these* middlemen the Drapier and Dean serve as examples par excellence, and both make clear their allegiance to this role in its various moral, literary, social, and economic ramifications. The Drapier adapts a rather traditional formulation to his own special situation when, after noting with some satisfaction that "my State is not altogether deplorable," he goes on to explain: "This I can impute to nothing but the Steddiness of *two impartial Grand Juries;* which hath confirmed in me an Opinion I have long entertained; That, as Philosophers say, *Vertue is seated in the*

Middle; so in another Sense, the little *Virtue* left in the World is chiefly to be found among the *middle* Rank of Mankind; who are neither *allured* out of her Paths by *Ambition,* nor *driven* by *Poverty"* (PW, 10:90).

The Dean too expressed his preference for, and suggested his affinities with, those in "the *middle* Rank of Mankind." It is not coincidental that his most famous protagonist, Gulliver, was the middle son of a man who, as owner of a small estate in Nottinghamshire, belonged to the "middling" gentry. In a letter to Pope, Swift explains that "There is another race which I prefer before [great people], as Beef and Mutton for constant dyet before Partridges: I mean a middle kind both for understanding and fortune" (C, 3:285), and he tells Chetwode, "Half a dozen middling clergymen, and one or two middling laymen make up the whole circle of my acquaintance" (462). It was not a matter of his uncritical embrace of the values and attitudes exemplified by this *"middle* Rank of Mankind"; his tracts, after all, contain many angry remarks about the indolence, greed, dishonesty, and outright corruption of a substantial proportion of the Irish working class, including weavers, woolen manufacturers, handicraftsmen, and drapiers (see, e.g., PW, 12:69–70; and PW, 13:89–92). Nevertheless, as Swift's disillusionment with the ruling elite increased as he grew older, he came to view members of this "middling race" as at least a potential source of moral virtue, positive political energy, and indispensable personal support.

While M. B. directed his appeal "To the *Tradesmen, Shop-Keepers, Farmers,* and *Country-People* in General" (PW, 10:3), the Dean spoke from the pulpit "chiefly to those of the lower Sort" (PW, 9:195), addressing "you of the lower Rank" (197) and assuring his audience, "When I say the people, I mean the bulk or mass of the people, for I have nothing to do with those in power" (234). In *A Letter to a Young Gentleman, Lately enter'd into Holy Orders,* Swift observes that ". . . Professors in most Arts and Sciences are generally the worst qualified to explain their Meanings to those who are not of their Tribe: A common Farmer shall make you understand in three Words, *that his Foot is out of Joint, or his Collar-bone broken;* wherein a *Surgeon,* after a hundred Terms of Art, if you are not a Scholar, shall leave you to seek" (66). Swift's remarks in this *Letter* are usually discussed in terms of his concern with rhetorical styles and proper use of language, but they possess an equally important ideological dimension having to do with Swift's art of ventriloquy (so to speak), which cut across class lines and linguistically collapsed, even as it implicitly acknowledged the existence of, clearly defined social hierarchies. Communication with the "lower Sort" was of particular importance: "For a Divine hath nothing to say to the wisest Congregation of any Parish in this Kingdom, which he may not express in a Manner to be understood by the meanest among them" (66). Thus the Drapier, in appealing to Ireland's uneducated, laboring classes, goes out of his way to put his argument in crystal-clear terms, promising that he will tell his readers "the *plain Story of the Fact*" (PW, 10:4). Swift's models for emulation included "that excellent Prelate," Dr. Tillotson, who knew "... the Difference between elaborate Discourses upon important Occasions, delivered to Princes or Parliaments, written with a View of being made publick; and a plain Sermon intended for the Middle or lower Size of People" (PW, 9:67); and Jesus himself, "who instead of a rich and honourable Station in this World, was pleased to chuse his Lot among Men of the lower Condition" (198). As Jonas Barish has suggested, the man who temporarily put aside his divine nature in order to act in the mortal world presents a paradigm of the ultimate role player.[57] He embodied a divinely sanctioned theatricality that must have proven irresistibly appealing to that consummate user of masks, Swift.

Swift occupied a fundamentally equivocal "middle state" in society, stemming largely from the fact that he was *both* a member of the Protestant Ascendancy, an Anglican dean automatically elevated above the Irish Catholic populace, *and* a member of the "inferior clergy," whom, indeed, he explicitly refers to as "the middling Rate of *Clergymen*" and foresees being reduced to "a Breed of Beggars" (PW, 12:193, 199) as a result of oppression by the bishops, men usually sent over from England who enjoyed close connections with the Court: "Our B[ishop]s puft up with Wealth and with Pride./To Hell on the Backs of the Clergy wou'd ride;/They mounted, and labour'd with Whip and with Spur,/In vain—for the Devil a Parson wou'd stir" (*On the Irish Bishops*, 17–20). Swift's "middle" position in Irish society allowed him to identify with both the haves and the have-nots. He was just poor enough to be able to support his assertions that "Money is not to be had, except they will make me a Bishop, or a Judge, or a Colonell, or a Commissioner of the Revenue" (C, 4:385) and that he could not finance a trip to England because of "the very bad posture of my private affairs in this oppressed and starving pennyless Country" (187). At the same time, he was sufficiently well off to enjoy the privileges of a more prosperous class—hence his admission to one correspondent that "with good Management I still make a shift to keep up; and am not poor, nor even moneyless" (379).

It seems clear, on the whole, that Louis A. Landa is right in arguing that Swift's living conditions in Ireland were not as personally disagreeable, and certainly not as impoverished or desperate, as he so often characterized them.[58] Had he wished, he could have largely dissociated himself from the Dublin "rabble" (as numerous other Anglican churchmen chose to do) and adopted a Pope-like stance of Olympian detachment from the dirty, crowded, urban scene nearby. That he chose to do the contrary by going out of his way to accentuate his ties to the rabble and by embracing this scene as his "home" was to some degree a conscious political choice. Swift's explicit identification with the most victimized groups in his "starving pennyless Country" was a means of locating himself within (or, to be more precise, outside) the existing social order, of expressing his relationship both to the ruling establishment and to the powerless classes. Although he never entirely repudiated his links to the ruling class and made certain that channels of communication with them remained open (Letter III of *The Drapier's Letters,* addressed *"To the Nobility and Gentry of the Kingdom of* IRELAND" [PW, 10:27], showed that he could speak to them in their own idiom about issues of vital concern for them), increasingly he displayed a far greater sense of identification and linguistic familiarity with the disinherited, oppressed groups in society, so that on those occasions when he (temporarily) took leave of his "middle realm," he generally moved *downward,* not upward, affirming his ties to weavers or shopkeepers rather than to ministers of state. As he asserted to Chetwode, "I have utterly done with all great names and titles of Princes and Lords and Ladies and Ministers of State, because I conceive they do me not the least honour. . . . I thank God that I am not acquainted with one person of title in this whole kingdom, nor could I tell how to behave myself before persons of such sublime quality" (C, 3:462).

Swift's deepening sense of alienation from, as well as growing contempt for, those in the upper classes was part and parcel of a thoroughgoing skepticism with regard to the very grounds upon which social distinctions are founded, a radical questioning of the legitimacy of titles and power relationships in society. As the eulogist in the *Verses on the Death of Dr. Swift* puts it, in describing Swift's mode of existence in Ireland:

> His Friendship there to few confin'd,
> Were always of the midling Kind:
> No Fools of Rank, a mungril Breed,
> Who fain would pass for Lords indeed:
> Where Titles give no Right or Power,
> And Peerage is a wither'd Flower,
> He would have held it a Disgrace,
> If such a Wretch had known his Face.

(435–42)

Swift's footnote to this passage clarifies the basis of his contempt for this "mungril Breed": "The Peers of *Ireland* lost a great Part of their Jurisdiction by one single Act [The Declaratory Act of 1720, which affirmed the English Parliament's right to legislate and to act as the final court of judicature for Ireland], and tamely submitted to this infamous Mark of Slavery without the least Resentment, or Remonstrance" (P, 2:570, n. 4).

The Irish upper classes, then, consisted of ersatz peers, men possessing empty titles and occupying meaningless, ineffectual positions in society despite their ostensibly elevated rank.

The peers of England, for their part, although they were presumably the "true" models whom the Irish peers parodically emulated, likewise underwent a process of cynical debasement when exposed to the withering eye and scathing pen of Swift. The poem *Directions for a Birth-day Song Oct: 30. 1729* (October 30 having been the birthday of King George II) satirically deflates all pretenders to title and rank, including the Prince of Wales, ". . . his little Highness Freddy,/Who struts like any King already" (187-88), and William Augustus, Duke of Cumberland, who "Will soon subdue the Realm of Lilliput" (208). Swift's satiric subversion is not limited to attacks on particular officeholders or on isolated instances of absurdity, false pretensions, or corruption. The ultimate object of his satire is often the emptiness of the traditional credentials invoked to justify the exercise of power:

> One Compliment I had forgot,
> But Songsters must omit it not.
> (I freely grant the Thought is old)
> Why then, your Hero must be told,
> In him such Virtues lye inherent,
> To qualify him God's Vicegerent,
> That with no Title to inherit,
> He must have been a King by Merit.
> Yet be the Fancy old or new,
> 'Tis partly false, and partly true,
> And take it right, it means no more
> Than George and William claim'd before.
>
> (129-40)

Throughout Swift's poetry of the late 1720s and early 1730s we find a radical questioning of the official sanctions supporting established forms of power, as well as a demythologizing of kingship itself. His verse *To Mr. Gay* describes the systematic erosion of the peerage through the corrupting "Arts" of the attorney, Peter Waters (Peter Walter), and maintains that ". . . Kings, like private Folks, are bought and sold" (136). Similarly, *A Panegyric on the Reverend D——n S——t*, after recalling the attributes of a former age, laments:

> But Things are strangely chang'd since then,
> And *Kings* are now no more than *Men;*
> From whence 'tis plain, they quite have lost
> God's *Image*, which was once their Boast.
>
> (163-66)

In a world where "Titles give no Right or Power" and "Kings, like private Folks, are bought and sold," the center (so to speak) can no longer hold; the traditional loci of authority have lost their mythic sanctions, hence their universally acknowledged legitimacy, the result being a dispersion of power throughout wider areas of society. This disintegration of a clearly delineated hierarchic structure is dramatized as well by the typical Swiftian catalog, which juxtaposes and intermixes a wide range of different social classes, ranks, and professions, conveying an image that combines anarchic dispersion with promiscuous fusion. We might recall, for example, Gulliver's comment at the end of his fourth voyage: "I am not in the least provoked at the Sight of a Lawyer, a Pick-pocket, a Colonel, a Fool, a Lord, a Gamester, a Politician, a Whoremunger, a Physician, an Evidence, a Suborner, an Attorney, a Traytor, or the like" (PW, 11:296). Another typical catalog appears in *On Poetry: A Rapsody:*

> A publick, or a private *Robber;*
> A *Statesman,* or a South-Sea *Jobber.*
> A *Prelate* who no God believes;
> A [Parliament], or Den of Thieves.
> A Pick-purse at the Bar, or Bench;
> A Duchess, or a Suburb-Wench.
>
> (161–66)

As Rawson observes, Swift's "satiric catalogues have in common a quality of teeming vitality, an exuberant profusion of ugliness and disorder. The moods which underlie this may range from the playful to the very bitter, but the sense of sheer anarchic energy is often strong." He adds that in certain of his works, "Swift goes even further than Flaubert in registering the radical unruliness of things."[59] Rawson, however, adopts an unnecessarily dark view of this "anarchic energy" and "radical unruliness," interpreting them as expressions of Swift's fundamental pessimism, perversity, and despair. If we consider them less in psychological and more in concretely political terms, we must conclude that Swift saw a good deal of positive potential in this fluid situation marked by the collapse of traditional hierarchic order.

It is precisely this situation and its profound sociopolitical implications that Swift comments upon in the *Intelligencer, No. IX,* which poses the question "... how it comes about, that for above sixty Years past, the chief Conduct of Affairs in [England] hath been generally placed in the Hands of *New-men,* with few Exceptions?" (PW, 12:47). In including in this group of *"New-men"* such diverse figures as Godolphin, Ashley-Cooper, Somers, Churchill, Harley, St. John, Walpole, and Addison, Swift indicates his awareness that the recently emergent social mobility and political dispersion is an ambiguous matter, possessing the potential for both good and ill, opening opportunities for political advancement to "Men of Art, Knowledge, Application and Insinuation" as well as to "Persons of the best private Families, but unadorned with Titles," at the same time that it has given power to members of the new capitalist class, those "retailers of fraud" castigated in the *Examiner* papers, and has allowed the meteoric rise of one whom Swift elsewhere describes as guilty of "oppressing true merit exalting the base/and selling his Country to purchase his peace" (*The Character of Sir Robert Walpole,* 7–8).

A further consequence of this displacement of power was the fact that even a member of the inferior Irish clergy and a lowly Dublin linen draper could exert an influence far exceeding their relative insignificance in the official political hierarchy and amass sufficient support to defeat a project promoted by the English prime minister himself. There can be no doubt that the Drapier-Dean enjoyed a very concrete and potent, not to mention at times awesome, influence, even though it did not express itself through formally constituted channels of governmental authority. As Bishop Nicolson noted several weeks after the formal revocation of Wood's patent, in September 1725, the Drapier "... is, at present, in great Repute; the Darling of the populace" (PW, 10:xxx). At the end of the following summer, a widespread public acclamation greeted Swift upon his return to Dublin from England, as was recorded by (among many others) Sheridan in his *Life of Swift:*

> ... several Heads of the different corporations, and principal citizens of Dublin, went out to meet him in a great number of wherries engaged for that purpose.... The boats adorned with streamers, and colours, in which were many emblematical devices, made a fine appearance; and thus was the Drapier brought to his landing-place in a kind of triumph, where he was received and welcomed on shore by a multitude of his grateful countrymen, by whom he was conducted to his house amid repeated acclamations, of *Long live the Drapier.* The bells were all set a ringing, and bonfires kindled in every street.[60]

Eight years later, his popularity and influence continued unabated, judging from a report in the *Dublin Journal* for June 11, 1734, which described how Swift, coming upon a large group of disgruntled weavers menacingly assembled in the street, who were intent upon searching out foreign manufactures, exhorted the mob to seek out a more peaceful solution to their problems: "... whereupon they immediately dispersed to their several Homes, crying out, Long live Dean Swift, and Prosperity to the Drapier, and returned him Thanks for his good Advice, which they said they would follow" (PW, 13:xxix).

Swift's very real if unofficial power was also attested to by his success in escaping punishment during the Drapier affair, despite the fact that a reward of £300 was offered for the Drapier's apprehension and that Lord Carteret had been hastily sent to Dublin as lord lieutenant of Ireland specifically to silence the pen of agitators like the Drapier. But, as Lecky puts it, ". . . that able, fearless, and experienced statesman found himself equally powerless" (as powerless as his weaker, less competent predecessor, the Duke of Grafton).[61] In the *Verses on the Death of Dr. Swift,* the eulogist in effect contrasts the Drapier's *successful* efforts to save Ireland from ruin with the *unsuccessful* efforts of those ". . . who at the Steerage stood,/And reapt the Profit, [and] sought his Blood" (413–14), exemplified by the thwarted attempts of Chief Justice Whitshed to silence the Drapier through arbitrary law enforcement: "Not Strains of Law, nor Judges Frown,/Nor Topicks brought to please the Crown,/Nor Witness hir'd, nor Jury pick'd,/Prevail to bring him in convict" (427–30).

The role of the Drapier, then, served as a means by which Swift's marginality and political insignificance from the point of view of established authority could be converted into an eminently formidable—and ultimately triumphant—political force. By the same token, the Drapier's role was a means by which Swift, the stranger in a strange land, became the beloved patriot and folk hero of a people who enthusiastically claimed him as their own. Although Swift's situation in life, as we have already seen, could lend itself to images of peripherality, of squatting in forgotten corners of the world far from the center of power, his activities as Drapier dramatized the fact that there were hitherto untapped sources of energy and pockets of potential force spread throughout society, any one of which could emerge as a center of effective political action given the right set of circumstances. We might think of these as provisional, ad hoc centers of power produced by specific historical situations and thus impermanent, but not any less real or significant for that. Swift suggested something very like this, though with a note of disingenuous modesty, when, four years after the event, he declared that the Drapier's success ". . . was not owing to my abilities, but to a lucky juncture, when the fuel was ready for the first hand that would be at the pains of kindling it" (PW, 12:85).

Thus we must significantly qualify Edward W. Said's contention that "after 1714, Swift occupied no place except as outsider to the Whig's monolithic machine. He had become the scribbler and projector he had once impersonated (in *A Tale of A Tub*) and attacked (in *The Examiner* and elsewhere)."[62] However much it may point to some interesting ironies in Swift's situation during the final three decades of his life, this statement unduly exaggerates the power of the official establishment while tending to dismiss the potential for political efficacy available to one on the "outside." Although historians like J. H. Plumb have stressed the monolithic aspect of the Whig Party's well-oiled machinery in drawing their picture of a stable, carefully regulated society founded upon the triumph of a Venetian oligarchy under the controlling genius of Robert Walpole,[63] the work of other recent historians conveys a rather different picture (or at least suggests a different emphasis) by reminding us that, for all the newly consolidated strength of England's political system under Walpole's ministry, the period was one of turbulence and often violent social unrest, marked by riots (such as those over food and corn) that Douglas Hay describes as "organized and often highly disciplined popular protest. . . ."[64] Although such protest hardly threatened to topple the Whig establishment, it did exert an impact on its policies and mode of functioning and did on occasion achieve definite if circumscribed successes. In his depiction of the Lindalinians' rebellion in Part III of *Gulliver's Travels* (inspired by Ireland's opposition to Wood's halfpence), Swift insightfully comments on precisely this situation by presenting, in the figure of the Flying or Floating Island, the very emblem of a highly centralized authority seemingly in command of all the techniques of organized state terror, complete with the most modern scientific instruments of repression at its disposal, which nevertheless proves impotent in the face of a determined grass-roots movement, concentrated in one particular area, that not only achieves its immediate goal but also hints at the possibility of regicide and complete revolution (PW, 11:309–10). Swift's own success as a political agitator, even (indeed, especially) when opposing the most powerful man in England, likewise reveals the paradoxical vulnerability of that country's well-regulated, efficient state machine. The latter's high degree of organization, although a major source of its strength, also contributed to its limited capabilities, for such machinery could be cumbersome (like the unwieldy armor of Goliath-Wood, ironically more a burden than a help) and slow to react (as in the case of the Laputian king, who only became aware of, and began taking steps to quell, the Lindalinians' rebellion a full eight months after the fact [309]). By contrast, a popular, spontaneous protest could (to use Swift's own image with regard to the Drapier affair) ignite suddenly and spread like wildfire through all levels of society, unobstructed by the bureaucratic apparatus and unyielding structures of the political establishment.

To be sure, there is a sense in which the Drapier *is* a Swiftian scribbler and projector, hence a direct descendant of the Tale-teller. His wildly fanciful flights into the airy realm of speculation as he spins out the imagined consequences of allowing Wood's halfpence to enter the country are fully a match for the Tale-teller's mental peregrinations or the Modest Proposer's bizarrely matter-of-fact computations. We may recall the scenarios the Drapier conjures up of the twelve hundred horses that would be required to transport a banker's cash payments (PW, 10:7) and of the coins that ". . . will run about like the *Plague* and destroy every one who

lays his Hands upon them" (12), as well as his comment on the story
"... of a *Scotch* Man, who receiving Sentence of Death, with all the
Circumstances of *Hanging, Beheading, Quartering, Embowelling,* and the
like; cried out, *What need all this* COOKERY?": "And I think we have
Reason to ask the same Question: For if we believe *Wood,* here is a *Dinner* getting ready for us, and you see the *Bill of Fare;* and I am sorry the
Drink was forgot, which might easily be supplied with *Melted Lead* and
Flaming Pitch" (67). Yet the Drapier is a very different kind of projector
from the Tale-teller or the Modest Proposer, for he replaces solipsistic
delusion with clear historical vision, having the good of his country, rather
than private obsessions or matters of mere self-interest, at heart. Moreover,
the Drapier's "scribblings" are not inherently and endlessly digressive;
being firmly anchored to concrete historical reality, they have a distinctly
centripetal character despite their speculative meanderings. Whereas the
Tale-teller's spiel is by its very nature a distraction, continually diverting
attention away from things of value and substance just as the empty tub
flung out by seamen lures the whale away from the ship (TT, 40), the
Drapier's commentary insistently zeroes in on, even as it circles around,
a central issue, striving to focus the reader's entire attention on one particular set of circumstances: "What I intend now to say to you, is, next to
your Duty to God, and the Care of your Salvation, of the greatest Concern to your selves, and your Children; your *Bread* and *Cloathing,* and
every common Necessary of Life entirely depend upon it. Therefore
I do most earnestly exhort you as *Men,* as *Christians,* as *Parents,* and
as *Lovers of your Country,* to read this Paper with the utmost Attention,
or get it read to you by others..." (PW, 10:3). Thus, whereas the *Tale*
is rooted in a process of dispersion, constituting a secular, linguistic form
of diaspora, *The Drapier's Letters* function through a process of concen-
tration and crystallization—a gathering together of thoughts and resources.
It is not that the Tale-teller's anarchic proclivities have been purged from
the later series of writings; rather, they have been carefully shaped by the
at once conservative and subversive Drapier, who deftly channels them into
a pointed form of political protest. Rather than viewing the course of
Swift's life as Said does, in terms of increasing digressiveness and a growing distance from the center of things,[65] we can therefore more accurately
see it as a rather paradoxical movement *toward* a center, that is, toward
a series of "occasional" centers snatched from the devouring jaws of time
and commemorated (to a certain extent actually defined, even constituted) by Swift himself.

Given the effectiveness and popularity of the Drapier, it is not surprising that Swift was loth to relinquish the role entirely. Although, after
learning of the formal cancellation of Wood's patent, Swift wrote to the
Reverend Worrall that "the work is done, and there is no more need of the

Drapier" (C, 3:93), the latter by no means completely disappeared from the Dublin scene. Not only did he survive in the popular imagination of his contemporaries, but he was actively kept alive by Swift's continued political activity during the next decade, mainly in the form of involvement with local elections and city government. When several candidates competed for the office of recorder of the city of Dublin in February 1733, Swift entered the fray by publishing a half sheet entitled *Some Considerations in the Choice of a Recorder,* which, although it avoided mentioning any names, offered implicit support for one of the candidates, Eaton Stannard, who had gained favor in Swift's eyes by being a staunch patriot in the House of Commons (see PW, 13:xxiv). Although Swift does not assume a persona in *Some Considerations,* the basic tone of the piece, as well as the particular audience it is appealing to, readily calls the Drapier to mind. Swift stresses the crucial consequences of the election for Dublin's middle-class population, for the Drapier's fellow tradesmen: "There is not a Dealer, or Shop-keeper in this City, of any Substance, whose Thriving, less or more, may not depend upon the good or ill Conduct of a Recorder" (PW, 13:70). Again invoking a familiar voice from the past, Swift concludes the brief paper with a call for unity from "the Commoners" in support of the candidate who "is most likely to advance the Trade of themselves and their Brother Citizens, [and] to defend their Liberties both in and out of Parliament, against any Attempts of Encroachment or Oppression" (70). Upon Stannard's success in winning the post of recorder, Lord Carteret wrote to Swift congratulating him on his victory and casting a glance back at an earlier, far greater victory over Carteret himself (in the latter's official capacity as lord lieutenant of Ireland): "I know by experience how much the City thinks itselfe under yr protection, & how strictly they usd to obey all orders Fulminated from the soverainty of St Patricks, I never doubted their complyance wth you in so trivial a point as a Recorder. . ." (C, 4:128).

The following July, one of the parliamentary representatives of the city of Dublin died, precipitating a struggle for the vacated office between the mayor of Dublin, Humphrey French, and Alderman John Macarell. Once again Swift became involved in the election, this time as a fervent supporter of the lord mayor. And again he printed a short paper, *Advice to the Free-Men of the City of Dublin, in the Choice of a Member to Represent them in Parliament,* directed at influencing the vote in favor of his candidate. French, like Stannard, seems to have earned Swift's respect on the strength of his patriotic commitment, for shortly after his death four years later, Swift promised his printer, George Faulkner, "When I shall have got a sufficient Information of all these Particulars [of French's character and actions] , I will . . . stir up all the little Spirit I can raise, to give the Public an Account of that great Patriot; and propose him as an

Example to all future Magistrates, in order to recommend his Virtues to this miserable Kingdom" (C, 5:84). In his *Advice to the Free-Men,* Swift compares the two chief candidates precisely with regard to their patriotic commitment and their actions on behalf of Ireland, rejecting Alderman Macarell's bid for the office largely on the grounds that he simultaneously held the royal post of registrar of barracks, and hence was eminently susceptible to political pressures from England. The Drapier's earlier depiction of William Wood is replaced by Swift's characterization of a certain Edward Thompson, member of Parliament for York and a commissioner of the revenue in Ireland, who, in supporting the bill for a general excise or inland duty, symbolizes the sacrifice of Ireland's economic well-being to the self-interests of an alien. Another such figure is Macarell himself, who, "though with good Reputation, is already engaged on the other Side" since "He hath 400 l. a Year under the Crown, which he is too wise to part with, by sacrificing so good an Establishment to the empty Names of Virtue, and Love of his Country" (PW, 13:84). Significantly, Swift concludes his pamphlet by resurrecting the Drapier as a living presence on the Dublin scene: "I can assure you, the DRAPIER is in the Interests of the present Lord-Mayor, whatever you may be told to the Contrary. I have lately heard him declare so in publick Company, and offer some of these very Reasons in Defence of his Opinion; although he hath a Regard and Esteem for the other Gentleman, but would not hazard the Good of the City and the Kingdom, for a Compliment" (84–85). Not surprisingly, French defeated Macarell in the election, occasioning widespread jubilation reminiscent of an earlier victory. As Herbert Davis puts it, "The Drapier and his supporters had again won" (xxvi).

Several years later, when the gold standard in Ireland was lowered at the urging of (among others) the powerful Archbishop Boulter, Walpole's confidant and a leading spokesman for the English interest in that country, the Drapier reemerged as a political agitator. As Mrs. Whiteway observed to Sheridan in reference to a protest meeting of Dublin merchants at the Guild Hall on April 24, 1736, "The *Drapier* went this Day to the *Tholsel* as a Merchant, to sign a Petition to the Government against lowering the Gold, where we hear he made a long Speech, for which he will be reckoned a Jacobite. God send Hanging does not go round" (C, 4:480). In this speech the Dean, like the Drapier more than a decade earlier, set up an opposition between the public welfare of the whole of Ireland and the private interests of a few: "Therefore, *Gentlemen,* I do entreat you, that, as long as you live, you will look upon all *Persons* who are for lowering the Gold, or any other Coin, *as no Friends to this poor Kingdom,* but such who find their private account in what will be most detrimental to *Ireland*" (PW, 13:119). The speech makes clear that his position on this issue was based largely on his conviction that lowering the gold standard would above all benefit the despised class of absentees, who "are in the strongest views, our greatest *Enemies*": "Can there be a greater folly than to pave a Bridge of Gold at your own Expence, to support them in their Luxury and Vanity abroad, while hundreds of thousands are starving at home, for want of Employment" (120). We may be reminded here of another popular political figure who, over a century and a half later, would oppose another (albeit very different) money policy through similarly impassioned statements that his enemies should not be allowed to "crucify mankind upon a cross of gold."

Nor did the Drapier limit his protest against the depressed gold standard to petition signing and speechmaking. In a display suggestive of guerrilla theater (another form of highly unorthodox and provisional political action reflecting, moreover, the theatricality so congenial to Swift's role-playing proclivities), Swift hung a black flag out of St. Patrick's Cathedral and ordered the bells to be rung in a muted tone, as if in mourning, an action he himself commemorated in a broadside mentioned earlier in this chapter:

> Arrah! who was him reading? 'twas a *jauntleman* in ruffles,
> And Patrick's bell she was ringing all in muffles;
> She was ringing very sorry, her tongue tied up with rag;
> Lorsha! and out of her shteeple there was hung a black flag.
>
> (*A Ballad*, 6-9)

A similar kind of action is instigated in Letter VI of *The Drapier's Letters,* addressed to Lord Chancellor Midleton (and signed "J. S.," rather than M. B., Drapier): "If the *Bell-man* of each Parish, as he goes his Circuit, would cry out, every Night, *Past Twelve a Clock; Beware of* Wood*'s Half-pence;* it would probably cut off the Occasion for publishing any more Pamphlets; provided that in Country Towns it were done upon Market-Days. For my own Part, as soon as it shall be determined, that it is not against Law, I will begin the Experiment in the Liberty of St. *Patrick*'s; and hope my Example may be followed in the whole City" (PW, 10: 114). We may also be reminded of Swift's little skit, *A full and true Account of the solemn Procession to the Gallows, at the Execution of William Wood,* which undoubtedly inspired new (even as it recorded already staged) mob demonstrations in which Wood's effigy was carried triumphantly through the streets, condemned by a mock trial to the gallows, and burned under "the fatal Tree" in St. Stephen's Green (145-49). These street happenings, at once seriously intended variations upon and parodies of more conventional political actions, staged and/or commemorated in print by Swift, embody quintessential aspects of Swift's temperamental as well as ideological affinities with the lower classes—affinities against which Baron Wainwright of the Irish Exchequer was perhaps unconsciously reacting when he petulantly noted to the Earl of Oxford how Swift involved himself in "strange, improper, insignificant oppositions to matters of a public nature, that, by hanging out black flags and putting his bells in mourning, he makes it impossible for one in my station to converse much with him" (P, 3:840).

Swift's unsuitability to converse with "one in [the baron's] station" was even more strikingly dramatized during his face-to-face encounter with Archbishop Boulter at the lord mayor's banquet on September 29, 1737. Commemorating the meeting in the poem *Ay And No. A Tale From Dublin,* Swift makes it clear that he associated his political opposition in this instance with the Drapier's earlier campaign against Wood's patent. Addressing Boulter, who complains that "This mischief arises from witty Dean *Swift*" (6), he declares: "Go tell your friend *Bob* [Walpole] and the other great folk,/That sinking the coin is a dangerous joke./The *Irish* dear joys have enough common sense,/To treat gold reduc'd like *Wood*'s copper pence" (13-16). The battle lines are clearly drawn here, and they are not simply between "pro-gold" and "anti-gold" factions but are, more profoundly, between the "great folk" exemplified by "*Bob*" on the one hand, and the "mob" (12) and "The *Irish* dear joys" on the other. Two different, although inevitably related, sets of oppositions are suggested here: the upper versus the lower classes, and English versus Irish interests. There is no doubt where the Drapier-Dean's sympathies reside in either case. Harold Williams dismisses Swift's standpoint on this issue as "mistaken" (P, 3:841) (perhaps the greater sin was that Swift's activism in this instance proved unsuccessful) and this entire incident has since been consigned to oblivion. But regardless of whether the lowering of the gold standard was a good thing, or whether Swift was accurate in his assessment of its consequences, what is significant is that Swift, in immediate response to this event, wholeheartedly allied himself with the interests of the merchants and traders, the groups most disturbed by the change; explicitly defined himself in opposition to powerful members of the English and the Anglo-Irish establishment (e.g., Walpole, Boulter, Lord Lieutenant Dorset, and Baron Wainwright); and in effect chose to speak once again in the voice of the Drapier.

Afterword

A persona in one of Swift's verses (appropriately enough, a crazy beggar) observes that *"The World consists of Puppet-shows"* and alludes to "... this Booth, which we call *Dublin"* (*Mad Mullinix and Timothy,* 134, 137). And Dublin did indeed provide Swift with a suitable stage— or, more accurately, a series of intersecting stages—on which he could enact the many roles of his life: roles that were at once an expression of his innermost character and a response to external circumstances. St. Patrick's, Fishamble, St. Kevan's, and St. Francis streets, with their teeming, raucous environs and their melting-pot atmosphere, were in many ways the perfect, indeed the only possible, "home" for Swift, providing a place where he had the option of either escaping into the anonymity of the crowd or asserting himself as its highly recognizable and vocal leader; a place where he could alternate roles in a continually shifting power hierarchy, on some occasions acting the part of "absolute Lord of the greatest Cathedral in the Kingdom," and on others, acting the part of a fellow subject and ordinary inhabitant of the Liberties who, as he explains to Charles Ford in language having more than metaphoric significance, "labor[s] for daily health as often and almost as many hours as a workman does for daily bread, and like a common laborer can but just earn enough to keep life and Soul together" (C, 4:91).

The deanery of St. Patrick's, along with such companion sites as Naboth's Vineyard, the Cabbage Garden, the draper's shop in St. Francis Street, and the printing shop in Molesworth's Court, becomes in Swift's eyes a testament to the precariousness of all human constructs and creations—to their inevitably tentative and at all times endangered status given the often arbitrary tides of human events. Swift's landscape tacitly denies the grounds of his Augustan contemporaries' rage for order as it expressed itself in the creation of a variety of enclosures—verbal, topographical, and architectural alike, heroic couplets as well as ha-ha's—designed to protect and control, to preserve a clear boundary between the chaos without and the organization within.

Swift too had his share to say about constructing fences and walls. Not only was he continually "fencing against" assorted hardships, inconveniences, and political factions, but he also advised Pope to get "a stronger fence" about his grounds (C, 3:250) and was himself seriously involved in erecting a wall around Naboth's Vineyard. Yet Swift's acts of fencing invariably signified struggle, not static containment; moreover, they were acts of simultaneous creation and destruction. (It is characteristic that his advice to Pope was accompanied by the counsel that Pope also "throw the Inner fence into the Heap," just as it is characteristic that the project to build the "cursed wall" in his orchard was disrupted by instances when entire sections of it had to be thrown down, much to the combined exasperation and glee of its owner.) Throughout his lifetime, as Dean, as Irish patriot, as poet and author, Swift engaged in setting up structures to enclose and define at the same time that he dramatized either the futility or the impermanence of these structures.

It is thus quite appropriate that Swift's final recorded words are in the form of the following epigram:

> BEHOLD! a proof of *Irish* sense!
>   Here *Irish* wit is seen!
> When nothing's left, that's worth defence,
>   We build a magazine.

In including the epigram in his edition of *Swift's Works,* John Nichols explained its context:

> The Dean, in his lunacy, had some intervals of sense; at which time his guardians, or physicians, took him out for the air. On one of these days, when they came to the Park [Phoenix Park], *Swift* remarked a new building, which he had never seen, and asked what it was designed for. To which Dr. *Kingsbury* [the physician who attended Swift in his last illness] answered, "That Mr. Dean, is the magazine for arms and powder, for the security of the city". "Oh! oh!" says the Dean, pulling out his pocket-book, "let me take an *item* of that. This is worth remarking: my tablets, as *Hamlet* says, my tablets—memory put down that!"—Which produced the above lines, said to be the last he ever wrote. (P, 3:844)

The *Annual Register* for 1759 adds that Swift, after writing the epigram, "laugh[ed] heartily at the conceit, and clinch[ed] it with, *After the steed's stolen, shut the stable door*" (843). The anecdote is entirely credible, for it is consistent with Swift's abiding sense that structures and fortifications were in and of themselves no more than empty shells, incapable either of repelling the undesirable elements outside or of protecting the valuable matter within. As Swift saw it, the living forces of reality inevitably either penetrate the defenses or else burst out from within. They remind us in this respect of the uncontrollable energies of his writings, which refuse to be contained within the literary forms and rhetorical constructions that convey them.

Swift's landscape tells us again and again that art is a lie, that all man's efforts to tidy up reality, to create a hermetically sealed zone of permanent comfort and absolute safety impervious to the daily disturbances of human existence, are doomed to failure. Instead of the eternal, transcendent verities commemorated in characteristic pieces of Augustan literature, Swift's landscape and writings stand as a witness to the radically provisional nature of all human structures, creations, and would-be solutions, and thereby testify above all to the continuing need for morally informed passion and political struggle: for a commitment to "perpetual revolution" both within the human heart—manifested by that "savage indignation" ready to be reignited at the spectacle of each new outrage—and on the larger stage of human history.

Notes

Chapter 1

1. See Barrell, *The Idea of Landscape and the Sense of Place, 1730–1840: An Approach to the Poetry of John Clare* (Cambridge: At the University Press, 1972), esp. pp. 1–63; and Turner, *The Politics of Landscape: Rural Scenery and Society in English Poetry, 1630–1660* (Oxford: Basil Blackwell, 1979).

2. Van Den Berg, *The Phenomenological Approach to Psychiatry*, American Lectures in Philosophy, No. 247 (Springfield, Ill.: Charles C Thomas, 1955), p. 32.

3. Mack, *The Garden and the City: Retirement and Politics in the Later Poetry of Pope, 1731–1743* (Toronto: University of Toronto Press, 1969), p. 232.

4. For works that presuppose, or attempt to define, some form of "Augustan outlook," see Paul Fussell, *The Rhetorical World of Augustan Humanism: Ethics and Imagery from Swift to Burke* (Oxford: Clarendon Press, 1965); James William Johnson, *The Formation of English Neo-Classical Thought* (Princeton: Princeton University Press, 1967); Donald Greene, "Augustinianism and Empiricism: A Note on Eighteenth-Century English Intellectual History," *Eighteenth-Century Studies* 1 (Fall 1967): 38–68; Martin C. Battestin, *The Providence of Wit: Aspects of Form in Augustan Literature and the Arts* (Oxford: Clarendon Press, 1974); and Pat Rogers, *The Augustan Vision* (London: Weidenfeld & Nicolson, 1974). Although these works are by no means identical in their conception of Augustanism, even those which are explicitly revisionary (Greene, for example, subtitles his article, "Toward a Demythologizing?") wind up making generalizations that gloss over crucial differences between individual writers like Pope and Swift.

The fallacies inherent in traditional assumptions about the Augustan world view, as well as the need to distinguish clearly between Pope and Swift, have best been argued by C. J. Rawson in two works: *Henry Fielding and the Augustan Ideal under Stress* (London: Routledge & Kegan Paul, 1972); and *Gulliver and the Gentle Reader: Studies in Swift and Our Time* (London: Routledge & Kegan Paul, 1973). A. B. England differentiates between Pope and Swift in rhetorical terms, partially on the basis of separate traditions of moral satire and burlesque, in *Byron's "Don Juan" and Eighteenth-Century Literature* (Lewisburg, Pa.: Bucknell University Press, 1975). England's study of Swift's poetry also points out "subversive" rhetorical aspects of Swift's verse and implies his differences from Pope; see *Energy and Order in the Poetry of Swift* (Lewisburg, Pa.: Bucknell University Press, 1980). England's discussion, however, is too narrowly rhetorical and stylistic in focus to make more than a very limited case for Swift's departures from traditional norms. Moreover, England's Swift turns out in the end to be remarkably orthodox and basically consistent with the views of a critic like Battestin. Like other recent reassessments of Augustanism, England's produces a Swift who is neither subversive nor demystifying, nor even significantly skeptical of authority, but only "ambivalent" in his adherence to traditional principles.

5. Battestin, *The Providence of Wit*, p. 55.

6. Rawson, "Order and Misrule: Eighteenth-Century Literature in the 1970's," *ELH* 42 (Fall 1975): 481–82.

7. See Kramnick, *Bolingbroke and His Circle: The Politics of Nostalgia in the Age of Walpole* (Cambridge, Mass.: Harvard University Press, 1968), especially pp. 1–7 and 205–35. Kramnick's study of Burke, however, displays a constructively critical attitude toward the kinds of generalizations and stereotypes he blithely reinforces in his discussion of Bolingbroke's Circle. The result is a significant and interesting reassessment of Burke's political thought. See *The Rage of Edmund Burke: Portrait of an Ambivalent Conservative* (New York: Basic Books, 1977).

8. All references to Pope's poems are to the relevant volumes of *The Twickenham Edition of the Poems of Alexander Pope*, 11 vols., ed. John Butt et al. (London: Methuen, 1939–1961).

9. Kramnick, *Bolingbroke and His Circle*, p. 214.

10. Hall, "'An Inverted Hypocrite': Swift the Churchman," in *The World of Jonathan Swift: Essays for the Tercentenary*, ed. Brian Vickers (Cambridge, Mass.: Harvard University Press, 1968), pp. 38–68. The quoted words appear on p. 64.

11. Traugott, "*A Tale of a Tub*," in *Focus: Swift*, ed. C. J. Rawson (London: Sphere Books, 1971), p. 78.

12. Steele, *Jonathan Swift: Preacher and Jester* (Oxford: Clarendon Press, 1978), p. 25.

13. Robbins, *The Eighteenth-Century Commonwealthman* (Cambridge, Mass.: Harvard University Press, 1959), p. 153. Robbins notes that Henry Yorke, ". . . a radical at the end of the century, and protagonist of the French revolutionary movements, declared that his republicanism had been enforc d by reading Swift."

14. Said, "Swift's Tory Anarchy," *Eighteenth-Century Studies* 3 (Fall 1969): 60. The term "Tory Anarchist" was earlier applied to Swift by George Orwell in "Politics vs. Literature: An Examination of *Gulliver's Travels*," in *Shooting an Elephant, and Other Essays* (New York: Harcourt, Brace, 1950), pp. 53–76.

15. Rawson, *Gulliver and the Gentle Reader: Studies in Swift and Our Time*, pp. viii, 52–53.

16. Ehrenpreis, *Swift: The Man, His Works, and the Age* (Cambridge, Mass.: Harvard University Press, 1962–   ).

17. Poulet, "Criticism and the Experience of Interiority," in *The Structuralist Controversy: The Languages of Criticism and the Sciences of Man*, ed. Richard Macksey and Eugenio Donato (Baltimore: Johns Hopkins Press, 1972), p. 61.

18. Discussions of Pope's landscape may be found in the following works: Maynard Mack, *The Garden and the City*; Edward Malins, *English Landscaping and Literature, 1660–1840* (London: Oxford University Press, 1966); James Sambrook, "Pope and the Visual Arts," in *Writers and Their Background: Alexander Pope*, ed. Peter Dixon (Athens: Ohio University Press, 1972), pp. 143–71; John Dixon Hunt, *The Figure in the Landscape: Poetry, Painting, and Gardening during the Eighteenth Century* (Baltimore: Johns Hopkins University Press, 1976); Jeffry B. Spencer, *Heroic*

Nature: Ideal Landscape in English Poetry from Marvell to Thomson (Evanston, Ill.: Northwestern University Press, 1973); and Morris R. Brownell, *Alexander Pope and the Arts of Georgian England* (Oxford: Clarendon Press, 1977). Also see Ronald Paulson's discussion of "The Poetic Garden" in *Emblem and Expression: Meaning in English Art of the Eighteenth Century* (Cambridge, Mass.: Harvard University Press, 1975), pp. 19–34.

19. Rogers, "Pope and the Social Scene," in *Writers and Their Background: Alexander Pope*, p. 107.

20. Barrell, *The Idea of Landscape and the Sense of Place*, p. 1.

21. The following is an example of such description: ". . . I am most charmed with [Hagley's] sweet embowered Retirements, and particularly with a winding Dale that runs thro' the Middle of it. This Dale is overhung with deep Woods, and enlivened by a Stream, that, now gushing from mossy Rocks, now falling in Cascades, and now spreading into a calm Length of Water, forms the most natural and pleasing Scene imaginable." *James Thomson: Letters and Documents*, ed. Alan Dugald McKillop (Lawrence: University of Kansas Press, 1958), p. 165.

22. Bush, *Hibernia Curiosa* (London: W. Flexney, 1768), pp. 64–65.

23. For a discussion of the links between eighteenth-century poetry and painting, see Elizabeth W. Manwaring, *Italian Landscape in Eighteenth-Century England* (New York: Russell & Russell, 1925); and Jean H. Hagstrum, *The Sister Arts: The Tradition of Literary Pictorialism and English Poetry from Dryden to Gray* (Chicago: University of Chicago Press, 1958). Ralph Cohen makes some telling points in arguing against the overly specific and literal interpretation of the poetry-painting analogy in *The Art of Discrimination: Thomson's "The Seasons" and the Language of Criticism* (Berkeley and Los Angeles: University of California Press, 1964), pp. 188–247, 251–52. But for a convincing answer to (or rather, qualification of) Cohen's objections, and a demonstration of the validity of the poetry-painting analogy, see Barrell, *The Idea of Landscape and the Sense of Place*, pp. 6–17

24. Quoted in John Dixon Hunt and Peter Willis, eds., *The Genius of the Place: The English Landscape Garden, 1620–1820* (London: Paul Elek, 1975), p. 11.

25. Spectator No. 477. In Addison and Steele, *The Spectator*, 5 vols., ed. Donald Bond (Oxford: Clarendon Press, 1965), 4:190. All subsequent references to *The Spectator* are to this edition.

26. Whately, *Observations on Modern Gardening*, 2d ed. (London: T. Payne, 1770), p. 1.

27. Hunt, *The Figure in the Landscape*, p. 69.

28. See Landa, *Swift and the Church of Ireland* (Oxford: Clarendon Press, 1954); and Ferguson, *Jonathan Swift and Ireland* (Urbana: University of Illinois Press, 1962). In addition to his biography, see Ehrenpreis, "Dr. S***t and the Hibernian Patriot," in *Jonathan Swift, 1667–1967: A Dublin Tercentenary Tribute*, ed. Roger McHugh and Philip Edwards (Dublin: Dolmen Press, 1967), pp. 24–37. Generally speaking, criticism dealing with Swift's connections with Ireland has consisted of short, specialized studies focusing on one or several specific works of Swift (such as *A Modest Proposal* and *The Drapier's Letters*), or else a single aspect of his life (e.g., his career as Church of Ireland clergyman). My own study, however, argues for the centrality and all-encompassing significance of Ireland for Swift's life, writings, and ideological outlook as a whole.

29. Malins and the Knight of Glin, *Lost Demesnes: Irish Landscape Gardening, 1660–1845* (London: Barrie & Jenkins, 1976), pp. 33, 37.

30. See Kenneth Woodbridge, *Landscape and Antiquity: Aspects of English Culture at Stourhead, 1718–1838* (London: Clarendon Press, 1970), pp. 39–40. That

Orrery viewed his estate in light of things English is shown by his proud assertion, "We have built, at the expence of five pounds, a root house, or hermitage, to which on Sunday the country people resort, as the Londoners to Westminster Abbey." Cited in Desmond Fitz-gerald, "Irish Gardens of the Eighteenth Century," *Apollo* (September 1968): 207.

Chapter 2

1. See Aldous Huxley, "Swift," in *Do What You Will: Essays by Aldous Huxley* (London: Chatto & Windus, 1929), pp. 93–106; Middleton Murry, *Jonathan Swift: A Critical Biography* (London: Jonathan Cape, 1954), pp. 432–48; and Norman O. Brown, "The Excremental Vision," in *Life against Death: The Psychoanalytical Meaning of History* (Middletown, Conn.: Wesleyan University Press, 1959), pp. 179–201.

2. See George Rudé, *Hanoverian London, 1714–1808* (Berkeley and Los Angeles: University of California Press, 1971), pp. 85–86, 134–35.

3. Young, *A Tour in Ireland, 1776–1779*, 2 vols., ed. A. W. Hutton (1892; Shannon: Irish University Press, 1970), 1:20–21.

4. Walsh, *Rakes and Ruffians: The Underworld of Georgian Dublin [Ireland Sixty Years Ago]* (Dublin: Four Courts Press, 1979), p. 63.

5. See Rudé, *Hanoverian London*, pp. 136–37.

6. Maxwell, *The Stranger in Ireland: From the Reign of Elizabeth to the Great Famine* (London: Jonathan Cape, 1954), p. 131.

7. Cited in Constantia Maxwell, *Dublin under the Georges, 1714–1830* (1937; rev'd. London: Faber & Faber, 1956), pp. 140–41.

8. Craig, *Dublin 1660–1860: A Social and Architectural History* (Dublin: Allen Figgis, 1969), pp. 85–86.

9. Thomas Cromwell, *Excursions through Ireland*, 3 vols. (London, 1820), 1:43.

10. Loveday, *Diary of a Tour in 1732 through Parts of England, Wales, Ireland, and Scotland* (Edinburgh: Roxburghe Club, 1890), p. 50.

11. Cromwell, *Excursions through Ireland*, 1:109.

12. Mason, *The History and Antiquities of the Collegiate and Cathedral Church of St. Patrick, Near Dublin* (Dublin, 1819), p. 205.

13. Malton, *A Picturesque and Descriptive View of the City of Dublin*, repro. from ed. of 1799 (Dublin: Dolmen Press, 1978), n.p.

14. Cited in Maxwell, *Dublin under the Georges*, pp. 140–41.

15. This fact was noted by John Loveday in his *Diary of a Tour in 1732*, p. 50.

16. Dunton, Letter No. 4, rptd. in Edward MacLysaght, *Irish Life in the Seventeenth Century* (1939; New York: Barnes & Noble, 1969), p. 353; and Burke, *Reformer No. 7* (10 March 1748), rptd. in Arthur P. I. Samuels, *The Early Life, Correspondence, and Writings of the Rt. Hon. Edmund Burke* (Cambridge: At the University Press, 1923), p. 315.

17. Young, *Tour*, 2:48.

18. Cited in Constantia Maxwell, *Country and Town in Ireland under the Georges* (1940; Dundalk: Dundalgan Press, 1949), p. 121.

19. Firth, "The Political Significance of 'Gulliver's Travels'" (1919–1920), rptd. in *Essays Historical and Literary* (Oxford: Clarendon Press, 1938), p. 228. I do not agree, however, with Firth's conclusion that Swift's attitude toward the native Irish was essentially negative and that "he reserved his sympathy for the new Irish—that is, the English colony in Ireland" (p. 230). In this connection, see also Donald T. Torchiana, "Jonathan Swift, the Irish, and the Yahoos: The Case Reconsidered," *Philological Quarterly* 54 (Winter 1975):195–212.

20. For a discussion of *Gulliver's Travels* in terms of England's colonialist policies and attitudes toward Ireland, see Ann Cline Kelly, "Swift's Explorations of Slavery in Houyhnhnmland and Ireland," *PMLA* 91 (October 1976):846-55.

21. Curley, *Samuel Johnson and the Age of Travel* (Athens: University of Georgia Press, 1976), p. 31.

22. See Young, *Tour*, 1:122-27.

23. Ibid., pp. 116, 119.

24. Williams, *The Country and the City* (New York: Oxford University Press, 1973), pp. 46-47.

25. Clifford, "Some Aspects of London Life in the Mid-Eighteenth Century," in *City and Society in the Eighteenth Century*, ed. Paul Fritz and David Williams (Toronto: Hakkert, 1973), p. 27.

26. Ibid., pp. 24-25. Architectural innovations in the English country house during the Restoration contributed to this widening class division and to the growing separation between those who dealt regularly with excremental matters and those who could maintain a comfortable distance from them. Mark Girouard observes:

> The ejection of servants from the hall revolutionized one aspect of the country house. Another was transformed by the equally revolutionary invention of backstairs . . . —and of closets and servants' rooms attached to them. . . . The gentry walking up the stairs no longer met their last night's faeces coming down them. Servants no longer bedded down in the drawing room, or outside their master's door or in a truckle bed at his feet. They became, if not invisible, very much less visible. . . . The servant often shared his room with a close-stool. . . . The servant, the contents of the close-stool, and anything that was undesirable or private could move or be moved up and down the backstairs, preferably to offices in the basement.

See *Life in the English Country House: A Social and Architectural History* (New Haven: Yale University Press, 1978), p. 138. Girouard's wording vividly underscores the intimate links between the lower classes and an excremental environment, as well as their joint consignment to a world of invisibility insofar as the upper class was concerned.

27. Selby, "The Cell and the Garret: Fictions of Confinement in Swift's Satires and Personal Writings," in *Studies in Eighteenth-Century Culture*, vol. 6, ed. Ronald C. Rosbottom (Madison: University of Wisconsin Press, 1977), pp. 143-44.

28. Rawson, *Gulliver and the Gentle Reader* (London: Routledge & Kegan Paul, 1973), pp. 66-83, 70.

29. Selby refers to the *Holyhead Journal* as a "prison record" in "The Cell and the Garret," p. 144. I do not, however, agree with her conclusion that the *Journal* "can only be viewed as a narrative of nonbeing."

30. For contemporary descriptions of the typical Irish cabin, see John Bush, *Hibernia Curiosa* (London: W. Flexney, 1768), pp. 30-31; Dunton, Letter No. 4 in MacLysaght, *Irish Life in the Seventeenth Century*, pp. 356-57; and Richard Twiss, *A Tour in Ireland in 1775* (London, 1776), pp. 29-30.

31. *Memoirs of Mrs. Letitia Pilkington, 1712-1750*, ed. Iris Barry (New York: Dodd, Mead, 1928), p. 67.

32. Cited in Maxwell, *Dublin under the Georges*, p. 304.

33. Carnochan, *Confinement and Flight: An Essay on English Literature of the Eighteenth Century* (Berkeley and Los Angeles: University of California Press, 1977), pp. 90, 94-95.

34. Craig, *Dublin 1660-1860*, p. 124; and Brian de Breffny and Rosemary ffolliot, *The Houses of Ireland: Domestic Architecture from the Medieval Castle to the Edwardian Villa* (London: Thames & Hudson, 1975), p. 96.

35. Paulson, *The Fictions of Satire* (Baltimore: Johns Hopkins Press, 1967), p. 167.

36. For a discussion of "priest hunting" and the general persecution of Catholics and other groups that the Protestant ruling class associated with them, see W.E.H. Lecky, *A History of Ireland in the Eighteenth Century*, 5 vols. (London: Longmans, Green, 1892), 1:266–84. For additional information concerning the harsh penal legislation enacted during the reigns of William III and Queen Anne to prevent the further growth of popery, along with its resulting oppressions, see Edith Mary Johnston, *Ireland in the Eighteenth Century*, The Gill History of Ireland, No. 8 (Dublin: Gill & Macmillan, 1974), pp. 27–29.

37. For a discussion of Molesworth's views, see Caroline Robbins, *The Eighteenth-Century Commonwealthman* (Cambridge, Mass.: Harvard University Press, 1959), pp. 91–133.

Chapter 3

1. See "A Discourse on Pastoral Poetry," in *The Twickenham Edition of the Poems of Alexander Pope*, 11 vols., ed. John Butt et al. (London: Methuen, 1939–1961), 1:27.

2. Cited in ibid., nn. 61–62.

3. Renato Poggioli, "The Oaten Flute," in *The Oaten Flute: Essays on Pastoral Poetry and the Pastoral Ideal* (Cambridge, Mass.: Harvard University Press, 1975), p. 2. See also the argument of John Barrell and John Bull that "the pastoral vision is, at base, a false vision, positing a simplistic, unhistorical relationship between the ruling, landowning class . . . and the workers on the land; as such its function is to mystify and to obscure the harshness of actual social and economic organization." Barrell and Bull, eds., *A Book of English Pastoral Verse* (New York: Oxford University Press, 1975), p. 4. For additional perspectives on the pastoral genre, see Harold E. Toliver, *Pastoral Forms and Attitudes* (Berkeley and Los Angeles: University of California Press, 1971); William Empson, *Some Versions of Pastoral* (London: Chatto & Windus, 1935); *Pastoral and Romance: Modern Essays in Criticism,* ed. Eleanor Lincoln Terry (Englewood Cliffs, N.J.: Prentice-Hall, 1969); and Laurence Lerner, *The Uses of Nostalgia: Studies in Pastoral Poetry* (London: Chatto & Windus, 1972). Further background information on eighteenth-century pastoral poetry may be found in James E. Congleton, *Theories of Pastoral Poetry in England, 1684–1798* (Gainesville: University of Florida Press, 1952). Richard Feingold examines some aspects of the relationship between pastoral fictions and social realities in the latter half of the eighteenth century in *Nature and Society: Later Eighteenth-Century Uses of the Pastoral and Georgic* (New Brunswick, N.J.: Rutgers University Press, 1978).

4. *The Twickenham Edition of Pope*, 1:32, 25.

5. References to *Paradise Lost* are to *John Milton, Complete Poems and Major Prose,* ed. Merritt Y. Hughes (New York: Odyssey Press, 1957).

6. References to Herrick's poetry are to *The Poetical Works of Robert Herrick*, ed. L. C. Martin (Oxford: Clarendon Press, 1956).

7. Frank Kermode, ed., *English Pastoral Poetry from the Beginnings to Marvell* (1952; New York: Norton, 1972), p. 228.

8. See Curtius, *European Literature and the Latin Middle Ages*, trans. Willard R. Trask, Bollingen Series 36 (New York: Pantheon, 1953), pp. 183–202.

9. Lerner, *The Uses of Nostalgia: Studies in Pastoral Poetry*, p. 246.

10. See Ehrenpreis, *Swift: The Man, His Works, and the Age* (Cambridge, Mass.: Harvard University Press, 1962–   ), 1:31, n. 4.

11. *The Collected Letters of Oliver Goldsmith*, ed. Katharine C. Balderston (1928; Folcroft, Pa.: Folcroft Press, 1969), pp. 28, 54.

12. Ibid., p. 30.

13. References to *The Deserted Village*—and, later in this chapter, to *The Traveller*—are taken from vol. 4 of *The Collected Works of Oliver Goldsmith*, 5 vols., ed. Arthur Friedman (Oxford: Clarendon Press, 1966). An interesting discussion of the significance of Goldsmith's early pastoral world for his perspective with regard to both city and country is presented by Richard Helgerson in his essay, "The Two Worlds of Oliver Goldsmith," *Studies in English Literature* 13 (Summer 1973):516–34. Regarding the question of the autobiographical dimension of Goldsmith's verse, see Robert Lonsdale, "'A Garden and a Grave': The Poetry of Oliver Goldsmith," in Louis L. Martz and Aubrey Williams, eds., *The Author in His Work* (New Haven: Yale University Press, 1978), pp. 3–30.

14. See *Collected Letters*, p. 29.

15. Bachelard, *The Poetics of Reverie: Childhood, Language, and the Cosmos*, trans. Daniel Russell (1960; Boston: Beacon Press, 1969), pp. 123–24.

16. Ibid., p. 118.

17. *The Compleat Angler*, in *The Universal Angler, Made so, by Three Books of Fishing* (London, 1676; repro. Menston, England: Scolar Press, 1971), pp. 5, 19.

18. References to Gay's poetry are taken from *The Poetical Works of John Gay*, ed. G. C. Faber (1926; New York: Russell & Russell, 1969).

19. Bachelard, *The Poetics of Space*, trans. Maria Jolas (1958; Boston: Beacon Press, 1969), p. xxxi.

20. Ibid., p. 7.

21. Landa, *Swift and the Church of Ireland* (Oxford: Clarendon Press, 1954), pp. 10–11, 18.

22. Ibid., p. 35.

23. Ibid., p. 37.

24. See John Bush, *Hibernia Curiosa* (London: W. Flexney, 1768), pp. 30–31, 44–45; and Arthur Young, *A Tour in Ireland, 1776–1779*, 2 vols., ed. A. W. Hutton (1892; Shannon: Irish University Press, 1970), 2:47–49.

25. Dunton, Letter No. 4., rptd. in Edward MacLysaght, *Irish Life in the Seventeenth Century* (1939; New York: Barnes & Noble, 1969), p. 356.

26. Landa, *Swift and the Church of Ireland*, p. 37.

27. *Memoirs of Mrs. Letitia Pilkington, 1712–1750*, ed. Iris Barry (New York: Dodd, Mead, 1928), p. 62. For the biblical source, see 1 *Kings* 21.

28. *Memoirs of Mrs. Pilkington*, pp. 62–63. In this connection see Poggioli, "Naboth's Vineyard: The Pastoral View of the Social Order," in *The Oaten Flute*, pp. 194–219. The article's relevance for Swift lies in its concern with the pastoral world's vulnerability to outside encroachments.

29. This statement appears in his essay, "Upon the Gardens of Epicurus; or, Of Gardening," in *The Works of Sir William Temple*, 4 vols. (London, 1757), 3:207.

30. The period following the Glorious Revolution witnessed radical innovations in Great Britain's economic system: the development of the Bank of England, the growth of the stock market, the accumulation of a huge national debt, and a growing dependency upon paper currency and credit, accompanied by a pervasive spirit of financial speculation symbolized for the Tory opposition by the South Sea Bubble. For background on the new economic situation, especially in terms of its effect upon writers of the period, see Isaac Kramnick, *Bolingbroke and His Circle: The Politics of Nostalgia in the Age of Walpole* (Cambridge, Mass.: Harvard University Press, 1968), pp. 39–55, 188–235. For a more technical and detailed analysis, see Peter Dickson,

The Financial Revolution in England: A Study in the Development of Public Credit, 1688–1756 (New York: St. Martin's Press, 1967).

31. For a relevant discussion of the South Sea Bubble, see Howard Erskine-Hill, "Pope and the Financial Revolution," in *Writers and Their Background: Alexander Pope*, ed. Peter Dixon (Athens: Ohio University Press, 1972), pp. 200–229. See also John Carswell, *The South Sea Bubble* (Stanford, Calif.: Stanford University Press, 1960).

32. Kermode, *English Pastoral Poetry*, p. 14.

33. Williams, *The Country and the City* (New York: Oxford University Press, 1973), p. 48.

34. Poggioli, "The Oaten Flute," in *The Oaten Flute*, pp. 4–5.

35. References to Marvell's poetry are to *The Poems and Letters of Andrew Marvell*, ed. H. M. Margoliouth, rev'd. Pierre Legouis with E. E. Duncan-Jones (Oxford: Clarendon Press, 1971), vol. 1.

36. Spenser, *A View of the Present State of Ireland*, ed. W. L. Renwick (Oxford: Clarendon Press, 1970), p. 104. Various periods of famine in Ireland were accompanied by historically recorded instances of cannibalism, including child eating. Moreover, popular tradition (as well as Swift himself) linked the Irish with the Scythians, particularly in their alleged common practice of drinking human blood and engaging in other cannibalistic activities. These historical and legendary accounts undoubtedly informed and helped shape Swift's depictions. See C. J. Rawson, "A Reading of *A Modest Proposal*," in *Augustan Worlds: Essays in Honour of A. R. Humphreys*, ed. J. C. Hilson, M.M.B. Jones, and J. R. Watson (Leicester: Leicester University Press, 1978), pp. 37–38 and 48, nn. 20 and 22.

37. Ferguson, *Jonathan Swift and Ireland* (Urbana: University of Illinois Press, 1962), p. 175.

38. Maxwell, *Country and Town in Ireland under the Georges* (1940; Dundalk: Dundalgan Press, 1949), pp. 204–5.

39. Loveday, *Diary of a Tour in 1732 through Parts of England, Wales, Ireland, and Scotland* (Edinburgh: Roxburghe Club, 1890), p. 58.

40. Bush, *Hibernia Curiosa*, pp. 31–32.

41. See Johnston, *Ireland in the Eighteenth Century*, The Gill History of Ireland, No. 8 (Dublin: Gill & Macmillan, 1974), p. 31.

42. Cited in Landa, *Swift and the Church of Ireland*, p. 154. Concerning this issue of Irish emigration and Swift's strong feelings about it, see Clayton D. Lein, "Jonathan Swift and the Population of Ireland," *Eighteenth-Century Studies* 8 (Summer 1975): 443–45.

43. Landa, *Swift and the Church of Ireland*, p. 154.

44. Berkeley, *The Querist*. In *A Reprint of Economic Tracts*, ed. Jacob H. Hollander (Baltimore: Johns Hopkins Press, 1910), p. 19.

45. Quoted as an epigraph to Maxwell, *Dublin under the Georges*.

46. Cullen, *An Economic History of Ireland since 1660* (1972; London: B. T. Batsford, 1976), p. 47.

47. Cited in Lecky, *A History of Ireland in the Eighteenth Century*, 5 vols. (London: Longmans, Green, 1892), 1:223–24, n. 4.

48. Kermode, *English Pastoral Poetry*, p. 180.

49. *The Collected Works of Oliver Goldsmith*, 3:26. All subsequent quotations from this essay may be found on pp. 24–30 of this volume.

50. Cited in *Collected Works of Oliver Goldsmith*, 4:280.

51. Lecky, *A History of Ireland in the Eighteenth Century*, 1:333. See also Eileen McCracken, *The Irish Woods since Tudor Times: Their Distribution and Exploi-*

tation, a publication of the Institute of Irish Studies, Queen's University, Belfast (Newton Abbot, Devon: David & Charles, 1971).

52. Cited in Lecky, *A History of Ireland in the Eighteenth Century,* 1:333–34, n. 3.

53. Ibid., pp. 334, 336.

54. Townshend, *The Life and Letters of the Great Earl of Cork* (London: Duckworth, 1904), p. 100.

55. Ibid., pp. 100–101.

56. Bush, *Hibernia Curiosa,* p. 41.

57. Hoare, *Journal of a Tour in Ireland in 1806* (London: W. Miller, 1807), pp. 310–11, 320.

58. Ibid., p. 82.

59. Jaffe, *The Poet Swift* (Hanover, N.H.: University Press of New England, 1977), pp. 132–33.

60. *Ovid's Metamorphoses, The Arthur Golding Translation,* ed. John Frederick Nims (New York: Macmillan, 1965), pp. 216–17.

61. *The Poems of John Dryden,* ed. James Kinsley (Oxford: Clarendon Press, 1958), 4:1569–70.

62. This incident is recounted by Edward Young, who accompanied Swift on his walk. See *Conjectures on Original Composition, 1759,* A Scolar Press Facsimile (Leeds: Scolar Press, 1966), pp. 64–65.

Chapter 4

1. Althusser, *For Marx,* trans. Ben Brewster (New York: Pantheon, 1969), p. 231. Althusser goes on to assert that ideology serves as "the relay whereby, and the element in which, the relation between men and their conditions of existence is settled to the profit of the ruling class." The nature of the relationship between ideology and a ruling-class outlook is problematical and has given rise to considerable differences of opinion, as has the question of whether ideology is an inherently pejorative term, designating an irrevocably false consciousness. Karl Mannheim identifies the concept of ideology specifically with the perceptions and thought processes of ruling groups, thereby distinguishing it from the "utopian" thinking of oppressed groups. See *Ideology and Utopia: An Introduction to the Sociology of Knowledge,* trans. Louis Wirth and Edward Shils (New York: Harcourt, Brace & Co., 1936), p. 40. Terry Eagleton, however, asserts that "an ideology is never a simple reflection of a ruling class's ideas; on the contrary, it is always a complex phenomenon, which may incorporate conflicting, even contradictory, views of the world." *Marxism and Literary Criticism* (Berkeley and Los Angeles: University of California Press, 1978), pp. 6–7. Raymond Williams distinguishes three basic meanings of the concept of ideology as it has commonly been used in Marxist writing: "(i) a system of beliefs characteristic of a particular class or group; (ii) a system of illusory beliefs—false ideas or false consciousness—which can be contrasted with true or scientific knowledge; (iii) the general process of the production of meanings and ideas." See *Marxism and Literature* (Oxford: Oxford University Press, 1977), pp. 55 et seq. James Turner includes a useful discussion of these and related issues in his "Conclusion" to *The Politics of Landscape: Rural Scenery and Society in English Poetry, 1630–1660* (Oxford: Basil Blackwell, 1979), pp. 188–95, 224–27. As my own discussion in the text suggests, although I associate the concept of ideology specifically with ruling-class doctrines and values, seeing it therefore as an inevitably distorted perception of historical reality whose overriding function is to legitimate the existing social order, I recognize that these ideological conceptions come to be

shared on some level by all (or at least other) classes in society, and that significantly different degrees of falsification—or, conversely, of clarity of vision—are possible both for particular groups and for individuals within them (hence the distinction I make between Pope and Swift in this chapter). E. P. Thompson indirectly points up the complexities surrounding the question of ruling-class ideology in his discussion of the extent to which the laboring poor in the eighteenth century (including so-called rioters) subscribed to a traditionalist view of society founded on economic paternalism. See "The Moral Economy of the English Crowd in the Eighteenth Century," *Past and Present* 50 (February 1971):76–136.

2. Girouard, *Life in the English Country House: A Social and Architectural History* (New Haven: Yale University Press, 1978), p. 2.

3. Hibbard, "The Country House Poem of the Seventeenth Century," in *Journal of the Warburg and Courtauld Institutes* 19 (1956):159.

4. Erskine-Hill, *The Social Milieu of Alexander Pope* (New Haven: Yale University Press, 1975), p. 281.

5. See Duckworth, *The Improvement of the Estate: A Study of Jane Austen's Novels* (Baltimore: Johns Hopkins Press, 1971); and idem, "Fiction and Some Uses of the Country House Setting from Richardson to Scott," in *Landscape in the Gardens and the Literature of Eighteenth-Century England,* ed. David C. Streatfield and Alistair M. Duckworth (Los Angeles: University of California, William Andrews Clark Memorial Library, 1981), pp. 91–138. Also see Richard Gill, *Happy Rural Seat: The English Country House and the Literary Imagination* (New Haven: Yale University Press, 1972).

6. Sackville-West, *English Country Houses* (London: W. Collins, 1947), p. 47.

7. Williams, *The Country and the City* (New York: Oxford University Press, 1973), pp. 9, 12.

8. Girouard, *Life in the English Country House,* p. 5.

9. Ibid., pp. 11, 184, 189.

10. Hibbard, "The Country House Poem of the Seventeenth Century," p. 174.

11. Erskine-Hill, *The Social Milieu of Pope,* p. 283.

12. Hibbard, "The Country House Poem of the Seventeenth Century," p. 172.

13. Mannheim, *Ideology and Utopia,* p. 96.

14. Althusser, *For Marx,* p. 233.

15. All references to Jonson's poetry are taken from *Ben Jonson: Poems,* ed. Ian Donaldson (Oxford: Oxford University Press, 1975).

16. Eagleton, *Criticism and Ideology* (London: NLB, 1976), p. 69.

17. See Craig, *Dublin 1660–1860: A Social and Architectural History* (Dublin: Allen Figgis, 1969), pp. 100–101. For a discussion of Conolly's loyalty to the English interest and to Walpole, see Oliver W. Ferguson, *Jonathan Swift and Ireland* (Urbana: University of Illinois Press, 1962), p. 93 and n.

18. A probably more reliable contemporary source put Conolly's annual income at £12,000 or £13,000 (see Craig, *Dublin 1660–1860,* pp. 101 and 105, n. 7). Swift's exaggeration of the figures, like his distortion of certain factual details (e.g., regarding Conolly's "illiteracy" and his having risen from a "shoe-boy"), serves to magnify the contempt with which Swift viewed the speaker.

19. Craig, *Dublin 1660–1860,* p. 101.

20. Breffny and ffolliott, *The Houses of Ireland: Domestic Architecture from the Medieval Castle to the Edwardian Villa* (London: Thames & Hudson, 1975), p. 95.

21. For verbal variants in this letter and deviations from Swift's text, see Williams's footnotes in C, 5:19 and 20.

22. That Swift's combined despair and outrage was an appropriate response to

the existing situation, as well as an expression of his characteristic mode of perceiving the world, may be inferred from G. E. Mingay's assertion that eighteenth-century Ireland represents "the darkest chapter in the history of English landlords." See *English Landed Society in the Eighteenth Century* (London: Routledge & Kegan Paul, 1963), p. 47. Noting that the absentees' neglect of their Irish lands and tenants "was in marked contrast with the attitude toward their English properties," Mingay concludes that the explanation "lay in the view of Ireland as a subordinate province or colony . . . and in the assumption that English proprietors drew their revenues by right of conquest over an alien people" (p. 47).

23. Young, *A Tour in Ireland, 1776-1779*, 2 vols., ed. A. W. Hutton (1892; Shannon: Irish University Press, 1970), 2:116-17.

24. Ibid., 2:53-54. See also Maria Edgeworth's scornful definition of middlemen in *Castle Rackrent*, ed. George Watson (London: Oxford University Press, 1964), pp. 20-21, n.

25. Lecky, *A History of Ireland in the Eighteenth Century*, 5 vols. (London: Longmans, Green, 1892), 1:214.

26. Ferguson has noted both thematic and verbal similarities between Swift's tract and William Molyneux's *Case of Ireland* (*Jonathan Swift and Ireland*, pp. 29, 32). In this regard see also Ehrenpreis, *Swift: The Man, His Works, and the Age* (Cambridge, Mass.: Harvard University Press, 1962-   ), 2:171-72. Molyneux's tract, published in 1698, was heavily influenced by Locke's political theories. (According to Ehrenpreis, "*The Case of Ireland* forms a kind of specialized appendix to the great *Second Treatise . . .*" [p. 171].) Molyneux's essential argument was that Ireland possessed the status of a sister kingdom rather than a colony, never having been conquered but instead, having voluntarily accepted the English king. His conclusion is that the Irish Parliament had as much authority (in its own geographic sphere of governance) as the English one and that settlers in Ireland possessed the same rights as their forefathers in either country. See Molyneux, *The Case of Ireland's Being Bound by Acts of Parliament in England, Stated* (Dublin, 1698). The tract has been reprinted in Irish Writings from the Age of Swift, vol. 5 (Dublin: Cadenus Press, 1977).

27. As Mingay notes, Burlington was one of the seventeen peers who drew £4,000 a year or more from their Irish holdings (*English Landed Society in the Eighteenth Century*, p. 44). For a brief discussion of the "Great" Earl of Cork's immediate descendants and the subsequent holders of his title, see Townshend, *The Life and Letters of the Great Earl of Cork* (London: Duckworth, 1904), pp. 443-54.

28. See Prior, *A List of Absentees in Ireland, and the Yearly Value of Their Estates and Incomes Spent Abroad, with Observations on the Present Trade and Condition of That Kingdom* (Dublin: R. Gunne, 1729).

29. Lees-Milne, *Earls of Creation: Five Great Patrons of Eighteenth-Century Art* (London: Hamish Hamilton, 1962), pp. 140-41.

30. *Correspondence of Pope*, 5 vols., ed. George Sherburn (Oxford: Clarendon Press, 1956), 2:239.

31. See, for example, John F. Ross, *Swift and Defoe: A Study in Relationship* (Berkeley and Los Angeles: University of California Press, 1941), esp. pp. 109-24; Kramnick, *Bolingbroke and His Circle: The Politics of Nostalgia in the Age of Walpole* (Cambridge, Mass.: Harvard University Press, 1968), pp. 205-17; and Myrddin Jones, "Swift, Harrington, and Corruption in England," in *Philological Quarterly* 53 (1974):59-70.

32. These imagistic motifs are noted by James T. Boulton in *The Language of Politics in the Age of Wilkes and Burke* (London: Routledge & Kegan Paul, 1963), pp. 111-12.

33. Samuels, *The Early Life, Correspondence, and Writings of the Rt. Hon. Edmund Burke* (Cambridge: At the University Press, 1923), p. 317.

34. Fischer, *On Swift's Poetry* (Gainesville: University Presses of Florida, 1978), pp. 88, 93. Peter J. Schakel likewise sees traditionally defined Augustan values functioning in the poem as a foil to Vanbrugh's house. See *The Poetry of Jonathan Swift: Allusion and the Development of a Poetic Style* (Madison: University of Wisconsin Press, 1978), pp. 37-41.

35. Fischer, *On Swift's Poetry*, p. 94.

36. Paulson, *Emblem and Expression: Meaning in English Art of the Eighteenth Century* (Cambridge, Mass.: Harvard University Press, 1975), p. 34.

37. Homer E. Woodbridge, *Sir William Temple: The Man and His Work* (New York: Modern Language Association of America, 1940), p. 214.

38. *The Works of Sir William Temple*, 4 vols. (London, 1757), 3:228-29. A bird's-eye view of Temple's estate, attributed to Leonard Knyf between 1690 and 1720, is reproduced in Christopher Hussey, *English Gardens and Landscapes, 1700-1750* (New York: Funk & Wagnalls, 1967), Plate 3 between pp. 16 and 17.

39. *The Works of Temple*, 2:552.

40. Erskine-Hill, *The Social Milieu of Pope*, p. 316.

41. Woodbridge, *Sir William Temple*, pp. 215-20.

42. Rptd. in ibid., pp. 232-33.

43. Schakel, *The Poetry of Jonathan Swift*, p. 19.

44. See *Abraham Cowley: Essays, Plays, and Sundry Verses*, ed. A. R. Waller (Cambridge: At the University Press, 1906), p. 395.

45. Williams, *Jonathan Swift and the Age of Compromise* (Lawrence: University of Kansas Press, 1958), p. 147.

46. Cited in Morris R. Brownell, *Alexander Pope and the Arts of Georgian England* (Oxford: Clarendon Press, 1977), p. 157.

47. Daniel Defoe, *A Tour through the Whole Island of Great Britain*, 2 vols. (New York: Everyman's Library, 1962), 1:164.

48. Lees-Milne, *Earls of Creation*, p. 71.

49. Brownell, *Pope and the Arts of Georgian England*, p. 159.

50. *Correspondence of Pope*, 2:257, 292.

51. Ibid., pp. 435-36.

52. All references to Thomson's poetry are from *James Thomson: Poetical Works*, ed. J. Logie Robertson (1908; New York: Oxford University Press, 1971).

53. See Hussey, *English Gardens and Landscapes*, pp. 80, 82.

54. Lees-Milne, *Earls of Creation*, p. 83.

55. See *Correspondence of Pope*, 2:259; 5:5.

56. Lees-Milne, *Earls of Creation*, pp. 84-85.

57. Defoe, *A Tour through . . . Great Britain*, 1:168.

58. Mack, *The Garden and the City: Retirement and Politics in the Later Poetry of Pope, 1731-1743* (Toronto: University of Toronto Press, 1969), p. 36.

59. *Correspondence of Pope*, 2:445.

60. Ibid., p. 386.

61. Horace, *Satires, Epistles, and Ars Poetica*, trans. H. Rushton Fairclough (Cambridge, Mass.: Harvard University Press, Loeb Classical Library, 1966), pp. 294-303. Pope's *Imitations of Horace, Epistle I, vii*, "Imitated in the Manner of Dr. Swift," vividly underscores the disparity between the two writers' perspectives vis-à-vis the country house tradition. In Pope's case it is precisely the *first* part of Horace's epistle that is focused upon, with no reference at all made to Mena's failed pastoral ideal. The

end of Pope's epistle portrays the poet's successful merging with the land, hence the viability of his rural vision. His ambitions in this respect, for all their humbleness, are expressed through a picture that conveys the central features of an aristocratic retreat: tranquillity, independence, continuity with one's ancestral past, and a reciprocal bond between the land and its inhabitants: "Can I retrench? Yes, mighty well,/Shrink back to my Paternal Cell,/A Little House, with Trees a-row,/And like its Master, very low . . ." (75-78). Pope here echoes, in a serious and respectful manner, the same sentiments from *Upon Appleton House* that Swift uses parodically in *Vanbrug's House.*

62. *The Twickenham Edition of the Poems of Alexander Pope*, 11 vols., ed. John Butt et al. (London: Methuen, 1939-1961), 4:249.

63. Reprinted in *The Works of Jonathan Swift*, 19 vols., ed. Sir Walter Scott, 2d ed. (London: Bickers & Son, 1883-1884), 14:164.

64. Percival's lampoon on Swift is reprinted by Scott in *The Works of Swift*, 1:255 n.

65. Cited in Malins and the Knight of Glin, *Lost Demesnes: Irish Landscape Gardening, 1660-1845* (London: Barrie & Jenkins, 1976), p. 13.

66. *The Works of Swift*, ed. Scott, 14:164.

67. Williams, "Swift and the Poetry of Allusion: 'The Journal,'" in *Literary Theory and Structure: Essays in Honor of William K. Wimsatt*, ed. Frank Brady, John Palmer, and Martin Price (New Haven: Yale University Press, 1973), p. 230.

68. For a discussion of Charles's significance for Swift, see F. P. Lock, *The Politics of "Gulliver's Travels"* (Oxford: Clarendon Press, 1980), pp. 56-65.

69. *Correspondence of Pope*, 1:234.

70. For information about Glasnevin in Swift's time, see F. Elrington Ball, *A History of County Dublin* (Dublin: A. Thom, 1902-1920), pt. 6:128-36.

71. For a description of one such visit to Rousham, see the *Autobiography and Correspondence of Mary Granville, Mrs. Delany*, 1st series, 3 vols., ed. Lady Llanover (London: R. Bentley, 1861), 2:220-21.

72. Cited in Malins and the Knight of Glin, *Lost Demesnes*, p. 37.

73. *Autobiography and Correspondence of Mrs. Delany*, 2:308-9.

74. Ibid., p. 315.

75. Copies of this and three other of Mrs. Delany's representations of Delville appear in Malins and the Knight of Glin, *Lost Demesnes*, p. 38. For a discussion of the relationship of the Claudian structure to eighteenth-century landscapes and the way in which they were perceived, see Ronald Paulson, "Toward the Constable Bicentenary: Thoughts on Landscape Theory," *Eighteenth-Century Studies* 10 (Winter 1976-1977):245-50; and John Barrell, *The Idea of Landscape and the Sense of Place, 1730-1840: An Approach to the Poetry of John Clare* (Cambridge: At the University Press, 1972), pp. 6-13, 15-17.

76. *Autobiography and Correspondence of Mrs. Delany*, 1:300.

77. Ibid., 2:309.

78. Ibid., p. 315.

79. *Memoirs of Mrs. Letitia Pilkington, 1712-1750*, ed. Iris Barry (New York: Dodd, Mead, 1928), p. 49.

80. Ibid., p. 47.

81. Ball, *A History of County Dublin*, pt. 6:140.

82. *Autobiography and Correspondence of Mrs. Delany*, 2:468.

83. Another verse, entitled "Dr. Delany's Villa," is of uncertain attribution but was probably written by Sheridan. Although conceptually and poetically inferior to

An Epistle upon an Epistle, it is Swiftian in tone and spirit. Through satiric deflation, it stresses both the villa's absurdly reduced dimensions and the sterility of its natural surroundings. Reprinted in *The Works of Swift*, ed. Scott, 14:170–71.

84. Horace, *Satires, Epistles, and Ars Poetica*, pp. 258–59. Pope, in his imitation of this epistle, puts it as follows: "I plant, root up, I build, and then confound,/Turn round to square, and square again to round" (lines 169–70).

85. Ball, *A History of County Dublin*, pt. 6:130.

86. *The Poems of Thomas Carew*, ed. Rhodes Dunlap (Oxford: Clarendon Press, 1970), p. 28.

87. Kavanagh, *The Green Fool* (1938; London: Martin Brian & O'Keeffe, 1971), p. 8.

88. Samuel Lewis, *A Topographical Dictionary of Ireland*, 2 vols. (London: S. Lewis, 1837), 2:344.

89. *Memoirs of Mrs. Pilkington*, p. 369.

90. See *The Works of Lord Bolingbroke*, 4 vols. (1844; rptd. London: Frank Cass, 1967), 3:45.

Chapter 5

1. *The Spectator*, 5 vols., ed. Donald Bond (Oxford: Clarendon Press, 1965), 3:538.

2. For an extended discussion by Addison of prospects and their appeal for the viewer, see ibid., pp. 540–41.

3. *Autobiography and Correspondence of Mary Granville, Mrs. Delany*, 1st series, 3 vols, ed. Lady Llanover (London: R. Bentley, 1861), 2:309, 314.

4. Ibid., 3:530–31.

5. Malins and the Knight of Glin, *Lost Demesnes: Irish Landscape Gardening, 1660–1845* (London: Barrie & Jenkins, 1976), p. 46.

6. Maxwell, *The Stranger in Ireland: From the Reign of Elizabeth to the Great Famine* (London: Jonathan Cape, 1954), p. 147.

7. *The Spectator*, 3:537.

8. For a sampling of such contemporary descriptions, see Maxwell, *Dublin under the Georges, 1714–1830* (1937; rev'd. London: Faber & Faber, 1956), pp. 297–308.

9. *The Rambler*, in 3 vols.; in *The Works of Samuel Johnson*, 3:i, ed. W. J. Bate and Albrecht B. Strauss (New Haven: Yale University Press, 1969), p. 10.

10. See Johnson, *A Dictionary of the English Language* (London: W. Strahan, 1755).

11. Cohen, *The Unfolding of "The Seasons"* (Baltimore: Johns Hopkins Press, 1970), p. 63. James Turner makes a similar point in discussing the seventeenth-century uses of the term: "The word 'prospective', in fact, could be used interchangeably for future options, distant views, telescopes, optical tricks and painted landscapes; it draws together all the new-found 'arts of prospect.'" *The Politics of Landscape: Rural Scenery and Society in English Poetry, 1630–1660* (Oxford: Basil Blackwell, 1979), p. 5.

12. Bush, *Hibernia Curiosa* (London: W. Flexney, 1768), p. 94.

13. Quotations from Cowper are taken from *Cowper: Verse and Letters*, ed. Brian Spiller (Cambridge, Mass.: Harvard University Press, 1968).

14. Bush, *Hibernia Curiosa*, pp. 93–94.

15. *The Works of the Right Honourable Edmund Burke*, 7 vols., Bohn's British Classics (London: Bell & Daldy, 1868–1872), 6:65–66.

16. See *Harper's Latin Dictionary*, founded on trans. of Freund's Latin-German

Lexicon, ed. E. A. Andrews, rev'd. and enl. by Charleton T. Lewis and Charles Short (1879; New York: American Book Co., 1907). The temple remained standing until quite recently. For a photograph of it taken in the 1940s, see Malins and the Knight of Glin, *Lost Demesnes*, p. 39.

17. MacLysaght, *Irish Life in the Seventeenth Century* (1939; New York: Barnes & Noble, 1969), pp. 327-28.

18. John Dixon Hunt and Peter Willis, eds., *The Genius of the Place: The English Landscape Garden, 1620-1820* (London: Paul Elek, 1975), p. 197.

19. Maxwell, *Dublin under the Georges*, pp. 306-7.

20. Ehrenpreis, "Poverty and Poetry: Representations of the Poor in Augustan Literature," in *Studies in Eighteenth-Century Culture*, vol. 1, ed. Louis T. Milic (Cleveland: Case Western Reserve University Press, 1971), p. 3.

21. Bush, *Hibernia Curiosa*, pp. 74-75.

22. See, for example, Ralph Cohen, *The Art of Discrimination: Thomson's "The Seasons" and the Language of Criticism* (Berkeley and Los Angeles: University of California Press, 1964), pp. 217-19.

23. Young, *A Tour in Ireland, 1776-1779*, 2 vols., ed. A. W. Hutton (1892; Shannon: Irish University Press, 1970), 2:48.

24. MacLysaght, *Irish Life in the Seventeenth Century*, pp. 356-57.

25. See, for example, Dorothy Marshall, *Industrial England, 1776-1851* (New York: Scribner's, 1973), p. 45; and M. D. George, *English Social Life in the Eighteenth Century* (London: Sheldon Press, 1923), pt. 1:48, 50.

26. Barrell, *The Idea of Landscape and the Sense of Place, 1730-1840: An Approach to the Poetry of John Clare* (Cambridge: At the University Press, 1972), p. 59.

27. Arthur P. I. Samuels, *The Early Life, Correspondence, and Writings of the Rt. Hon. Edmund Burke* (Cambridge: At the University Press, 1923), p. 315.

28. MacLysaght, *Irish Life in the Seventeenth Century*, p. 356.

29. Samuels, *The Early Life, Correspondence, and Writings of Edmund Burke*, p. 315.

30. Ibid., pp. 315-16.

31. The significance of spectacles for Swift—specifically in connection with Gulliver's dependency upon them because of his "weak eyes"—is discussed in W. B. Carnochan, *Lemuel Gulliver's Mirror for Man* (Berkeley and Los Angeles: University of California Press, 1968), pp. 135-37; and in Pat Rogers, "Gulliver's Glasses," in *The Art of Jonathan Swift*, ed. Clive T. Probyn (London: Vision Press, 1978). Carnochan sees Gulliver as a "myopic hero," to whom spectacles are symbols of man's blindness after the Fall, as well as of man's "pride in his ability to overcome it" (p. 135). Rogers, on the other hand, believes that the spectacles "represent visual over-development, hypertrophy of the sight" (p. 183), as well as "the intrusive intellect; the over-intent scrutiny of what is better left unexamined because it causes pain and revulsion when pried into by the modern empiricist" (p. 187). As my discussion suggests, I strongly disagree with Rogers's identification of Swift with this latter point of view and with his argument that ". . . on another level Swift shares Gulliver's instincts, to hide and to peer out, to avoid bodily contact which squeezes and pains us. He wants to do this while at the same time negotiating a safe distance with the physical world, through his sight" (p. 187). On the contrary, Swift tended to be contemptuous of those who sought this kind of visual refuge. Although the example of Gulliver is a somewhat complicated and paradoxical one, for Swift in general spectacles were instruments not for probing deeply into, but precisely for glossing over, empirical realities.

32. This view is put forth by Robert M. Adams in *Strains of Discord: Studies in Literary Openness* (Ithaca, N.Y.: Cornell University Press, 1958), pp. 158-60.

33. Interestingly, Swift in actual life eschewed the use of glasses despite his failing eyesight. As Harold Williams observes in a footnote to a letter in which Swift's correspondent expresses fears that her writing "shoud inconvenience [his] Eyes": "Swift's eyesight had begun to trouble him but he consistently refused the aid of spectacles" (C, 4:17, n. 1). Swift's refusal apparently persisted into old age.

34. Berger, *Ways of Seeing* (Harmondsworth, England: Penguin, 1972), p. 16.

35. See Donoghue, "The Eye as Benevolent Despot," *Art International* 15 (20 May 1971):28-31.

36. See my article, "Pope's Portraits of Women: The Tyranny of the Pictorial Eye," in *Women and Men: The Consequences of Power*, ed. Dana V. Hiller and Robin Ann Sheets (Cincinnati: University of Cincinnati, Office of Women's Studies, 1977), pp. 74-91.

37. *The Spectator*, 1:87.

38. Berger, *Ways of Seeing*, p. 16.

Chapter 6

1. Spence, *Observations, Anecdotes, and Characters of Books and Men*, 2 vols., ed. James M. Osborn (Oxford: Clarendon Press, 1966), 1:52.

2. *Autobiography and Correspondence of Mary Granville, Mrs. Delany*, 1st series, 3 vols., ed. Lady Llanover (London: R. Bentley, 1861), 2:457-58.

3. Ibid., p. 459.

4. Bush, *Hibernia Curiosa* (London: W. Flexney, 1768), p. 8.

5. *Autobiography and Correspondence of Mrs. Delany*, 2:306.

6. Lecky, *A History of Ireland in the Eighteenth Century*, 5 vols. (London: Longmans, Green, 1892), 1:222.

7. Cited in ibid., pp. 227-28.

8. Ibid., pp. 242, 244-46.

9. Johnson, *A Journey to the Western Islands of Scotland* (London, 1775; rptd. Menston, England: Scolar Press, 1968), p. 17.

10. *The Works of the Right Honourable Edmund Burke*, 7 vols., Bohn's British Classics (London: Bell & Daldy, 1868-1872), 5:125.

11. Cited in Lecky, *A History of Ireland in the Eighteenth Century*, 1:246-47.

12. Ibid., p. 247, nn. 1, 4.

13. See Oliver W. Ferguson, *Jonathan Swift and Ireland* (Urbana: University of Illinois Press, 1962), pp. 161-62.

14. Orrery, *Remarks on the Life and Writings of Dr. Jonathan Swift* (London: A. Millar, 1752), p. 34.

15. *Autobiography and Correspondence of Mrs. Delany*, 2:321.

16. See Patrick Delany, *Observations upon Lord Orrery's "Remarks on the Life and Writings of Dr. Jonathan Swift"* (London: W. Reeve, 1754), pp. 135-36.

17. See Appleton, *The Experience of Landscape* (London: Wiley, 1975), pp. 85-101.

18. For a discussion of the significance and implications of the feminized landscape in the eighteenth century, see my article, "Binding and Dressing Nature's Loose Tresses: The Ideology of Augustan Landscape Design," in *Studies in Eighteenth-Century Culture*, vol. 8, ed. Roseann Runte (Madison: University of Wisconsin Press, 1979), pp. 109-35.

19. Bush, *Hibernia Curiosa*, pp. 95-96.

20. Ibid., p. 99.

21. "And, having thus got safely over the bogs, which, in general, are hardly firm

enough to carry a man without sinking into the surface, we will now enter upon a survey of another and much more pleasing species of natural curiosity in this Kingdom, which will particularly engage the attention, and afford scope for the highest entertainment to the English traveller . . ." (Bush, *Hibernia Curiosa*, pp. 84-85).

22. An English translation of Swift's Latin inscription (part of which appears in parentheses in the text) was published in the *Dublin Intelligence* for April 17, 1731; rptd. in *The Correspondence of Jonathan Swift*, ed. F. Elrington Ball (London: G. Bell, 1912), 4:218 n.

23. This same point was made even more emphatically by the Dean from the pulpit of St. Patrick's: "I verily believe, that, since the beginning of the world, no nation upon earth ever shewed (all circumstances considered) such high constant marks of loyalty in all their actions and behaviour, as we have done . . ." (PW, 9:234).

24. Beckett, "Swift and the Anglo-Irish Tradition," in *Focus: Swift*, ed. C. J. Rawson (London: Sphere Books, 1971), p. 155.

25. See Orrery, *Remarks on the Life and Writings of Swift*, p. 7.

26. *Memoirs of Mrs. Letitia Pilkington, 1712-1750*, ed. Iris Barry (New York: Dodd, Mead, 1928), p. 62.

27. Jackson, "Dean Swift, The Liberties King," in *The Liberties of Dublin*, ed. Elgy Gillespie (Dublin: O'Brien Press, 1973), p. 41.

28. For some perceptive observations about Swift's penchant for role playing, see Peter Steele, *Jonathan Swift: Preacher and Jester* (Oxford: Clarendon Press, 1978), pp. 7-10, 60-117. According to Steele, "However much of his energy goes into unmasking and denouncing, [Swift] is vividly aware of the world as scenic array. And, once again of a piece with Erasmus, he is painfully conscious of how entirely the roles may be reversed. . . . He is to some extent Erasmus's 'manager,' determining the roles; and an actor-manager, participating in what he has initiated. He contrives the motley he condemns" (p. 61).

29. Delany, *Observations upon Lord Orrery's "Remarks,"* p. 10. A similar perception is expressed by Harry C. Payne in his discussion of the eighteenth-century French philosophes and their way of looking at the world: "The people were not hard to see, but they were hard to see clearly and sympathetically. . . . The philosophes viewed the people, as did most of the elite, from the upper story of a mansion, from the window of a carriage, from a road passing swiftly through the fields of France or the working quarters of Glasgow. Neither the means nor the will to see the life of the people at close hand existed." *The Philosophes and the People* (New Haven: Yale University Press, 1976), pp. 3-4.

30. Latocnaye, *Rambles through Ireland: By a French Emigrant*, trans. by an Irishman (Cork: M. Harris, 1798), p. iii.

31. *The Correspondence of Jonathan Swift*, ed. Ball, 3:85, n. 3.

32. See Constantia Maxwell, *Country and Town in Ireland under the Georges* (1940; Dundalk: Dundalgan Press, 1949), p. 328.

33. Craig, *Dublin 1660-1860: A Social and Architectural History* (Dublin: Allen Figgis, 1969), p. 116.

34. Preu, "Swift and the Common Man," *Florida State University Studies* 11 (1953):24.

35. Critics writing about this poem have consistently overlooked the essential distinction it makes between the English and the Irish phases of Swift's life. As a result, they have failed to define accurately the relationship between the poem's ironic and panegyric aspects or to characterize the precise nature and role of the eulogist. The credibility of the latter's laudatory portrait of Swift lies at the center of the debate over the verse's meaning. Ronald Paulson sees him as a wholly reliable narrator—one

with no personal stake in the matter who, on the strength of sufficient temporal perspective (a year after Swift's death), is able to deliver a detached, objective verdict on Swift's accomplishments in life. See *The Fictions of Satire* (Baltimore: Johns Hopkins Press, 1967), pp. 189-94, 197-99. For Paulson, in other words, the eulogy is a serious apologia, to be taken largely at face value. Barry Slepian, on the contrary, interprets the eulogy in an ironic fashion, as a demonstration of Swift's own pride ("The Ironic Intention of Swift's Verses on His Own Death," *Review of English Studies* 14 [August 1963]:249-56). These two views represent the two poles of interpretation of the poem. Other critics have attempted to steer a middle course between them. Arthur H. Scouten and Robert D. Hume, for example, see the poem as a "half-genuine apologia," mingling elements of serious praise and comic exaggeration ("Pope and Swift: Text and Interpretation of Swift's Verses on His Death," *Philological Quarterly* 52 [1973]:205-31). John Irwin Fischer, although acknowledging that the eulogist is in certain ways biased and untruthful, ultimately views his narration as serious praise since the lies it contains " . . . do not undermine but rather support that large bulk of the panegyric which, if flattering to Swift, is biographically sound." See *On Swift's Poetry* (Gainesville: University Presses of Florida, 1978), p. 170. My own view of the poem, although also recognizing its ironic and its panegyric elements, rejects both Fischer's heavily tendentious and overly depersonalized interpretation, which places the verse in the tradition of formal seventeenth-century meditations on death (pp. 156-59), and the implication in Scouten's and Hume's essay that the verse is largely a playful rhetorical game on Swift's part. It seems clear to me that the poem is dealing with matters of the utmost seriousness to Swift and that he is presenting in it an apologia intended to be accepted as genuine. But its seriousness—the true validity and force of the eulogy—is rooted not in a general meditation on man's mortality, nor in the metaphysical contemplation of what Paulson terms "the disinterested spiritual" aspect of man (p. 194), but in a concretely political vision that implicitly rejects the "golden dreams" of defeated idealists for the potent deeds of practical-minded political activists—a distinction that corresponds to the English and the Irish phases of Swift's public life.

36. Schakel, *The Poetry of Jonathan Swift: Allusion and the Development of a Poetic Style* (Madison: University of Wisconsin Press, 1978), pp. 144-46.

37. Ibid., pp. 157-80.

38. Ibid., p. 41.

39. Jaffe, *The Poet Swift* (Hanover, N.H.: University Press of New England, 1977), pp. 1-3. See also Herbert Davis, "Swift's View of Poetry," in *Fair Liberty Was All His Cry: A Tercentenary Tribute to Jonathan Swift*, ed. A. Norman Jeffares (New York: St. Martin's Press, 1967), pp. 62-97. Davis argues that, whereas Pope "looks upon poetry as the special activity of a privileged and well-trained hierarchy, which professes and believes literally in a creed that has been handed down by the great founders and leaders of the order," Swift "had none of this professional pride, and never showed the least inclination to set much value on the business of writing poetry" (pp. 63, 65).

40. See popular anti-Puritan satires from the mid-seventeenth century, such as the *Rump Songs* (London, 1662; rptd. 1874); and *Poems on Affairs of State: Augustan Satirical Verse, 1660-1714*, 7 vols., ed. George deF. Lord et al. (New Haven, Yale University Press, 1963-1975). Paulson discusses anti-Puritan satire in connection with techniques such as travesty and parody, with anti-Court satire of the Restoration, and with Swift's use of impersonation (*The Fictions of Satire*, pp. 92-97, 105-8, 136-37). Jaffe points out ways in which Swift's poetry resembles Butler's and, describing Swift as "a Restoration wit," suggests various links between his satire and Rochester's (*The*

Poet Swift, pp. 31–42, 157–63). See also Harold Love, "Rochester and the Traditions of Satire," in *Restoration Literature: Critical Approaches*, ed. Harold Love (London: Methuen, 1972), pp. 145–75; and Donna G. Fricke, "Swift and the Tradition of Informal Satiric Poetry," in *Contemporary Studies of Swift's Poetry*, ed. John Irwin Fischer and Donald C. Mell, Jr. (Newark: University of Delaware Press, 1981), pp. 36–45.

41. Somerville-Large, *Dublin* (London: Hamish Hamilton, 1979), p. 201.

42. Lecky, *A History of Ireland in the Eighteenth Century*, 1:322.

43. Cited in Maxwell, *Dublin under the Georges*, p. 150.

44. Speaking of this "noble achievement to abolish the Irish language," Swift declares: "Yet I am wholly deceived if this might not be effectually done in less than half an age, and at a very trifling expence, for such I look upon a tax to be, of only six thousand pounds a year, to accomplish so great a work" (PW, 12:89). Although six thousand pounds may sound to us like "a very trifling expence," Swift's tracts throughout this period stressed the fact that raising any amount of money in impoverished Ireland was a nearly impossible task. As he told the author of a "Paper, called 'A Memorial,'" "Your Scheme for a *Tax* for raising such a Sum, is all visionary[,] and owing to a great want of Knowledge in the *miserable State* of this Nation. . . . so præternatural a Sum, as one Hundred and ten Thousand Pounds, raised all on a sudden, (for there is no dallying with Hunger) is just in Proportion with raising a Million and a half in *England* . . ." (pp. 20–21). According to the rate of equivalency Swift set up here, even a much smaller sum like six thousand pounds would represent substantially more than "a very trifling expence" when translated into its comparable value in England at the time.

45. *The Collected Works of Oliver Goldsmith*, 5 vols., ed. Arthur Friedman (Oxford: Clarendon Press, 1966), 3:118–20.

46. See Donal O'Sullivan, *Carolan: The Life, Times, and Music of an Irish Harper*, 2 vols. (London: Routledge & Kegan Paul, 1958), 1:76-88.

47. Ibid., pp. 84–85.

48. Craig, *Dublin 1660–1860*, pp. 122–23.

49. Mercier, "Swift and the Gaelic Tradition," in *Fair Liberty Was All His Cry*, p. 279.

50. Rawson, "The Injured Lady and the Drapier: A Reading of Swift's Irish Tracts," *Prose Studies* 3 (May 1980):28.

51. Ewald, *The Masks of Jonathan Swift* (Oxford: Basil Blackwell, 1954), p. 3.

52. The most detailed and valuable map of Dublin (including the Liberty of St. Patrick) during this period is John Rocque's *An Exact Survey of the City and Suburbs of Dublin* (Dublin, 1756). Throughout the remainder of the century it was frequently reprinted with additions.

53. Beckett, *The Anglo-Irish Tradition* (London: Faber & Faber, 1976), p. 54; and Speck, *Swift* (London: Evans Bros., 1969), pp. 29–30.

54. McHugh, "The Woven Figure: Swift's Irish Context," *University Review* (Dublin) 4 (1967):41.

55. Donoghue, *Jonathan Swift: A Critical Introduction* (Cambridge: At the University Press, 1969), p. 153.

56. Paulson, *The Fictions of Satire*, p. 148.

57. Barish, "The Antitheatrical Prejudice," in *Critical Quarterly* 8 (1966):340–42.

58. See Landa, "Swift's Deanery Income: A New Document," in *Pope and His Contemporaries: Essays Presented to George Sherburn*, ed. James L. Clifford and Louis A. Landa (New York: Oxford University Press, 1968), pp. 159–70.

59. C. J. Rawson, *Gulliver and the Gentle Reader: Studies in Swift and Our Time* (London: Routledge & Kegan Paul, 1973), pp. 89, 99.

60. Sheridan, *The Life of the Rev. Dr. Jonathan Swift*, 2d ed. (London, 1787), p. 225.

61. Lecky, *A History of Ireland in the Eighteenth Century*, 1:455.

62. Said, "Swift's Tory Anarchy," *Eighteenth-Century Studies* 3 (Fall 1969):56–57.

63. See Plumb, *The Growth of Political Stability in England, 1675–1725* (Boston: Houghton Mifflin Co., 1967). Plumb sums up his argument as follows: "To those who lived within [the world of government after 1715], and fought for the highest office, it must have seemed a precarious and fickle world; to us who can view it in relation to what went before and what came after, however, it possesses an almost monolithic stability, a political system more secure than England had ever known or was to know" (p. 189). Also see Plumb, *Sir Robert Walpole*, 2 vols. (Boston: Houghton Mifflin Co., 1956). Other studies that emphasize the consolidation of Whig power into a political machine include H. T. Dickinson, *Walpole and the Whig Supremacy* (Clarendon: English University Presses, 1973); and Basil Williams, *The Whig Supremacy, 1714–1760*, 2d ed., rev'd. C. H. Stuart, The Oxford History of England, vol. 11 (Oxford: Clarendon Press, 1962). According to Williams, "between 1714 and 1760 the English people, wearied with struggles and sated with glory, was content to stabilize the results of the Revolution . . . and accept an oligarchic system of government which for the time being seemed exactly suited to its needs. It was an age of stability in politics, in religion, in literature, and in social observances, a stability needed to enable the nation to recover its poise after more than a century of excitement" (p. 1). W. A. Speck, although explicitly dealing with elements of "strife" during this period, does so specifically within the context of the power struggles within the ruling circles, and presents a picture of the Whig supremacy that corresponds in its essentials to the picture conveyed in the preceding histories. See *Stability and Strife: England 1714–1760*, The New History of England, vol. 6 (London: Edward Arnold, 1977).

64. Hay, "Property, Authority, and the Criminal Law," in Hay, Linebaugh, Rule et al., *Albion's Fatal Tree: Crime and Society in Eighteenth-Century England* (New York: Pantheon, 1975), p. 21. Other essays in this volume, without necessarily questioning the power of the governmental system, likewise point to the stubborn persistence and at least periodic effectiveness of criminal activity and social protest (the two not always being clearly separable) throughout the period. See, e.g., Peter Linebaugh, "The Tyburn Riot against the Surgeons," pp. 65–117; and Cal Winslow, "Sussex Smugglers," pp. 119–66. Noting "the inability of the authorities to suppress the illicit [smuggling] trade"—despite Walpole's fierce personal campaign against it—Winslow explains: "Smuggling, far from being seen as an illegal activity by the Sussex poor, was considered a legitimate part of the local economy. It was one of the many methods used by the eighteenth-century rural poor to maintain themselves, regardless of legal prohibitions" (pp. 147, 149). For further insights into the nature and extensiveness of social protest in eighteenth-century England, see George Rudé, *The Crowd in History: A Study of Popular Disturbances in France and England, 1730–1848* (New York: Wiley, 1964).

65. Said, "Swift's Tory Anarchy," pp. 55–58.

Index

For the reader's convenience, all titles have been italicized even if they are not italicized in the text. Individual titles of Swift's works are listed solely under the author's name with the exception of *Gulliver's Travels* and *A Tale of a Tub*.

293

of Commons, referred to in Swift poem, 155

Grafton, Charles Fitzroy, second Duke of, Lord Lieutenant of Ireland, Carteret's predecessor, 262

Grant, Francis, Swift's letter to, 232

Grattan, Henry, Ireland's illustrious son, 232

Grattans, the (Charles, James, Robert et al.): absence from Dublin lamented, 153; portrayed as Swift's "fav'rite Clan," 231-32

Greene, Donald, 273 n.4

Gullivers's Travels (Swift), 8, 159; anarchic and deconstructive elements in, 6-7, 15; confinement in, 46-47, 175-76; and colonialism, 35, 48, 263, 277 n.20; excremental landscape in, 34-36, 41, 227; Gulliver as wanderer, 218, 220; and language, 17, 119; and satiric catalogs, 260; and shifting perspectives/modes of perception, 2, 175-76, 186, 198-99, 203-4; and Swiftian/Irish landscape, 32, 62-63, 81-82, 95-96, 227

Gyllenborg, Count Karl, Jacobitism and Swift's dedication of work to, 146-47

Hagstrum, Jean H., 275 n.23

Hall, Basil, 5

Harding, John, printer of *The Drapier's Letters*, 250

Harley, Robert. *See* Oxford, Robert Harley, first Earl of

Harrington, James, Country Party principles and Swift, 113

Hay, Douglas, 263

Helgerson, Richard, 279 n.13

Herrick, Robert: and country house ideal, 106, 171; and pastoral, 60-61

Hibbard, G. R., 96, 98, 99

Hibernia Curiosa. *See* Bush, John

History of Carolan, the Last Irish Bard, The (Goldsmith), 247

Hoare, Henry: and Lord Orrery, 20; and Stourhead, 71

Hoare, Richard Colt, *Journal of a Tour in Ireland in 1806*, 92

Hock-cart; or, Harvest home, The (Herrick), 60-61

Hogarth, William, 139; depiction of Gulliver by, 47; on London, 24; Swift's poetic allusion to, 14

Holderness, Lady Frederica, Countess of,

and monument for her grandfather in St. Patrick's Cathedral, 112-13

Holyhead: and Swiftian landscape, 10; Swift's journeys on foot from, 220; Swift's verse description of, 62. *See also* Swift, Jonathan, prose works of, *Holyhead Journal*

Homer, and Pope, 132

Horace: retirement theme and country house poem, 121, 122, 123; Swift's departures from, 136; Swift's echoes of, 151-52. *See also* Pope, Alexander, works cited, *Imitations of Horace; and* individual titles of Swift's adaptations of Horace, *under* Swift, Jonathan, poetical works of

Howard, Henrietta. *See* Suffolk, Henrietta Howard, Countess of

Hume, Robert D., 290 n.35

Hunt, John Dixon, 14, 274 n.18

Hussey, Christopher, 284 nn.38, 53

Huxley, Aldous, 276 n.1

Ideology, 3-4, 95-100, 281-82 n.1. *See also* Cosmic Toryism; Country house ideal; Swift, Jonathan, characteristics of mind, temperament, and writing, anarchic elements *and* political and ideological outlook of

Imitations of Horace. *See* Pope, Alexander, works cited

Ireland. *See also* Dublin; Swift, Jonathan, and Ireland *and* political and ideological outlook of, attacks on colonialism

—country houses of: Brackdenstown (Swords), 52, 54; Castletown House (Celbridge), 103-4; Delville (Glasnevin), 148-51, 152-53, 181; Gaulstown House (co. Westmeath), 140-42; Glaslough (co. Monaghan), 139; Howth Castle (co. Dublin), 174; Laracor (co. Meath), 13, 69-70, 136; Loughgall (co. Armagh), 142, 222; Market-Hill (co. Armagh), 39, 160-61; Quilca (co. Cavan), 33, 156-60; Wood-Park (co. Meath), 137

—geographical areas of: (co.) Armagh (Drumlack, Market-Hill, Newry), 39, 139, 142, 160-61, 166, 168; Cavan, 19, 21, 157-60, 227-28; Celbridge (co. Kildare), 104; Clonfert (co. Galway), 222; Coleraine (co. Derry), 105, 170-71; Connaught, 221; (co.) Cork ("Carbery Rocks," Schull, Youghal), 12, 91, 222-

135, 137, 161, 198, 284-85 n.61, 286 n.84; *Pastorals*, 14, 86; *Windsor-Forest*, 11-12, 33, 66, 90

Popish Plot, 50

Popular satiric tradition. *See under* Swift, Jonathan, and satire

Poulet, Georges, 9

Poussin, Nicholas, 13, 14

Prendergast, Sir Thomas, second Baronet, 22; as satirized by Swift, 33, 51

Preu, J. A., 237-38

Prior, Thomas, list of absentees, 110

Prospects. *See* Landscape, prospects

Protestant Ascendancy, 180-82, 253-54, 257, 278 n.36. *See also* Anglo-Irish gentry; Class society; Swift, Jonathan, political and ideological outlook of, on gentry and nobility

Querist, The (Berkeley), 83

Quilca. *See under* Ireland, country houses of; Swift, Jonathan, and Ireland, and Cavan/Quilca

Rambler, The (Johnson), 176

Rambles through Ireland (Latocnaye), 236-37

Rawson, C. J.: on anarchic elements in Swift, 7-8, 260; on Augustan outlook, 273 n.4; on Battestin, 3; on confinement in Swift, 43, On the Drapier, 249; on Irish and cannibalism, 280 n.36

Reynolds, Joshua, and privy, 41

Richardson, William, of Summerseat near Coleraine, Swift's letter to, 170-71

Richmond Lodge, 125-26. *See also* Swift, Jonathan, poetical works of, *A Pastoral Dialogue between Richmond-Lodge and Marble-Hill*

Robbins, Caroline, 6, 274 n.13, 278 n.37

Robinson, Richard, first Baron Rokeby, Archbishop of Armagh, and architectural improvements, 39

Rochester, John Wilmot, second Earl of, similarities with Swift's poetry, 58, 242, 248, 290-91 n.40

Rochfort, George: exchange of trifles with Swift, 248-49; and Swift's *Journal*, 142, 143

Rochfort, Robert, Chief Baron of Irish Court of Exchequer: Swift's depiction of, in *The Journal*, 144, 145, 147, 163; as Swift's host at Gaulstown House, 141, 142

Rocque, John, map of Dublin, 291 n.52

Rogers, Pat, 10, 273 n.4, 287 n.31

Romney, Henry Sidney, first Earl of, false friendship to Swift, 178

Rosa, Salvator, and eighteenth-century landscape, 13

Ross, John F., 283 n.31

Rudé, George, 276 n.2, 292 n.64

Rump Songs, 290 n.40

Rural Sports (Gay), 66, 67

Sackville (Germain), Lord George, on confrontation between Swift and Archbishop Boulter, 244

Sackville-West, Vita, on English country house, 97, 98

Said, Edward W., 7, 262, 264

St. Patrick's Cathedral, 25, 28-30, 32, 44, 111, 112, 247, 267. *See also* Swift, Jonathan, and Ireland, and Dublin

Sambrook, James, 274 n.18

Sanitary conditions, in eighteenth-century England and Ireland, 23-34, 40-41, 277 n.26

Satire. *See* Pope, Alexander, and satire; Swift, Jonathan, and satire

Sawbridge, Thomas, Dean of Ferns, satirized by Swift, 85

Schakel, Peter J., on Swift's poetry, 122, 239, 241-42, 284 n.34

Schomberg, Frederick Herman, Duke of: proposed monument for in St. Patrick's Cathedral, 112-13; Swift's epitaph for, 229

Scouten, Arthur H., 290 n.35

Seasons, The. See Thomson, James

Selby, Hopewell R., 43, 277 n.29

Shaftesbury, Anthony Ashley Cooper, first Earl of, as one of Swift's "Newmen," 260

Sheridan, Thomas, 44, 132, 266; poetic trifles of, 140, 246, 248-49, 285-86 n.83; Swift's depictions of, 33, 104-5, 157; Swift's letters to, 17, 30, 33, 44, 104, 133, 161, 222, 230; Swift's visits to (at Quilca), 4, 70, 157-59, 222, 227

Sheridan, Thomas, the younger, *Life of Swift*, 261

Slepian, Barry, 290 n.35

Smedley, Jonathan, Dean of Clogher and of Killala, satirized by Pope, 38

Smollett, Tobias, and country house ideal, 96

THE JOHNS HOPKINS UNIVERSITY PRESS

Swift's Landscape

*This book was composed in Baskerville text
by Horne Associates, Inc., and Caslon Antique
display type by The Composing Room of Baltimore
from a design by Cynthia W. Hotvedt. It was
printed on S. D. Warren's 50-lb. Sebago Eggshell
paper and bound in Joanna Arrextox A by
Universal Lithographers.*